MANZANAR MOSAIC

The George and Sakaye Aratani Nikkei in the Americas Series
Series Editors Valerie Matsumoto and Tritia Toyota

This series endeavors to capture the best scholarship available illustrating the evolving nature of contemporary Japanese American culture and community. By stretching the boundaries of the field to the limit (whether at a substantive, theoretical, or comparative level), these books aspire to influence future scholarship in this area specifically and Asian American studies more generally.

Barbed Voices: Oral History, Resistance, and the World War II Japanese American Social Disaster, Arthur A. Hansen

Beyond the Betrayal: The Memoir of a World War II Japanese American Draft Resister of Conscience, Yoshito Kuromiya, edited by Arthur A. Hansen

Distant Islands: The Japanese American Community in New York City, 1876–1930s, Daniel H. Inouye, with a foreword by David Reimers

Forced Out: A Nikkei Woman's Search for a Home in America, Judy Kawamoto

The House on Lemon Street, Mark Howland Rawitsch

Japanese Brazilian Saudades: Diasporic Identities and Cultural Production, Ignacio López-Calvo

Manzanar Mosaic: Essays and Oral Histories on America's First World War II Japanese American Concentration Camp, Arthur A. Hansen

Relocating Authority: Japanese Americans Writing to Redress Mass Incarceration, Mira Shimabukuro

Starting from Loomis and Other Stories, Hiroshi Kashiwagi, edited and with an introduction by Tim Yamamura

Taken from the Paradise Isle: The Hoshida Family Story, edited by Heidi Kim and with a foreword by Franklin Odo

MANZANAR MOSAIC

Essays and Oral Histories on America's First World War II
Japanese American Concentration Camp

ARTHUR A. HANSEN

UNIVERSITY PRESS OF COLORADO
Denver

© 2023 by University Press of Colorado

Published by University Press of Colorado
1624 Market Street, Suite 226
PMB 39883
Denver, Colorado 80202

All rights reserved
First paperback edition 2023

 The University Press of Colorado is a proud member of the Association of University Presses.

The University Press of Colorado is a cooperative publishing enterprise supported, in part, by Adams State University, Colorado State University, Fort Lewis College, Metropolitan State University of Denver, University of Alaska Fairbanks, University of Colorado, University of Denver, University of Northern Colorado, University of Wyoming, Utah State University, and Western Colorado University.

ISBN: 978-1-64642-421-4 (hardcover) | ISBN: 978-1-64642-515-0 (paperback) |
ISBN: 978-1-64642-422-1 (ebook) | https://doi.org/10.5876/9781646424221

Library of Congress Cataloging-in-Publication Data

Names: Hansen, Arthur A., author.
Title: Manzanar mosaic : essays and oral histories on America's first World War II Japanese American concentration camp / Arthur A. Hansen.
Other titles: George and Sakaye Aratani Nikkei in the Americas series.
Description: Denver : University Press of Colorado, [2023] | Series: The George and Sakaye Aratani Nikkei in the Americas series | Includes bibliographical references and index.
Identifiers: LCCN 2022061333 (print) | LCCN 2022061334 (ebook) | ISBN 978-1-64642-515-0 (paperback) | ISBN 9781646424214 (hardcover) | ISBN 9781646424221 (ebook)
Subjects: LCSH: Hansen, Arthur A.—Interviews. | Embrey, Sue Kunitomi—Interviews. | Yoneda, Karl G., 1906–1999—Interviews. | Yoneda, Elaine Black, 1906–1988—Interviews. | Ueno, Harry Y. (Harry Yoshio), 1907–2004—Interviews. | Tanaka, Togo, 1916–2009—Interviews. | Manzanar War Relocation Center. | Japanese Americans—Forced removal and internment, 1942–1945. | World War, 1939–1945—Japanese Americans—Personal narratives. | World War, 1939–1945—Japanese Americans—Interviews. | World War, 1939–1945—Evacuation of civilians—United States. | BISAC: HISTORY / United States / State & Local / West (AK, CA, CO, HI, ID, MT, NV, UT, WY) | HISTORY / Wars & Conflicts / World War II / General
Classification: LCC D769.8.A6 H3563 2023 (print) | LCC D769.8.A6 (ebook) | DDC 940.53/1779487—dc23/eng/20230127
LC record available at https://lccn.loc.gov/2022061333
LC ebook record available at https://lccn.loc.gov/2022061334

This publication was made possible, in part, with support from the University of California Los Angeles's Aratani Endowed Chair in Asian American Studies.

Cover photograph by Ronald C. Larson.

To the very special memory and legacy of Sue Kunitomi Embrey (1923–2006),

and

To the members of the Manzanar Committee and the staff and volunteers at the Manzanar National Historic Site, both past and present,

and

In commemoration of the remarkable lives and legacies of Lane Ryo Hirabayashi (1952–2020), Lloyd Inui (1930–2021), Roger Daniels (1927–2022), and Michel Wehrey (1940–2018).

Contents

Foreword
    Bruce Embrey, Co-chair, Manzanar Committee   ix

Preface   xv

A Note on Editing   xix

Prelude   3

Introduction   16

PART 1: ESSAYS   21

Doho: The Japanese American "Communist" Press, 1937–42
    Ronald C. Larson and Arthur A. Hansen   26

The Manzanar "Riot": An Ethnic Perspective
    Arthur A. Hansen and David A. Hacker   74

PART 2: ORAL HISTORIES   135

Progressive: An Interview with Sue Kunitomi Embrey   138

Thinker: An Interview with Togo W. Tanaka   161

Advocate: An Interview with Karl G. Yoneda   185

Partisan: An Interview with Elaine Black Yoneda   235

Martyr: An Interview with Harry Y. Ueno   284

Coda   293

Acknowledgments   295

Selected Bibliography   297

Index   301

Foreword

BRUCE EMBREY
CO-CHAIR, MANZANAR COMMITTEE

In this notable selection of essays and oral histories, Art Hansen has once again provided us with a collection of material to deepen our understanding of the forced removal and unjust incarceration of 120,000 Americans of Japanese ancestry during World War II. While this work includes some of Hansen's early efforts, it is also a reexamination of the scholarship with some of the most advanced analyses of today. In particular, his treatment of two essays—"The Manzanar 'Riot': An Ethnic Perspective" (coauthored by David Hacker) and *"Doho*: The Japanese American 'Communist' Press, 1937–42" (coauthored by Ronald Larson)—offer new insights into the political turmoil within the Japanese American community in the pre–World War II years and explain how this situation impacted subsequent events at the Manzanar War Relocation Center.

Manzanar Mosaic includes two of Hansen's first oral history subjects, my mother Sue Kunitomi Embrey (an interview transacted with David Hacker), and Togo Tanaka. Conducted back in the early 1970s when Hansen launched the Japanese American Oral History Project at California State

University, Fullerton, the interviews reveal two narrators who could not have been further apart in demeanor and world view. My mother, an educator, civil rights activist, and author, went on after World War II to lead the Manzanar Pilgrimage for thirty-seven years and was instrumental in preserving Manzanar as a National Historic Site. Tanaka was a prewar Japanese American Citizens League leader who collaborated with the War Relocation Authority at Manzanar and then, in the postwar period, turned his attention primarily to profitable business pursuits and international travel.

Hansen also selected for inclusion in *Manzanar Mosaic* the oral history interview he did with some of the most consequential figures incarcerated at Manzanar: Karl Yoneda (done with Ronald Larson), Elaine Black Yoneda, and Harry Ueno (done with Sue Kunitomi Embrey). All of these individuals were central figures in the Manzanar Revolt of December 1942 who many years later became important figures in the Japanese American Redress and Reparations movement.

Each person's story in *Manzanar Mosaic* adds to the growing body of work that helps us understand the many intricacies of the involuntary exclusion and unmerited imprisonment of our families. These oral histories offer perceptive insights, invaluable stories, and illuminating recollection to our collective history. The respective narrators were very different people with varied outlooks who at times stood on the opposite side of divisive issues, but they were all bound together by being inmates in America's first Japanese American concentration camp. Thankfully, Hansen brings all of them together once again in the pages of this volume.

These oral histories are told from the vantage point of those who directly experienced life behind barbed wire. These are not sociological studies, nor are they clinical observations of detached outsiders. Rather, they are reflections by onetime Japanese American inmates on how Executive Order 9066, issued by President Franklin Roosevelt on February 19, 1942, and its inherently racist, undemocratic nature impacted their lives and their broader racial-ethnic community.

As my mother noted in her introduction to *Manzanar Martyr: An Interview with Harry Y. Ueno* (1986), one must not "pass judgment on any one's story, regardless of the perspective from which it comes." While describing the importance of Harry Ueno's story, she went on to say: "I strongly believe that it is imperative that our stories, those of former 'internees,' be recorded.

Whether one agrees or disagrees with Harry Ueno's version of what happened at Manzanar, it is important that we hear from him."

Several of the oral histories in *Manzanar Mosaic* are somewhat unique in that they feature lifelong progressive activists. Oral histories are more than simple recollections. What one chooses to remember, deem important, or evaluate as just or unjust flows from a world view. What differentiates the oral histories of these progressive activists is that their individual stories are framed by and rooted in a broader political framework. For example, my mother and Karl and Elaine Yoneda were all driven by a deep commitment to social justice. They demanded and fought for equal rights for all, regardless of the cost to them personally or to their families. This preoccupation added a depth and breadth to their oral histories and to their work in the Redress and Reparations movement. All three of these people dedicated themselves to preserving Manzanar while actively participating in the broader civil rights and peace movements. They understood that Manzanar was truly a site of conscience, a civil rights site as well as America's first Japanese American concentration camp.

Through their insider's perspective, we can see that Executive Order 9066 and the mandatory eviction and penal confinement of Japanese Americans that it set in motion during World War II was not an aberration or deviation of American policy. Instead, these progressive narrators viewed Manzanar as part of the general pattern and practice of American racism, embedded in and created by settler colonialism and chattel slavery. My mother often mused upon and recounted that the policies in Manzanar were shaped by the fact that most of the early staff and administrators at Manzanar had not only transferred there from the Office of Indian Affairs but also brought with them a colonial mentality and racist mindset. These social justice activists understood that the racial animus directed against people of Japanese ancestry during World War II was not some misguided deed or mistake. Indeed, my mother believed that fighting for redress and reparations and for the creation of the Manzanar National Historic Site was essential to help prepare the younger generations of Japanese Americans to face what she described as the "inherent racism" and discrimination that they would face throughout their lives.

The two essays in part 1 of *Manzanar Mosaic* provide significant factual and analytical value to our understanding of the dynamics within the Japanese

American community on the eve of and at the outbreak of World War II. Both essays thoroughly examine the political and social tensions within the Japanese American community and explore how they foreshadowed ominous developments within the barbed wire confines of Manzanar. Upon reading these essays in conjunction with the oral histories, we can see the logical through line of *Manzanar Mosaic* emerge with striking clarity.

The essay examining the impact of the Manzanar Revolt on the activists within the Manzanar Committee and others in the Redress and Reparations movement deserve attention. At the time of its original publication in 1974, little had been written about resistance in the World War II Japanese American camps. In fact, widespread scholarship about the camp and the forced removal in general was then barely developing. Previously, almost all of the scholarship and popular narrative focused on the "loyal" Americans of Japanese descent. By exploring the revolt in Manzanar and examining this significant and lethal mass resistance event, Hansen and Hacker broke with the dominant historiography at a time when the Redress and Reparations movement was in its early development stages. Their scholarship added fuel to the emergent righteous anger among many activists to demand that our national government address and redress the flagrant injustice of Executive Order 9066.

Hansen's persisting exploration of and reflection on the Manzanar Revolt of December 1942 within *Manzanar Mosaic* is of special interest. True to form, he thoughtfully examines and ruminates on critiques of this early groundbreaking work by him and David Hacker in a thoroughly principled manner while simultaneously explaining each position with care and respect. In so doing, he encourages the reader to understand some of the many complexities of the Manzanar Revolt.

Hansen has been a significant force in the life of the Manzanar Committee, the Manzanar Pilgrimage, and the Manzanar National Historic Site. His comradery, wise counsel, and skilled historical analysis have for a long time buoyed the resolve and proceedings of our committee and, in past years, my late mother's spirit. A colleague and consistent friend, he was unwavering in his support of my mother's life work to tell the story of the unwarranted eviction and undeserved incarceration so as to further the fight for democracy and against racial and governmental oppression everywhere. Simply put, he has made us stronger. That said, it is important to remember that his contributions extend well beyond Manzanar.

Both pioneer and visionary, Hansen's recording and documenting of the unsung heroes of the Japanese American community—particularly those driven by a refusal to tolerate blatantly racist treatment—translates into a long and distinguished track record. His steadfast and dogged determination in chronicling the life and contributions of those "unquiet Nisei"—those resisters and principled individuals who demanded that the wrongs of camp be recognized, damned, and made right, regardless of whether the perpetrator was from within or outside of the Japanese American community—is truly commendable.

Manzanar Mosaic is an excellent collection and exploration by one of the most consequential historians of Japanese American history. And for that, Art Hansen deserves our deep gratitude and appreciation.

Preface

This book, *Manzanar Mosaic*, is in accord with the main currents of my five decades of scholarship on Japanese American history, particularly that focused on the eviction and imprisonment of people of Japanese ancestry during World War II. Its major thematic topic has been the resistance mounted by Americans of Japanese ancestry to their oppression from whatever source, whether external or internal. Up to the present, I have peer-reviewed and/or written book reviews on a substantial array of studies falling broadly within this category. Additionally, I have served as a consultant on multiple documentary films of the same nature. When I launched my research and writing in this vein in the early 1970s, I was influenced primarily by two historical scholars. While both of them have achieved truly eminent careers, one was my senior, Roger Daniels, and the other my junior, Gary Okihiro.

Unlike these two greatly admired and highly respected colleagues, I have not produced a dizzying profusion of exemplary books, but merely a steady stream of historical essays or articles, the major ones of which appeared in an anthology titled *Barbed Voices: Oral History, Resistance, and the World War II*

Japanese American Social Disaster (Louisville: University Press of Colorado, 2018). Readers of the eight essays in that volume will find my theme of resistance to oppression pervasive. In addition, those who peruse my epilogue to *Barbed Voices* will be privy to those resistance-themed books I read and judged to be unusually noteworthy over the previous ten years. Resistance activity is also paramount in two recently published autobiographical works edited by me, one in relation to James Omura, *Nisei Naysayer: The Memoir of Militant Japanese American Journalist Jimmie Omura* (Stanford, CA: Stanford University Press, 2018), and the other pertaining to Yoshito Kuromiya, *Beyond the Betrayal: The Memoir of a World War II Japanese American Draft Resister of Conscience* (Louisville: University Press of Colorado, 2021). Moreover, those who peruse *Barbed Voices* and *Nisei Naysayer* will appreciate how deeply they are grounded in and sustained by oral historical interviews transacted chiefly, though not exclusively, by me.

Since *Manzanar Mosaic* consists of a combination of essays and oral history interviews carried out either by me alone or in tandem with a former colleague of mine in the Japanese American Oral History Project of the Oral History Program (now the Lawrence de Graaf Center for Oral and Public History) at California State University, Fullerton, I want here to discuss briefly my brand of essay writing and oral historical interviewing.

With respect to historical essays, I typically approach them in the manner so compellingly set forth by the prominent essayist Katharine Fullerton Gerould (1879–1944) in her 1935 piece titled "An Essay on Essays," most recently reproduced in Phillip Lopate's *The Glorious American Essay: One Hundred Essays from Colonial Times to the Present* (New York: Pantheon, 2020). According to Gerould, the explicit object of an essay is persuasion. Accordingly, it necessarily must state a proposition. Because the essay's basis is meditative, not polemical, potential readers must be admitted to the meditative process. The task of the essayist, then, is to show readers precisely how and why he/she made up his/her mind as to a given proposition and then engage them in reviewing the steps taken by which he/she reached his/her conclusions.

As to my mode of oral history interviewing, put simply it is a threefold process: (1) to produce an absorbing and useful conversational narrative developed by two parties, an interviewer and an interviewee, both of whom are knowledgeable about a common subject, the former mainly by dint of research and the latter principally by personal experience; (2) to undertake topical interviews that are embedded in full life histories, thereby avoiding the instrumental strip mining of factual information enacted by many interviewers for their narrow utilitarian purposes, while concurrently granting interviewees an opportunity to place their reflections on a part of their lives into the enlarged sphere of their complex biographical trajectory and providing other researchers with possibly useful information for their respective projects; and (3) to deposit the interviews, both tapes and transcripts, in a certified public archive so that they are available to all researchers on an equal and transparent basis and not be subject to the multiple pitfalls of those interviews cited within interpretive studies as being "in the possession of the author." In this connection, I want to register one additional point. Although I am a lifetime member and former president of both the regional Southwest Oral History Association (SOHA) and the national Oral History Association (OHA), as well as a past editor of the OHA's scholarly journal, the *Oral History Review*, I do not regard myself as an oral historian per se. Rather, I am a US intellectual, social, and cultural historian who employs oral history as one of many tools of historical inquiry and interpretation while being acutely aware that, like every other tool, it possesses special strengths and decided limitations.

A Note on Editing

All matters of style within *Manzanar Mosaic* follow the guidelines set forth in the 17th edition of *The Chicago Manual of Style*. As for the vocabulary utilized in relation to the World War II exclusion and detention experience of Japanese Americans, the essays in part 1 reflect the comparatively recent terminological shift in Japanese American studies from euphemistic to accurate descriptive language. However, in part 2 (Oral Histories) inappropriate terminology, such as "evacuation," employed frequently by interviewers and narrators alike owing to the interviews having been transacted in the 1970s, has been placed within quotation marks to signify its outdated character.

Readers of this book should also be aware of a few unavoidable inconsistencies within the text and the notes owing to historical peculiarities and changes in institutional nomenclature and classification. With respect to the first category, the detention center at Manzanar utilized idiosyncratic designations for its iterations as both a Wartime Civil Control Administration "assembly center" (Owens Valley Reception Center) and a War Relocation Authority "relocation center" (Manzanar War Relocation Center). As to the second category, the Oral History Program at California State University, Fullerton, first altered its appellation in 2003 to the Center for Oral and Public History and then again in 2017 to the Lawrence de Graaf Center for Oral and Public History.

To avoid possible confusion by readers over the use of Japanese American generational terms, their respective meanings are as follows: *Issei*, immigrant generation, denied, until 1952, US citizenship; *Nisei*, US-born citizens, children of Issei; *Kibei*, Nisei educated in Japan; *Sansei*, third-generation Japanese Americans; *Yonsei*, fourth-generation Japanese Americans. Less familiar than any of these generational terms is that of *Yobiyoshi*, a subgeneration between the Issei and Nisei signifying those Japanese immigrants who came to the United States as children to join their parents, older siblings, or other relatives. As for the term *Nikkei*, it is employed generically to designate all Americans of Japanese ancestry.

MANZANAR MOSAIC

In the early part of World War II, 110,000 persons of Japanese ancestry were interned in relocation centers by Executive Order no. 9066, issued on February 19, 1942.

Manzanar, the first of ten such concentration camps, was bounded by barbed wire and guard Towers, confining 10,000 persons, the majority being American citizens.

May the injustices and humiliation suffered here as a result of hysteria, racism and economic exploitation never emerge again.

—*California Registered Historical Landmark no. 850 plaque placed by the State Department of Parks and Recreation in cooperation with the Manzanar Committee and the Japanese American Citizens League, April 14, 1973*

Prelude

In 1972, at the urging of one of my mature California State University, Fullerton (CSUF), reentry students, Betty E. Mitson, I launched the Japanese American Oral History Project within the CSUF Oral History Program (now the Lawrence de Graaf Center for Oral and Public History). Thanks to Mitson's able tutelage, I was prepared to conduct interviews for this project, the first of its kind in the United States. A year later I was emboldened to transact my first oral history interview. It was a two-part interview, done by me on August 24, 1973, and November 15, 1973, in conjunction with two CSUF history majors, David A. Hacker and David J. Bertagnoli, both Japanese American Oral History Project affiliates. The narrator in question for that interview was Sue Kunitomi Embrey, one of this volume's dedicatees, who was then employed at the Asian American Studies Center at the University of California, Los Angeles, in a community outreach capacity while also serving as the chair of the activist Los Angeles–based Manzanar Committee.

At the conclusion of the interview with Embrey, she referred to a new and very popular work of historical fiction coauthored by Jeanne Wakatsuki

Houston and James D. Houston and entitled *Farewell to Manzanar: A True Story of Japanese American Experience during and after the World War II Internment* (Boston: Houghton Mifflin, 1973). Because Embrey, like Jeanne Houston, had been a wartime inmate at the Manzanar War Relocation Center, I was moved to ask her as my final question: "What exactly does it mean to say, 'Farewell to Manzanar'?" The essence of her response was this: "I think that the most important thing about saying 'Farewell to Manzanar' is facing the fact that there is racism in America.... Once you've faced it and know it's there, [and] possibly find ways and tools to cope with it, then you can let go of the past and say, 'Farewell.'"

In a very different sense, up until the mid-1980s, I myself struggled with the challenge of saying farewell to Manzanar—as both a historical topic and a geographical place—and I still, at least to a certain extent, wrestle with this ordeal right up to this present publication. I was first drawn to Manzanar while a 1960 senior at the University of California, Santa Barbara, while writing a term paper for a sociology class on what was then euphemistically styled as the "Japanese American Evacuation." In the course of preparing this paper, I had some assistance from informal interviews with the dentist father and housewife mother of a close Santa Barbara friend and classmate of mine, Norm Nakaji. Whereas Dr. Yoshio Nakaji related to me his experience of having himself and his family uprooted from their Terminal Island residence and incarcerated at the Manzanar concentration camp, his wife Lillian told me mostly about her resettlement out of Manzanar, with her two young sons, to rejoin her earlier resettled husband in Cincinnati, Ohio.

But Manzanar did not become much more than an abstraction to me until 1972, when I switched my scholarly focus from Anglo-American intellectual history to the World War II Japanese American experience. At that juncture I first began to teach classes in which my students wrote research papers on assorted dimensions of that experience. To prepare them, I exposed them to two guest lecturers, both CSUF colleagues of mine who had lived at Manzanar—one, a female Caucasian dean (Dr. Hazel Jones) and a former high school English teacher; the other, a male Japanese American history professor (Dr. [Kinji] Yada), who was once an adolescent inmate.

That same year I accompanied Yada, my best friend and boon companion, along with two other CSUF History Department colleagues (Jack Elenbaas and Tom Reins), on his personal thirtieth anniversary pilgrimage back to

FIGURE 1. Kinji Yada (center), a World War II inmate at the Manzanar War Relocation Center, with Jack Elenbaas (left) and Art Hansen, 1972. The three colleagues from the history department at California State University, Fullerton, were attending a pilgrimage to the Manzanar site. Photo by Tom Reins. Courtesy Lawrence de Graaf Center for Oral and Public History, California State University, Fullerton.

the Manzanar site, where his family had been incarcerated in 1942. Walking around the grounds of that mile-square camp and seeing the scant number of still-standing buildings, the concrete footprints of thirty-six barracks apartments and other structures that housed and serviced 10,000 inmates and their governmental keepers, and the exposed artifactual remnants of an imprisoned population's daily lives, all framed by the spectacular beauty of snowcapped 14,379-foot Mount Williamson, the second-highest mountain in the Sierra Nevada range, stamped an indelible impression on my mind. This imprint was burnished by my viewing, shortly thereafter, the stellar array of camp photos appearing in *Born Free and Equal: The Story of Loyal Japanese Americans* (New York: U.S. Camera, 1944) that famed photographer Ansel Adams had shot in 1943–44 when visiting Manzanar at the invitation of his friend Ralph P. Merritt, the camp's director.

Beginning in the 1973–74 academic year, I commenced the near-annual practice of taking a class of my students on an intensive weekend field trip to the Manzanar area. Lodged in the nearby town of Lone Pine at a motel consisting of refurbished camp barracks, the students and I were treated to a whirlwind tour by a pair of wartime Manzanarians, typically Shiro and Mary Kageyama Nomura or Sue Embrey and Wilbur Sato. They led us to the Lone Pine railroad depot, where many of the inmates had been transported from Los Angeles in 1942, took us on a hand-mapped and narrated excursion around the Manzanar site, and escorted us to the Eastern California Museum in the proximate community of Independence to see a Shiro Nomura–curated exhibit showcasing Manzanar memorabilia and to talk to local Owens Valley people who were connected to the Manzanar War Relocation Center during World War II. By the end of the weekend, the students were duly expected to select some aspect of Manzanar life to use as a topical foundation for fulfilling their culminating class assignment of an original historical research paper.

In addition to working with my students on their Manzanar-based writing projects, I partnered with several members of the Japanese American Oral History Project on a number of undertakings related to Manzanar. With Betty Mitson's assistance, I coordinated a 1973 University of California, Irvine, extension program lecture series designated as "Japanese American Internment during World War II: A Socio-Historical Inquiry." The first such event in the country, it included presentations by two of the notable Manzanar personalities whose oral histories are featured in *Manzanar Mosaic*, Togo Tanaka and the aforementioned Sue Kunitomi Embrey. With Mitson as my coeditor, I also published the first oral history book to pursue the topic of the World War II experience of Americans of Japanese ancestry, *Voices Long Silent: An Oral Inquiry into the Japanese American Evacuation* (Fullerton: Japanese American Oral History Project, Oral History Program, California State University, Fullerton, 1974).

Then too, during this 1973–74 interval, I coauthored with two of my especially capable students, David Hacker and Ronald Larson, a pair of in-depth research studies impinging on the Manzanar situation. The first of these, with Hacker, resulted in a published reassessment of the bloody Manzanar uprising of December 6, 1942 ("The Manzanar Riot: An Ethnic Perspective," *Amerasia Journal* 2 [Fall 1974: 112–57]); the second, with Larson, yielded an unpublished appraisal of the prewar Los Angeles Japanese American

FIGURE 2. Togo Tanaka (left), a documentary historian at Manzanar, speaks on the topic "How to Survive Racism in America's Free Society" in a extension class organized by Professor Art Hansen (right), University of California, Irvine, April 3, 1973. Courtesy Lawrence de Graaf Center for Oral and Public History, California State University, Fullerton.

"Communist" newspaper *Doho*, an organ that included several key staff members who would later play significant roles at Manzanar. Both of these treatises appear in the Essays section of *Manzanar Mosaic*.

Within this same two-year interval, I joined up with four of the above-named members of the Japanese American Oral History Project (Hacker, Bertagnoli, Mitson, and Larson) to conduct taped-recorded interviews with three Manzanarians, Sue Kunitomi Embrey, Karl Yoneda, and Elaine Black Yoneda. All three of these interviews are represented in the Oral Histories section of *Manzanar Mosaic*. I also transacted with Bertagnoli a few of the many fieldwork interviews we together as a team recorded with Owens Valley townspeople in regard to their World War II memories of Manzanar. These interviews constituted the core of a later publication edited by Larson with still another Japanese American Oral History Project member, Jessie A. Garrett: *Camp and Community: Manzanar and the Owens Valley* (Fullerton: Oral History Program, California State University, Fullerton, 1977), for which I provided the foreword.

FIGURE 3. Japanese American Oral History Project members at California State University, Fullerton, journey to the Manzanar War Relocation Center for the annual Manzanar Committee–sponsored pilgrimage, April 19, 1975. Left to right: (bottom row) Susan McNamara and Ronald Larson; (middle row) Mary Reando, Jessie Garrett, and Tonja Larson; and (top row) David Hacker, Art Hansen, and Reed Holderman. Courtesy Lawrence de Graaf Center for Oral and Public History at California State University, Fullerton.

Throughout the years spanning 1973 and 1978 I interviewed seven other Manzanarians, one of whose camp experiences are highlighted in the Oral Histories portion of *Manzanar Mosaic*: Harry Y. Ueno, whom I interviewed with Sue Kunitomi Embrey in 1976. This interview was subsequently published as a book coedited by Embrey, myself, and Betty Mitson under the title *Manzanar Martyr: An Interview with Harry Y. Ueno* (Fullerton: Oral History Program, California State University, Fullerton, 1986). Within this same time frame, I interviewed numerous other former Manzanarians whose stories are not included within *Manzanar Mosaic*. One other Manzanar-related activity I participated in during this interval was the collective creation of a Manzanar Committee–rooted critique of director John Korty's 1976 nationally televised and groundbreaking film *Farewell to Manzanar*.

Prelude 9

FIGURE 4. Cover photo for *Manzanar Martyr* depicts the central figure in the Manzanar Revolt, Harry Ueno (crouching with pipe), along with four other Manzanar inmates who were branded as "troublemakers" and imprisoned at the high-security Leupp Isolation Center in Arizona. Courtesy Lawrence de Graaf Center for Oral and Public History, California State University, Fullerton.

During the years between 1978 and 1983 I was drawn away from my near-exclusive preoccupation with Manzanar as a consequence of two developments. In 1978 I opted to topically orient one of my Japanese American–themed classes to the Poston Relocation Center (consisting of three camps) in southwest Arizona, which was located about equidistant as Manzanar from the CSUF campus. Part of the motivation for my decision was that the overwhelming number of the 2,000 pre–World War II Japanese Americans in Orange County had been incarcerated during the war at Poston. Instead of having the ten enrolled students write research papers, however, I assigned each of them to dedicate part of their spring break to enacting the following agenda: while lodging in a motel converted from a former Poston barrack in the Colorado River town of Parker, Arizona, to collectively tour the Poston site and a curated exhibit about it in a local La Paz County museum, and then, individually, to conduct an oral history interview with a pre-selected person about his or her 1942–45 interactions with the Poston camp. The edited and indexed transcripts of these ten interviews (plus two others done by David Hacker and me) were published in a volume I coedited with another Japanese American Oral History Project member, Nora M. Jesch, as "Part V: Guards and Townspeople" in *Japanese American World War II Evacuation Oral History Project* (Munich: K. G. Saur, 1993).

In the wake of this experience, in 1980 I became involved with another undertaking related to Poston as co-director of the Honorable Stephen K. Tamura Orange County Japanese American Oral History Project. Jointly sponsored by the Japanese American Council of the Historical and Cultural Foundation of Orange County and the Japanese American Oral History Project at CSUF, this project generated oral history interviews, converted into bound and indexed volumes, with about a dozen pioneering Orange County Japanese Americans of the first-generation (Issei) and second-generation (Nisei)—with the former being rendered bilingually and the latter exclusively in English. In virtually all of these interviews the narrators related their World War II experiences at the Poston Relocation Center.

But what was mostly responsible for my bidding "farewell to Manzanar," leastwise temporarily, occurred in March 1983 when I attended the International Conference on Relocation and Redress at Salt Lake City, Utah. The proceedings of this event, which attracted a panoply of prominent participants in the burgeoning field of Japanese American studies, were later collected in a publication edited by the conference organizers, Roger Daniels, Sandra C. Taylor, and Harry H. L. Kitano, *Japanese Americans: From Relocation to Redress* (Salt Lake City: University of Utah Press, 1986). There I met people whom previously I had only heard about or, at best, whose books, articles, and reviews I had come across in my research and teaching. One of them was Daniels, an endowed professor of history at the University of Cincinnati and the dean of World War II Japanese American history. The author by then of three landmark books in the field—*The Politics of Prejudice* (Berkeley: University of California Press, 1962); *Concentration Camps USA* (New York: Holt, Rinehart and Winston, 1971); and *The Decision to Relocate the Japanese Americans* (Philadelphia: Lippincott, 1975)—Daniels had recently served as a consultant to the congressional Commission on Wartime Relocation and Internment of Civilians. We had been in touch by mail but had never met in person. I was pleased when he invited me up to his hotel room one night for a chat. I don't recall much of what we talked about on that occasion except for one thing: before wishing me a good evening, Daniels tendered this piece of advice: "You *must* get well beyond Manzanar in your research and writing." Which is precisely what I did, in a small but significant way, the very next day when I boarded a bus that took conferees on a guided tour of the Topaz Relocation Center, located in west-central Utah, 140 miles southwest of Salt Lake City and just north of the town of Delta.

In the forty years since that Salt Lake City conference, I have visited the remaining seven WRA centers—in California (Tule Lake), Arizona (Gila River), Wyoming (Heart Mountain), Idaho (Minidoka), Colorado (Amache), and Arkansas (Rohwer and Jerome). In relation to the first four of these centers, I have produced multiple publications and oral history interviews, while in connection with the Colorado and Arkansas camps, I have, through my affiliation with the Japanese American National Museum, first as its senior historian and then as a historical consultant, staged national conferences that spotlighted them. Moreover, I have led organized grant-funded tours around the Gila River camp and on my own toured the two WRA isolation centers in Moab, Utah, and Leupp, Arizona (which imprisoned a contingent of Manzanarians in 1943) as well as a good share of the sites constituting the Wartime Civil Control Administration (WCCA) and Department of Justice (DOJ) facilities that incarcerated Americans of Japanese ancestry during World War II.

However, my strongest identity has remained with Manzanar, which is the Japanese American camp where, far and away, I have spent the most time as a visitor, consultant, volunteer, and invited speaker. While I have attended (and contributed my services to) pilgrimages at two other camps, Tule Lake and Heart Mountain, and found these occasions to be truly enlightening and exceedingly memorable experiences, I have participated in Manzanar pilgrimages for five decades and have become, as my dedication for this book intimates, closely allied and deeply indebted to the members of the Manzanar Committee and the staff and volunteers at the Manzanar National Historic Site.

Even though my work over the last half century as a student of the World War II Japanese American experience has taken me well beyond Manzanar, this sacred place has always continued to be a staple in my life and career. I have directed Manzanar-focused theses and projects done by my CSUF graduate students, one of which gained publication, Jane Wehrey's *Voices from This Long Brown Land: Oral Recollections of Owens Valley Lives and Manzanar Pasts* (New York: Palgrave Macmillan, 2006); consulted on Manzanar-related books and documentary films; coedited a 1995 National Park Service–funded annotated bibliography on the Manzanar site with Jane Wehrey, Sue Embrey, Debra Gold Hansen, Garnette Long, and Kathy Frazee; keynoted a 2008 Manzanar Pilgrimage address; delivered both a 2012 Day of Remembrance presentation and, six years later, a talk on my book *Barbed Voices* (Louisville: University Press of Colorado, 2018) at Manzanar's interpretive center; published a book within my Michi and Walter Weglyn Multicultural Publication Series on Manzanar's Children's Village, Catherine Irwin's *Twice Orphaned* (Fullerton: Center for Oral and Public History, California State University, Fullerton, 2008); written the forewords for two Manzanar-oriented books: Samuel Nakamura's *Nurse of Manzanar* (Bellingham, WA: self-published, 2008) and Naomi Hirahara and Heather C. Lindquist's *Life after Manzanar* (Berkeley, CA: Heyday, 2018); guided the publication of Frank F. Chuman's memoir *Manzanar and Beyond* (San Mateo, CA: Asian American Curriculum Project, 2011); and penned reviews for San Francisco's *Nichi Bei Weekly* newspaper of two Manzanar books—Hank Umemoto's *Manzanar to Mount Whitney* (Berkeley, CA: Heyday Books, 2013) and Arthur L. Williams's *Reflecting on WWII, Manzanar, and the WRA* (Victoria, BC: Friesenpress, 2014). On one occasion, in 2011, I even served on a Manzanar National Historic Site selection committee for the hiring of two National Park Service interpretive rangers. In truth, being at Manzanar or even driving past the site on historic US Route 395 unfailingly moves me intellectually, emotionally, and spiritually.

The temporal center of gravity for *Manzanar Mosaic* is the year of 1942, extending from the late-winter and early-spring planning and construction of the camp, to its subsequent populating by US citizens and law-abiding alien inmates (overwhelmingly of Japanese ancestry) and administrative and appointed personnel (preponderantly of Euro-American descent), and proceeding down through the assorted developments within the camp's evolution that led to the climactic riot (or revolt) that erupted in the early days of

December. Although some of the material in this volume necessarily deals with events that occurred both prior to and after 1942, that situation is decidedly the exception and not the rule.

What makes this book a mosaic, per its title, is that it is composed of two diverse genres. Part 1 (Essays) consists of two items. The first essay, coauthored by Ronald C. Larson and me in 1975, treats the 1937–42 history of the Los Angeles–based Japanese American Communist newspaper *Doho*. When we submitted this piece for publication consideration as an article by the relatively new and already respected *Amerasia Journal*, it was rejected by the editors on the grounds that, whereas *Doho* was published in both a Japanese-language edition and an English-language edition, our article paid attention only to the latter, much smaller of these two editions. Accordingly, we did not pursue publication further but simply set the manuscript aside, and in time it even became misplaced. Only recently was it discovered in the Japanese American Oral History Project archival files housed in the Lawrence de Graaf Center for Oral and Public History at CSUF by its archivist, Natalie Garcia. Upon reading this composition anew, Larson and I were convinced that, notwithstanding its purported linguistic limitation, it still possessed a great deal of historical value, especially in the context of *Manzanar Mosaic*. This is because some of *Doho*'s significant contributors were incarcerated at Manzanar, where a number of them became affiliated with the *Manzanar Free Press* camp newspaper and, along with other ideological cohorts, spearheaded controversial camp organizations and championed unpopular policies that landed them, along with prominent prewar Japanese American Citizens League leaders from Los Angeles, on the blacklist and death list compiled by inmate adversaries at the time of the December 1942 Manzanar Riot.

It is this event, which David Hacker and I interpreted from a revisionist ethnic perspective, that serves as the second document in part 1. Although this essay has previously been published, most recently in my book *Barbed Voices*, without it, the oral histories constituting part 2 of *Manzanar Mosaic* would be greatly diminished in significance and power. This is because all five of these conversational narratives had the overarching purpose of clarifying and comprehending this cataclysmic incident. In fact, readers of this book might seriously consider perusing the oral histories in part 2 before tackling the Manzanar Riot article. If the year 1942 is indeed this volume's temporal center of gravity, then the Manzanar Riot article is assuredly its experiential epicenter.

Readers of these two essays should keep in mind the several ways in which they overlap and interpenetrate one another. First, both of them focus on the Japanese American community of Los Angeles: its prewar experience in the late 1930s and early 1940s (in the *Doho* piece) and its wartime camp experience in 1942 (in the Manzanar Riot piece). Second, both of these essays are resistance-themed interpretive studies: in the *Doho* essay, the oppression that the so-called Communist newspaper addresses and aims to redress within the Nikkei community is hegemonic Japanese Fascist propaganda and the capitalist exploitation of proletarian workers; in the Manzanar Riot essay, the oppression that an increasing number of camp inmates mobilize to confront and overcome is the unjust racist policies of the US government and its WRA administration and the collaborative support for these policies by an incongruous yet opportunistic coalition of two markedly opposing prewar groups, the Japanese American Citizens League and far-left political progressives. Third, both of these essays are revisionist in character: on the one hand, the *Doho* essay argues that the Communist newspaper, notwithstanding its ideological underpinnings, functioned as a much-needed alternative community newspaper in the prewar Los Angeles Japanese American community; on the other hand, the Manzanar Riot essay makes the case that what occurred at the Manzanar War Relocation Center in eastern California in 1942 was not a "riot" but rather a "revolt."

The narrations in the five oral history interviews that constitute part 2 are ordered in the following sequence: Sue Kunitomi Embrey (Nisei, *Manzanar Free Press* journalist), Togo Tanaka (Nisei, documentary historian), Karl Yoneda (Kibei, block leader), Elaine Black Yoneda (Jewish American social and political activist), and Harry Ueno (Kibei, Kitchen Workers Union leader). Each of these five people were noteworthy Manzanar inmates. All of their interviews were tape-recorded in the 1970s, and each of them provide exceedingly important information bearing on camp life in 1942, including the "riot" at that year's end. Of the five inmate interviewees, Tanaka, the two Yonedas, and Ueno, for one or another reason, had departed Manzanar before the end of 1942, while Embrey left camp the following year.

The interview transcripts that appear in part 2 represent only the portions that predominantly bear directly or, in a few instances, indirectly on the narrators' 1942 imprisonment at Manzanar. As indicated on the first page of each interview, the full transcripts are available to researchers at the Lawrence de Graaf Center for Oral and Public History at CSUF. Three of these interviews (Sue Kunitomi Embrey, Togo Tanaka, and Harry Ueno) have appeared previously in print, but those with the Communist couple Karl Yoneda and his Caucasian wife, Elaine Black Yoneda, are published here for the first time.

Because all of the interviews in part 2 were designed to produce life-history research documents and not merely specialized topical ones, they were necessarily of considerable length, with some of them requiring multiple days of taping, which was the case for the interviews with Sue Kunitomi Embrey, Karl Yoneda, and Elaine Black Yoneda. In order to provide readers with background information about the interviewees' pre-Manzanar lives, I have supplied a biographical profiles at the beginning of each oral history. Thereafter, the documents, save for the interview with Harry Ueno, are rendered as question-and-answer dialogues. To save space, the post-Manzanar experiences of those interviewed are not provided, though in the Selected Bibliography section of *Manzanar Mosaic* I have listed sources in which this information can be found for all five of the narrators.

In reading the transcribed oral histories, readers should keep in mind what the Lawrence de Graaf Center for Oral and Public History provides as a cautionary note for users of its archival holdings: "The reader should be aware that an oral history document portrays information as recalled by the interviewee. Because of the spontaneous nature of this kind of document, it may contain statements and impressions that are not factual."

In scrutinizing the interviews in part 2 of *Manzanar Mosaic*, you should be able to appreciate how this section of the book best embodies the metaphor of "mosaic" in its title, for by so doing you will have lodged in your mind the pieces of information and impressions that in combination serve to present you with a subjective holistic portrayal of the conflicted World War II Manzanar experience, with particular reference to the 1942 year of turmoil.

Introduction

Manzanar was the first of ten detention centers created for "national security" by the US government in 1942, following Japan's bombing of Pearl Harbor on December 7, 1941, and the entrance of the United States into World War II. Incarcerated in these camps were more than 120,000 US-resident Japanese Americans, approximately one-third of whom were law-abiding Japanese aliens (Issei) denied US citizenship and two-thirds US citizens (preponderantly second-generation Nisei, but also some third-generation Sansei and even a few fourth-generation Yonsei). Located inside the West Coast military zones in eastern California's Inyo County, 212 miles north of Los Angeles and nearly equidistant between the Owens Valley towns of Lone Pine and Independence on US Route 395, the Manzanar site had been home for centuries to the Paiute and Shoshone Indians. They were displaced by homesteaders, who in turn sold out to developer George Chaffey in the early 1900s. Chaffey planted fruit trees, subdivided the property into small ranches, and marketed it as Manzanar (Spanish for "apple orchard"). By 1930, the orchard owners had sold the land to the Los Angeles Department of Water and Power.

https://doi.org/10.5876/9781646424221.c002

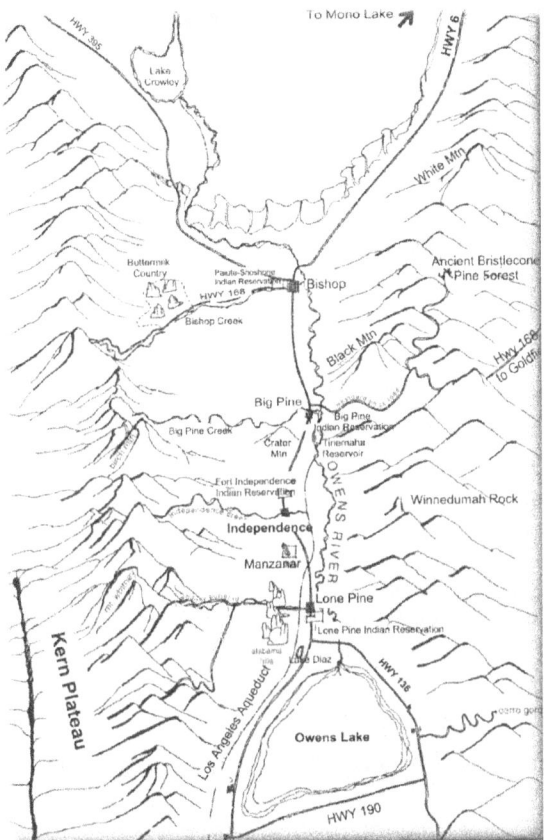

FIGURE 5. Map of Owens Valley, adapted from Julian Steward, "Ethnography of the Owens Valley Paiute," *American Archaeology and Ethnology* 33, no. 3 (1933): insert between pages 324 and 325. Courtesy Lawrence de Graaf Center for Oral and Public History, California State University, Fullerton.

The Manzanar camp was established initially by the US Army as an "assembly center" and managed by the Wartime Civil Control Administration (WCCA) as the Owens Valley Reception Center from March 21 through May 31, 1942. On June 1, 1942, Manzanar became the only one of fifteen total "assembly centers" to be constituted as a "relocation center" administered by the War Relocation Authority (WRA), and it was renamed the Manzanar War Relocation Center. As a WCCA unit, Manzanar had one project director (Clayton Triggs). In its "relocation center" phase, which extended to its shutdown on November 21, 1945, Manzanar's directors were Roy Nash and Ralph P. Merritt, along with two acting directors, Harvey N. Coverley and Solon T. Kimball (extending until November 24, 1942). The overwhelming majority of the camp's peak population of 10,121 (nearly equally divided between male and female with one-quarter of them school-age children) derived primarily from prewar Japanese American communities in Los Angeles County, particularly the city of Los Angeles, which was the prewar population, commercial, and sociocultural capital of mainland Japanese America.

Situated in the rain shadow of the imposing Sierra Nevada range at the base of 14,375-foot Mount Williamson on some 6,000 acres of land leased from the Los Angeles Department of Water and Power, Manzanar experienced a harsh climate of extreme temperature, high winds, and severe dust storms. The camp proper consisted of a 550-acre rectangle dominated by thirty-six blocks of 504 tar-paper residential barracks for the incarcerated population, most of whom lived within twenty-by-twenty-five-foot family apartments. This area encompassed communal mess halls, laundry facilities, and latrines for each inmate block, as well as considerably upgraded living facilities for the appointed personnel. Additionally, it contained a modern 150-bed hospital, schools, churches, recreational and cultural facilities, cooperative stores, and most other amenities found in a "normal" American city of comparable size. Also located in this central area were war-related industries (for example, a camouflage net factory), an experimental plantation for producing natural rubber from the guayule plant, and the Children's Village orphanage. Immediately outside this main camp were 1,500 acres of agricultural land, which not only contributed to Manzanar's food supplies but also augmented those of several of the nine other WRA camps. The camp's core was surrounded by barbed wire and overlooked by eight sentry towers and manned by armed military police, a battalion of which was quartered a half-mile south of the Manzanar center and, in 1942, was equipped with twenty-one rifles, eighty-nine shotguns, six machine guns, and twenty-one submachine guns.

Although relative peace and harmony generally prevailed within the center, inmate resistance to unpopular administrative policies—manifested as work slowdowns and strikes as well as through cultural politics and noncompliance with regulations—was not uncommon. The most dramatic incident of resistance occurred on December 6, 1942. Sparked by the jailing of the Kitchen Workers' Union's popular head (Harry Ueno) for his alleged participation in the beating of an unpopular inmate (Fred Tayama) prominent in the Japanese American Citizens League (JACL), whose leaders were widely assumed by inmates to be collaborators and informers, the so-called

Manzanar Riot climaxed in the death of two inmates and the wounding of at least nine others by MP-fired bullets. Its aftermath involved the roundup and ultimate imprisonment (without formal charges or hearings) of Ueno and other suspected "pro-Japanese" advocates and camp "troublemakers" in WRA citizen isolation centers in Moab, Utah, and Leupp, Arizona, and the "protective custody" consignment to an abandoned Civil Conservation Corps (CCC) camp, known as Cow Creek, in nearby Death Valley National Monument, of JACL and allied "pro-American" spokespersons and their families. A more pervasive and protracted show of resistance was set in motion two months later, in February 1943, when the US Army and the WRA imposed a mandatory registration of the adult population of Manzanar (and the other WRA centers) for the joint purpose of establishing eligibility for leave clearance and securing volunteers for a special Japanese American combat team. At Manzanar only forty-two persons (2 percent of the eligible citizen males) volunteered for military service, while approximately 50 percent of all eligible male citizens and 45 percent of all eligible female citizens either answered "no" to the professed "loyalty questions" on the registration questionnaire or refused to answer the questions. The latter situation led to 1,322 allegedly "disloyal" Manzanarians and their families (a grand total of 2,165 individuals) being transferred in late 1943 to the WRA's newly established Tule Lake Segregation Center in Northern California.

For the remaining two war years, Manzanar was a more accommodating camp. Thus, in early 1944, when the War Department's resumption of the Nisei draft was challenged by a widespread inmate resistance movement, it was one of only two WRA camps (the other was Gila River in Arizona) not to log a solitary draft resister. With the departure of its "disloyals" to Tule Lake (along with expatriates and repatriates to Japan) and an increasing number of its "loyals" entering the military and resettling throughout the United States as war workers and college students, Manzanar became a community largely of elderly and youthful residents. Notwithstanding limited self-government and an improved physical appearance and social ambience, Manzanar retained constant reminders that it was a concentration camp; its residents were not free to leave, its newspaper (*Manzanar Free Press*) was censored, and its boundaries were patrolled by soldiers with loaded weapons.

After its November 21, 1945, closure, the Manzanar site reverted to its prewar "natural" state, save for three surviving inmate-built structures (two

1942 pagoda-like stone security posts at the camp's eastern entrance and a 1944 auditorium on the northeast perimeter) plus scattered remnants of the constructed and botanical environment. Beginning in 1969 annual pilgrimages to the site have been held under the sponsorship of the Manzanar Committee, a Los Angeles-based community activist group. Manzanar was declared a state historical landmark in 1972 and a national historical landmark in 1985. On March 3, 1992, President George H. W. Bush signed a law passed by the US Congress that established Manzanar National Historic Site and provided for government purchase of the site and National Park Service administration, under the Department of the Interior, for preservation and historical interpretation.

Part 1
ESSAYS

Both of the essays in this section are rooted in a single report, "A Report on the Manzanar Riot of Sunday, December 6, 1942," by Togo Tanaka. He wrote it for the University of California, Berkeley (UCB)–based Japanese American Evacuation and Resettlement Study (JERS) on January 19, 1943, while in protective custody at the Cow Creek camp in Death Valley, California, following the December 6, 1942, riot/revolt at the Manzanar War Relocation Center, in which as an inmate he was a participant-observer. This report along with several addenda to it, including one on the *Doho* newspaper, are archived at the Bancroft Library, UCB, JERS, O 10.12.

After Tanaka's 1943 report, *Doho* was accorded significant attention in memoirs by two of its pre–World War II staff members, James Oda, in *Heroic Struggles of Japanese Americans: Partisan Fighters from America's Concentration Camps* (North Hollywood, CA: Self-published, 1980), 258–66, and Karl Yoneda, in *Ganbatte: Sixty-Year Struggle of a Kibei Worker* (Los Angeles: Asian American Studies Center, UCLA, 1983). However, the sole extant substantial treatment of this newspaper to appear in print is chapter 6 ("The *Doho*:

An American Guardian," 246–83), of Takeya Mizuno's 2000 University of Missouri doctoral dissertation entitled "The Civil Libertarian Press, Japanese American Press, and Japanese American Mass Evacuation."

None of these three studies, all by Japanese-English bilingual authors, had been written when Ronald Larson and I penned our unpublished *Doho* essay of 1975 that is reprised in the present volume. However, James Oda, who had declined to have his November 14, 1974, interview with Larson tape-recorded, was permitted to read the final draft of our *Doho* essay. As he noted in *Heroic Struggles of Japanese Americans* (258–59), Oda disagreed with Larson and me on two major points. "Despite their contentions, the *Doho* never claimed to be a Communist organ, nor did it ever endorse the platform of the Communist Party. Secondly, the *Doho* fought pro-Japan sentiment almost to the extent of Uncle Tomism, in the hopes of retaining Japanese-American citizenship." Also, as opposed to our assertion that *Doho*'s staff members were "heirs to an impressive heritage of Japanese-American socialists," Oda felt that their greatest inheritance was their "sense of radicalism—the sense of fundamental truth, the essential ingredient in the leap for progress." Another point of concern for Oda was that our manuscript was based exclusively on the smaller English section of *Doho*, which in his opinion "by no means represented the paper as a whole."

As for Takeya Mizuno's account of *Doho*—a tabloid-sized paper in which the English section comprised one page compared to eight Japanese pages—its liberal, progressive editorial policy was community-oriented: "to serve the welfare of the U.S. Japanese in general, [and] the nisei in particular." Prior to Japan's December 7, 1941, attack on Pearl Harbor, *Doho*'s position was "anti-militarism and anti-Japan," and it was committed to exposing un-American activities of "die-hard fascists." As for Japanese Americans, according to *Doho*, they had only two choices: the United States or its Axis enemies, and it was a must for them to "identify themselves as unequivocally and exclusively as 'Americans.'" Genuine Americanism for Japanese Americans could only be gained through "one hundred percent cooperation with the war policies of the United States government." All Japanese Americans, Issei and Nisei alike, had to abandon their old ethnic identities and unconditionally adopt the American way of life. After Pearl Harbor *Doho* insisted upon the expulsion of the pro-Japan faction from the Japanese American community and zealously supported the FBI's sweeping apprehensions of Japanese nationals. The paper fully endorsed President Roosevelt's issue of his February 19, 1942, Executive Order 9066, setting in motion the forcible mass eviction and incarceration of the West Coast population of people of Japanese ancestry and called for patriotic Nisei to aid the government in implementing this objective. *Doho* even went so far as to advocate for Japanese Americans to give up their First Amendment rights of speech, press, and assembly. It furthermore argued that Japanese Americans had a collective responsibility to go to incarceration camps. The many problems that this imposed for Japanese Americans were purely secondary to their primary responsibility to facilitate national defense. While *Doho* requested that the US government conduct its policy of mass removal and detention of people of Japanese ancestry as "humanly and compassionately" as possible, it forcefully impressed upon its readers the need to support this policy as evidence of their assimilation as loyal, self-sacrificing Americans, which *Doho* defined in terms of a "total detachment from Japan." *Doho* voiced and justified this controversial editorial position based strictly upon its overriding commitment to serve the Japanese American community as the guardian of its well-being.

As for the literature produced on the subject of the Manzanar "Riot" in the years since Togo Tanaka's 1942 treatment of it, although numerous studies accorded attention to it in the ensuing years, the first in-depth assessment of it came about when David Hacker and I published our article in the *Amerasia Journal* in 1974. Twenty-six years later, a two-volume US government–sponsored work, authored by Harlan D. Unrau, *Manzanar National Historic Site, California: The Evacuation and Relocation of Persons of Japanese Ancestry during World War II: A Historical Study of the Manzanar War Relocation Center* (Washington, DC: U.S. Department of the Interior, National Park Service, 1996) was published. Chapter 11, "Violence at Manzanar on December 6, 1942: An Examination of the Event, Its Underlying Causes, and Historical Interpretation," provided a wide-ranging and detailed assessment of the event in question. This comprehensive study, which defies easy summarization, merits examination and is available online at https://www.nps.gov/parkhistory/online_books/manz/hrs11.htm (accessed March 20, 2011).

It was not until the opening of the present century that our analysis of this bloody event met with fundamental criticism in the form of Lon Kurashige's penetrating and consequential article, "Resistance, Collaboration, and Manzanar Protest," *Pacific Historical Review* 3 (August 2001): 387–417. According to Kurashige, although our study represented a revisionist challenge to previous interpretations of the riot, it was seriously flawed by its similarity to those by earlier analysts of our generation in being preoccupied with cultural conflict. "In sympathizing with internee protesters," explained Kurashige, "revisionists have exposed the ideological underpinnings of triumphalist narratives on internee cooperation. But, in the process, they have missed the opportunity to explore deeper social and cultural formations among the internees. One of these was a historically precedented yet virtually ignored class conflict among Japanese Americans." The year following the publication of this article, Kurashige buttressed his position within his groundbreaking book *Japanese American Celebration and Conflict: A History of Ethnic Identity and Festival in Los Angeles, 1934–1990* (Los Angeles: University of California Press, 2002), particularly chapter 3, "War and the American Front: Collaboration, Protest, and Class in the Internment Crisis." It was with this chapter in mind that Scott Tang, in his 2003 online review of Kurashige's book (H-California, H-Net Reviews, http://www.h-net.org/reviews/show rev.php?id=8333 [accessed March 19, 2021]) offered this cogent observation: "Kurashige portrays the Manzanar protest as a challenge to the ethnic orthodoxy maintained by the JACL and argues that class, education, and cosmopolitanism influenced whether one was against or for the protest. By analyzing the social backgrounds of those involved, he claims that the pro-WRA faction included college-educated urban Nisei who had the skills, the opportunity, and the cultural capital to succeed in the world outside the ethnic community. The protesters, on the other hand, remained detached from white America and tended to come from the farming classes. Kurashige also suggests that white racism's persistence embittered the Nisei and led some of them to criticize those who implemented and supported the internment. Kurashige's interpretation thus revises earlier studies that characterized the Manzanar protest as primarily a struggle between the Americanized Nisei and the Issei and Kibei, two social groups which were thought to have stronger cultural ties with Japan."

Two years later, Brian Masaru Hayashi, a generational colleague of Lon Kurashige, in *Democratizing the Enemy: The Japanese American Internment* (Princeton, NJ: Princeton University Press, 2004), offered another variant of criticism. Here Hayashi took Hacker's and my work to task, as well as that of other historical authors of our generation, such as Gary Okihiro and Michi Weglyn, for failing to consider "the wider, global context influencing decision makers and victims in events such as the Manzanar 'Riot.'" "After observing 'disloyal' behavior in Manzanar, such as the singing of the Japanese national anthem and the Imperial Navy marching song during a riot," observed Hayashi, "[Hansen and Hacker] interpreted it as evidence of a Japanese American desire to create 'Little Tokyos in the desert,' where their prewar culture of 'group solidarity' and 'the predominance of elements of Japanese culture' could survive."

A few years later Eileen H. Tamura produced a first-rate biographical book, *In Defense of Justice: Joseph Kurihara and the Japanese American Struggle for Equality* (Urbana: University of Illinois Press, 2013), based on the life of Joe Kurihara, a Hawai'i Nisei and World War I veteran, who not only denounced the US government's unwarranted eviction and imprisonment of 120,000 Nikkei in the wake of Japan's attack on Pearl Harbor, but allegedly was chiefly responsible for the Manzanar Revolt. At one point in her narrative, Tamura offered a footnote juxtaposing two explanations by historians for what underlay the conflict between the anti-administrative protesters and the pro-administrative JACL that precipitated the explosive event, and then provided her own interpretation. "Lon Kurashige challenges the emphasis on cultural differences [by Hacker and me] and instead highlights differences in class backgrounds.... My view is that social class interacted with and fed into the different cultural perspectives of the Nikkei."

In the 2001 article referenced above, Kurashige concluded with this provocative message: "More work needs to be done on the Manzanar riot.... Dichotomizing Manzanar internees into protesters and collaborators, pro-America and pro-Japan factions, has concealed as much as it has revealed about the inner history of Japanese Americans." I agree wholeheartedly with every dimension of this exceedingly insightful assessment. What future studies by historical scholars of the "riot," replete with new social theories, methods, and analytical tools, will produce is certainly interesting to behold in terms of the fresh insights they might yield in the form of historical explanation.

Doho

The Japanese American "Communist" Press, 1937–42

RONALD C. LARSON AND ARTHUR A. HANSEN

During the 1930s and 1940s the international Communist movement became a pawn of the Russian Foreign Office. Accordingly, the policies of the American Communist Party closely adhered to those laid down in Moscow. This audience is clearly reflected within Communist publications of the period. Rather than pursuing relatively unswerving editorial policies, these organs invariably shifted their policies to coincide with the radically fluctuating line of the Soviet Union, which swung from patriotic anti-fascism to pacifist isolationism and back again to a patriotic anti-fascism, pro-Ally stance. A case in point is the Japanese American "Communist" newspaper *Doho*, whose editorial policy evolved through these three stages during its short-lived existence between 1937 and 1942.

This essay has a twofold purpose. First, it seeks to demonstrate the correspondence between *Doho*'s policy orientation and Communist ideological objectives. Secondly, and more significantly, it attempts to show that *Doho* was much more than a mere echo of Comintern politics within the Japanese American pre–World War II community. Rather, it is herein posited that *Doho*

https://doi.org/10.5876/9781646424221.c003

was indeed a viable "community" newspaper, offering a much-needed alternative to the established vernacular press and providing realistic solutions for a wide assortment of pressing social issues and concerns.

This study has a quadripartite organization. The opening section surveys the parallel evolution during the 1930s and 1940s of the international Communist movement and that of the Communist Party of America (CPUSA). The second section traces the background of the Japanese American Left from the turn of the century up to the appearance of *Doho*. The third and longest section focuses upon *Doho* itself, illuminating its editorial position, examining its personnel, and assessing its impact. The concluding section offers a new interpretive perspective for understanding *Doho* and, by implication, the entire leftist movement within the prewar Japanese American community.

COMMUNIST PARTY POLICY, 1935-41

In 1935, 510 delegates from sixty-five Communist parties met in Moscow to participate in the Seventh World Congress of the Communist International. The main report was developed by Bulgarian Georgi Dimitrov, general secretary of the Comintern, while Premier Josef Stalin took a prominent part in the preparation and proceedings of the Congress.[1] As William Z. Foster, longtime president of the CPUSA, explains in his *History of the Three Internationals*, "The congress worked on the assumption that the world's peoples had the power to prevent war if they acted together."[2] The older Marxist axiom of class struggle was now de-emphasized, and a new policy of cooperation with the bourgeois—"the Popular Front"—was begun. "Ours has been a congress," Dimitrov proclaimed, "of a new tactical orientation of the Communist International." Seeing the development of the Fascist offensive as drastically altering the world situation, the Seventh Congress recognized that new tactics were required.[3] The united front policy adopted meant that Communists would now be forced to work within the framework of capitalism. Temporarily setting aside ideological purity for pragmatic expediency, Communists now were to participate in world governments elected under bourgeois democracy.[4]

The subsequent Popular Front era witnessed rapid growth for the CPUSA and ushered in relative popularity for Communists. Even many American liberals came to join the ranks of "front" groups.[5] While the majority of these "fellow travelers" never became official members of the party, they were absorbed within and supportive of the Popular Front coalition. The CPUSA, following the dictates of the Seventh Congress to utilize progressive democratic bourgeois statespersons as Popular Front leaders, championed President Franklin D. Roosevelt as their helmsman.[6] This alignment with the New Deal gained the CPUSA still more power and popularity. Another result of the Popular Front's flirtation with the Democratic Party was a deep split between the CPUSA and the American Socialist Party, which saw the Popular Front as a move to the Right and criticized the Communists on these grounds.[7] The CPUSA defended its strategy, however, by arguing that the international movement had to face the threat of Nazism and that there was a need both for "collective security" among "anti-fascist powers" and for unity on the Left.[8] In spite of continued Socialist Party opposition, the Popular Front emerged as a coalition of anti-Fascist, anti-militarist peoples and organizations. Indeed, the CPUSA became interested in all mass organizations and used them according to Popular Front policies.

On August 24, 1939, however, the growing membership and new respectability gained as a result of Popular Front tactics came to an abrupt halt with the signing of the Nazi-Soviet Non-Aggression Pact. This action caused many anti-Fascist Popular Front followers to become disenchanted with the CPUSA. Once again, though, the CPUSA showed its flexibility and dedication to the International Communist Party by shelving Popular Front policies and assuming a new stance of world peace and noninvolvement. Adopting the slogan "Keep America Out of War," the CPUSA now styled the impending war as a capitalist one. The watchword of the Popular Front, "Embargo Japan and Germany for the defeat of the fascist aggression," now gave way to such bywords as "Capitalism is the root cause of the great evils of war, hunger and oppression."[9] This period of isolationist noninvolvement ended on June 22, 1941, when Hitler's armies invaded the Soviet Union.

With the Soviet Union endangered, a reorientation of policy was now necessary. From this date until the end of the war, Communists the world over dedicated themselves totally to defeating the Axis powers. Once again the official policy of the CPUSA became super-patriotic, urging total war upon the Axis powers, advocating that the United States enter the war to create a Second Front, and calling for complete cooperation within the United States—even to the point of not allowing strikes by workers affiliated with

CPUSA-controlled labor unions.[10] The CPUSA was so fully committed to supporting US actions that Earl Browder, the de facto head of the CPUSA, proposed that the word "Communist" be dropped from the title of the CPUSA (and he was defeated by only *one* vote in the Political Committee).[11]

THE JAPANESE AMERICAN LEFT, 1904–37

Although *Doho* was not published until 1937, its staff members were heirs to an impressive heritage of Japanese American socialists, and the paper itself evolved from a long line of leftist publications. Among the twelve original founders of Japan's first socialist party in 1901, five played important roles in the socialist movement in the United States.[12]

One of these, Katayama Sen, first came to America in 1884 because he had heard that it was possible here to work one's way through college. After attending Oakland Hopkins Academy for eleven months, Katayama became the first Japanese student to attend Maryville College in Tennessee. From Maryville, he transferred to Grinnell College, Iowa, where he earned his BA and MA degrees (thus becoming the first Japanese to receive a graduate degree in the United States).[13] Katayama burned to better this world; indeed, this was the motivating force behind his dedication to the myriad causes he fought for along his political odyssey. His first cause was Christianity; following his attendance at Andover Theological Seminary, he received his BD degree in 1895 at Yale Divinity College.[14] But his religious impulse was channeled into secular concerns upon his return to Japan the following year, evolving from a trade unionist to an ardent socialist. His widening political activism ultimately provoked the authorities to sentence him to nine months in jail for antiwar activities.[15] After his release in 1904, he returned to the United States en route to Amsterdam as Japan's representative to the Sixth Congress of the Second International.

While in America, Katayama met with other Japanese socialists and members of the Socialist Party of America (SPA), then began a speaking tour entitled "The Socialist and the Anti-War Movements in Japan." This tour took him through many major American cities: Milwaukee, Chicago, Houston, Oakland, Sacramento, Portland, Los Angeles, San Francisco, and Seattle. In the last of these, assisted by Kawakami Kiyoshi, Katayama, he formed the Seattle Nihonjin Shakaito (Seattle Socialist Party).[16] In the Bay Area the two organized still another socialist society, the Soko Nihonjin Shakaito (San Francisco Japanese Socialist Party).[17] His tour over, Katayama sailed for Amsterdam, where he became famous among socialists by shaking hands with George Plekanov, the Russian delegate, as a symbolic gesture of friendship and socialist solidarity at a time when their two countries were involved in an "imperialistic" war.[18]

The next leading Japanese socialist to arrive in the United States was Abe Isoo, who, curiously enough, landed in San Francisco in 1905 in the nonpolitical role of manager for Waseda University's baseball team. He soon perceived that, despite Katayama's efforts, the cause of Japanese socialism had not made significant headway in America. With an eye toward changing this situation, Abe addressed several Japanese and socialist groups; but the results did not match his ambition, for apparently the moderate type of Christian socialism he espoused lacked sufficient appeal within the Japanese American community.[19]

The Japanese anarchist Kotoku Shusui continued the procession of prominent leftists across the Pacific. Silenced and sentenced to five months' imprisonment for violating Japan's National Press Law, Kotoku decided upon his release in 1905 from Sugamo Prison to seek refuge in the United States. Here, he explained in a letter to a California anarchist, he could continue his criticism of Japan's governmental policies "where the pernicious hand of 'His Majesty' cannot reach." Indeed, Kotoku envisioned the United States becoming a "sanctuary" and a "logistical base for operations" for Japan's revolutionaries in much the same way as Switzerland had for Russia's.[20]

Kotoku's initial American activities were propagandistic and educational in nature. They included writing a series of newspaper articles for San Francisco's vernacular newspaper, the *Nichibei Shimbun* (Japanese American News), which argued the need for socialism in Japan, and, after becoming a member of the SPA, conducting several "study sessions" on socialism in the Japanese immigrant communities of San Francisco and Oakland. Discussion soon led to action, however, and in 1906 Kotoku organized the Shakai Kakumeito (Social Revolutionary Party) in Oakland.

Although the original membership of the Shakai Kakumeito numbered fifty-two, only a handful of these—perhaps fifteen—resided in the Bay Area. As with most organizations, the active core was still smaller, consisting of Takeuchi Tetsugoro, Konarita Tsunero, Kuramochi Zensaburo, Hasegawa

Ichimatsu, Uyeyama Jitaro, Ogawa Kinji, and Iwasa Sakutaro. While not the first Japanese American socialist group, the Shakai Kakumeito was certainly the first to become visible to the larger community.

Shortly after its formation, the group staged a rally that gained it wide publicity. Further attention, even notoriety, followed publication of its official journal, the *Kakumei* (Revolution), commenced on December 20, 1906. Among the contents of this Japanese-language paper's first edition appeared one item in English: "Our policy is toward the overthrow of Mikado, King, President as representing the Capitalist Class as soon as possible, and we do not hesitate as to means."

This policy statement became a cause célèbre, and the Shakai Kakumeito, a term of opprobrium almost overnight, for the major Bay Area newspapers, exploiting the implied threat on President Theodore Roosevelt's life, responded with outrage and alarm. "Japs Favor Killing of President Roosevelt" and "Japanese Anarchists Publish Paper Urging President's Death" headlined the stories respectively in the *San Francisco Chronicle* and the *San Francisco Examiner*, while a similar brand of sensationalism, seasoned by anti-radical and anti-Japanese chauvinism, characterized the reportage dealing with the incident in the *San Francisco Call* and the *Berkeley Daily Gazette*.

Such journalistic fanning of the Yellow Peril fear quickly threw into jeopardy the very existence of the Shakai Kakumeito, and the man who assumed responsibility for the issue, Takeuchi Tetsugoro, was ordered to appear before a Special Board of Inquiry of the San Francisco Immigration Commission for deportation hearings. Though Takeuchi was spared deportation, his public identification with the cause of anarchism and the *Kakumei*'s repeated attacks on the emperor system won few friends within the Japanese immigrant community for the group.

Finally, on November 3, 1907, a faction within the group overstepped the threshold of the community's tolerance by issuing a mimeographed "Open Letter to Mitsuhito Emperor of Japan" on the occasion of Emperor Meiji's birthday. The letter declared that the emperor and the letter's authors had "evolved from 'monkeys' and hence were 'peers'"; that he was "responsible for the poverty and suffering of the poor; that he was 'vanity' personified if he believed the 'fabrications' scholars related about his origins." The circular also promised that a bomb would be planted to blow up the emperor. The combination of content and timing proved suicidal. It was offensive enough to speak of bombing the emperor, but to do it on his birthday was akin to sacrilege. Due to the community's negative reaction, the group was forced to disband, with its members either returning to Japan or dispersing throughout the Bay Area.[21]

During 1906, when the Shakai Kakumeito was experiencing difficult times, another leftist group was finding favor within the Japanese immigrant community. Founded by Abe Yoyoji, the Japanese Labor Union set up headquarters in Seattle and began publishing a newspaper, *Doho* (Brother, Brotherhood, Comrade), for its 600 members.[22]

Two years later, with the help of the Industrial Workers of the World (IWW), several Japanese socialists formed the Fresno Rodo Domei Kai (Fresno Labor League), which successfully organized 2,000 to 4,000 grape pickers. Spearheaded by Takeuchi Tetsugoro, the controversial ex-member of the Shakai Kakumeito, the league encountered opposition not only from the grape growers but from Japanese labor contractors as well.

In California a labor contracting system had evolved whereby the grower hired migrant farm workers. To restrict harmful competition, fifty-three Japanese labor contractors organized themselves into the Central California Contractors' Association on June 7, 1908. The association set the rate charged growers at $1.65 per ton of grapes picked, thereby guaranteeing the workers a higher salary than customarily received.

Trouble came, however, when the association attempted to contract with the Tarpey Ranch, one of the area's largest vineyards. This was because this ranch chose instead to contract with three renegade Japanese contractors who charged the lower rate of $1.25 per ton of grapes picked. It was precisely with the intention of giving the workers a lever against these three contractors that the Rodo Domei Kai was formed. Takeuchi and others quickly carried their fight to the surrounding area, persuading Japanese American pickers to boycott the three renegade contractors. Their efforts were successful, for thereafter no Japanese would work for the contractors; in order to live up to their commitment to the Tarpey Ranch, the three were forced to hire Mexican, Indian, and Korean laborers.

Fortified by this victory, the Rodo Domei Kai began publication of its official organ, the *Rodo* (Labor) on November 20, 1908. Takeuchi was joined by Matsushita Zenpei in the capacity of editors for the Fresno area, while Iwasa Sakutaro, Konarita Tsuenero, Kuramochi Zensaburo, and Ogawa

Kinji shared the *Rodo*'s editorial responsibilities for the Bay Area. Significantly, the paper's editorial staff was composed of many ex-members of the Shakai Kakumeito.[23] Publication of the *Rodo* continued until September 14, 1909.

Five years after the *Rodo* ceased its operations, another important development occurred in the Japanese American Left: Katayama returned to the United States and organized the Zeibei Nihonjin Rodo Domeikai (Japanese Labor League of America). By this time, Katayama was one of the most renowned socialists in this country, someone American socialists spoke of often and respectfully. Indeed, it is not an exaggeration to say that he had become "a legend in his own lifetime."[24] While here on this occasion he lived in San Francisco (where he worked as a cook) and started, in 1916, a monthly magazine called the *Heimin* (Commoner).[25]

The previous year a group of Japanese gardeners in Southern California formed the Seiren Rodo Doshikai (Brotherhood of Hollywood Laborers).[26] Still another labor association among Japanese workers came into existence in 1917 when Kagawa Toyohiko organized several hundred Japanese sugar beet sharecroppers in Ogden, Utah, into the Sharecroppers Union. The union lost no time in showing its strength, for within the year it had carried out a successful strike against the landowners in the area.[27]

Somewhat later, in 1926, a group of Japanese gardeners allied themselves with farm, domestic, and restaurant workers under the aegis of the Rafu Nihonjin Rodo Kyokai (Los Angeles Japanese Laborers Association) and started a journal, the *Kaikyu Sen* (Class War).[28] In these years, the CPUSA utilized "foreign language sections" as a device for organizing aliens and foreign-speaking peoples, and so the Rafu Nihonjin Rodo Kyokai functioned as a subsidiary of the Los Angeles CPUSA[29]—with the *Kaikyu Sen* serving as the Japanese section's house organ. After being published in Los Angeles for three months, the *Kaikyu Sen* moved to Berkeley, where it continued publication until early 1928. Throughout its history this paper covered current political issues as well as "educational articles on Marxism-Communism doctrines."[30]

Once the *Kaikyu Sen* was terminated, its staff launched a new journal, the *Zaibei Rodo Shimbun* (American Labor News). Since the Issei (first-generation Japanese Americans) were disallowed by law from becoming naturalized US citizens, they were not deemed attractive targets for voting drives.[31] Thus, the *Zaibei Rodo Shimbun* attempted to rally all Nisei (second-generation Japanese Americans) to vote for the Communist ticket of William Z.

Foster for president and Benjamin Gitlow for vice president.[32] When, in 1930, *Zaibei Rodo Shimbun* changed its name to *Rodo Shimbun* (Labor News), it also became the official organ of the Japanese Language Section of the American Communist Party. The next year, Teuchi Kenmotsu, the *Rodo's* first editor, was arrested and deported as an undesirable alien-Communist, and in 1933 Karl G. Yoneda—who would later serve as *Doho's* Bay Area correspondent—took over the paper's editorship.[33]

The year 1933 also witnessed the formation of the Rafu Nihonjin Yoshokuten Jugyoin Kumiai (Los Angeles Restaurant Workers Union).[34] Then, the following year, a counterpart organization to the Rafu Nihonjin Yoshokuten Jugyoin Kumiai was begun in San Francisco. Named the Soko Rodo Kyokai (San Francisco Labor Association), it gained a membership of some 300 Japanese domestic workers.[35]

It will be recalled that the Seventh Congress of the Communist International saw fascism as an emergency requiring a "popular front" strategy. It was Communist Party policy to align with virtually all mass organizations when, in 1936, the *Rodo Shimbun* staff found itself "making no headway." Thereupon they decided to change the format of the paper so as to appeal more to progressives and liberals. They also agreed at this time to move the newspaper's home from the Bay Area to Los Angeles because of the larger Japanese American population in Southern California.[36] With the new location came a new staff and a new editor.

DOHO: 1937-42

Doho, under the name *Zenshin* (Progress), began publication on January 1, 1937.[37] Edited by Shuji Fujii—who assumed the pseudonym Henry Shimura—*Zenshin* was an exclusively Japanese-language newspaper (as was its successor, in name, *Doho*), until the appearance of an English-language section on June 10, 1938.[38] In the first, and last, issue of *Zenshin*, readers were asked to select a permanent name for the newspaper from among a list of four: *Zenshin*, *Toso* (Struggle), *Zen Sen* (Frontline), and *Doho*. Because the last of these received the greatest reader support, the paper's next issue changed its masthead from *Zenshin* to *Doho*.[39]

Since all Los Angeles–based vernacular newspapers utilized a single personality to identify themselves in the community's mind, Shuji Fujii

FIGURE 6. *Doho* editor Shuji Fujii (left), his journalist wife Kikue Ukai Fujii, and typesetter George Matsui look over the historic December 7, 1941, issue bearing the headline "Defeat Militarist Japan." Courtesy Bancroft Library, University of California, Berkeley.

(who resorted to his own name once *Zenshin* gave way to *Doho*) was a judicious choice as *Doho*'s editor.[40] His family's journalistic reputation—his father was a well-known editor of a Japanese vernacular newspaper in San Francisco—endowed the paper with much-needed public acceptability.[41] *Doho*'s acceptability was also enhanced by its leftist coalition base. Whereas subscribers and newsstand operators had shied away from the blatantly Communist *Rodo Shimbun*, *Doho* circulated quite freely and found a considerably wide reading audience.[42]

That *Doho* endorsed the CPUSA's Popular Front policy of supporting the New Deal became apparent in its first English-language edition. One article predicted a large Nisei turnout for California's Democratic Party in the upcoming gubernatorial election, while another displayed typical Popular

Front allegiance and rhetoric: "Oregon's primaries showed that a broad Democratic Front can defeat a reactionary candidate when New Dealer Henry Hess won over the labor-hating Governor [Charles] Martin recently."[43]

Also evident in this edition was a theme which would reappear in virtually every subsequent edition: the exploitation of the Japanese people by the militarists in Japan. This theme, like most others appearing in *Doho*, probably reflected editor Fujii's own opinion and experience, because from its first issue, *Doho* was largely a one-man affair, with Fujii functioning as "publisher, editor, reporter, typesetter, composer, circulation manager, booster and promoter."[44] As a Kibei (a native-born American citizen who had received a significant portion of his education in Japan), Fujii had observed the militarists coming to power in Japan before his return to the United States sometime during the early 1930s, and this firsthand experience undoubtedly shaped both his and *Doho*'s anti-militarist outlook.[45]

While *Doho*, a relatively small voice in Los Angeles's Little Tokyo community, argued this anti-Japan perspective, the *Kashu Mainichi* (Japan-California Daily News), one of California's largest vernacular papers, presented the opposite view.[46] The *Kashu*'s editor, Sei Fujii (no relation to Shuji Fujii), glorified the military accomplishments of Japan. Predictably, therefore, a "David and Goliath–like" feud erupted between these two community organs, and this journalistic "war" represented still another theme that reverberated throughout the pages of *Doho* throughout its brief life.[47] Whereas the *Kashu* stigmatized *Doho* as an "*Aka* (Red) paper" because of its anti-militarist position, *Doho* assailed the larger paper for its pro-Japan—and thus "anti-democratic"—"propaganda."[48]

Among the editorial staffs of the Japanese vernacular newspapers in Los Angeles—the *Rafu Shimpo* (Los Angeles Japanese Daily News), the *Kashu Mainichi*, and the *Sangyo Nippo* (Southern California Industrial Daily)—there were many areas of agreement, with *Doho* being the only "rebel." Because of their greater circulation, the larger papers, particularly the *Rafu* and the *Kashu*, enjoyed greater power in the community. Nonetheless, due to its unique editorial positions, *Doho* served a vital function both within the Los Angeles and the larger West Coast Japanese American community.

The *Rafu*, the *Kashu*, and the *Sangyo* shared a common taboo against any criticism of the imperialist policies of Japan. Violators of this "conspiracy" of silence, like *Doho*, were quickly tagged with the dreaded *Aka* label by the

Little Tokyo press community.[49] The three major papers also acted as cultural custodians (i.e., protectors of the status quo) in matters of local politics; serving as the unofficial voice of the community's businessmen, the *Rafu*, *Kashu*, and *Sangyo* upheld conservative interests by indiscriminatingly applying the term *Aka* to anyone who championed the cause of labor organizing or unionism.[50] In addition, these papers were not reluctant to use their formidable leverage with the residents of Little Tokyo to place and perpetuate leaders within the community's governing hierarchy.[51]

Doho, as an alternative press, took radical exception to the underlying assumptions and common practices of the "established" papers. Consequently, it served as a voice for many within the community who had previously gone unrepresented—the working class and liberal "progressives." In taking up the cudgel for the workers, a substantial segment of the community, *Doho* undertook an especially challenging task. Organizing workers of any sort was hard enough during the Depression years, but Japanese American workers were probably the most difficult among the various ethnic groups.[52] Typically, the Japanese shop owner was a self-made man who, understandably enough, was committed to the conservative notion that others, including his employees, should also be able to work hard, save, and eventually attain a status commensurate with his own.[53] This idea, reinforced by the deference owed a superior within the traditional Japanese hierarchical system, had a powerful hold on Nikkei employees, especially the Issei and the Kibei. Still, an increasing number of the laboring class during the late 1930s were American-raised Nisei who were anxious for self-advancement and who gave the traditional deferential system less allegiance. *Doho*, seeing in this situation the basis for a more active labor movement, volunteered as its spokesperson.

Consistent with the CPUSA's Popular Front tactic of Americanization, *Doho* represented labor unions as being part of the "American Way." In response to charges from the establishment community press that *Doho*'s alliance with labor stemmed from its *Aka* character, *Doho* ingeniously turned the accusations around, pointing out that these papers were anti-labor, and hence un-American. And the more the established papers treated *Doho* as a subversive pariah for its unionizing enthusiasm, the more it was inclined to become venomous in its attacks on "exploitive" employers.

The first victim of *Doho*'s venom was the Three Star Produce Company, a chain of forty-five retail fruit and vegetable stores employing some 300 Nikkei employees. *Doho*'s first English edition featured an article by "a Three Star Employee" who urged his fellow workers to join the American Federation of Labor's Japanese Retail Clerks' Union. "As long as we stick together with other Japanese workers," explained the union advocate, "we can get some protection from losing our jobs left and right."[54] To assure job security for these unorganized fruit stand workers, *Doho* devoted a series of editorials during the summer of 1938 to exposing the labor practices of the Three Star concern and promoting unionization. In this campaign the enemy was personified in George Hasuike, the owner of the Three Star Produce Company.

As *Doho* explained to its readers, Hasuike had originally signed a contract with the American Federation of Labor (AFL), an agreement that destroyed the hopes of those supporting the Southern California Retail Produce Workers Union (SCRPWU), an independent all-Nikkei union. The SCRPWU retaliated by "blacklisting" those of its members who dropped their affiliation in favor of membership in the AFL union. Hasuike, charged *Doho*, took advantage of this dispute between the two unions to justify termination of his contract with the AFL and the establishment of the Three Star produce markets as "open shops."

Doho further reported that Hasuike had cut the wages of his nonunion employees, had "laid-off old-timers" and replaced them with "young high school kids," and had extended working hours from ten to thirteen a day. To alleviate this situation, *Doho* said, the Three Star employees must organize, whether it be under the AFL, the Congress of Industrial Organizations (CIO), or an independent union. But even though *Doho* included an independent union as an option, the paper adamantly opposed the SCRPWU, blasting it as a company union and a pawn of the employers. Rather than taking refuge in an independent union based on ethnic background, the Nisei should exercise their strength as Americans and join the larger American labor movement—the established AFL or the CIO. In addition, support should be given to all friends of labor in the political arena. "Workers of the Three Star Produce Company," enthused *Doho*, "here is your real chance! Register for the coming State election and vote for a progressive labor candidate, who supports such labor legislations . . . to ensure your rights to bargain collectively."[55]

Doho's interest in the "American Way" was not limited to the progressive labor movement, as can be seen in the editorial policy statement which appeared in the June 10, 1938, number:

[*Doho* is the] only Japanese progressive publication in America. . . . Our policy is to protect the welfare of the Second Generation Japanese in America, exposing the tactics of reactionary elements and to unite the Japanese people with a broad democratic front for peace, progress and Democracy.[56]

Given its patriotic posture, *Doho* was especially sensitive to "those who think the paper is a 'red' publication, [and] hence, n[o] g[ood]." "There is no Moscow Gold behind us," argued John Kitahara defensively in a July 1, 1938, editorial, "and there is no special interest financing us."[57]

However expedient *Doho*'s Americanism, it does indeed seem to have been self-financed. Costs were minimal; aside from editor Fujii's monthly salary of $90, the only other significant outlay of cash was the union-scale weekly wages, for two hours' work, paid to *Doho*'s printer. According to James Oda, the paper's non-Communist, ex-treasurer, 95 percent of *Doho*'s funds derived from Issei. And although Oda was occasionally obliged to pay Fujii's salary out of his own pocket, *Doho* was able to perpetuate itself on subscription revenue and contributions from some 200 individuals.[58]

Another dimension to *Doho*'s "American Way" was support for the Japanese American Citizens League, a staunchly patriotic Nisei organization.[59] Side by side with Kitahara's editorial in the July 1 issue there appeared a featured article supporting the JACL's drive to register Nisei voters. Somewhat prophetically, in light of what would befall Nisei in a few short years, the article counseled that "the registration of Nisei for the election is not only the fulfillment of his [and her] rights as American citizens, but will also be valuable for him [and her] in identification should any controversy over his [and her] citizenship arise."[60]

During *Doho*'s Popular Front period, Americanism, as indicated before, frequently became translated into an endorsement of New Deal policies, both at home and abroad. In the domestic sphere *Doho* dismissed as "reactionary" any group who opposed the New Deal. For example, in the September 1, 1938, issue, *Doho* coupled a statement of support for California gubernatorial candidate Culbert Olson and other Democratic aspirants with a condemnation of the "reactionary anti–New Deal Republicans of the [Frank] Merriam-[George] Hatfield-[Harry] Chandler-[William Randolph] Hearst brand."[61] With respect to foreign affairs, *Doho*, following the lead of Moscow, applauded President Roosevelt's unyielding stand against Fascist imperialism and drew invidious comparisons with the appeasement policies of Prime Minister Neville Chamberlain of Britain. Fascists like Hitler needed to be resisted, not accommodated. To drive this point home, *Doho* reprinted a moral lesson that originally appeared in *Pravda*: "Chamberlain has been taught a lesson . . . that concessions only increase the appetite of aggressors."[62]

No doubt feeling that Japan's fascism would more likely be excused within the Japanese American community than that of the other Axis powers, *Doho* focused its attention chiefly on the former. In a January 1939 editorial, Fumio criticized those Little Tokyo residents who identified with Japanese militarists merely because they were *Japanese* militarists. Of greater importance than national or ethnic identity was an awareness that all imperialist wars were based upon the exploitation of the working class; it was, after all, the poor in the Axis countries who were "paying for the fascist war."[63] Because of Japan's war against China, reported *Doho* in a later issue, the suffering of the Japanese people was growing in terms of impoverished homes, the malnutrition of children, and inadequate food and clothing.[64] Nisei should properly view Imperial Japan as an enemy to the goals of equality, peace, and progress. Prophesying a future war between the United States and Japan, John Kitahara declared editorially that he would side with "progressive" America and not "reactionary" Japan. "It is about time," exhorted Kitahara, "that we in America . . . took a definite stand on the side of peace and democracy by renewing our pledge of loyalty to this country and by actively taking part for the cause of world peace and democracy."[65]

Throughout this Popular Front period, *Doho*, in spite of its attention to international developments, devoted its major energies to safeguarding democratic values, beliefs, and practices within the Japanese American community. Those in the community who endangered them needed to be exposed. Although friendly to the cause of unionization, *Doho* saw danger in the deviationism of the independent SCRPWU. Noting the appearance of the union's new monthly magazine, *Doho* was disturbed by the publication's silence on the "Three Star controversy." "Surely, we thought, the editor could tell us how the affair was settled. But, instead, we found a great big advertisement from Mr. Hasuike of the Three Star. Or perhaps, the editor didn't like to remember that the Three Star boys are still working under the intolerable conditions that the union deplored so long ago."[66]

In a later issue, after the SCRPWU had drawn up a new contract with the fruit stand owners, *Doho* offered "suggestions" that virtually called for a complete rewriting. Under the terms of the new contract, the owners were to pay the same wage scale as before; this did not meet with the approval of the owners, who held out for a reduction in wages. During the resulting deadlock, *Doho* advised the union to exercise firmness tempered by restraint. "What the union should do and can do is to refrain from signing any agreement (except the union's offer) until the union's rank-and-file is more closely knit together and business begins to pick up. It is impossible for the union to take the offensive now, we believe."[67]

Whereas *Doho* advised deviationists, it attacked reactionaries. Through February 1939 *Doho*'s number one nemesis remained George Hasuike,[68] but thereafter he was supplanted by Fred Tayama,[69] owner of the U.S. Cafes in Little Tokyo. In March *Doho* launched a long series of attacks against Tayama, a leader in the Southern California Japanese American community and first vice president of the Los Angeles JACL chapter. While he enjoyed a "favorable press" within the larger vernacular papers, *Doho* characterized him as the incarnation of exploitive capitalism.

War on Tayama surfaced in *Doho*'s March 1 issue, with the first offensive captioned "Fred Tayama: Hypocrite?" It was indeed paradoxical that Tayama, a leader in an organization professedly working on behalf of Japanese Americans should be at the same time exploiting Japanese-ancestry workers through his restaurants' deplorable conditions of labor. But the seeming paradox was not real: Tayama was a hypocrite. There was no room in his limited definition of Americanism for labor unions, such as the Oriental Restaurant Employees Union Local 646 (AFL). Although those who formed this union "were working for America . . . were a part of America . . . [and] wanted to live like good Americans," the first to resist their "Americanism" was Fred Tayama, who was "successful in locking the union out of his stores."[70]

An extension of *Doho*'s solicitude for the community's workers could be seen in this same issue, which announced that a "united front" would be used to solidify the various union factions in the Alaskan canneries. Seeing the Sailors' Union of the Pacific as the main obstacle to a peaceful settlement, *Doho* favored the new coalition's adoption of CIO leadership. Unless this jurisdictional trouble ended, cautioned *Doho*, the 700 Japanese migrant workers going to Alaska would lack a means of achieving higher

FIGURE 7. Fred Tayama (left), a prominent JACL leader in Los Angeles with two JACL spokesmen, Kay Sugahara (center) and Kei Matsumoto, 1941. Courtesy Special Collections, Charles E. Young Research Library, University of California, Los Angeles.

pay and better working conditions through "peaceful negotiations with the employers."[71]

In its next issue *Doho* redirected its journalistic battlefront to a defense of the fruit stand workers and the AFL. A situation had arisen whereby *Doho* was placed in the middle. The AFL, believing that working conditions in the Little Tokyo produce stores had progressively deteriorated, had ordered a boycott against them. Joe DeSilva, secretary of the Retail Food Clerks' Local 770 (AFL), dismissed the rival independent SCRPWU as a company union incapable of representing the employees' interests. In a countercharge the SCRPWU, intimating racism, declared that the AFL had ignored the special conditions existing in Little Tokyo. Assuming a mediating role, *Doho* urged that the two unions quickly reach common ground so that "peace among the laboring ranks of the Japanese and American workers may be found." As in the case of the Alaskan canneries, *Doho* evidenced its belief that a coalition of fruit stand unions was of paramount importance. "The emphasis today, in the current tendency of the national labor scene, is on peace. And peace between the two unions may go a long way in promoting the mutual benefits."[72]

This peaceful coalition theme echoed throughout *Doho*'s next few issues, with letters from AFL members imploring those of Japanese ancestry to work for unity on the labor front and to join "American trade unions."[73] So, in light of the fact that the SCRPWU remained recalcitrant toward coalition, *Doho* came out in support of the AFL boycott. Though mindful of the special circumstances within Little Tokyo, *Doho* nonetheless felt that a boycott was necessary to correct the deplorable conditions existing there.

Doho's faith in the boycott as a means of achieving democratic progress extended to international affairs. It will be recollected that during the Popular Front period, the CPUSA had called for a boycott by the United States of all goods from both Japan and Germany. Accordingly, when in April 1939 the *Rafu Shimpo* expressed its opposition to such a boycott, *Doho* reacted with an admonishment:

> The war in China that has been raging for the last eight years has not only created misery for the Chinese people who are fighting to maintain their independence, but has brought untold misery and suffering to the majority of the Japanese people.
>
> The slogan "Boycott Japanese Made Goods" does not mean boycotting the Japanese people. It means boycotting war makers.[74]

As part of its unceasing war on fascism, *Doho* announced on May 20, 1939, its sponsorship of a huge anti-Fascist rally in Los Angeles on June 3: "So put on your dogs and come to the *Doho* party."[75] In a later issue the rally was declared a huge success. "It raised its voice among the cowed people oppressed by the threats of Japanese super-patriots and reactionaries."[76]

That Fascist activity was rife within the Japanese American community did not escape *Doho*'s watchful eye. In July 1939 *Doho* criticized those Japanese Americans who were sending money and "junk" to militarist Japan, and also called upon all Nisei to support the JACL's campaign for the abolition of dual citizenship.[77] In the following month *Doho* angrily "exposed" a letter that had been sent to all Japanese-language school principals calling for the "recruitment" of twenty to thirty Japanese propagandists to support the war effort. These agents were to be "appointed immediately," then sent to Japan for two years of training before returning to the United States. In the face of such treachery, *Doho* warned that "all Nisei must remain here as loyal Americans."⁷⁸

If these developments discouraged *Doho*, its staff could take heart that at least one of its democratic campaigns had achieved success. For in June 1, 1939, *Doho* triumphantly announced a "Final Victory Won in Alaska." Using the united strength of 7,000 members, the CIO had succeeded in breaking the three-month deadlock and gaining a net wage increase for cannery workers of approximately $1.5 million.⁷⁹

Nonetheless, other labor matters remained unsettling. Later in the month *Doho* listed areas of concern for Japanese American labor organizers and union members. Those deemed worst were retail vegetable stands, restaurants, and wholesale markets. As a step toward remedying conditions at these establishments, *Doho* forwarded copies of its list of their respective problems to the Los Angeles Chamber of Commerce, the Japanese Association, the Japanese Fruitstand Union, and the JACL; affixed to each list was a one-word admonishment—"SHAME."⁸⁰

Doho's Popular Front phase came to a sudden end with the news of the Nazi-Soviet Pact of August 24, 1939. Following the lead of the CPUSA, *Doho* now altered its policy toward one of peace and noninvolvement. On the same day as the pact's signing, CPUSA head Earl Browder applauded the wisdom of the Soviet Union's peace-inspired action.⁸¹ "The pact," wrote Browder in the *Daily Worker*, "is a smashing blow at Munich treachery.... By compelling Germany to sign a non-aggression pact, the Soviet Union tremendously limited the direction of Nazi war aim...."⁸² *Doho*'s stand in its first issue following the pact was remarkably similar—with one important difference: "Throughout the world one tangible result is apparent. The Fascist Axis has been dealt a shattering blow.... But it is in Japan that the severest blow has been dealt upon the aggressive military jingoists as the result of the agreement...."⁸³

While thereafter taking a more pacifistic stance toward Germany, *Doho* continued to criticize Japan for its saber-rattling in Asia. This policy orientation no doubt reflected the fact that, although the Soviet Union was now "at peace" with Germany, it still viewed Japan as a real threat. The Soviet Union could not rest as long as the militarists held sway in Japan; and with Japanese forces fighting along its Manchurian border, the Soviet Union's (and hence, *Doho*'s) anxiety was particularly acute.

Now committed to an antiwar policy, *Doho* assailed all countries showing signs of war preparation. Nisei were asked to reexamine the war motives behind US-aided Britain. "Nisei," editorialized *Doho* in its October 5, 1939, issue, "might as well ask this question: Is [Prime Minister Neville] Chamberlain defending democracy as the British propagandists so nobly expostulate? Is this really a fight between democracy and dictatorship and not an imperialist war for a redivision of the world? And Nisei together with their fellow Americans, will answer 'No!' "[84] If support for the Allies against the Axis countries had characterized the policies of the CPUSA and *Doho* prior to the Nazi-Soviet Pact, the new key phrase was now "noninvolvement." *Doho* could well agree with the CPUSA belief, as expressed in an interview with Browder, that *every* nation should sign a nonaggression pact with the Soviet Union because the war was a war of capitalist expansion and the country of the workers should not be involved.[85]

As part of its campaign against Japan's threat to world peace, *Doho* hammered away at Japanese "fifth column" activities within the Little Tokyo community. Following up on its earlier report of a "secret" letter from Japan asking language school principals to secure recruits for espionage work, *Doho* announced on October 15, 1939, that four Nisei had now been selected for training in Japan: Kay Tateishi, a local newspaperman; Isamu Masuda, a JACL patriotic oratory winner from Orange County; Tamaye Tsutsumida, from Santa Barbara County; and Louis Furuya, a student at UCLA. *Doho* wondered aloud why the other vernacular newspapers had not covered this "scandal." "Why are the *Rafu Shimpo*, whose editor champions Nisei in aggressively demonstrating their desire to be recognized as good American citizens, and the *Japan-California Daily* [*Kashu Mainichi*], whose English editor meekly echoes the voice of his big boss [Sei Fujii], remaining so silent? Is it that the 'unofficial censorship' of the Japanese community newspaper is functioning [once] again?"[86]

In addition to blasting the community's press leadership, *Doho* denigrated the "do-nothingism" of two organizations—the JACL and the Nisei Business Bureau—which purportedly represented Nisei interests. "If the nisei are to be successful in business," argued John Kitahara in his editorial for September 20, 1939, "they should not adopt the same attitude the issei adopted in regard to their employees." "The issei," he continued, "brought their traditional Japanese feudalistic conceptions of master-servant relationship from Japan and carried it with them into their business.... The present and future business results from better purchasing power of the people. Trade unions help to maintain the decent wage level for the American workers."[87]

In urging the Nisei to affiliate themselves with the labor union movement, *Doho* was calling upon them first to "progressivize" and "democratize" their organizations.[88]

By the 1940 election campaign, the CPUSA's pacifist policy was well underway. Directing his party away from cooperation with the New Deal, Earl Browder anathematized both major parties as bourgeois promoters of the "predatory interests of American imperialism."[89] Similarly, *Doho*, in its March 15, 1940, edition, noted Roosevelt's transformation into an imperialist and called for Nisei voters to support a third-party candidate.[90] Instead of lauding Roosevelt, as it had during its Popular Front days for being the nation's peace-loving helmsman, *Doho* now took him to task for his nefarious warmongering and equated his activities with those of his counterparts in Imperial Japan.

When the American people denounced Japanese aggression and sympathized with China, President Roosevelt, in spite of his verbal denouncement of Japan as aggressor, did not even "raise a finger" to "quarantine" Japan or give substantial aid to China, railed *Doho*. It is this "criminal" connivance of the Roosevelt administration and the imperialist ambitions of Japanese rulers that are now bringing destruction and human misery into the Pacific.[91] Confronted with this situation, Nisei had "no other alternative than to seek alignment with a third party of workers, liberal[s] and farmers who must unite against threats to their livelihood at home and involvement in the war abroad."[92]

Doho's solicitude both for the Nisei's livelihood at home and possible involvement in a war abroad was reflected in its opposition to the Peace Time Conscription Bill (the Selective Training and Service Act of 1940). On the one hand, the measure smacked of Hitlerian tactics—violating civil liberties, imposing oppressive taxation, and creating social confusion. On the other hand, it stimulated the martial mind by making American involvement in the "capitalist war" a self-fulfilling prophecy. "Whether or not the people can prevail over Wall Street influences," worried *Doho*, "is yet to be seen."[93]

Criticism of inordinate governmental authority carried over into the labor arena upon the arrest of *Doho*'s Stockton area correspondent, Louis

Yamamoto. After successfully organizing the area's farm workers, Yamamoto was arrested for "vagrancy" and sentenced to six months' imprisonment. Although his sentence was suspended contingent upon his leaving San Joaquin County, Yamamoto was again picked up because he had remained in the county to await the hearing of his appeal. Charged with "contempt of court," his bail was set at $1,000. Thereupon, the International Labor Defense (ILD) announced its intention to assist him by applying for a court-issued writ of habeas corpus and to use his predicament as a test case toward repealing California's "vagrancy" laws.[94] On behalf of this cause, *Doho* dispatched a resolution to all labor unions in the Stockton area that called for the release of Yamamoto, the repeal of the "vagrancy" laws, and financial donations in support of the ILD.[95]

Two months later, in June of 1940, *Doho* turned its scrutiny of the labor arena to problems within the Little Tokyo community. Once again *Doho*'s ire was excited by the "cooperationism" of the independent SCRPWU. This time the provocation derived from the Japanese American union's election of officers from a slate of candidates composed solely of managers and buyers. "Rank and file workers were, as usual, absent from the list of candidates," complained *Doho*, "and in the case of the presidency the incumbent was the sole candidate." Moreover, *Doho* revealed that its latest survey of fruit stands left no doubt that the worst conditions prevailed in those controlled by the SCRPWU.[96]

In spite of *Doho*'s unflagging efforts on behalf of the community during its (and the CPUSA's) "peace" period, the paper nonetheless succeeded in alienating many of its liberal supporters. Since these readers and backers were becoming increasingly interventionist, they could no longer look with favor upon *Doho*'s mandate for noninvolvement. *Doho*'s financial state was perennially precarious; although during the best of times the paper may have had a circulation of more than 1,000, it never could claim more than about 200 paying subscribers. Given this situation, *Doho* could not afford the luxury of becoming too ideologically narrow—not if it was to continue with its customary format of having both Japanese and English sections. Thus, when the paper abandoned its coalition politics, it cut itself adrift from its economic underpinnings. Though not all liberals dropped their support for *Doho* at this time, enough did to force a temporary suspension of its English section from September 15, 1940, to March 1, 1941.[97]

Upon restoration of the English section, *Doho* carefully avoided disaffecting any more of its supporters by modulating its pacifism vis-à-vis the European war and by emphasizing its opposition both to the United States' anti-Asian discriminatory practices and to Japan's militarism and related "fifth-column" activities in the Japanese American community. The first of these emphases was apparent when *Doho*, in its April 1, 1941, issue, cheered a bill being introduced in the House of Representatives by Vito Marcantonio of New York (American Labor Party) that would aid Nisei in receiving defense training. Encouraged by the fact that the bill's supporter was probably the most powerful Communist Party member in a government position,[98] *Doho* was even more exultant over the bill's foreseen results: to prohibit any type of discrimination based on race, color, or creed in work contracted by the government or paid for by government agencies.[99]

Doho's anxiety over Japan's escalating bellicosity pervaded all its issues throughout this period,[100] but its tone became particularly shrill when exposing the alleged fifth-column actions of resident Japanese Americans. On March 1, 1941, *Doho* charged that an identifiable minority in the community were pro-Japan. "Though small in number," cautioned Shuji Fujii in his column "A Nisei Speaks," "the . . . ideas are exceedingly harmful under the circumstances existing today."[101]

Within the same issue, *Doho* floated a warning in the direction of the JACL, alerting it to the potential danger within its ranks posed by the Kibei division. Under no circumstances should the Kibei branch be allowed, through the mechanism of constitutional amendments, to achieve independent status. It was "common knowledge," declared *Doho*, that the Kibei "are shying away from the Americanization program" of the JACL "and separating themselves from general nisei ideas and activities."[102] These activities, reported *Doho* in a subsequent edition, were being watched with "keen interest" by the FBI (thereby affirming *Doho*'s printed suspicions).[103]

Alongside this reassuring note on surveillance, however, there appeared one of a disquieting nature. Disputing the claim of Togo Tanaka,[104] English-section editor of the *Rafu Shimpo*, that anti-American feelings were rare in Little Tokyo, Fujii revealed the existence of a well-organized plot in Little Tokyo to aid Japan.[105] The identical dual theme—that the majority of Little Tokyo's residents were loyal Americans while a minority posed a potential threat of subversion—appeared in one of Fujii's May editorial columns. "The presence of some 900 Japanese, Issei and Nisei, at the JACL's patriotic rally in Hollywood May 10th," reassured Fujii, "shows undoubted determination to make America their homeland, adherence to American principles of democracy and preference to Americanization over Japanization."[106] This situation notwithstanding, warned Fujii in a later editorial, pro-Japan elements were still too strong, and "further Americanization" was needed.[107] This dictum customarily found fulfillment through *Doho*'s disclosures of un-American activities by members of the Japanese American community. The June 1, 1941 issue, for example, reported FBI efforts to locate Shunsei Kanchi (alias Toshi Miyajima), the "racist-minded Hitler-admiring former reporter on San Francisco's *Japanese American Daily*. . . . [who] may be organizing a Japanese-American branch of Col. Kingaro Hashimoto's Youth Party of Japan."[108] And a month later, in July 1941, *Doho* alerted Nisei to the presence of "traitors" among them.[109]

A signal victory for the forces of Americanization over those of Japanization was jubilantly announced by *Doho* on April 15, 1941. For months *Doho* had argued that the AFL was the answer for those workers seeking a race-blind union. Now, under the headline "Fruit Workers Acclaim New AFL Local: Pay Up," *Doho* reported that the SCRPWU, its old punching bag, had affiliated with the AFL to become the Fruit and Vegetable Store Employees, Local 1510. The large majority of Japanese American workers, explained the article, were glad to have joined the mainstream of the American labor movement and looked forward to achieving the American standard of living. *Doho* could not resist taking a swipe at its long-standing adversary, George Hasuike, who had just ratified a contractual agreement with the new union. Searching for an explanation for Hasuike's sudden turnabout, *Doho* insinuated that he was probably planning to "freeze out the smaller markets with lower prices, thus solidifying and completing his domination and monopoly of the retail fruit and vegetable industry." But, added *Doho*, if this could be prevented, the new union would assuredly be a success—in the American tradition.

It will be remembered that on June 22, 1941, Germany invaded the Soviet Union. With Germany now attacking from the west, this meant that Japan, to the east, posed an even greater threat than before to the Soviet Union. Thus, the CPUSA now not only abandoned its nonaggression position but also took an even harder line toward Imperial Japan. This new official line was reflected within *Doho*'s intensified campaign against what it regarded as fifth-columnist subversion within the Japanese American community. In September, for example, *Doho* implored the JACL to adopt a "program and immediate action to root out by publicly denouncing every sign of organization, activity, policy and propaganda that inclines to promote the pro-Nazi elements among us."[110]

The reiteration of this and other warnings sounded by *Doho* reverberated in Washington, DC, for on October 2, 1941, Senator Guy M. Gillette of Iowa issued the following alert to his colleagues in the Senate:

> In the western portion of the United States there are some groups of American citizens of Japanese ancestry who are doing their earnest best to prove their loyalty to America by exposing un-American, Japanese-governed, Japanese-inspired, and Japanese-controlled activities against the United States. . . . These young American citizens have been left practically alone to face the united and tremendously powerful force of pro-Japanese organizations.
>
> In an issue of the publication *Doho Sha* [Doho Incorporated], published in Los Angeles, dated September 1, 1941, the editor, Mr. Shuji Fujii . . . urged immediate action to root out, by publicly denouncing every sign of organization, activity, policy, and propaganda that inclines to promote the pro-Nazi elements in the Japanese [Americans] among us. . . .
>
> The same fearless editor in the same publication, September 1, 1941, demanded the dissolution of the Japanese Military Service Men's League, and decried the denials of Fred Toyania [?], president of the league, that such a league existed as "deplorable ignorance; an asinine attempt at concealment of facts," and further states that "due to the character of its membership, it has often been regarded as a potential 'fifth columnist' organization against the United States of America."[111]

Senator Gillette also lent credence to *Doho*'s continuing suspicions of subversive activity within the JACL's Kibei branch by reporting that Takashi Kubota, editor of the Los Angeles chapter's monthly journal, the *Shimin no Tomo* (Citizens' Friend), had successfully engineered "the cooperation and collaboration of the Citizens League with the Heimusha-kai [Japanese Military Servicemen's League] and the Gunyudan [Japanese Imperial Comradeship Society]."[112]

Consistent with this vein of "fascist exposing," *Doho* devoted several pieces in its fall 1941 issues to indicting Sei Fujii, owner-publisher of the

Kashu Mainichi, for his unceasing promotion of pro-Japan sentiment. On one occasion, *Doho* denounced Sei Fujii for having claimed that US citizenship was unimportant for resident Japanese, while on another it assailed him as Little Tokyo's leader in the campaign to raise war funds for Japan.[113] *Doho*'s prewar patriotism reached a peak, however, on December 5, 1941—just two days before the Japanese bombing of Pearl Harbor—when it presented the community an ultimatum in the form of a blaring headline: "U.S. JAPANESE MUST MAKE CHOICE—Democracy or Hitlerism."

While *Doho* was keeping a close eye on pro-Japan elements, it was also monitoring the Little Tokyo labor scene. In July it proudly announced the formation of a restaurant workers' union and the achievement of a better wage scale for members of the Alaska Cannery Workers Union. It mattered little to *Doho* that the prolabor forces (including *Doho*) responsible for these advances were deprecated by being called such epithets as "Red." Dismissing such "red-baiting," *Doho* boasted, "We can take it."[114]

Behind the boast lay a series of successes. In its very next issue *Doho* praised the early successes of the new Oriental Restaurant Employees Union. Having won an increase for those employees covered by union contracts with a number of Little Tokyo restaurants, the union's next target for an organizing drive, declared *Doho*, should be Fred Tayama's chain of U.S. Cafes. Echoing its two-year-old charge that Tayama was a hypocrite (he had since been elevated to the presidency of the Los Angeles JACL chapter), *Doho* pointed out that this mouthpiece for Americanism paid the lowest wages and that his "treatment of his workers is . . . far from American."[115] For *Doho*, Tayama symbolized the oppressor Oriental.

Pearl Harbor symbolized a far more formidable oppressor for *Doho*. December 7, 1941, the date of the Japanese attack, not only ushered in a worldwide conflagration but also represented a tragic turning point for Japanese Americans. From that time until the end of World War II, they were considered a dangerous people. This date, however, did not mark a major shift in *Doho*'s editorial policy. But it did herald a shift in emphasis, because the new importance of international affairs forced *Doho* to all but drop labor news and causes. While declaring peace with Tayama and the "anti-union" forces, it now escalated its verbal aggression against Japan and redoubled its Americanization campaign. With the community undergoing a period of crisis, a revised program of community action was deemed necessary.

The new emphasis became apparent on the very day of Pearl Harbor. In the issue for December 7, *Doho*'s headlines screamed at its readers: "DEFEAT MILITARIST JAPAN." *Doho* also bit at Sei Fujii. "There is no doubt," disclosed *Doho*, "that agents of Japan in our community—amongst them Mr. Sei Fujii (self-named 'uncle'), publisher of the *Kashu Mainichi*—have been deluding Li'l Tokyo with demagogic militarist propaganda, and misleading many a trusting soul."

In this same issue *Doho* combined its commitment to defeating Japan and exposing community subversives by printing a copy of a telegram it had sent earlier in the day to President Franklin Roosevelt, Vice President Henry Wallace, Secretary of State Cordell Hull, Secretary of the Navy Frank Knox, Secretary of War Henry Stimson, Attorney General Francis Biddle, and House of Representatives Speaker Sam Rayburn.

> As editor-publisher of "DOHO," Japanese-American newspaper, I urge immediate declaration of war on Japan and pledge fullest support to the U.S. government and towards extermination of un-American elements amongst us. Stop. May I request reiteration of promise of fair and democratic treatment of loyal resident and citizen Japanese? Stop. Shall call upon Japanese American Citizens League and other organizations to cooperate with such program.
>
> *Shuji Fujii*

In addition, *Doho* printed similar telegrams that it had dispatched to California's governor, Culbert Olson, and to the governors of the other western states having a considerable number of resident and citizen Japanese.

In spite of this display of pro-Americanism, *Doho*'s staff members did not escape the December 7 evening roundup of "potentially dangerous" members within the Japanese American community by government authorities. In San Francisco *Doho*'s Bay Area correspondent, Karl Yoneda,[116] was arrested and held overnight before the FBI became convinced of his opposition to Japan's military efforts.[117] Shuji Fujii and his "right-hand man," George Ban, underwent a similar experience in Los Angeles and were also detained overnight at the Central Police Station on East First Street.[118]

Once exonerated, Shuji Fujii returned to his offensive against "subversives" with added vituperation. Blaming Sei Fujii for "a great deal of the grief and sorrow and confusion now rife among resident Japanese," he called for a boycott of the *Kashu Mainichi* and challenged its owner-publisher to debate his allegation that *Doho* had blackmailed innocent and loyal American Japanese.[119]

More positively, *Doho* took steps to redeem the promissory note contained in its December 7 telegram to national leaders. In keeping with its pledge of "fullest support to the U.S. government," *Doho* began in early January to interlard its editions with the slogan "Buy U.S. Defense Bonds." And an item that appeared in *Doho* on January 9, 1941, signified that the paper was also fulfilling its stated intention to "call upon [the] Japanese American Citizens League and other organizations to cooperate with [our] program." For the item in question announced a forthcoming radio broadcast on the topic of "The Nisei in War Time" to be jointly sponsored by *Doho*, the JACL Anti-Axis Committee, and the Nisei Writers and Artists Mobilization for Democracy group.

But the depth of *Doho*'s dedication to coalition politics at this juncture could best be gauged through its altered disposition toward Fred Tayama. Because this foe of labor was now, as chairman of the Los Angeles JACL's Anti-Axis Committee, a foe of Japanized thought and action within the Japanese American community, *Doho* no longer deprecated his Americanism as being "hypocritical." Indeed, Shuji Fujii willingly accepted his appointment by Tayama to the Anti-Axis group's subcommittee on publicity.[120]

Doho's revitalized patriotism assumed an even higher profile once it seemed possible that the government might impose mass wartime "relocation" (exclusion and incarceration) upon the West Coast Japanese American population. The paper's first editorial dealing with this matter appeared in Shuji Fujii's column at the end of January. Typically, it took a "cooperationist" stand:

> We must accept restrictions . . . [for] democracy is being menaced abroad as well as at home. Abroad by the dastardly military attack on our territory and at home by the fifth columnist infiltration.
>
> Therefore, how to treat Americans of Japanese descent, citizens or non-citizens, must be carried out with this basic principle.
>
> Why should America allow freedom to those fellow anti-American propagandists, though they may be unconscious tools of the fascist militarists?
>
> Why should America protect those whose stand is still doubtful or whose words and deed are now harmful to the very existence of democratic America?[121]

Doho's accommodative spirit could also be gleaned in this issue through reproduction of a letter it had sent Los Angeles's mayor, Fletcher Bowron, supporting the dismissal of all city and county employees of Japanese extraction. "To win this war," declared the letter in part, "every American must make sacrifices . . . America cannot afford to allow even one single fifth columnist abroad in this time of our crises. [Therefore] such precautionary measures are of grave necessity, and we must willingly support such measures."[122] *Doho* elaborated on this "defense first" theme until its demise. Seemingly obsessed with the sinister activities of fifth-columnists in the community, *Doho* persisted in airing its conviction that as long as there were "bad eggs amongst the good," precautionary measures were necessary.[123]

On February 6 Governor Olson conferred with twenty Japanese American leaders at the state capitol in Sacramento, urging the cooperation of the state's Nisei residents and mapping out plans for the voluntary "evacuation" (forced removal) of those of Japanese ancestry. At this meeting Shuji Fujii read a prepared statement that called for an investigation of Japanese language schools and control of the vernacular press. "The press today," cautioned Fujii, "is and will be vulnerable to fifth column infiltration or at least to such influence. In this case it can do incalculable harm to America."[124]

To buttress its support for "voluntary evacuation," *Doho* reproduced on February 20 the tentative principles and means for such a program, which the Nisei Writers and Artists group, headed by noted sculptor Isamu Noguchi, had recently drafted. This proposal embraced the following points: All Issei and Nisei should voluntarily "evacuate" to show their patriotism; "evacuees" should be decentralized so that they could be absorbed by the local communities; "evacuation" was to be considered temporary; and a rehabilitation program should be established for "evacuees" before they returned to their home. That *Doho* was in accord with this plan was made obvious by its prefatory notation: "DOHO is happy to print the . . . [draft] in its entirety." Moreover, in March, *Doho* added one supplement to this scheme—that a government-controlled vernacular press be allowed for the "evacuees."[125]

In its March 13 issue *Doho* reported on the Los Angeles hearings of the Tolan Committee,[126] emphasizing the statements made by Tokie Slocum,[127] the chauvinistic successor to Fred Tayama as chairman of the Anti-Axis Committee. (During his tenure in office, Tayama, owing to political pressure, had been forced to suspend Shuji Fujii from the subcommittee on publicity,

FIGURE 8. Tokutaro "Tokie" Slocum outside the Los Angeles office of the JACL, April 1942. As part of the JACL's counterespionage activities, he aided the FBI in imprisoning Issei leaders in the wake of Japan's attack on Pearl Harbor. Photo by Clem Albers. Courtesy National Archives, photo no. 217-G-B56.

but Slocum had reactivated him and enlarged his duties to encompass the subcommittee on press control as well.) In line with *Doho*'s position, Slocum argued that while most Japanese Americans were loyal to the United States, there nonetheless existed a pro-Japan minority. He also shared *Doho*'s opinion that "evacuation" was justifiable, perhaps even necessary: "We haven't been tough enough. Any price we must pay is not high enough to win this war. And if evacuation is what you want, evacuation is what you'll get and I'll lead it myself, by golly!"[128]

That "evacuation" was what the government wanted became clear in the next issue of *Doho*. "The army's first order of evacuation," reported *Doho*, "came to the people of the Los Angeles area when 1,000 Nisei and one

Issei, single and without dependents and nineteen years old or over, were enlisted for construction work at 'reception centers' in Owens Valley [eastern California]. The first working crew is scheduled to leave Saturday and Monday (March 21, 23) and will include bakers, cooks, dishwashers and such general construction workers as carpenters, electricians, etc."[129]

On Tuesday, March 24, the *Doho* staff paid a visit to the Manzanar center, which was coined "Li'l Tokyo of the desert" and described as "quite beautiful, exciting and promising."[130] In the next issue *Doho* cited the opinion of two new "residents" at Manzanar that the reception center promised to be "extremely successful." *Doho* was proud to report that these correspondents saw in Manzanar a potentially successful experiment in American living. More distressing, however, was the news that a subversive minority had already infiltrated the transplanted community and had come to occupy strategic positions. For heading the inmate-manned information center at Manzanar were David Akira Itami, the "pro-Axis" *Kashu Mainichi* columnist and vice president of the Kibei division of the Los Angeles JACL,[131] and Roy Takeno, another *Kashu* staffer.[132]

Time was running out on *Doho*. In its April 23 edition, *Doho* announced that it had fallen under the army's Exclusion Order Number 10 and was thus required to evacuate by April 29. Still, it held out a faint hope of continuance in a relocated setting by expressing the need for a vernacular press in the camps.[133]

Doho's last gasp as a publication came on May 5, 1942. Fittingly, this edition, bringing the paper full circle to its initial stance, contained an urgent plea to all Japanese Americans to support the Allied countries in the war effort. But *Doho* had not really expired, for its spirit continued into the camps and beyond. Its last issue announced that twelve block leaders had been chosen at Manzanar, including *Doho*'s Bay Area correspondent, Karl G. Yoneda. Both Yoneda and James Oda, *Doho*'s treasurer and labor writer, were to remain prominent in camp policies throughout their "internment" at Manzanar, particularly in events leading up to and surrounding the "Manzanar Riot" of December 6, 1942.[134] Following their voluntary enlistment in the armed forces, Yoneda and Oda had distinguished military careers. Oda worked for military intelligence in Washington, investigating international Japanese-language publications,[135] while Yoneda rendered heroic service in the Burma Theater, often behind enemy lines.[136] As for *Doho*'s editor-publisher, Shuji Fujii, he

FIGURE 9. Karl Yoneda at Manzanar, July 3, 1942. Photo by Dorothea Lange. Courtesy National Archives, photo no. 210-G-C711.

first went to the Santa Anita Assembly Center (where he was involved in the Santa Anita "Riot") and thereafter saw duty in the Office of War Information in New York City.[137]

CONCLUSION

This essay, as declared at the outset, has been governed by two objectives. The first of these—to explicate the nexus between *Doho*'s editorial policies and those of the Communist Party—has been assuredly realized. While the demonstration of this correspondence is of considerable interest, it must not, as with much Cold War scholarship on Communist institutions and ideas, seduce us into ideological reification at the expense of systematic historical inquiry. Too often historians have unconsciously (and sometimes consciously) assumed the role of defensive cultural custodians and displayed an incapacity to understand Communist phenomena in other than un-American, uncharitable, or unrealistic terms. Mindful of this historiographical pitfall, we have directed our attention away from abstract polemics and toward concrete accomplishments. The second objective has been to show that, viewed from the perspective of the immediate prewar Japanese American community, *Doho*'s Communist orientation was not incompatible with its function as an authentic community newspaper addressing itself to real and urgent problems and needs.

To fully appreciate *Doho*'s role as a much-needed alternative press, it is necessary to comprehend the structural and ideational composition of the West Coast Japanese American communities, especially Los Angeles's Little Tokyo, during the late 1930s. Those communities, according to one anthropologist, can be defined in terms of six basic cultural themes, each representing an element of traditional Japanese culture modified by the American setting.[138] The effect of all of these themes was to promote group solidarity and Japanese cultural traits. From the time of their arrival in the United States at the end of the nineteenth century, the Issei had experienced a series of attacks—both legal and extralegal—which necessitated the development of self-sufficient "Little Tokyos." Each anti-Japanese attack forced the Issei to retreat further from American cultural values and to depend increasingly on their traditional Japanese culture. This, in turn, reinforced group solidarity. Thus, by the outbreak of World War II, the two most significant characteristics of the Issei-dominated Japanese American community were group solidarity and the predominance of elements of Japanese culture.[139]

These characteristics were not only reflected within but also promoted and strengthened by the community press. As Togo Tanaka, former English-language editor of the *Rafu Shimpo* has observed in a study of the prewar vernacular press, "In a highly organized community they [the vernacular press] exerted an influence greater than is generally attributed to the press in American life. In creating popular attitudes and views on issues affecting the community, the Japanese vernaculars played a primary role."[140]

Tanaka's study clarifies what these attitudes and views were by offering an anatomy of the prewar Little Tokyo press community. Tanaka, who has also written the only extant comprehensive account of *Doho*, was in an ideal position to analyze the staffs and editorial policies of the several vernacular papers, for in addition to his editorial duties with the *Rafu Shimpo* he had

FIGURE 10. Togo Tanaka (right), editor of the *Rafu Shimpo*, George Waki, circulation manager, and Louise Suski, English editor, scan the last issue of the newspaper on April 11, 1942, just prior to the eviction of Americans of Japanese ancestry from the Little Tokyo district. Photo by Clem Albers. Courtesy Bancroft Library, University of California, Berkeley.

previously served in a similar capacity with the *Kashu Mainichi*. Since Tanaka also possessed a rare ability for detached criticism (his studies were written under the direction of Morton Grodzins for the Japanese Evacuation and Relocation Study at the University of California, Berkeley), his analysis merits respectful consideration.

In addition to the *Rafu* and *Kashu*, there was a third major vernacular newspaper in Little Tokyo, the *Sango [Sangyo] Nippo* (Japanese Industrial Daily). Together these papers had 17,000 subscribers, with a great deal of overlapping in subscription lists. Indeed, writes Tanaka, it is probable that "the average Japanese family in Southern California subscribes to two out of the three newspapers."[141] All three newspapers were owned by an Issei.

Each was primarily a Japanese-language medium, though supplemented by an English-language section. While competitive in seeking subscribers, the members of all three (Japanese) staffs were informally organized into Little Tokyo's "Press Club," a fraternal organization.

As to similarity in editorial policy, all three newspapers were pro-Japan in foreign policy and anti-labor in domestic policy. With respect to the first, this orientation was fortified by an extensive reliance upon the Domei Japanese News Agency's wireless dispatches originating from Tokyo. This news source had relevance not only for the Japanese sections but the English sections as well. For although Tanaka maintains, for instance, that "the English editors of the Rafu Shimpo made no use of Domei," he also confesses that the *Rafu*'s "telegraph editor" had the responsibility of selecting "for the English editors each day the dispatches culled from the day's Domei Japanese Agency releases those items of likely interest to English section readers."[142]

Over and beyond a slavish adherence to the Domei Japanese News Agency, there is additional evidence in the papers' selection and interpretation of the news "to indicate that the political ideology of Japan in the late thirties found reflection in the controlling leadership of the vernacular dailies in Los Angeles."[143] This ideology, as *Doho* vehemently and repeatedly charged, was most vigorously displayed within the *Kashu Mainichi*. As "a one-man-dominated publication reflecting the personality and influence of its publisher and editor, Sei Fujii,"[144] the *Kashu*, Japanese and English sections alike, reflected Fujii's "wide assortment of editorial excursions to instill an intense pride in the Japanese race and achievements of that race." On the one hand, the *Kashu* treated the Sino-Japanese War from a strictly Japanese perspective—extolling Japan's "humane pacification" of "bandit-ridden" China, glorifying Japanese military victories, and suppressing Japanese atrocity stories such as the "Rape of Nanking"; on the other hand, it expressed a growing resentment "against the encroaching and meddlesome hand of the United States in the Far East."[145]

Though not as blatantly, the *Rafu Shimpo* also espoused this ideology. Since its publisher, H. T. Komai, took little active part in shaping editorial policy, the *Rafu*'s editors determined its direction. The two senior editors, Hiroshi Suzuke (managing editor) and Kokichi Shimozuma (telegraph editor), both regarded themselves as sojourners in America and interpreted events in the Far East "from the point of view as expressed in official dispatches and releases from the Tokyo Foreign Office."[146] Although Yoneo Sakai, the

Rafu's third in command, challenged the opinions and beliefs of his superiors, their outlook generally prevailed.¹⁴⁷ Essentially a farm publication, the *Sango [Sangyo] Nippo*, insofar as it took up questions of foreign policy, closely followed the persuasion of the older two newspapers.

Until August 1939, when the US State Department announced its intention to abrogate the Treaty of Commerce and Navigation of 1911 with Japan, the stance of the English sections on world affairs closely conformed to that found in the Japanese sections. Thereafter, the newspapers acquired a dual character (though this was less true for the *Kashu*), with the Japanese sections retaining their established perspective. "The ideological gap between Japanese and English sections, imperceptible at first," says Tanaka, "gradually widened until, by fall of 1941, the two departments were editorially committed on different sides of two potential belligerents. The Japanese sections had stuck by Japan, the English sections had gone American."¹⁴⁸

Tanaka also clarifies the unified anti-labor disposition of the community's establishment press. As in the case of those few Issei who spoke out or wrote about the "militarism" of Japan, those, whether Issei or Nisei, who promoted the cause of unionizations were dismissed as *Aka*.

> Whatever else may be said about acceptable views that could safely be embraced by . . . staff members, it was generally acknowledged that to become tainted with the label "Aka" or Communist was a cardinal sin. Editorial direction and policy-making were, within all three newspaper offices, in the hands of conservative men with fairly characteristic Japanese antipathy toward any views favorable to Soviet Russia. *The term "Aka," in the more common parlance of the community, included not only those intellectuals who acknowledged merit in the Russian experiment, but those who actively campaigned to unionize hotel and restaurant employees, fruit stand workers, and others of the community's proletariat.*¹⁴⁹

This "don't rock the boat" frame of mind found expression outside of the area of business-labor relations. Most notably, by the near silence of newspapers on incidents of anti-Japanese discrimination by the dominant society, it provided tacit acceptance of racism in questions of employment, housing, and other sociocultural matters.

The foregoing community profile explains both why *Doho* chose to mute its Communist ideology and why it was truly an alternative press. Springing into existence at a time when a virtual monolith prevailed in the community's information system,[150] *Doho* was confronted with the monumental task of overcoming not only the inordinate attachment of those in the Japanese American communities on the West Coast to the mother country but also "the traditional paternalism and anti-organized-labor attitude generally existing among the older Japanese who comprised the employer class."[151] In light of this burdensome situation, it is hardly surprising that *Doho* at times should have been driven into a shrill tone, an editorial policy characterized by pragmatic expediency, and an alarmist preoccupation with fifth-column activity in the Little Tokyo community. In spite of its understandable excesses, *Doho* represented a "progressive" voice in a "reactionary" wilderness. In addition to lashing out at the Fascist militarist activities of Japan and exploitive practices of the community's businessmen, *Doho* consistently upheld the conviction that American democracy must necessarily embrace racial equality for all and attacked all departures from this standard (especially those involving Japanese Americans).

It must also be kept in mind that numerous non-Communists—antimilitarists and prolaborites—took an active role in *Doho*'s publication. Many, including scholars, might too easily dismiss these people as "Communist dupes," but such an interpretation would be much too simplistic. During the late 1930s the options for expression were so limited as to be almost nonexistent. As a consequence, the *Doho* type of coalition served this wide range of leftists within the Japanese American community by allowing them to have greater impact through an organ that combined their efforts. As an alternative press, *Doho* was an authentic community newspaper filling a large gap left open by the larger and more established vernacular papers. Whether it was also "Communist" would seem to be, however interesting, quite immaterial.

NOTES

1. William Z. Foster, *History of the Three Internationals* (New York: International Publishers, 1955), 390.
2. Foster, *Three Internationals*, 392.
3. Foster, *Three Internationals*, 396.
4. Foster, *Three Internationals*, 397.

5. Irving Howe and Lewis Coser, *The American Communist Party* (New York: Praeger, 1962), 319–86.
6. Foster, *Three Internationals*, 403.
7. Howe and Coser, *American Communist Party*, 327.
8. Howe and Coser, *American Communist Party*, 323.
9. Howe and Coser, *American Communist Party*, 388, 391.
10. Howe and Coser, *American Communist Party*, 408.
11. Howe and Coser, *American Communist Party*, 429.
12. Yuji Ichioka, "Early Issei Socialists and the Japanese Community," *Amerasia Journal* 1 (July 1971): 2. These five were Kawakami Kiyoshi, Katayama Sen, Abe Isoo, Kaneko Kiichi, and Kotoku Shusui. Throughout the background portion of this essay, we have followed the Japanese style with respect to names, giving the family name first and the given name last.
13. Karl G. Yoneda, "The Heritage of Sen Katayama," *Political Affairs* 4 (March 1975): 39.
14. Yoneda, "Heritage of Sen Katayama," 39.
15. Theodore Draper, *The Roots of American Communism* (New York: Viking Press, 1957), 78.
16. Yoneda, "Heritage of Sen Katayama," 42.
17. Ichioka, "Early Issei Socialists," 3.
18. Yoneda, "Heritage of Sen Katayama," 43. "With great enthusiasm," writes Yoneda, "Katayama went on to Amsterdam to participate in the Second International Congress proceedings. George Plekhanov, a Russian delegate, and he were chosen co–vice chairmen. Upon being introduced to the assemblage, they shook hands, each pledging to fight against the Russo-Japan War. After Katayama's address, which he delivered in English, was translated into German by Clara Zetkin and into French by Rosa Luxemburg, everyone stood and applauded for several minutes. Thus, was his international anti-war reputation established." Actually, George Plekhanov was more than simply "a Russian delegate." At this time, as the clear leader of the Mensheviks, the majority faction of the Social Democratic Party of Russia, he enjoyed greater power than his Bolshevik counterpart, V. I. Lenin. See Leonard Schapiro, *The Communist Party of the Soviet Union* (New York: Vintage Books, 1970), 74.
19. Ichioka, "Early Issei Socialists," 3.
20. Ichioka, "Early Issei Socialists," 3–4.
21. Ichioka, "Early Issei Socialists," 3–8.
22. Karl G. Yoneda, "Yoneda Updates History Asian Workers," *New York Nichibei*, December 21, 1972. This *Doho* had no direct relation to the later paper printed in Los Angeles, the subject of this essay.

23. Ichioka, "Early Issei Socialists," 10.
24. Draper, *Roots of American Communism*, 77.
25. Yoneda, "Heritage of Sen Katayama," 47.
26. Karl G. Yoneda, "Outline: 100 Years of Japanese Labor in U.S.A.," Yoneda Papers, box 152, folder 6, Japanese American Research Project (JARP), Special Collections, Charles E. Young Research Library, UCLA. Hereafter material drawn from this folder will be cited as Yoneda, JARP.
27. Yoneda, "100 Years of Japanese Labor."
28. Yoneda, "100 Years of Japanese Labor." See also Karl G. Yoneda, interview by Ronald C. Larson and Arthur A. Hansen, March 3, 1974, Oral History 1376b, Japanese American Oral History Project, Lawrence de Graaf Center for Oral and Public History, California State University, Fullerton. Hereafter interviews from this collection will be cited as CSUF-COPH O.H.
29. Karl G. Yoneda, interview by Betty E. Mitson, March 2, 1974, CSUF-COPH O.H. 1376a. Yoneda was associated with and active in the undertakings of the *Nihonjin Rodo Kyokai*.
30. Karl G. Yoneda, "A Brief Summary of the Political Activities of Japanese Refugees and Japanese Socialists in America" (1880–1934), March 26, 1965, Yoneda, JARP.
31. Yoneda, CSUF-COPH, O.H. 1376b.
32. Yoneda, "A Brief Summary."
33. Yoneda, CSUF-COPH, O.H. 1376b.
34. Yoneda, "100 Years of Japanese Labor." In 1936 this organization, as with many other leftist labor groups, affiliated with the American Federation of Labor, thereby becoming the Culinary Workers Union, Local 646 (AFL).
35. Yoneda, "100 Years of Japanese Labor."
36. Yoneda, CSUF-COPH, O.H. 1376b.
37. The *Zenshin* was unquestionably the transition newspaper between the blatantly Communist *Rodo Shimbun* and the non-Communist *Doho*. While the *Rodo Shimbun* was an official Communist Party organ and carried the hammer and sickle on its masthead, *Doho* never published news of Communist Party activities and, in fact, was careful to disassociate itself from CPUSA editorials and news stories. Contained within the one issue of *Zenshin* (before giving way to *Doho*) was an article which explained (1) the CPUSA's shift to Popular Front policies and (2) the fact that the CPUSA, Japanese Language Section, would hereafter support the Communist Party of Japan's efforts to fight Japanese imperialism. See "Beikoku Kyosanto Nihongo Bu—Zembai Yuiuin Kaigi," *Zenshin*, January 1, 1937.
38. Yoneda, CSUF-COPH, O.H. 1376b.
39. Yoneda, CSUF-COPH, O.H. 1376b.

40. Sei Fujii, the publisher-owner of the *Kashu Mainichi*, was a prime example of a man who personified his newspaper. See Toga Tanaka, "The Vernacular Newspapers," 31, folder A1.11, Japanese Evacuation and Relocation Study (JERS), Barnhart Collection, Bancroft Library, University of California, Berkeley. Hereafter cited as JERS, Barnhart.

41. Yoneda, CSUF-COPH, O.H. 1376b.

42. Yoneda, CSUF-COPH, O.H. 1376b. According to Yoneda, *Doho*'s audience was still further augmented through the formation of *"Doho* readers' circles," which discussed the paper's contents and forwarded suggestions for improvement back to the editorial offices in Los Angeles. The organization, therefore, was structured along soviet lines, with *Doho* serving as the nucleus and the respective reading circles as satellites. This system allowed for a two-way flow of information, thereby incorporating participatory democracy into the shaping of editorial policy.

43. *Doho*, June 10, 1938. A complete run of *Doho* is available in the JARP collection at UCLA and at the Gardena Branch Library of the Los Angeles County Public Library.

44. Togo Tanaka, "A Report on the Manzanar Riot of Sunday, December 6, 1942: Addenda—'The Newspaper Doho,'" 8, folder O10.16, JERS, Barnhart. This report is also available online at https://digitalassets.lib.berkeley.edu/jarda/ucb/text/cubanc6714_b211010_0012_2.pdf.

45. Yoneda, CSUF-COPH, O.H. 1376b. Yoneda, also a Kibei, remarked that his return to the United States prior to the upsurge of Japanese militarism allowed him to retain his leftist ideas. By contrast, said Yoneda, those Kibei who returned from Japan during the 1930s generally remained pro-Japan. Yoneda, CSUF-COPH, O.H. 1376a.

46. Tanaka, "Vernacular Newspapers," 32–35.

47. *Doho*'s first English edition, in an article by John Kitahara, pointed out its differences from the rest of the vernacular press, particularly from the *Kashu Mainichi*: "In the Japanese press, no one attempts to write a feeble protest in fear of the eagle eye of the publishers. Pages after pages are just covered with news of Japanese victories, derogatory remarks about the Chinese nation, coming mostly from the government propaganda dispatch. [*Doho* never used the Domei dispatch service.] The man responsible for this strict unofficial censorship is Sei Fujii, jingoist extraordinary and the publisher of the *Japan-California Daily*." John Kitahara, "Views and Reviews," *Doho*, June 10, 1938.

48. Tanaka, "Report on the Manzanar Riot: Addenda," 13–14.

49. Tanaka, "Vernacular Newspapers," 8.

50. Tanaka, "Vernacular Newspapers."

51. Tanaka, "Vernacular Newspapers," 1.

52. Yoneda, CSUF-COPH, O.H. 1376a.
53. Yoneda, CSUF-COPH, O.H. 1376a.
54. June 10, 1938.
55. "'Three Star' Hasuike Labor Tactics Bared; Fairly Malodorous," *Doho*, August 1, 1938.
56. Karl Yoneda confirmed *Doho*'s claim to being the only progressive Japanese American vernacular paper in America during this time. Yoneda, CSUF-COPH, O.H. 1376b.
57. "Views and Reviews."
58. In an unrecorded interview with Ronald C. Larson, November 14, 1974. Hereafter cited as Oda/Larson.
59. For information on the JACL, see Cherstin M. Lyon, "Japanese American Citizens League," *Densho Encyclopedia*, https://encyclopedia.densho.org/Japanese%20American%20Citizens%20League/ (accessed February 16, 2021).
60. "Nisei Voters Will Go 'Democrat' in Election, Says Observer."
61. "Nisei Voters Back Olson."
62. October 1 (?), 1938. This represented one of the rare times when *Doho* cited a Communist source.
63. "Views and Reviews." *Doho* was careful to elucidate that its opposition was to the militarist government of Japan and not the Japanese people. Indeed, *Doho* saw itself as spokesperson for all Japanese people, whether in Japan or overseas.

Fumio Tanaka and John Kitahara, whose by-lines frequently appeared over the "Views and Reviews" editorial column, seem to have been pseudonyms for Joe Koide. According to Karl Yoneda, Koide, the son of a Christian minister in Tokyo, graduated from the University of Colorado and then joined the CPUSA in New York. Seeing him as "cadre material," the party sent him to Moscow, where he graduated in 1928 from the Lenin School. Upon returning to the United States, he was placed in charge of the Japanese Language Section of the CPUSA. Most party members did not trust him, however, because "he didn't look like a worker and he spoke differently." These suspicions, said Yoneda, were justified because Koide was later discovered to be an agent of the Japanese government. Yoneda, CSUF-COPH, O.H. 1376b.

James Oda, in Oda/Larson, also maintained that, although Koide acted as *Doho*'s Communist International representative during the paper's history, he was a Japanese agent. The Communist International, according to Oda, oftentimes hindered *Doho*'s staff operation, with Shuji Fujii being caught between Joe Koide, on the one hand, and Oda and the liberals, on the other hand.

In a 1973 interview Togo Tanaka implied that Koide was not an agent for the Japanese but for the American government: "There was this local bilingual weekly Japanese paper, the *Doho*, edited by Shuji Fujii; it was a small paper, and Communist. I say so now because a staff member was a man I subsequently met and came to know—Joe Koide. This man was a double agent, a member of the Communist Party and trained in Moscow. He came over here and got his U.S. citizenship by working for our Office of War Information during the war." Togo Tanaka, interview by Arthur A. Hansen, August 30, 1973, CSUF-COPH, O.H. 1271b. It appears unlikely that the Office of War Information would welcome a Japanese agent as an employee. While that office hired many Japanese Americans, invariably, says James Oda, in Oda/Larson, leftists or left-leaning anti-militarists were chosen because their loyalty to the Allied cause was unquestionable. If Koide had been an agent for Japan, he would surely not have revealed himself to Tanaka.

64. April 25, 1939.

65. October 15, 1938. In the November 20, 1938, issue, Kitahara warned: "Each report from Nazi Germany of new brutal oppression of the Jews should give a serious thought to the nisei. Most nisei are still unaware of what would be their fate when fascism comes to California. Fascists must have a scapegoat for their own shortcomings and that scapegoat may easily be the Japanese people. Oppression of racial minority is the program of the fascists."

66. November 20, 1938. According to *Doho*, this magazine, the *S.C.R.P.W.U.*, printed a pro-employer article written by Tomomasa Yamazaki, the English-section editor. There is a certain irony in this situation, because later, during his wartime confinement at the Manzanar War Relocation Center, Yamazaki was notable for his espousal of and affiliation with leftist causes.

67. December 20, 1938.

68. "Glamor Boss 3-Star Brenda Throws Party," *Doho*, June 15, 1939.

69. For a biographical profile of Tayama during the prewar years, see Arthur A. Hansen and David A. Hacker, "The Manzanar Riot: An Ethnic Perspective," *Amerasia Journal* 2 (Fall 1974): 138–39. See also Brian Niiya, "Fred Tayama," *Densho Encyclopedia*, https://encyclopedia.densho.org/Fred_Tayama/ (accessed March 12, 2021).

70. Hansen and Hacker, "The Manzanar Riot," 138–39.

71. "Nisei Canners Join United Front This Year."

72. March 15, 1939.

73. April 5, 1939.

74. April 5, 1939.

75. "Huge Rally to Present L.A. Japanese Anti-Fascists."

76. "Doho Party Draws Huge Gay Crowd," *Doho*, June 15, 1939.

77. July 15, 1939. Equating the sending of junk to Japan with treason, *Doho* cautioned: "Already an arrangement between the pro-militarist group and the Japanese

naval oil tankers has been made to ship this junk to Japan to add to the war fund. We warn all nisei not to participate in such an un-American activity."

78. "Japan Calls for Nisei to Act as Propagandists," *Doho*, August 15, 1939.

79. "Besides boosting wages 5 to 43 per cent over the previous high year, which was 1937," reported *Doho*, "this year's agreement covers all cannery men hired from California, Oregon and Washington—signifying industry-wide recognition of the CIO as a coastwide unit for the first time. Hitherto, [in] agreements being negotiated separately by packer and union locals at San Francisco, Portland and Seattle, uniform wages and working conditions had never been established."

80. "Japanese Workers' Condition Made Worse by Misleaders," *Doho*, June 15, 1939.

81. "When Joachim von Ribbentrop and Vyacheslav Molotov shook hands over the Nazi-Soviet pact . . . ," Irving Howe and Lewis Coser observe, "the leaders of the American Communist Party were at least as surprised as anyone else. Stalin, contemptuous as always of the Comintern, had seen no need to give advance warning to his American—or European—followers." *American Communist Party*, 37.

82. Howe and Coser, *American Communist Party*, 37.

83. September 5, 1939. In addition, *Doho* viewed the pact as a great victory against pro-Japan militarists in Little Tokyo:

> Just as the militarists have been discredited in Japan, so in our own Japanese communities in the United States the rabid pro-militarist leaders who have been beating the drum of military alliance, now stand completely exposed and discredited. Sei Fujii, jingoist publisher of the Japan-California Daily, and one of the most ardent supporters of the Japanese mil[i]tarists, and others are now hurriedly offering apologies and excuses. These gentlemen are attempting to push the entire blame on Hitler without questioning their own irresponsibility in trying to peddle the alliance to the Japanese people here. Whatever following these jingoists may have had among Japanese here is now lost.

84. "Views and Reviews."

85. Howe and Coser, *American Communist Party*, 387.

86. "Japanese Government Enlists Four American Citizens."

87. "Views and Reviews."

88. "Views and Reviews." Shuji Fujii, later, in the May 15, 1940, issue of *Doho*, took Togo Tanaka, English-section editor of *Rafu Shimpo* and head of the Nisei Business Bureau, to task for his traditional Japanese approach to Nisei labor dealings. Fujii's rebuke derived from an incident in Hawai'i in which two Nisei were refused work in an airfield construction project by naval authorities. When their case was taken up and made public by the CIO, Tanaka, according to *Doho*,

allegedly thought that it was unwise of the CIO to bring the matter to public attention, commenting that, "Nothing can be gotten out of such publicity." "Mr. Tanaka," retorted Fujii editorially, "offers no alternative. Perhaps he thinks the best solution to such a problem of discrimination against American citizens of Japanese ancestry is to keep still about it—bury it in silence and wait until enlightenment and tolerance strike men in high places."

89. Howe and Coser, *American Communist Party*, 391.
90. "Third Party for Nisei Needed in 1940 Election."
91. July 1, 1940.
92. *Doho*, March 15, 1940.
93. August 15, 1940.
94. *Doho*, February 15, 1940.
95. *Doho*, March 15, 1940.
96. June 1, 1940.
97. The peak circulation figure derives from Karl Yoneda, while the paid subscriber estimate comes from James Oda. See Yoneda, CSUF-COPH, O.H. 1376b, and Oda/Larson. The September 1940 issue, the last before expansion of the English section, contained a column called "Between Ourselves." Appearing in only this issue, the column utilized a light and humorous narrative that perhaps was designed to expand the paper's sagging circulation.
98. Howe and Coser, *American Communist Party*, 420. Roger Daniels, in *Concentration Camps USA: Japanese Americans and World War II* (New York: Holt, Rinehart and Winston, 1971), 79, dealing with the later Japanese American wartime incarceration experience, notes that "on the national scene party-lining Congressman Vito Marcantonio of New York gave tacit support to the evacuation by repeating the canard that the disaster at Pearl Harbor was made possible by 'the Japanese fifth column.'"
99. June 1, 1941.
100. See, for example, the following issues: March 1, 1941, April 15, 1941, June 15, 1941, and July 1, 1941.
101. Fujii singled out the Kibei for harboring especially dangerous ideas: "among the Kibei, Japanist tendencies are more evident."
102. "L.A. Kibei Insist on Independence in Amended Laws."
103. April 1, 1941. *Doho*'s "keen interest" in Kibei activities was apparent in its May 15, 1941, issue. It warned of the danger presented by the Kibei division of the Los Angeles JACL, disclosing that Shunsei Kanchi, a Japan-born student at the University of Southern California and a former student of Waseda University in Tokyo, led the "Japanist faction" of the Kibei body. "In view of the present Los Angeles kibei's Japanistic leadership," *Doho* ominously predicted, "the coming Kibei convention of Southern California may be likely to have militaristic tendencies."

104. See Brian Niiya, "Togo Tanaka," *Densho Encyclopedia*, https://encyclopedia.densho.org/Togo%20Tanaka/ (accessed February 16, 2021).
105. "A Nisei Speaks."
106. May 15, 1941.
107. September 21, 1941.
108. "A Nisei Speaks."
109. July 1, 1941.
110. September 1, 1941.
111. *Congressional Record*, vol. 87, pt. 7 (August 12, 1941–October 20, 1941), 7591–92. Subsequent to Gillette's alert, a Senate committee of five was charged to make a "full and complete investigation" of all possible pro-Axis activities within the United States.
112. October 25, 1941. In spite of its repeated attacks on the activities of the Kibei division of the JACL and the actions of specific Kibei in the community, *Doho* was careful to draw distinctions between those isolated incidents and the good citizenship practiced by the majority of Kibei. For example, in the October issue cited above, *Doho* came to the defense of this majority: "Although it is quite natural to expect strong pro-Japanese influence among kibei because of their early Japanese education and background, most of them fully appreciate their status as American citizens and actively demonstrate their sincerity." It should be kept in mind that many key *Doho* staff members were themselves Kibei. In addition to editor Fujii, other Kibei included James Oda, treasurer; Karl Yoneda; Bay Area correspondent; and George Ban, who, according to Togo Tanaka, served in the role of the editor's "man Friday." Tanaka claims that Ban was "allegedly the black-sheep son of a travelling Christian minister." Tanaka, "Doho," 8. This description coincides with the one offered by Karl Yoneda for Joe Koide. Yoneda, CSUF-COPH, O.H. 1376b. But Yoneda maintained that Koide was born in Japan, which would contradict Tanaka's assertion that Ban (i.e., Koide) was a Kibei. Yet James Oda, in Oda/Larson, insisted that George Ban was but another pseudonym for Joe Koide. If this was indeed the case, then Ban could not have been a Kibei, since as Tanaka later indicated, Koide (i.e., Ban) "got his citizenship by working for our Office of Information during the war." Tanaka, CSUF-COPH, O.H., 1271b. Notwithstanding this unresolved mystery, the point remains that the staff of *Doho* was dominated by Kibei.
113. October 25, 1941; November 5, 1941.
114. July 1, 1941.
115. "Tayama, Skidrow Café Man, On Spot," *Doho*, July 15, 1941. The Oriental Restaurant Employees Union later became known as the Oriental Restaurant Employees Association (OREA).

116. See Glenn Omatsu, "Karl Yoneda," *Densho Encyclopedia*, https://encyclopedia.densho.org/Karl%20Yoneda/ (accessed February 16, 2021).

117. Yoneda, CSUF-COPH, O.H. 1376b. The irony of Yoneda's arrest is pointed out by Betty E. Mitson, "Looking Back in Anguish: Oral History and the Japanese-American Evacuation," *Oral History Review* 2 (1974), 43–44.

118. Tanaka, "Doho," 8.

119. "Doho Challenges You, Mr. Sei Fujii!!," *Doho*, December 26, 1941.

120. January 2, 1942. For a discussion of how this alliance between *Doho* and JACL leadership groups continued into the wartime incarceration experience, see Hansen and Hacker, "Manzanar Riot," 127–28, 149–50.

121. January 30, 1942.

122. January 30, 1942.

123. January 30, 1942.

124. *Doho*, February 13, 1942.

125. March 6, 1942. "There must be considered," explained *Doho*, "the effect false rumor can have on the people. Only a government-sponsored newspaper can cope with such a situation."

126. The Select Committee Investigating National Defense Migration was chaired by Representative John H. Tolan of California. For details about this committee and its proceedings, see Robert Shaffer, "Tolan Committee," *Densho Encyclopedia*, https://encyclopedia.densho.org/Tolan_Committee/ (accessed March 14, 2021).

127. See Brian Niiya, "Tokutaro Slocum," *Densho Encyclopedia*, https://encyclopedia.densho.org/Tokutaro_Slocum/ (accessed February 16, 2021).

128. Slocum's flamboyant brand of patriotism stemmed in large measure from the fact that he had gained his US citizenship (he was an Issei) by virtue of his participation in World War I. For a biographical sketch of his background, see Togo Tanaka, "A Report on the Manzanar Riot of Sunday, December 6, 1942: Addenda—'Personality Sketches of Principals Involved: Sketch Number Five, Tokutaro Nishimura Slocum," 33–44, folder O10.12, JERS, Barnhart. At this time, although *Doho* joined Slocum in urging exclusion, it did not advocate or endorse incarceration.

129. March 20, 1942.

130. *Doho*, April 1, 1942.

131. Although *Doho* referred to Itami as a "pro-Axis" columnist, evidence suggests that his ideological outlook was not necessarily of this persuasion or that it was then undergoing a transformation. According to Togo Tanaka, Itami "served on the Kashu Mainichi staff for most of its nine years of publication, except for a few months leave of absence he once took to try out a position in Washington, D.C. with the Japanese Embassy, from which he returned in short order. . . . In his

writings, he shared some of the racial ideology of his chief [Sei Fujii] but seems to have parted company—largely through silence—in a number of significant issues." Tanaka, "Vernacular Newspapers," 34–35. And James Oda recollected, in Oda/Larson, that prior to Pearl Harbor Itami had come to see him and had asked him if he would accept him as a brother. Moreover, Itami's pro-Americanism is testified to by his later wartime experience. Not only did he go to Manzanar with the first group of family volunteers on March 23, 1942, but in mid-November of the same year he also became the first inmate from Manzanar to serve in a military-related capacity when he was appointed an instructor at the Camp Savage (Minnesota) Military Intelligence Language School. Eventually he became liaison officer with General Douglas A. MacArthur's command in occupied Japan. For biographical information on Itami, see the following: Togo Tanaka and Joe Masaoka, "Historical Documentation: Project Report No. 28," July 16, 1942, folder O10.06, JERS, Barnhart; Morris E. Opler, "A History of Internal Government at Manzanar, March 1942 to December 6, 1941," collection 122, Manzanar War Relocation Center Records, box 12, folder 1, 107, US War Relocation Archive, Relocation Center, Manzanar, California; and Robert L. Brown and Arch W. Davis, "Reports Division," *Final Report Manzanar Relocation Center* (available at the interpretive center of the Manzanar National Historic Site in Independence, California), 2:13.

132. April 10, 1942. Actually, Takeno served as the *Kashu*'s English-section editor. He, like Itami, appears not to have warranted *Doho*'s suspicions, for he shortly thereafter became closely associated with the rabidly pro-Americanist *Manzanar Free Press* (and later, after the December 6, 1942, Manzanar Riot, its editor). See Tanaka, CSUF-COPH, O.H. 1271b.

133. This goal was partially achieved, at least at the Manzanar camp. There the camp paper, the *Manzanar Free Press*, was dominated by leftists. See Hansen and Hacker, "Manzanar Riot," 150.

134. Hansen and Hacker, "Manzanar Riot," 127–42; Mitson, "Looking Back in Anguish," 45–50. See also Brian Niiya, "Manzanar Riot/Uprising," *Densho Encyclopedia*, https://encyclopedia.densho.org/Manzanar_riot/uprising/ (accessed March 12, 2021).

135. Oda/Larson.

136. Yoneda, CSUF-COPH, O.H. 1376b.

137. Yoneda, CSUF-COPH, O.H. 1376b. James Oda has published a study in Japanese on the subject of Japanese American war heroes. He was also the author of *Heroic Struggles of Japanese Americans: Partisan Fighters from America's Concentration Camps* (North Hollywood, CA: Self-published, 1980).

138. Toshio Yatsushiro, "Political and Socio-Cultural Issues at Poston and Manzanar Relocation Centers: A Themal Analysis" (PhD diss., Cornell University, 1953), 41.

139. See Hansen and Hacker, "Manzanar Riot," 122.
140. Tanaka, "Vernacular Newspapers," 1.
141. Tanaka, "Vernacular Newspapers."
142. Tanaka, "Vernacular Newspapers."
143. Tanaka, "Vernacular Newspapers."
144. Tanaka, "Vernacular Newspapers."
145. Tanaka, "Vernacular Newspapers," 20, 18.
146. Tanaka, "Vernacular Newspapers," 16.
147. Tanaka, "Vernacular Newspapers," 21.
148. Tanaka, "Vernacular Newspapers," 39.
149. Tanaka, "Vernacular Newspapers," 8; emphasis added.
150. Explaining to what extent this monolith operated, Tanaka writes that even if all three vernacular dailies in Little Tokyo had interpreted Tokyo headlines dealing with Japan's military ventures in an objective way, "it was questionable as to how much good they could accomplish in the face of the flood of magazine and other publications from Japan which were sold in the numerous books stores and stationery shops of west coast Japanese business districts." See Tanaka, "Vernacular Newspapers," 25.
151. Tanaka, "Doho," 8.

The Manzanar "Riot"

An Ethnic Perspective

ARTHUR A. HANSEN AND DAVID A. HACKER

In his book *American Historical Explanations*, Gene Wise reproves American historians for naively assuming that "the real aim of historical scholarship is to discover just what happened in the past; that what happened has been recorded here and there in what historians call 'primary documents'; and that the only true scholarship in the field of history must be based directly on only those primary documents."[1] While granting that this approach has eliminated much flagrant bias and derivativeness, Wise nonetheless maintains that it has led historians into some profound epistemological fallacies. First, it has fostered the scholarly ideal that "objective history"—the whole Truth, nothing but the Truth—can be realized once historians learn to behave as "ideal observers," that is, cease viewing reality through existential frames of reference. Second, this approach has promoted the correlative notion that the way for historians to attain this ideal is to devote themselves to an intensive examination of primary sources, for in these documents the original experiences repose in pure and unfiltered wholeness.

https://doi.org/10.5876/9781646424221.c004

To refute these nostrums, Wise explains that "objective" history is impossible precisely because the historian's mind is grounded ineluctably in experience, and therefore she/he observes through selected frames of reference. This same relativism pertains to primary documents since they too are merely commentaries upon original phenomena by similarly bounded minds. Accordingly, Wise suggests an alternative model of historical inquiry—the "perspectivist" model—which he believes more realistic and productive than the "ideal observer" one. This new model would ask different questions of its sources. Because the ideal-observer model is preoccupied with what happened in the past, its questions are designed to untangle the objective truth of history from the snares and delusions of assorted interpreters. On the other hand, since the perspectivist model discounts what happened as its sole or even fundamental concern, it queries its sources in a different manner. Although mindful of what happened, its chief concern, according to Wise, "is with the question, 'How do particular people experience what happened?' And further, 'How do they put form on their experience?' And yet further, 'How do these forms connect into their particular locations in time and place?'"[2]

The present essay utilizes the perspectivist approach in studying one celebrated episode occurring during the incarceration experience of Japanese Americans in the World War II, the so-called Manzanar Riot.[3] We have given our study a tripartite division. The first section offers a brief summary of the event itself. The second attempts to delineate and account for the dominant perspective influencing the interpretation of this event in the past. The third and longest section offers a new perspective for interpreting the Manzanar Riot. Although this portion of the study adds considerably to the existing stock of information about the riot (and relies heavily on primary documentation), we feel its major contribution is that it presents a strategy for explaining this information in a significantly different way.

THE MANZANAR RIOT

On the evening of December 5, 1942, some unidentified inmates at the Manzanar War Relocation Center assaulted Fred Tayama, a Nisei who had returned the previous day from Salt Lake City, where he had served as the center's representative at the national convention of the Japanese American Citizens League (JACL).[4] The beating administered to Tayama, formerly a Los Angeles restaurateur and chairman of the JACL's Southern District Council, was severe enough to hospitalize him and prompt the camp authorities to arrest three Kibei. Two of these suspects were taken into custody at the Manzanar jail and released after questioning, but the remaining one, Harry Ueno, head of the Kitchen Workers Union, was removed from the camp and jailed in nearby Independence, California.[5]

Ueno's arrest aroused widespread hostility and resistance among the inmates. Contrary to the War Relocation Authority (WRA) rationale for this action—that Ueno had been identified positively by Tayama as one of his assailants—many inmates charged that Ueno was innocent and was being victimized due to his recent allegation that certain WRA officials were appropriating meat and sugar intended for the inmates in order to sell them for profit outside the camp.[6]

At 10:00 a.m. on Sunday, December 6, about 200 inmates assembled in the mess hall of Block 22, Ueno's block, to discuss his arrest and consider ways of effecting his return to the camp. This meeting, consisting of Block 22 inmates and a sprinkling of Kitchen Workers Union members, entertained several plans of action, including the imposition of a centerwide strike of kitchens. After about twenty minutes, the meeting was adjourned, and a second meeting of block managers, mess hall workers, and Kibei groups was arranged for 1:00 p.m. in Block 22.

News of the one o'clock meeting apparently spread throughout the entire camp population, for the crowd that subsequently arrived was so large (estimates place it in excess of 2,000 people) that the gathering had to be moved outside the mess hall to the adjacent firebreak area. Following the delivery of some fiery speeches over a hastily constructed public address system, a Committee of Five was selected to negotiate Ueno's reinstatement with project director Ralph P. Merritt.[7] This committee included two Issei and two Kibei who were associated in some way with the Kitchen Workers Union. Its principal spokesman, however, was Joe Kurihara,[8] a Hawai'i-born Nisei and World War I veteran who, while a friend of Ueno's, was unaffiliated with the union but was outspoken in his opposition to the incarceration, the camp administration, and suspected inmate collaborationists.

Director Merritt, a recent appointee, was so alarmed by police reports of the huge assemblage that he asked the military police to form outside the center's gate in case trouble threatened. To ward off this contingency, he then accompanied the center police chief to the meeting, which was just concluding. In fact, the Committee of Five had already left to confer with Merritt. Accordingly, he returned immediately to the staff area to await them.

Presently the mob arrived in front of the Administration Building, where it was confronted by a massed rank of armed soldiers. When attempts by the authorities to disperse the crowd proved useless, Director Merritt agreed to hear its demands. Urged on by the large throng, the committee informed him that he must immediately obtain release of Ueno from the Independence jail and return him to Manzanar. Merritt refused to capitulate, but he did express his willingness to air this and other grievances with the committee, provided that the crowd disperse and return to its quarters.

The highly volatile mob was determined, however, to stay put until the officials had satisfied its demands. Perhaps sensing that it was no longer in control of the crowd, the committee urged Merritt to concede before matters got completely out of hand. Although the project director publicly reiterated his earlier refusal to this demand, a private conference with the police chief and the commander of the military police convinced him that this concession was necessary in order to avoid bloodshed. Out of the crowd's earshot, Merritt then met with the committee and informed it that Ueno would be returned to the Manzanar jail within one hour after the crowd had returned home if the committee agreed to certain conditions: (1) that Ueno stand trial before Manzanar's Judicial Committee; (2) that no attempt be made to release Ueno from the camp jail; (3) that the Committee of Five meet with Merritt to decide on any other matters it wished to discuss; (4) that there would be no more mobs or mass meetings of any sort until the center had resumed normalcy; and (5) that the Committee of Five help maintain law and order in the center and assist the police in apprehending Tayama's assailants. Merritt also announced that a subsequent statement pertinent to Ueno's return would be issued at six o'clock that evening at Mess Hall 22.

That afternoon Ueno was returned to the camp jail. When the Committee of Five appeared at Mess Hall 22 at six o'clock to affirm this fact, it encountered a crush of 2,000 to 4,000 inmates. Again the meeting was transferred outside. On the grounds that it had accomplished its objective, the committee attempted to resign. This suggestion was shouted down by the crowd, which felt that the administration had not gone far enough by merely returning Ueno to the Manzanar jail. Ueno should be unconditionally released, even if release required his enforced removal. Moreover, the crowd demanded that inmates like Fred Tayama, whom they suspected of collaborating with the administration and informing the FBI about pro-Japan activities in camp, be killed. Having degenerated into an uncontrolled demonstration, the meeting broke up when a hurried plan of action was outlined. The crowd divided itself into two main groups, one to ferret out Tayama in the camp hospital and finish the job begun the night before, and the second to liberate Ueno from jail.

After failing to locate Tayama, the first group broke into splinter groups bent on searching out and killing Tokie Slocum and Togo Tanaka, two other JACL leaders reputed to be stooges. This quest also proved fruitless. By now the second group was approaching the jail. At this point, Director Merritt ordered in the military police, which immediately placed a protective barricade between the crowd and the jail.

From seven o'clock to nine-thirty, the administration attempted to negotiate with the inmate representatives. At first the crowd contented itself with singing Japanese songs and gesturing menacingly at the soldiers. But when some of the inmates began throwing stones and bottles, the military police were ordered to fire tear gas into their midst. Shortly thereafter, for reasons never clearly established, the soldiers opened fire on the crowd, killing a young Nisei and wounding ten other inmates, one of whom died several days later.

During the night the camp remained in a turbulent state. Kitchen bells tolled continuously, beatings of alleged informers ensued, and military police units patrolled the camp, breaking up numerous inmate gatherings. Those whose names appeared on the inmates' blacklists and death lists were spirited out of camp and placed in protective custody, and the administration began a roundup of those believed responsible for the disruption. Within the next few days, the first group and its families were sent to an abandoned Civilian Conservation Corps (CCC) camp in Death Valley, while the latter group was imprisoned in local jails and then transferred to a temporary isolation center in Moab, Utah.[9]

THE PREVAILING "WRA-JACL" PERSPECTIVE

To date, most of the accounts of the Manzanar Riot have been filtered through what might be labeled the "WRA-JACL" perspective.[10] The appellation is apt because nearly all of the original documentation was prepared by WRA or JACL affiliates and because secondary compilers almost have without exception simply buttressed this official version. This perspective has resulted in uniform meanings being drawn from disparate information. The reasons for this stylization of form inhere within the historical experience of its creators and custodians. But before tracking down these connections, let us first outline the most conspicuous features of the WRA-JACL perspective.

One dimension can be glimpsed through analysis of the language used to describe the event. As a general rule, the primary sources refer to it as an "incident," while the secondary works term it a "riot." Since the former denotes an "occurrence" and the latter signifies a "violent disorder," these designations, at first glance, appear radically different. This impression is reinforced when one encounters statements like the following, which appears in an account written from a modified WRA-JACL perspective: "The incident, properly called a riot, at Manzanar early in December, 1942, was handled quite differently from the Poston strike."[11] In perspectivist terms, however, the difference is more apparent than real. What places both words within the WRA-JACL perspective is that each trivializes the event's cultural significance.[12] "Incident" accomplishes this effect by scaling down the affair to commonplace proportions, while "riot" achieves the same by inflating it to melodramatic ones. Because neither term allows for meaningful contextual inquiry, both invite descriptive treatment but discourage explanatory analysis.

A second, closely related feature of this perspective is its tendency to view the "riot" episodically.[13] This myopia has stamped itself upon the literature in various ways. First, it has militated against sustained, in-depth analyses of causation. Most accounts practically ignore the causative factor, and even those aspiring to explain cause have confined their investigation within the parameters of the immediate pre-exclusion, exclusion, and camp experience. Secondly, it has caused the riot to be misconstrued as a denouement rather than seen as one development along a continuum of inmate resistance. Thus, for example, in direct violation of the available evidence, one account concludes that "the easing of tension, and a return to normal life [at Manzanar] came shortly after Christmas of 1942";[14] another posits that "events which [subsequent to the riot] occasioned conflict in other centers, such as [loyalty] registration, segregation and selective service, occasioned no conflict in Manzanar."[15] Thirdly, it has unduly parochialized the riot; that is, the riot has often been reduced to a purely local phenomenon instead of being related to the meta-pattern of resistance activity within all the detention centers.[16]

Another distinguishing mark of this perspective is its chauvinistic orientation. As a result, the riot has been viewed as a microcosm of World War II. This outlook has hampered seriously an understanding of the event in its own terms. It has, for instance, dramatized the riot as an ideological confrontation between pro-American and pro-Japanese factions. This interpretation can be seen vividly in newspaper accounts of the period, like that in the *Los Angeles Times*: "Shouting 'Pearl Harbor, banzai, banzai' an estimated 1,000 pro-Axis Japanese, many of whom are Kibei, adherents of Japan, demonstrated in a firebreak and hooted down Japanese American Nisei . . . who protested their antics."[17] But even the secondary work that dismisses the *Times*' version as "fanciful or at least exaggerated," prefaces its own description with the similar assertion that "trouble broke out around the first anniversary of Pearl Harbor, between pro-American and pro-Japanese factions."[18] The above quotations reveal two additional by-products of this filiopietistic outlook. First, it has confused the aggressively patriotic posture of the JACL—a small minority—with that of the Nisei as a whole (excepting, of course, the Kibei, who have been represented indiscriminately as "troublemakers"). Second, it has betrayed an inability to understand ethnic identity in terms other than subversive. This fact explains why most accounts of the riot minimize or ignore the massive participation of inmates and instead focus exclusively on the actions of selected groups like the Kibei and colorful personalities like Joe Kurihara.[19]

With this picture in mind, we now must see how the WRA-JACL perspective derives from its promoters. Our task is a dual one. We must account for its origination in the primary sources as well as explain its survival in the secondary literature. It would be a pointless tautology to say merely because WRA and JACL representatives compiled the original accounts of the riot, they were written from the WRA-JACL perspective. More pertinently, we need to inquire into the connection between their interpretation of the riot and their overall attitude toward incarceration and to relate both to their conception of American society.

Although different in some respects, the WRA and JACL viewpoints on incarceration were fundamentally the same. Roger Daniels has summarized the WRA stance: "Although some of the staff, particularly those in the upper echelons of the WRA, disapproved of the racist policy that brought the camps into being, the majority of the camp personnel . . . shared the contempt of the general population for 'Japs.'"[20]

Attitude, of course, is extremely difficult to evaluate, but the documentation—both written and oral—pertinent to the Manzanar staff suggests that perhaps "contempt" is too strong a word to label their outlook. The staff member most frequently cited by inmates for his contemptuous attitude toward them is Ned Campbell, the assistant project director. For instance, after the Manzanar Riot, Harry Ueno is quoted as remarking, "Every time Ned Campbell speaks he thinks he talks to a slave."[21] When an interviewer asked another inmate, Togo Tanaka, whether he thought Ueno's appraisal of Campbell an accurate one, he replied, "Maybe that was the way he [Ueno] reacted. I just thought he [Campbell] was a loud, obnoxious someone who, you know, in another setting I wouldn't hire, period. But he was a big shot."[22] Perhaps Campbell himself provides the clearest insight into why his manner may have been construed as contemptuous. The following exchange is drawn from an interview with him:

> Hansen: Had you known Japanese Americans prior to taking this job?
> Campbell: If so, maybe one or two in my lifetime.
> Hansen: You have been criticized by former inmates for not having understood the Japanese psychology. Would you care to comment on that estimate?
> Campbell: Well, that is one hundred percent valid. . . . I went out there a real babe, believe me, a real babe. I went out there with the idea that here was a job to be done. I shall never forget how distressed I was when, because of being the assistant project director here, I was assigned a big Chrysler—which I liked; everybody likes a big car to drive around. And I felt happy about it. But then to have a boy, a young man, come up one day and say, "You know, you're driving my car." He just wanted to look at it and touch it again. It was the first time I realized just how hard we were stepping on these people's toes. Not only stepping on their toes but rubbing it in their faces. And I think probably that was my first realization that I was dealing with human beings, and this was just not a job to be done with so many bodies out there. Certainly I was very guilty of the fact of going out first with the notion that we have so many people—so many bodies, if you will—and we have a job to do: we've got to feed so many mouths, and we have so many people we have to get into the hospital, and we've got this and that and the other. But they were just numbers to me. And I think probably that instance was the beginning of my realization that I did have a human quotient to deal with.[23]

Similarly, Alexander Leighton has divided the staff into those who were "people-minded" (i.e., who regarded the inmates as people first and as Japanese second) and those who were "stereotype-minded" (i.e., who regarded the inmates as Japanese first and people second).[24] For our purposes, the distinction is less significant than it appears. Whether or not an individual staff member possessed a humanitarian outlook assuredly did significantly affect his/her day-to-day treatment of the inmates; however, it mattered little with respect to his/her overall perspective, for the decision to affiliate with the detention program implicated one, at least tacitly, in upholding the policy objectives of the WRA.[25] These objectives were concerned with social control and social rehabilitation—that is, with developing protective communities where the evicted Japanese American population could be detained and imbued with American principles and practices. Staff members who resisted these objectives were eliminated. For those who remained, active participation in the camp bureaucracy effectively instilled these corporate goals within them so that ultimately they came to measure their own worth in terms of their fulfillment of the goals.

The JACL posture complemented that of the WRA: while the JACL leadership certainly was not contemptuous of "Japs," its identification with Americanized behavior and attitudes was complete enough to cause disavowal of and dissatisfaction with traditional Japanese customs, social organization, and values. This helps to account for what Douglas Nelson has described as the JACL's policy of "deliberate and calculated compliance" with the detention program. JACL compliance, according to Nelson, began from the outset of that operation. "JACL members assisted the FBI in the initial roundup of suspect Japanese aliens. They were usually among the first volunteers to go to the assembly centers and later to the interior concentration camps, [and] in November 1942, the JACL, meeting at Salt Lake City, resolved to endorse the administrations and goals of the War Relocation Authority."[26]

In return for their cooperation, JACL leaders were accorded a measure of responsibility and influence in the camps. Not infrequently, they were selected for the preferred jobs, chosen to edit the camp newspapers, and granted other social, political, and economic perquisites. As a result of their integration into the WRA administration, however, they too came to evaluate their personal status in terms of the successful realization of WRA objectives.

Behind the WRA's and JACL's shared attitude toward the detention objectives rested a common social ideology. Put simply, both subscribed to a "progressive" view of American history. Central to this persuasion was the idea that the American past made sense only if read as a triumphant progression toward the fulfillment of the nation's democratic potential. This view acknowledged the existence of a long line of reactionary persons and groups who, for selfish ends, had attempted to thwart the advance of democracy. But it took succor from the fact that liberal, humane individuals always had emerged who transcended themselves and rallied the nation into overcoming anti-democratic challenges.[27]

Given these situational and philosophical considerations, we are better able to comprehend the WRA-JACL perspective on the Manzanar Riot. We can now appreciate, for example, why the original accounts chose to describe it innocuously as an "incident." Like all good bureaucrats, the administrators (a term used here to embrace the JACLers [i.e., aggressive pro-American Nisei] as well as the WRA staff) intuitively sensed the wisdom of the adage that "no news is good news." For them even to have intimated that what happened on December 6, 1942, was more than slightly nonroutine would have been tantamount to admitting that WRA policies were wrong or unsuccessful.

In keeping with this psychological imperative, it followed that causal explanations were largely unwarranted. Interpreting the disturbance as the outgrowth of serious, underlying grievances would have called into question the administration's oft-repeated claim that Manzanar was a "model" American community. That a resistance movement could arise in such a "happy camp" was unthinkable. It made better sense, therefore, to perceive the "incident" as either a transitory release from unanalyzable "frustration" or, as was more often the case, the pernicious work of a small but committed minority of pro-Axis sympathizers.[28]

The latter explanation gained currency among WRA-JACL analysts because they could readily incorporate it into their Manichean view of history. Envisioning themselves as selfless inheritors of America's democratic heritage, they justified their complicity in the detention program by the belief that their efforts furthered the democratic cause. The WRA could argue that the attendant loss of civil liberties was unfortunate but that perilous times sometimes necessitated short-term undemocratic means to promote long-range democratic ends. The JACL could uphold exclusion and detention by the argument that it would provide Japanese Americans an opportunity to prove their loyalty, thereby paving the way for the enjoyment of democratic liberties in the postwar world. Given that the administration equated the existence of the camps with the cause of democracy, it is hardly surprising that they should interpret the riot as engineered by an anti-democratic faction.

Such an interpretation occasions even less surprise when one considers the Manzanar administration's relative unfamiliarity with all inmate groups except for the JACLers. Robert L. Brown, who as reports officer supervised the substantially JACLer-staffed *Manzanar Free Press*,[29] provides a case in point:

> *Brown:* I might have been isolated by the kids that I had working on the newspaper, and the people that were around me. The girls in the office, the Block Leaders, the guy we finally made "mayor" . . . an old Issei.
>
> *Hansen:* You felt, then, that you might have been isolated maybe from what was going on in the population at large, so you couldn't account for, say, the people who were in the Kitchen Workers Union; they wouldn't have been people you were in contact with in the camp?
>
> *Brown:* No, I wasn't in contact with that group; I didn't know a damned thing about them.[30]

And Ned Campbell recollected that "the young fellows around the newspaper office were the ones I was more frequently in contact with, and I think they became more friendly to me, and therefore came to me with, not tattletaling, but forewarning."[31]

Before considering a new perspective for interpreting the riot, we must account for the persistence of the WRA-JACL perspective in the secondary literature. The most obvious reason is documentary in nature: later writers had access to copious materials about the riot, but practically all of them were compiled by WRA-JACL personnel. Nonetheless, this fact does not explain why these writers have not penetrated beyond the existing documentation and staked out different interpretative frameworks. We need, therefore, to explain why their own experiential situations caused them to be receptive to the established perspective.

A caveat needs to be entered at this point: it must not be assumed that, because these writers have disseminated the WRA-JACL perspective, they have a similar attitude toward the Japanese American Incarceration (JAI) experience. They have not, in other words, acted as outright apologists for the JAI. On the contrary, most have bristled with righteous indignation at what they consider a deplorable and unjustified departure from America's traditional democratic practices. Eschewing the official view that the "relocation centers" were necessary security precautions, almost unanimously they have redefined them as "concentration camps" and attributed their existence to public hysteria, virulent racism, and economic and political opportunism. In light of this condemnatory attitude, it seems paradoxical that these writers have been so obeisant to the entrenched WRA-JACL notion that the riot was inspired by dark, anti-democratic elements.

The paradox can be resolved, however, when we consider another factor. Earlier we noted that the primary accounts of the riot were grounded in the progressivist view of history held by their compilers. This same view, with slight modification, has also informed the secondary writers. While this view was heightened by the overarching wartime distinction between pro- and anti-democratic belligerents, it has continued to thrive in the "Cold War" atmosphere of emphasizing the ideological juxtaposition of the American-led "free world" and the "Communist bloc." One of the liabilities of this persuasion is its criterion that all historical experience emerges as democratic progress. The impossibility of seeing the incarceration of 120,000 Japanese Americans as consonant with the advance of democracy has caused the secondary writers to style the inmates as the unsung torchbearers of the democratic mission. Thus, they have been depicted as 100 percent Americans who set aside their grievances, miraculously transformed their camps into models of democratic life, and contributed to the defeat of fascism by unstinting allegiance to the war effort at home and abroad. Preoccupied with constructing this heroic portrait, secondary writers have been blinded to the existence of inmate resistance. In cases where evidence of resistance is too blatant to be ignored, as with the Manzanar Riot, these writers have seen them either as highly atypical episodes or situations provoked by a handful of subversives.[32]

THE ETHNIC PERSPECTIVE

In contradistinction to the foregoing perspective on the Manzanar Riot, we propose an "ethnic" perspective. Whereas the WRA-JACL perspective, as we have seen, has interpreted the riot in terms of its ideological meaning within American society, the ethnic one focuses upon the riot's cultural meaning within the Japanese American community (with particular reference to Manzanar's inmate population). Although ours is a "new" perspective toward the Manzanar Riot, it conforms closely to and draws much sustenance from a small number of general studies—mostly unpublished—on the JAI.[33] We believe it is a perspective that, unlike the WRA-JACL's, promotes analysis and understanding rather than ideological reification.

As a first step in this direction, we replace the word "riot" with "revolt." Terming the event the "Manzanar Revolt" forces us to see it not as an uncaused and inconsequential aberration but as one intense expression of a continuing resistance movement. This change also credits the participants in the action with a greater degree of purposeful behavior. For while a riot's members are momentarily conjoined because they do not like where they have been, those involved in a revolt have some sense of where they want to go.[34] Overall, then, this redefinition of the collective manifestation encourages us to view it in relation to social change within a larger structural framework, thereby affording a more sociologically meaningful analysis. Instead of dismissing the "riot" as an isolated, spontaneous, and unstructured phenomenon, we now must locate its causes or determinants in the social system.[35]

It will be recalled that while a few accounts written from the WRA-JACL perspective deal with causation, even these restrict their inquiry within the social system to the period bracketed by the immediate pre-exclusion crisis and the "riot." Because the ethnic perspective is predisposed to see the revolt as an expressive moment within a process of cultural development, it is more farsighted. On the one hand, it looks backward to the prewar West Coast Japanese American community in search of explanatory antecedents for the revolt. On the other hand, it looks beyond the revolt to ascertain its connection to subsequent subcultural evolution.

First, we must turn to the prewar community. A heretofore largely ignored study by Toshio Yatsushiro—"Political and Socio-Cultural Issues at Poston and Manzanar Relocation Centers: A Themal Analysis"[36]—is especially useful for our purposes. Its thesis is that prewar Japanese American culture contained a limited number of themes—dynamic affirmations controlling behavior and stimulating activity—that were strengthened by pre-exclusion discriminatory practices, reinforced by the exclusion crisis, and expressed within the concentration camp culture.[37]

Yatsushiro identifies six basic cultural themes that define the prewar community. Each represents an element of traditional Japanese culture, modified by the American setting. The first four themes relate to personal and collective obligation, the governing of human relationships and conduct by precise rules, and the use of go-betweens to avoid possible embarrassment in social relations. The two remaining themes have special relevance to the present study. The first of these is contained in the following proposition: "Society is an ordered social hierarchy in which status is ascribed largely on the basis of biologically determined factors of sex, age, and generation."[38] This theme was clearly manifest in every aspect of family and community life. Within the family the male Issei wielded near autocratic power; in the community, he controlled political, economic, and social activities by leadership in associations like the Japanese Association and the *kenjinkai* (prefectural organization). The second theme maintains that "the welfare of the group is far more important than that of any single individual."[39] Diametrically opposed to the American cultural strain of individualism, this theme promotes cultural homogeneity by granting the group omnipotence. Thus, the Japanese American community tended to minimize distinctions between personalities and social classes, to attribute all accomplishments to the group, and to seek group aid and advice in all social and economic undertakings.[40]

The importance of these themes lies in their influence on group solidarity. From the time of their arrival in the United States at the end of the nineteenth century, the Issei had experienced a series of attacks—both legal and extralegal—that necessitated the development of self-sufficient "Little Tokyos." Each anti-Japanese attack forced the Issei to retreat further from American cultural values and to depend increasingly on their traditional Japanese culture. This, in turn, reinforced group solidarity. Thus, by the outbreak of World War II, the two most significant characteristics of the Issei-dominated Japanese American community were group solidarity and the predominance of elements of Japanese culture.[41]

These characteristics prevailed less among their children. During the 1930s the Nisei generation was maturing and represented a potential challenge to the group's solidarity and to its cultural orientation. As citizens, Nisei came into greater contact with American society and consequently underwent increased Americanization. Their attendance in public schools led them to emulate activities of the American teen culture, and not uncommonly they resisted their parents' attempts to direct their lives in accordance with traditional Japanese values and practices. Some Nisei, in their anxiety to be accepted as typical Americans, began to resent their parents and to ridicule their Japanese ways. All this conflict served to widen the "social distance" between Issei and Nisei.[42]

On the other hand, the usual picture of Nisei as thoroughly Americanized is far from accurate, for countervailing forces were diminishing the social distance and returning the Nisei to the Japanese American community. One form of pressure emanated from the Issei, who, in addition to asserting ordinary parental influence, mandated Nisei participation in cultural agencies—such as Japanese clubs—that undermined the Americanization process. The result for many Nisei was confusion. Sue Kunitomi Embrey recalls that during her youth in Los Angeles's Little Tokyo, the bilingual instructor in her Japanese language school told her that "he thought that my direction in life was going different from the others, that he didn't think I would be too happy within the Japanese community."[43] Additional pressures came from without. Socially, the Nisei encountered barriers to their assimilation into the larger society and found it necessary to participate in social organizations, residential patterns, and marital arrangements along ethnic lines. Economically, they discovered upon graduation from high school and college that the only available employment opportunities existed within their own communities. Therefore, while the Nisei returned to the community perhaps more from necessity than desire, the result was a partial restoration of their ethnicity and a consequent maintenance of group solidarity.[44]

Because of their influence on prewar solidarity as well as their later involvement in the Manzanar Revolt, two Nisei subgroups deserve special consideration. The first is the Kibei. Applied literally, the term *Kibei* denoted any Nisei who had gone to Japan, for however short a time, and had returned to America. In some instances, it was employed to describe any Nisei, whether he had gone to Japan or not, who "spoke Japanese . . . preferably to English and who otherwise behaved in what the Nisei regarded as a 'Japanesy' manner."[45] But its usual meaning was restricted to those whose residence in Japan exceeded two years and who received a portion of their education there.

Many Kibei, especially those whose stay in Japan was brief, experienced little difficulty in adjusting to the American milieu, and their behavior was indistinguishable from that of other Nisei. Other Kibei chose to repress their Japaneseness and exhibited hyperbolic American behavior. But for those who had spent considerable time in Japan, the situation was somewhat different. Although Kibei studies customarily emphasize that those in this category were treated as "pariahs within the larger minority group of the Japanese Americans," this remark is at best a half-truth.[46] True, the more Americanized Nisei often derided and even scorned them for their linguistic and social ineptitude, but by no means were they considered "pariahs" by the Issei. After all, many Issei parents originally had sent them to Japan precisely to allow them to absorb Japanese cultural habits deemed essential for economic and social success within the ethnic community. Their Nisei contemporaries might have found them strange and maladjusted, but on the whole the Issei applauded them as "model" Japanese children. One Nisei, recalling her prewar attitude toward Kibei, offered the following response in an interview:

Were Kibei frowned upon by most of the Nisei?
They were considered odd, and I guess it was mostly because of their language problem. And they really didn't make an adjustment into the community.[47]

These Kibei were mostly nonassimilationists. They formed their own clubs and recreational groups, actively led Buddhist and other cultural organizations, and willingly joined the community business structure; Kibei women married either Kibei or Issei men. For this reason, they strengthened group solidarity.[48]

The same cannot be said of the second Nisei subgroup—the JACLers. Properly, this term applied only to Nisei affiliated with the Japanese American Citizens League, an organization formed in 1930 as "a reaction against the Japanese orientation of the Issei leadership."[49] Generally, however, it was applied to Nisei who most fully accepted the attitudes, values, practices, and goals of the American culture. Matthew Richard Speier has observed that while the Issei "retained ethnic perspectives and took account of the dominant society only in the form of a valuation group (i.e., a reference group whose standpoint is not adopted as one's own). . . . Nisei took on Caucasian American society as their reference group . . . and adopted its perspective as their own in the form of an identification group."[50] While this distinction is partly valid for Nisei as a whole, it is more valid with respect to the JACLers. They, to a larger degree, penetrated into the dominant society through social, political, and economic activities. Emotionally they moved increasingly away from their parents and community. Still, at no time prior to the war did they pose a serious threat to group solidarity. Like other Nisei, the JACLers were young, uninfluential, and almost wholly dependent on the Issei-dominated Japanese community for their economic livelihood.[51]

With this sketch of the psychosocial makeup of the prewar community in mind, we must now see how it was altered by the combined impact of Pearl Harbor and the subsequent exclusion and incarceration of Japanese Americans. For the Issei, who were subjected to a barrage of restrictions, harassments, and indignities—including the precipitous internment of their leaders in federal detention centers—the effect of Pearl Harbor and its aftermath was a pronounced increase in social solidarity. For them, the repressive measures exercised by the government represented only the latest and most serious of a long series of discriminatory actions, and they responded in their customary manner—with cultural retrenchment.[52]

The Nisei responded ambiguously. In a study centering on this period, Tamotsu Shibutani points out that while "there was increased social solidarity [among Nisei] in the sense that everyone recognized the cleavage between the Japanese and the out-group quite clearly . . . there was increased disunity among the Nisei after the outbreak of the war."[53] In other words, we can summarize their dilemma by stating that the crisis forced them to choose between their identification group—as symbolized by their citizenship—and their ethnic group—as actualized by their families and community. Many were too traumatized by the swirl of events to choose one way or the other, though this attitude was less common among JACLers.

Even before Pearl Harbor, when war with Japan seemed all but inevitable, some JACLers zealously advertised their Americanism. Unfortunately, their patriotic boosterism sometimes included a repudiation of Issei leadership. Togo Tanaka, a national office holder in the JACL and the English language editor of the Los Angeles–based *Rafu Shimpo*, provides a case in point. As Roger Daniels has related, Tanaka, in a speech early in 1941, "insisted that the Nisei must face . . . 'the question of loyalty' and assumed that since the Issei were 'more or less tumbleweeds with one foot in America and one foot in Japan,' real loyalty to America could be found only in his generation."[54] Moreover, according to Daniels, during this period Tanaka consistently voiced this sentiment editorially.[55]

Daniels's assertion is not, however, clearly documented. In an effort to clarify this point, the authors, in a telephone conversation with Tanaka on August 29, 1974, queried him about the reputed speech. His response was that, while he had possibly said something of this sort, he very much doubted it and would like to be confronted with evidence to allay his doubt. He also denied another action attributed to him by Daniels: "On the very evening of Pearl Harbor, editor Togo Tanaka went on station KHTR [sic], Los Angeles, and told his fellow Nisei: 'As Americans we now function as counter-espionage. Any act or word prejudicial to the United States committed by any Japanese must be warned and reported to the F.B.I., Naval Intelligence, Sheriff's Office, and local police.'"[56] Tanaka absolutely denied this allegation, claiming that he had never been on the radio. Yet Daniels has firm evidential grounds here for his attribution. A perusal of the minutes of the Japanese American Citizens League Anti-Axis Committee for December 8, 1941, reveals that on December 7, 1941, at 11:00 p.m. Tanaka broadcast such a message over KMTR, although the statement was released on behalf of Joe Grant Masaoka, chairman of the Coordinating Committee for National Defense of the JACL's Southern District Council and an older brother of the JACL's foremost leader, Mike Masaoka.[57] (By way of foreshadowing their later involvement in the Manzanar Revolt, it is interesting to note that Tanaka was joined on the *Rafu*'s editorial board by Fred Tayama and Tokie Slocum.)

Bill Hosokawa, a prominent JACL figure, has written about how JACL leaders were summarily seized and interrogated by federal authorities in the wake of Pearl Harbor. Tanaka, for instance, was arrested under a presidential warrant and placed in Los Angeles jails for eleven days.[58] Such persecution, however, only prompted JACLers to redouble their efforts to "prove" their loyalty as American citizens. They fought their campaign on two fronts. On the one hand, they utilized the limited political influence they possessed to alleviate personal hardship and to exonerate the Japanese American community from irresponsible charges of subversion being leveled against it. More ominously, they cooperated with the authorities as security watchdogs. In this connection, an Anti-Axis Committee was established in Los Angeles, headed first by Fred Tayama and later by Tokie Slocum (and also including Togo Tanaka, Joe Grant Masaoka, and Tad Uyeno—names that would appear on the death list announced on the evening of the Manzanar Revolt—as members), to serve as a liaison with the FBI to help flush out "potentially dangerous" Issei.[59]

FIGURE 11. Four members of JACL's Anti-Axis Committee testifying before the Tolan Committee during its Los Angeles hearings, March 6, 1942. Left to right: Tokutaro "Tokie" Slocum, Togo Tanaka, Fred Tayama, and Joseph Shinoba. Courtesy Special Collections, Charles E. Young Research Library, University of California, Los Angeles.

However well-intentioned its efforts and helpful its services, the JACL came under heavy fire from the Japanese American community. Issei resented the manner in which JACLers, whom they regarded as young and irresponsible, seemed to arrogate the role of community spokesmen. They were angered further by the JACL's apparent complicity with the FBI in Issei arrests. Nor were the Kibei kindly disposed toward the JACL. The Kibei were disturbed that the JACL apparently had forgotten that they too were citizens. They also believed that JACLers were informing on them as well as on Issei, a suspicion that hardened into conviction after the JACL undertook a Kibei survey in mid-February 1942.[60] There even existed widespread dissatisfaction with the JACL among certain Nisei elements. Leftist groups, for example, "looked upon the J.A.C.L. as a large organization controlled by a small minority of 'reactionary' businessmen who used the body as a means of getting business connections and personal prestige."[61] Other Nisei were disgruntled that the JACL should presume to "represent" the community: in Los Angeles the JACL totaled 650 members out of an eligible community population of 20,000.[62] Whatever their grievances against the JACL, Issei, Kibei, and Nisei generally believed that the league was sacrificing the community's welfare for its own aggrandizement.

During the period from President Roosevelt's issuance on February 19, 1942, of Executive Order 9066 (which authorized the secretary of war to establish "military areas" and exclude therefrom "any and all persons") until March 21, when the first contingent of Japanese American voluntary inmates arrived from Los Angeles at the Manzanar Reception Center, the Japanese American community was rife with rumors about the complicity and duplicity of the JACL. For example:

> The J.A.C.L. was instructed by Naval Intelligence to send questionnaires to all members to report on their parents.
>
> The J.A.C.L. started their survey on the Kibei in order to turn in information to the F.B.I. They are taking this as a protective move to whitewash themselves by blaming others.
>
> The J.A.C.L. is trying to be patriotic and they are supporting the evacuation program. They do not have the welfare of the Japanese people at heart.
>
> The J.A.C.L. is supporting the idea of cooperating with the government and evacuating voluntarily because then they could go in and buy up all the goods in Japanese stores at robbery prices and make a substantial profit.
>
> The J.A.C.L. big shots have their fingers in the graft. They are getting something out of the evacuation.
>
> The J.A.C.L. is charging aliens for information that the aliens could get anywhere.
>
> The J.A.C.L. is planning the evacuation with the officials. They are mixing with high government officials.
>
> All J.A.C.L. leaders are *inu* (dogs; informers).[63]

The content of these rumors is less important (many had little basis in fact; others were clearly apocryphal) than their function. As Tamotsu Shibutani has observed, rumors function as mechanisms of social control (i.e., they keep errant individuals in line) and social definition (i.e., they disseminate a common mood).[64] At a time when governmental actions threatened the very existence of the community and government policies were fraught with ambiguity and inconsistency, the shared belief in rumors about the JACL buttressed group solidarity and provided some certitude within the confusion. Therefore, the community's branding of the JACLers as "deviants" must be construed not as a simple act of censure but rather as a cultural rite by which the community attempted to define its "social boundaries"—what Kai Erikson has denoted as the symbolic parentheses a community draws around its permissible behavior—vis-à-vis a hostile world, thereby insuring its cultural integrity.[65]

JACLers themselves employed rumors during this critical time, though for contrary purposes. Identifying with the larger American community, they guarded its cultural boundaries by exposing "deviants" in the ethnic community. At times they cast Issei in this role, but more commonly the deviants were Kibei, whom they distrusted as hot-tempered, pro-Japan enthusiasts who were "willing to do almost anything, even at the risk of their lives, for the emperor of Japan."[66] Rumors about the Kibei reflected and underscored this suspicion, as the following reactions illustrate:

> I hear those god damn Kibei bastards botched up our chances in the Army. If those son of a bitches like Japan so much why did they come over here in the first place? I never did like those guys anyway. They came over here with their Japanesy ideas and try to change all America to suit themselves. They don't seem to realize that 130,000,000 people might be right.

> I really don't blame the Army for booting the Kibei out. I wouldn't trust those guys either. Some of them are O.K., but a lot of them don't belong in this country. You can't tell what they'd do. They might shoot the guns in the wrong way. But Jesus Christ, they didn't have to wreck everything for us Nisei by burning the [U.S. Army] barracks.

> Those Kibei are the guys we have to watch. They're so damned hot-headed they will do anything. Then all the rest of us have to suffer just because

they happened to be technically American citizens. It'll get so the *hakujin* (Caucasians) won't trust any Nisei.

I hear those Kibei ran wild after December 7. I'd like to castrate some of those bastards.[67]

Again, like rumors concerning the JACL, many of these were patently untrue. The important point, however, is that if the JACL rumors seemed logical from the community's perspective, these Kibei rumors seemed equally plausible from a JACL perspective.

Having examined the prewar community and charted the changes undergone as a result of the Pearl Harbor and eviction crises, we now must focus upon the situation that unfolded at Manzanar. In keeping with our ethnic perspective, we need to connect prewar and camp developments and determine their cumulative impact on the inmate population. More specifically, we must ascertain the extent to which, in cultural terms, the Manzanar Revolt represented a logical, even "necessary" outgrowth of these developments.

First, however, we will relate some basic facts about the Manzanar Center. Situated in the Owens Valley of east-central California, Manzanar was the first of the centers to be established. From March 21 to June 1, 1942, it was known as the Owens Valley Reception Center, controlled by the military Wartime Civil Control Administration (WCCA) and administered by a staff drawn predominantly from the Works Progress Administration.[68] After June 1, when it came under the jurisdiction of the WRA, its name was changed officially to the Manzanar War Relocation Center. Its population was chiefly urban in background. Out of an approximate total of 10,000 inmates, 88 percent originated from Los Angeles County, with 72 percent from the city of Los Angeles. Located between the small communities of Lone Pine and Independence, Manzanar's climatological conditions were oppressive and its physical accommodations substandard.[69] Moreover, the administrative personnel were badly splintered, and between the time of the camp's opening and the Manzanar Revolt the camp directorship changed four times.[70]

More pertinent to this study than any of these outward conditions was the internal struggle waged over control of the inmate community. From the outset it was clear that the cultural division that emerged during the exclusion period had carried over into the camp. In line with their decision to accept the JAI as their contribution to the war effort, JACLers readily volunteered to assist in the establishment of the camp. In this enterprise they were joined, actually preceded, by a cadre of left-wing Nisei—and some Kibei—intellectuals who, for ideological and strategic reasons, chose to pursue a similar brand of superpatriotism. Because of their early arrival and their avowed pro-Americanism, the administration rewarded JACLers by granting them the white-collar, supervisory, and generally favored jobs, according them what little power was available to inmates and allowing them a voice in shaping policy. In addition, they were placed in key positions of the camp newspaper, the *Manzanar Free Press*, which afforded them an opportunity to influence public opinion.[71]

This administration-sponsored JACL hierarchy was deeply resented by Issei and Kibei who often were relegated to subordinate and menial jobs. It was bad enough to witness the JACLers' usurpation of community authority, but worse to see the purposes for which that authority was used. One can imagine how galling it was for Issei and Kibei to read in the *Free Press* of April 11, 1942, the following "appreciation":

> The citizens of Manzanar wish to express in public their sincere appreciation to General John L. DeWitt and his Chiefs of Staff, Tom C. Clark and Colonel Karl R. Bendetsen, for the expedient way in which they have handled the Manzanar situation.
>
> The evacuees now located at Manzanar are greatly satisfied with the excellent comforts the general and his staff have provided for them. "Can't be better," is the general feeling of the Manzanar *citizens*. "Thank you, General!"[72]

Nor could the JACL's flaunted citizenship and unctuousness toward Caucasian authorities have pleased Nisei. The mass extirpation and confinement in concentration camps permitted Nisei to reflect upon "their past hostility towards the ways of their 'Japanesy' parents . . . the long years of hardships suffered [by Issei] in their behalf . . . [and] they became extremely respectful of the Issei, their judgment, their advice, and their ways."[73] Thus, a growing number of Japanized Nisei increasingly viewed the JACLers' behavior as "patricidal" and "treasonable."[74]

Notwithstanding the JACLers' ostensible authority, the Issei managed quietly to resume the leadership they had occupied within the prewar community. There was, for example, a gradual ascendancy of the Issei-dominated block leaders over the JACL-headed Information Center throughout March, April, May, and June. Initiated at the request of two JACL leaders, Roy

Takeno and David Itami, the Information Center emerged in late March in order to answer perplexing questions and supply basic services for new arrivals. It developed branch offices and subsections, eventually numbering fifty-three persons on its roll. In early April the system of block leaders came into existence, whereby each block selected three men, one of whom was appointed block leader by the camp manager. For the most part, those selected were Issei.[75] It soon became apparent that the inmates preferred to query the block leaders rather than the Information Center, which by the end of June had been displaced by the block leaders. Moreover, it was determined by the camp authorities that now the block leaders should be directly elected instead of being appointed by the administration. At the grassroots level, then, power was gravitating back into Issei hands.[76]

Just as the Issei were beginning to consolidate their power in the Block Leaders Council in late June, a disquieting directive arrived from Washington declaring that only citizens could elect and serve as block representatives. Naturally, the Issei saw this action as another attempt to undermine their leadership and subordinate them to Nisei. Fortunately, project director Roy Nash, recognizing the Issei's important role in Manzanar's government and fearing the consequences of stripping them of that role, obtained a stay on the ruling. Nonetheless, as community analyst Morris E. Opler pointed out, "Considerable damage had been done by the debate and the division which had followed the announcement of the ruling."[77]

The damage was compounded on July 4 by another policy decision from Washington. In a memorandum to Ted Akahoshi, temporary chairman of the block leaders, assistant project director Ned Campbell made the following request: "Will you please get over to all Block Leaders that it is against the policy of the War Relocation Authority to allow meetings to be conducted in Japanese. We have no objection to having meetings held in English interpreted so that all can understand, but we feel that all meetings should be primarily conducted in English."[78] Again the Issei, and many Kibei, interpreted this measure as a device to render them politically impotent. The following week, the council registered its displeasure by passing a motion that "when a meeting is attended by more Issei then Japanese will be used and brief translation in English be made."[79]

More important, however, was the debate that preceded the motion, for it depicted vividly the evolving Issei-Kibei frame of mind. Chairman Akahoshi, an Issei graduate of Stanford University known for his cooperation with the administration, set the tone with his opening remarks.[80]

> I think this letter [Campbell's memorandum] is very important, because majority of those who come to the meetings are Issei and they want to conduct the meetings in Japanese. When I saw this letter I told Mr. Campbell "that the Japanese people are greatest nation in the world for sacrifice"—many of us are day laborers and in spite of low income are able to send our children to university. No nation sacrificed as hard as Japanese. We have, I think, no saboteurs among us, why restriction on Japanese speaking?[81]

Among the following speakers, only two—an Issei and Karl Yoneda, a Kibei Communist who aligned himself with the JACLers, outdoing them in his advocacy of pro-Americanism—approved the policy.[82] The rest, all Issei and Kibei, dissented with emotion! The debate was recorded by Karl Yoneda:

> *An Issei:* I am in favor to conduct meeting in Japanese, because we cannot express ourselves ably in English. (3 or 4 people clapped hands)
>
> *A Kibei:* I believe all block leaders are very responsible people and they should be trusted by the Administration. You know that once we, the Japanese, decide to carry certain duty, we do accomplish it, that is the nature of us Japanese. (Big applause)
>
> *A Kibei:* Mr. Yoneda said that he is an American citizen, but he have to give up that right. Same thing true to me too, I am American but I cannot use my citizenship, therefore we must depend on Issei for leadership and certainly I am in favor for Japanese meeting. (Big applause)
>
> *An Issei:* My son is in U.S. Army and when he obtained furlough and came home, he was arrested by the FBI in spite of fact that he is American. (Spoken with tears in his eyes) We are always discriminated against here and only one who protect Nisei is we the Issei. I can speak only Japanese and if it must be English, I must resign as block leader. Don't forget we are Japanese and we are the people who can unite to do anything. (Big applause)
>
> *Chairman Akahoshi:* I think we, the Issei, know what's bad and what's good. Some Nisei have stool-pigeoned on us—some Nisei is boasting that he turned in 175 of us Japanese to the FBI. Other is boasting that he turned in so many and they are boasting each other. I am quite sure that only 2 or 3 out of the 175 are guilty. Roosevelt spoke about national unity—these Nisei are the ones who disrupt national unity and they are the traitors to this country. (Big applause)

An Issei: Those Nisei are lazy bunch and they are no good. We, the Issei, are doing everything. Look at those janitors. None of the Nisei are cleaning toilets. We Issei have to do all the work.[83]

Equally interesting is that Yoneda offered his written account to the administration in a confidential report. The recommendations that Yoneda appended and his cautionary advice also deserve attention since they reflect an opposing JACL viewpoint:

... may I suggest the following: 1. All meetings in camp must be held in English. 2. Stenographic minutes be made of Block Leaders Council Meetings unless some one of the Administrators attends meeting. 3. Qualification for Block Leader should be that he must understand English and preferably Nisei. (Some Nisei are just as pro-axis as Issei but one can argue with them easier because of their knowledge of American institutions.) 4. The instruction that all meetings are to be conducted in English should be widely publicized.

If we allow another meeting such as was held this morning, the block leaders' meetings will be turned into germinating nest for undesirable elements and pro-axis adherents. Crystallization of pro-Axis sentiment is getting stronger every day and if we don't guard against it, eventually there will be a clash between pro-axis and pro-America groups in camp such as occur[r]ed at Santa Anita.[84]

This issue was resolved temporarily by the administration's interpretation of the WRA policy as allowing Japanese to be spoken at meetings if followed by an English translation, but a legacy of acrimony and widened division between Issei-Kibei and JACLers resulted.

These feelings were exacerbated by the announcement on July 27 that a new Manzanar Citizens Federation would meet the following evening. The leaders at the meeting were Hiro Neeno, Joe Grant Masaoka, Karl Yoneda, and Togo Tanaka, all closely allied with JACL objectives, who spoke about "improving conditions in camp," "educating citizens for leadership," "participating in the war effort," and "preparing evacuees for postwar conditions."[85] As Director Merritt later observed, the meeting represented "an attempt to organize American citizens into a federation which would aid the administration and which probably would also help the Nisei get more power and political strength in opposition to the Issei."[86]

FIGURE 12. Joe Kurihara (standing) in his World War I US Army uniform with an unidentified man, ca. 1918. Courtesy Henry Fujita.

This strategy ultimately backfired. The meeting itself, packed with pro-American Nisei supporters of the JACL leadership, turned into a rally. Following the general meeting, an open forum took place in which Joe Kurihara, who would later figure prominently in the Manzanar Revolt, took the floor:

> "I'm an American citizen," he cried. "I served under fire in France. Now I'm in this prison. You're all here, too, with me. I've proved my loyalty by fighting over there. Why doesn't the government trust me?" "If you please, Mr. Chairman," shouted back Tokie Slocum, a self-styled patriot and former Chairman of the JACL's Anti-Axis Committee, "I was a Sergeant-Major in the last war. That was the highest position any Japanese ever attained. Sergeant Alvin York served under me. I was in some of the hottest fighting that took place. For this loyalty

FIGURE 13. Tokie Slocum, proudly wearing his World War I veteran's hat, Los Angeles, 1942. As a sergeant major, he fought in the same outfit with military hero Sergeant Alvin York and was mainly responsible for getting Congress to pass a 1935 citizenship law for World War I vets previously unqualified for this status. Courtesy Bancroft Library, University of California, Berkeley.

the Government gave all of us veterans American citizenship. We're here because of military necessity. I've had three chances to go to other places."
"Tokie," challenged Kurihara, "why are you in here? Isn't it because you couldn't go any place? Isn't it because you're a Jap? Isn't it because the government doesn't trust you?" Overriding the Chairman's vain attempts to restore order, Slocum hollered back at Kurihara: "I'll tell you why I'm here. I'm here because my commander-in-chief, the President, ordered me in here."[87]

Shortly thereafter the meeting was adjourned.

Although it is customarily emphasized that this meeting provoked Kurihara into accepting the Issei point of view, its conversion of many other Nisei as well is more significant. Kurihara declared that "he was a Jap and not an American, and . . . [that] he wanted to go . . . to Japan where he belonged."[88] However, other Nisei, "who had had their patriotism dampened by evacuation . . . [grew] cynical over the Federation's petition for a second front and for the drafting of Japanese-Americans."[89]

The following excerpts from an interview with Karl Yoneda shed light both on the purpose of the Manzanar Citizens Federation and on the petition drive for a second front and also suggest that the real moving force in both was the leftist faction in the pro-American coalition, not the JACL leaders:

> *Hansen:* You mean they [the JACL] didn't have much input into the Block Leaders Council so they really set up an alternative organization [the Citizens Federation] that would be able to have some policy statements voiced at the camp?
>
> *Yoneda:* That's the way, I guess, they started. But when James Oda and myself came in, we turned it around and made it into an entirely different organization altogether, which they didn't like. As soon as we got in, we took over the leadership—Koji Ariyoshi,[90] Jimmy Oda, and myself. Togo Tanaka, Joe Grant Masaoka, and Fred Tayama, they didn't say boo.
>
> *Hansen:* What were the differences in philosophy with respect to the Citizens Federation? How did the JACL look at its purpose? And how did the people in your group look at its purpose differently?
>
> *Yoneda:* One of the purposes was to push the petition drive [to open a second front]. This was not done in the name of the federation. But through the Citizens Federation we saw that we could muster more support among the evacuees. . . . [We wanted to] open a second front and utilize manpower of the Japanese Americans in the camps. We obtained 218 signatures, among them Fred Tayama, Togo Tanaka, Joe Grant Masaoka and some forty women.
>
> *Hansen:* And what was the JACL's philosophy? How did that differ? What do you think they wanted out of the organization?
>
> *Yoneda:* Well, the JACL people—actually, they don't know what to do, you see. Many times they asked us, you know, "What do you think?" Because we were really the driving force within the Manzanar Citizens Federation. While opening the second front was a Communist Party campaign, it was also our thinking and that of the bulk of the American people's contention,

because the US and British governments refused to open such a front. This would be a way to help the Russian front, which was being beaten by the Nazis, and the Russian people [were] retreating. If opened, then Hitler would have to divert more of his troops toward Europe and the Soviet Union could recoup.

Hansen: So you, in a sense, maneuvered the JACL into certain policies through the Citizens Federation. They really didn't know what they were doing at this point.

Yoneda: Yes. Circulating the petition was a good idea, said Tanaka and Masaoka. And I still think so. Further, they [JACL leaders] were in the same quandary, but we had a better understanding of the true nature of World War II. Of course, one of the driving forces was Koji Ariyoshi, the president of the Citizens Federation, who had been approached by JACLers to head the MCF because of his non-JACL status.[91]

Increasingly, the Issei-Kibei point of view was expanding into an Issei-Kibei-Nisei point of view.[92] From the beginning of August until the revolt in December, the Kibei formed the spearhead of the opposition to the JACLers. Once again, a ruling from Washington galvanized underlying discontent into retaliatory action: Bulletin 22 was issued, which excluded all Kibei from participation in the leave program. This discriminatory measure further reduced the depreciated value of Kibei citizenship and robbed them of an important economic perquisite. When Kibei leader Ben Kishi announced that a meeting of Kibei would be held on August 8, the Nisei secretary of the block leaders voiced the fear that they might "try to find [a] scapegoat among Nisei Leaders and blame them for descriminating [*sic*] against Kibei and [that] this [would] . . . further aggravate sectional strife among Japanese."[93] Kishi's idea was that "if the government do[es] not recognize the citizenship right of Kibei and continues to treat them as dangerous element it might as well revoke citizenship of Kibei"; in response, the secretary reasoned that "this line of thinking is very dangerous and goes to show that at least some Kibeis are more inclined to forfeit Citizenship and would rather be regarded as aliens."[94]

The proceedings of this famous Kibei meeting were recorded by Fred Tayama in another JACL "confidential" report directed to the administration. In Mess Hall 15 gathered approximately 400 of the camp's Kibei population of over 600, augmented by a large contingent of Issei and roughly

70 Nisei. Five speakers were scheduled. The first was Raymond Hirai, who outlined inmate complaints concerning medical care, educational facilities, food, housing, wages, and self-government. We concern ourselves only with his remarks on the last two subjects:

> Look, for example, [at] the rate of pay for Camouflage workers. Camouflage is a war production. They are using minors: many around the ages of 15 and 16. . . . I demanded many more things of Nash. And Nash told me, "I am the Project Director here and I can do anything the way I want it to be done." So I told Nash, "You are like Hitler and Mussolini combined," and Nash replied, "I am." So I demanded what he had said in writing and immediately Nash turned around and said that he had never said such a thing. That's the type of Director we have here. I got so mad that I told him that I'd get a rock and hit him right on his bald spot (his head). (Laughter and applause from the audience)
>
> We must demand re-election of all Block Leaders. We have people now in control who are unable to say anything and are just taking orders from the Administration. *This is our Camp and the Japanese people should decide for themselves how this Camp should be governed; we should not listen to those prejudiced whites.* (great Applause)[95]

The next speaker, Kiyoshi Hashimoto, entitled his talk "Kibei Nisei *no tachiba*" (The Stand of the Kibei Nisei) but confessed that he was unsure of what he wanted to say. Several persons in the audience shouted "*wakatteoru*" (we understand). Then Joe Kurihara exclaimed: "I was born in Hawai'i. I have never been in Japan but in my veins flows Japanese blood; a blood of *Yamato Damashii* [Japanese Spirit]. We citizens have been denied our citizenship; we are 100% Japanese"; this statement elicited "roaring applause" and a "stamping of feet." The third speaker, Bill Kito, directed his commentary to the Manzanar Citizens Federation, charging that certain Nisei had completely disregarded the Issei—a remark that precipitated great applause and provoked someone in the audience to demand that those Nisei ought to be struck down. The fourth speaker, Karl Yoneda, was greeted by sustained booing and cries of "Sit down! Get out! Shut Up!" The last scheduled speaker, Masaji Tanaka, received more sympathy:

> I am a Kibei Nisei, but the Kibei Nisei are not Americans; they are Japanese. (big applause) The Kibei are not loyal to the United States and they might as

well know about it. (roaring applause) But the Kibei should use their citizenship rights for their own benefit. (everybody looking around the room; no applause) I cannot understand why there are a few Nisei who still talk about their citizenship rights; and about American democracy. I have heard that there are a few who even send reports outside. (boo and down with those rats) Those fools can holler all they want, but in the eyes of the American people they too are Japanese and nothing but Japanese.[96]

Following some extemporaneous speeches from the floor, Chairman Ben Kishi, declaring that he would assume personal responsibility for the meeting, adjourned the gathering by stating, "We may never be able to hold a meeting like this again, and Japanese soldiers will be here soon to liberate all of us."[97]

Several factors about this meeting command notice: the stress of nativistic themes, the aggressive criticism of the camp's administration, the intolerance of dissenting viewpoints, and the heightened determination to punish suspected informers. The circle around the community was drawing tighter.

August witnessed further in-group solidarity. As a result of the Kibei meeting, Director Nash issued an official bulletin reinstating the WRA ban on the use of Japanese in public meetings.[98] This decision revitalized earlier Issei grievances and further aroused the Kibei's anti-administration stand. This month also saw the "enforced" resignation of those block leaders deemed cooperative with administrative policy.[99]

The Issei-Kibei coalition had developed an effective organization. On August 21, when elections were held to select block leaders in those blocks whose incumbents previously had been appointed, JACLers were ousted and supplanted by Issei or Kibei. In Block 4, for example, Karl Yoneda was defeated by an Issei who amassed 93 percent of the votes cast. Yoneda correctly evaluated the reasons behind his defeat in a communication forwarded to the administration, explaining that the Issei-Kibei bloc had criticized him on the following grounds:

1. Circulated petition for Second Front and wanted to send all Japanese American soldiers on front line duty and let the enemy shoot them first.
2. For America's war effort and urged many citizens in the block to work on camouflage nets.
3. That he is a dangerous "red."

4. Married to white woman and does not follow Japanese customs. He washes son's clothes, while wife works on camouflage, let's [sic] wife go to meetings, etc.
5. Stooge for administration and also informer because he has been seen with [Tokie] Slocum on many occasions.
6. Spoke at Kibei meeting against them.
7. Spoke at Citizens Federation meeting for America.
8. Responsible for all meetings, in camp, to be conducted in English.[100]

Viewing himself as a scapegoat for pro-Japan elements, Yoneda believed this opposition to him *politically* significant. The overriding significance, however, is *cultural*; from the perspective of the inmates in his block, Yoneda was a quintessential deviant, representative of all those characteristics the subculture abhorred. A cultural anti-hero, he symbolized for the inmate population its need of social cohesion.[101]

This need grew urgent when on August 24 the WRA, through Administrative Instruction No. 34, began enforcing the ruling that only citizens could hold office (though aliens might vote and fill appointive posts). The full impact of this ruling occurred in September when the Block Leaders Council learned that it was to be supplanted by a Community Council structured along the above lines. Issei were incensed, arguing that "they had lived long in the United States and that denial of the right to naturalize was unjust [and] to prevent them now from holding office in their own evacuee community was simply to emphasize this injustice."[102] Moreover, they charged that JACLers had inspired the decree and had poisoned the Issei case with the WRA. That is, here was another attempt to diminish their influence. Opler summarized their perspective this way: "As a result of evacuation they had lost heavily in property and in prestige. Their places in the old Japanese community were gone. Now they feared that they would be entirely at the mercy of the less sympathetic among the Nisei and of the American government."[103]

Their worst fears materialized, therefore, when the project director appointed a seventeen-man Self-Government Commission composed entirely of Nisei to draft a charter for the new government. Their tolerance disappeared completely on September 25 when the new acting project director, Harvey Coverley, announced that at the end of the month the block leaders would become block managers, exchanging their legislative functions for administrative ones. A rash of resignations followed. Indeed, by mid-October the position of block manager had become so undesirable that the administration could hardly find substitutes for those who had resigned.[104]

Another threat that alarmed Issei was the formation of the Manzanar Work Corps. Designed to include a Representative Assembly and a Fair Practices Committee, it aroused their suspicion because the same JACLers who had formed the detested Citizens Federation also were sponsoring the Work Corps. Thus, when the election of representatives took place in late September, Issei registered little interest in the proceedings.

But it was the Kibei, smarting from their recent exclusion from the Charter Commission, who emerged as the most vociferous opponents of the Work Corps. At the first meeting of the Representative Assembly Harry Ueno, a Kibei representing the kitchen workers of Mess Hall 22, clashed with Fred Tayama, chairman of the Work Corps. Upon questioning Tayama regarding Work Corps functions, Ueno became convinced that it represented an administrative tool that would not fully protect the interests of kitchen workers. Consequently, Ueno organized the Kitchen Workers Union to "wring concessions from the administration, rather than have the administration wring more work out of the evacuees, as they believed would happen under the Work Corps."[105] Since most Kibei were employed as mess workers and approximately 1,500 of the Manzanar work force of 4,000 were kitchen employees, the Kitchen Workers Union provided Kibei a powerful base for mobilizing community action.[106]

Karl Yoneda's recollection on Ueno and the Kitchen Workers Union deserves careful attention:

> He [Ueno] is such an unknown figure. He talks about organizing Kitchen Workers Union. To me, through my experience in organizing, he just had a handful [of followers] in his kitchen and among the strong pro-Japan kitchen crew in my block, Block 4. . . . Actually, they don't have an organization such as the Kitchen Workers Union; they merely name themselves.
>
> *You mean few kitchen workers really identified in any strong sense with the Kitchen Workers Union?*
>
> I don't think so, because I was there. If they had such a force, I am sure not only I, but others would have detected it right away.[107]

If the formation of the Kitchen Workers Union represented one index of rising anti-JACL sentiment, another was the swelling opposition to the JACL-dominated Charter Commission, headed by Togo Tanaka. One form of resistance was passive: few bothered to register for the charter's ratification vote of November 9. When an "educational" meeting on the charter was held, outraged speakers assailed its citizen-alien distinction and cast aspersions on the commission members. The same evening an ominous message appeared on mess hall bulletin boards:

> Attention: We do not recognize any necessity for a self-government system. We should oppose anything like this as it is only drawing a rope around our necks. Let the Army take care of everything. Stop taking action which might bring trouble to our fellow residents.
>
> *Blood Brothers Concerned About the People*[108]

The administration, responding to the cumulative pressure, rescheduled the ratification election for November 30. The postponement did not have the desired "cooling" effect, however, for the charter had come to symbolize the deep cultural division between the para-administrative JACLers and, in effect, the rest of the camp population. Using their subsidized press, the charter supporters attempted to mollify the inmates' widespread fears and convince them of the advantages of speedy ratification. To counter the influence of the *Free Press*'s campaign, the oppositional forces established what Morris Opler has termed the "Manzanar Underground."[109] Soon the community was inundated with posters, bulletins, and other communiqués, variously signed "Manzanar Black Dragon Society," "Southern California Blood Brothers Corps," "Southern California Justice Group," and "Patriotic Suicide Corps." Primary attention was given to undermining the self-government scheme by including intimidating letters to each member of the Charter Commission, but in time the camp's underground branched out to criticize every aspect of Manzanar life.

As the date of the ratification grew closer, it became apparent that the charter was doomed to defeat. Seeking to rid the self-government plan of its JACL stigma, the administration disbanded the Charter Commission and announced that "before the final charter was submitted to the people, a city-wide election was to take place on November 22, and two persons from each block were to be elected to a committee to study the charter and make adjustments."¹¹⁰ (At the same time, the administration called in two FBI agents to investigate Manzanar's underground, thereby hoping to eliminate a major source of opposition to the charter.) Once again, however, the administration was confronted by passive resistance, for on November 22 the turnout of voters was embarrassingly meager.

Nonetheless, on November 30 the new project director, Ralph P. Merritt, scheduled a meeting of the elected block representatives. This meeting proved even more embarrassing to the cause of the charter. Indeed, only about half of the representatives attended. As a first item of business, the group decided to poll how many opposed the self-government plan. All but one—Togo Tanaka, the JACL head of the commission—raised their hands. This lopsided division was mirrored by the subsequent discussion, which deserves our attention for its representation of the general mood of the camp population:

> *Harry Ueno (who was in attendance as an interested visitor):* In my block we didn't even elect delegates; we see no necessity for such a joke of a thing, we should organize a strong Japanese Welfare Group in this camp. It will furnish the representation for us. I think it is a plot of the government to use those who can be used when they talk about self-government.
>
> *Togo Tanaka:* I do not feel that we have anybody capable of speaking in support of 10,000 people. The self-government arrangement would fill that need.
>
> *The chairman, Genji Yamaguchi, an Issei block leader [and later a member of the Committee of Five]:* I wish to differ with Mr. Tanaka. We do have a body capable of speaking for the population and representing them. That is the Block Managers. We can do everything that any Council of Nisei can do. What have you to say to that?
>
> *Tanaka:* The Block Managers have their role to perform. They are important in the scheme of things. But their job is administrative. You do not represent the people so much as you do the Administration, *at least in theory*. The Managers have no power to legislate. That is the difference.
>
> *Chairman Yamaguchi:* There is one question that I would like to put before Mr. Tanaka, if he will be good enough to answer. I don't know whether it's rumor or not, but I have heard that the reason why the W.R.A. decided on the policy of discriminating against the Issei in holding office in the proposed Council is because Mike Masaoka [executive secretary] of the national JACL got together with Dillon Myer [WRA national director] and had that discriminatory clause put in. What do you know about that?

Tanaka: Now that you tell that to me, I've heard it too. Why don't you write to Washington, D.C. and Mr. Myer and ask him?

Another Issei: I would like to ask Mr. Tanaka why it is that the Nisei seem to want to control this camp? Why is it that they are out to persecute the Issei?[111]

Another vote followed on the self-government question—this time with a unanimous negative response.[112] The circle around the community had all but closed.

Two interesting sidelights to this meeting are the role of "spokesman for the people" assumed by Harry Ueno and the attribution to JACL leaders of influence in shaping WRA policy. From the time of his formation of the Kitchen Workers Union two months earlier, Ueno had emerged as a cultural hero. In part, this development stemmed from his style of leadership. A fluent, persuasive, and straightforward speaker in Japanese who customarily spoke in a high-pitched, excitable voice, his actions personified the traditional Japanese cultural theme emphasizing group welfare over personal aggrandizement.

Ueno was not interested in control merely as an end in itself, this he told to all, and his friends were convinced of his sincerity when he said that "everything which I do, I am doing for the sake of the people of Manzanar. I have no selfish motives, and this unselfishness on my part will be recognized by the people."[113]

While his opposition to the Work Corps and the Charter Commission enhanced his reputation in the community, what catapulted Ueno into a position of public stature was his charge that two administrators—assistant project director Ned Campbell and chief steward Joe Winchester—were misappropriating and selling inmate sugar supplies for personal gain. This charge had led to a full-scale investigation by the block managers. Although insufficient evidence was uncovered to implicate the two, the investigation did expose the fact that the inmates were being shortchanged in their sugar allotment.[114] This finding alone guaranteed Ueno's popularity, for it confirmed the inmates' deep-seated conviction that the administrators were capable of the most unscrupulous behavior.

JACL-WRA collusion rumors had been commonplace, but their credibility became intensified by a recent development. While the meeting on self-government was in progress, Fred Tayama and another JACL leader, Kiyoshi

FIGURE 14. Michi Nishiura Weglyn, author of *Days of Infamy*, and Harry Ueno, one of the book's most celebrated figures of World War II Japanese American resistance. This photo was taken in 1993 when Weglyn was being honored with the establishment of an endowed chair in multicultural studies at California Polytechnic State University, Pomona. Courtesy Lawrence de Graaf Center for Oral and Public History, California State University, Fullerton.

Higashi (inmate police chief), were serving as Manzanar's delegates to the JACL National Convention in Salt Lake City. Tayama's departure for that city in mid-November had outraged the inmates, for he, even more than Karl Yoneda, Tokie Slocum, and Togo Tanaka, typified the antithesis of the "Japanese spirit." From the standpoint of the community, "no more unrepresentative person could be chosen to present the views of Manzanar at the convention."[115] Antipathy toward Tayama stretched back to pre-eviction days. As the president of the Los Angeles JACL chapter and chairman of the Southern District Council of JACL, "it was almost axiomatic that [he should have been] the most-criticized Nisei in Los Angeles."[116] But the community's animosity for Tayama was seasoned by other factors as well. At a time when the economic and social fortunes of Japanese Americans were at a low ebb, he was conspicuously prosperous. The proprietor of a chain of restaurants employing thirty-five to fifty workers, Tayama owned a large home, drove around the community in a late-model Buick sedan, "played golf with the Japanese Consul (Tomokazu Hori), and was frequently asked by Nisei clubs to serve, with his wife, as patron and patroness at numerous social functions."[117] Whereas his JACL circle of associates regarded him "as a 'regular guy' who played a stiff hand at poker, traded gusty jokes with the best of 'em and won more than his share of golf trophies," in the pages of *Doho*, a leftist Nisei newspaper, he was accused of "operating [his cafes] under 'sweat shop conditions,' underpaying his help, and of obstructing the unionization of his employees."[118] Nor did his penchant for self-assertiveness and aggressive opportunism endear him to the community. For example, he reputedly announced to his classmates in a public speaking class: "You know, I have been raised to always do my very best and to rise to the very top. I firmly believe that one should always strive to be top. Even if I were to be a bandit, I would expect to be the Chief Bandit."[119]

Tayama's activities during the eviction period further compounded his unpopularity. It was rumored—and generally believed—that in his capacity as a JACL official and as co-owner of the Pacific Service Bureau he exploited Issei, "making exorbitant profits from high charges for services [filing alien travel permits required by the Department of Justice, transferring business licenses, and the like] which could be obtained free" through federal channels.[120] Another damaging rumor circulated to the effect that Tayama had mishandled a relief fund collected for beleaguered Terminal Island fishermen.[121]

Over and beyond these personal endeavors, Tayama was vilified for his "witch hunting" efforts in behalf of the JACL. A vigorous proponent of Americanization and undivided loyalty, Tayama, in March 1941, had been instrumental in the formation of the Southern District Council's Coordinating Committee for Southern California Defense (CCSCD), whose animating purpose of "making patriotism vital" entailed gathering information on subversive activities (which was turned over directly to Naval Intelligence).[122] After Pearl Harbor, Tayama organized the Anti-Axis Committee to enlarge upon and to step up the work of the CCSCD. His subsequent appointment of Tokie Slocum, a frenetic chauvinist who reportedly accompanied FBI agents on their post–Pearl Harbor sweep of "potentially dangerous" Issei in Los Angeles's Little Tokyo, darkened Tayama's reputation still further. Indignation toward him reached a fever pitch when, following a meeting with army officials and JACL leaders in San Francisco, Tayama broke the news of total exclusion and detention to Southern Californians at a mass meeting at the Maryknoll Catholic Church auditorium, located just outside the heart of Little Tokyo.[123] His actions at Manzanar did nothing to mitigate the community's detestation for him:

> Indeed, if anything, he fell into even greater displeasure. At Manzanar his most unpopular antics were those concerned with his demonstration of his Americanism. As one observer put it, "Tayama was not content to be a 100% American; he was a 350% American." Specifically, Tayama was very loose in his talk about disloyal Americans, openly informing the Administration about manifestations of disloyalty on the part of particular individuals at Manzanar. Tayama is said to have worked off his personal prejudices by accusing those he disliked of being pro-Japanese. He is also said to have informed on the basis of completely inadequate evidence. Tayama did his informing with some secrecy, but the Japanese grapevine kept the community informed of his activity.[124]

Tayama seemed to be accorded special privileges by the camp staff: According to Opler, "Rumors circulated freely about the sugar, canned foods and fine furniture with which his home was filled, and . . . it was assumed that the sugar said to be in his home was a portion of the amount the kitchen workers claimed had mysteriously disappeared."[125] Nor did his role as a leading spirit in both the Citizens Federation and the Work Corps win him anything but more intense hatred. And now he had the audacity to name himself, through political manipulation, Manzanar's "representative" at the Salt Lake City meeting where WRA national leaders would gather and policy decisions would be made. Indeed, word had filtered back to Manzanar that Tayama, in addition to repeating his loose accusations of un-American activities in camp and proposing measures for their elimination, had, along with other JACL delegates, "in the name of the Japanese people in and out of the Centers, asked that Nisei be inducted into combat units of the U.S. Army."[126] The mere mention of his name evoked profound disgust. If anyone endangered the group's existence and threatened its solidarity, it was Fred Tayama.[127]

In the words of Morton Grodzins, "[It] can be said without doubt that the majority of the people at Manzanar did not believe anyone, guilty or not, should be punished for beating Fred Tayama. Tayama was a public nuisance. His assailants were to be praised, not punished." Grodzins cites the following inmate reactions as typical: "It was hard to find a single person at Manzanar who expressed sympathy for Tayama." "Even the highly Americanized and cooperative Nisei were of the opinion that though the approach was unorthodox, Tayama deserved the beating. Since there was no other way of his getting punished, the beating fit the situation perfectly."[128] Grodzins' report, "Manzanar Shooting," is the best account of the social psychology of the Manzanar camp at the time of the revolt. Written immediately after the disturbance, it makes no attempt to judge ideology or morality but merely tries to reflect public opinion. In so doing, it too is written from an ethnic (i.e., community) perspective.

It will be recollected that Tayama was beaten upon his return to the center, thereby setting in motion the Manzanar Revolt. What must be emphasized is that there is strong reason to believe that the overwhelming majority of inmates fully endorsed this beating. Historians writing from the WRA-JACL perspective may see the attack on Tayama as the unwarranted work of a few pro-Axis Kibei troublemakers, but such an analysis construes the action too restrictively. Even if one concedes pro-Japan terrorism as the basis for the assault and accepts the idea that only a small band of hooligans participated in it, one still has to account for the thousands who protested the arrest of Harry Ueno and who were willing to defy the administration to have him released from jail. Nor did they simply believe him innocent of involvement in Tayama's beating. Indeed, one might say that Ueno was lionized because of his alleged connection with the attack. For the inmates—Issei, Kibei, and Nisei—the time had come when something had to be done to prevent the corrosive effects of the JACLers. Seen through the ethnic perspective, the beating of Tayama was both necessary and good.

Similarly, what transpired on December 6, 1942, must not be seen in isolation or ascribed solely to ideological motivations. When viewed within the ethnic perspective, all of the occurrences of that day—the massive crowds, the membership of the Committee of Five, the composition of the death lists and blacklists, the demands for the dismissal of specified members of the appointed staff, and the character of the inmates' evening demonstration at the jail—assume a definite cultural logic.

While WRA-JACL sources attribute the huge assemblages to the fact that most present were merely curious onlookers, this interpretation stems from narrow wish fulfillment.[129] It appears to us that a more satisfactory explanation is that the mounting discontent of the inmate population, which heretofore found sporadic expression through grumbling about camp conditions, work slowdowns, strikes against war-related industries and profit-oriented camp enterprises, and pervasive gang activity and *inu* beatings, became crystallized into concerted resistance action through the symbolic juxtaposition of Harry Ueno and Fred Tayama.[130] As Grodzins has perceptively observed:

> The situation was made to order for a popular anti-administration demonstration. The issue cut through political and cultural lines. The question could be put as one involving administrative integrity and fairness to the inmates. Loyalty to America had nothing to do with it. . . . The demonstrations that followed, though in part engineered by the genuine pro-Japanese elements in the camp, were not pro-Japanese demonstrations. Rather, they were simply demonstrations against an administrative policy that according to the trend of thought in the camp, jailed on flimsy evidence one of the community's benefactors.[131]

The cultural significance of the Committee of Five is also noteworthy. In consonance with the Japanese cultural theme mandating that community status be ascribed by factors of sex, age, and generation, the committee was composed largely of mature male Issei. Moreover, all of the members embodied the cultural theme positing the paramount importance of the community's welfare. Four of them were aligned with the Kitchen Workers Union, while the remaining one, Joe Kurihara, was primarily identified by inmates for his attacks on the Citizens Federation and his championship of an alternative organization, the Manzanar Welfare Association.[132]

Likewise, there is a cultural logic informing the death lists and blacklists read off to the crowds by the committee. While the precise membership and order of priority of these lists is somewhat vague, it seems clear that the primary targets were Fred Tayama, Tokie Slocum, Karl Yoneda, Koji Ariyoshi, James Oda, Togo Tanaka, and Joe Masaoka.[133] In addition, the lists included inmates prominently associated with the *Free Press* and the camp internal security force, particularly its special investigative branch.[134] Significantly, all of these individuals were identified with JACL-sponsored organizations and objectives and/or anti-subversive activities.

The choice of the particular three members of the administration whose removal was called for by the crowd also made cultural sense. The individual most frequently named, assistant project director Ned Campbell, not only failed to understand the Japanese psychology but epitomized the *keto* (white man, hairy beast) to the inmates. Loud, stubborn, overbearing, and given to making physical threats against those who disagreed with him, Campbell in his very demeanor evoked the racism undergirding the entire incarceration program.[135] Chief steward Joe Winchester, whom Ueno had accused of being in collusion with Campbell in shorting inmates of their rightful supplies, compounded his culpability in the community's eyes by his penchant for making snap judgments and for treating incarcerees in accordance with simplistic, pejorative stereotypes. For Winchester, inmates were either "good Japs" or "troublemakers." The remaining staff member whose ouster was demanded was Hervey Brown, chief engineer in charge of public works. Like Campbell and Winchester, Brown projected a high-handed manner and appeared to transfer or fire inmate employees for what seemed to them very arbitrary reasons.[136]

Finally, the behavior of the crowd at the evening gathering before the camp jail prior to the shooting—heckling directed at the military police, speaking almost exclusively in Japanese, and singing the Japanese national anthem and other Japanese songs—is culturally revealing.[137] For the inmates the jailing of Ueno became a rallying point for their willingness to resist those (like the WRA, the JACL, and the military police) who appeared to threaten their cultural heritage and identity. Thus, in response to their endangered ethnicity, they exhibited heightened ethnic consciousness and behavior.

This was also true with the entire Manzanar Revolt. The events of December 6 were but a logical culmination of developments originating with the administration's decision to bypass the community's natural Issei leadership to deal with its own artificially erected JACL hierarchy and to embark on a program of Americanization at the expense of Japanese ethnicity. When the WRA moved the JACLers out of the camp after the revolt, the Issei took a step toward restoring the dominance they had enjoyed before the JAI, and the entire community served notice that its self-determination and ethnic identity would not be relinquished without a struggle. Through the operation of continuing resistance activity, Manzanar would eventually be transformed into a Little Tokyo of the desert where, as in prewar days, the most salient community characteristics were group solidarity and the predominance of elements of Japanese culture.[138]

NOTES

1. Gene Wise, *American Historical Explanations: A Strategy for Grounded Inquiry* (Homewood, IL: Dorsey, 1973), vii.

2. Wise, *American Historical Explanations*, 34. Unlike Wise, who derives his inspiration for perspectivist history from the novelistic technique and from recent conceptual breakthroughs in a multiplicity of scientific and humanistic disciplines, we have been led to adopt the perspectivist approach in this study chiefly through our involvement in oral history. This tool of inquiry, with its emphasis on the taped interview, has confirmed our suspicion of "objective" history and directed us to seek answers to the very questions that Wise depicts as central to the perspectivist model of historical explanation.

3. For an overview of the camp, see Glen Kitayama, "Manzanar," *Densho Encyclopedia*, https://encyclopedia.densho.org/Manzanar/ (accessed March 13, 2021).

4. Our account of the Manzanar Riot is drawn from primary materials in the US War Relocation Archive, collection 122, Manzanar War Relocation Center Records, boxes 16 and 17, Special Collections, Charles E. Young Research Library, UCLA; and Japanese American Evacuation and Resettlement (JAER) Records, folders E2.332, O7.00, O7.50, O8.10, O.10.00, O10.04, O11.00, R30.00, R30.10, S1.10, and S1.20 A, B, and C, Bancroft Library, University of California, Berkeley. Collection 122 consists of the files collected and maintained by Ralph Palmer Merritt, project director of the Manzanar War Relocation Center. Hereafter cited as MWRCR. The Berkeley archives were prepared and indexed in 1958 by Edward N. Barnhart. Hereafter references from this collection will be cited as JAER. We have purposely avoided controversial points of detail in our overview of the events surrounding the riot. On such issues as whether Ueno was one of Tayama's assailants (but his admission was not forthcoming until many years later, something I clarify in profuse detail in three appendixes in "A Riot of Voices," *Barbed Voices*, 127–39) or why the military police fired upon the inmate crowd, there is a plethora of documentation to support conflicting, even contradictory interpretations. Instead of expending our energy in historical sleuth work, we have contented ourselves with arriving at a consensual summary of the Manzanar Riot that could serve as a springboard for perspectivist analysis.

5. See Arthur A. Hansen, "Harry Ueno," *Densho Encyclopedia*, https://encyclopedia.densho.org/Harry_Ueno/ (accessed February 16, 1942).

6. See Greg Robinson, "War Relocation Authority," *Densho Encyclopedia*, https://encyclopedia.densho.org/War_Relocation_Authority/ (accessed March 13, 2021).

7. See Brian Niiya, "Ralph Merritt," *Densho Encyclopedia*, https://encyclopedia.densho.org/Ralph%20Merritt (accessed February 18, 2021).

8. For a biography of Kurihara, see Eileen Tamura, *In Defense of Justice: Joseph Kurihara and the Japanese American Struggle for Equality* (Urbana: University of Illinois Press, 2013); see also Tamura, "Joe Kurihara," *Densho Encyclopedia*, https://encyclopedia.densho.org/Joe%20Kurihara/ (accessed February 16, 2021).

9. See Arthur A. Hansen, "Moab/Leupp Isolation Centers" (detention facility), *Densho Encyclopedia*, https://encyclopedia.densho.org/Moab/Leupp_Isolation_Centers_(detention_facility)/ (accessed February 16, 2021).

10. The primary accounts are contained in MWRCR, box 16, and JAER, folder 07.00. See also *Pacific Citizen*, December 10, 1942. Secondary treatment of the Manzanar Riot from this perspective includes Allan R. Bosworth, *America's Concentration Camps* (New York: Bantam, 1968), 152–56; Audrie Girdner and Anne Loftis, *The Great Betrayal: The Evacuation of the Japanese-Americans during World War II* (London: Macmillan, 1969); Bill Hosokawa, *Nisei: The Quiet Americans* (New York: William Morrow, 1969), 361–62; Norman Jackman, "Collective Protest in Relocation Centers" (PhD diss., University of California, Berkeley, 1955), 170–83, 211–19; Dillon S. Myer, *Uprooted Americans: The Japanese Americans and the War Relocation Authority during World War II* (Tucson: University of Arizona Press, 1971), 63–66; and Thomas Brewer Rice, "The Manzanar War Relocation Center" (master's thesis, University of California, Berkeley, 1947).

11. Girdner and Loftis, *Betrayal*, 263.

12. One primary account of the riot written from the WRA-JACL perspective that reflects an awareness of the event's cultural significance is that authored by Janet Goldberg (under the supervision of Robert L. Brown, Reports Officer, Manzanar War Relocation Center), "The Manzanar 'Incident,' December 5 to December 19," n.d., MWRCR, box 16, and JAER, folder 07.00. Still, while this account concludes that one of the two main contributing factors to the uprising was "the inherent conflict between those culturally Japanese and those culturally Americans," nowhere in this thirty-one-page report is there evidence presented that would warrant such a conclusion.

13. For convenience, throughout the discussion of the WRA-JACL perspective, this term will be employed without quotation marks, though the sense should be understood.

14. Rice, "Manzanar," 69.

15. Jackman, "Collective Protest," 183. If anything, the year 1943 was even stormier than the preceding one. Manzanar was the only center, for instance, where over 50 percent of the adult male citizens answered no to the question on loyalty, qualified their response, refused to answer, or refused to register at all (by contrast, at Minidoka these groups constituted only 8 percent of the male citizen population). See Morton Grodzins, "Making Un-Americans," *American Journal of Sociology* 60 (May 1955): 570–82. Moreover, this period saw widespread resistance to the imposition of the draft for Nisei and a mounting number of applications for repatriation and expatriation. See MWRCR, boxes 15 and 26, especially the reports prepared by Morris E. Opler, the WRA community analyst at Manzanar. On the general unrest and inmate resistance during this time, see MWRCR, boxes 10, 11, and 31–39, which contain the block managers' reports.

16. By contrast, Gary Y. Okihiro, in "Japanese Resistance in America's Concentration Camps: A Re-evaluation," *Amerasia Journal* 2 (Fall 1973): 20–34, posits a Manzanar Model of Resistance as an explanatory tool for correlating forms of resistance—work slowdowns, struggles for inmate self-determination, lack of cooperation with Americanization programs and war-related industries—that operated within many of the camps.

17. December 7, 1942. Similar accounts appearing in various West Coast newspapers, along with official WRA press releases, can be found in MWRCR, box 17.

18. Girdner and Loftis, *Betrayal*, 263. Togo Tanaka's account of the riot, which shares some of the features of the WRA-JACL perspective, deflates the ideological interpretation: "The impression given in most newspaper accounts of the Manzanar disturbance, that the instigators were all 'pro-Japan' or 'pro-Axis' . . . and that the intended victims of violence were 'pro-American'—all of them—is not necessarily an accurate picture . . . Undoubtedly, differences in ideology and position on the war played an important part; but these were . . . incidental to the riot itself." Togo Tanaka, "A Report on the Manzanar Riot of Sunday, December 6, 1942," 95, Bancroft Library, UCB, JERS, O10.12.

19. The inordinate attention paid Kurihara's role is reflected in the Berkeley collection. See JAER, folders O.810, R30.00, and R30.10. This preoccupation with Kurihara has been extended further by such secondary accounts as Paul Jacobs and Saul Landau's *To Serve the Devil: Colonials and Sojourners* (New York: Vintage, 1971), 166–270.

20. Daniels, *Concentration Camps USA*, 105.

21. Board of Review, "Harry Yoshio Ueno," December–January 1942–43, MWRCR, box 16.

22. Tanaka, 28–29, CSUF-COPH O.H. 1271b.

23. Ned Campbell, interview by Arthur A. Hansen, August 15, 1974, CSUF-COPH O.H. 1329. For an uncharacteristically favorable impression of Campbell by an inmate, see Tad Uyeno, "Point of No Return," *Rafu Shimpo* (Los Angeles), 1973, 12. Uyeno's story, which focuses upon the post–Manzanar Riot experiences of those "pro-American" inmates sent to the Cow Creek camp in Death Valley, was originally serialized in fifty installments in the *Rafu Shimpo* between August 22 and October 20, 1973.

24. Alexander H. Leighton, *The Governing of Men: General Principles and Recommendations Based on Experience at a Japanese Relocation Camp* (Princeton, NJ: Princeton University Press, 1946). Leighton's comments pertain specifically to the Poston staff, though they certainly have general applicability for all of the camps' staffs.

25. Recounting an occasion when he had sided with the inmates against the WRA in a labor dispute, Ned Campbell has confessed that his action "might have been a mistake, a basic mistake in organization. If the boss tells you to do something, you either quit or go ahead and do what the boss tells you to do." Campbell, CSUF-COPH O.H. 1329. That Campbell did not make many such "basic mistakes" is attested to by one inmate, Koji Ariyoshi, in "Memories of Manzanar," *Honolulu Star-Bulletin*, April 9, 1971.

26. Douglas Nelson, "Heart Mountain: The History of an American Concentration Camp" (master's thesis, University of Wyoming, 1970), 103–4.

27. For a more detailed explanation of how this "progressive" idea has manifested itself within American historiography, see Wise, *American Historical Explanations*, 86–89, 97–100.

28. Cf. Okihiro, "Japanese Resistance." Okihiro's article is central to systematic inquiry into the phenomenon of resistance movements in the camp.

29. See Patricia Wakida, "Manzanar Free Press (newspaper)," *Densho Encyclopedia*, https://encyclopedia.densho.org/Manzanar_Free_Press_(newspaper)/ (accessed March 12, 2021).

30. Robert L. Brown, interview by Arthur A. Hansen, December 13, 1973, 53, CSUF-COPH O.H. 1375.

31. Campbell, CSUF-COPH O.H. 1329. The experiences of Brown and Campbell are especially significant since the latter, in his interview, also explained, "The camp was a two- or three-man operation. I mean, two or three personalities or philosophies [ran the camp]: the police chief, Bob Brown, and me."

32. Okihiro, "Japanese Resistance," 20–21.

33. Three of these works have already been cited: Daniels, *Concentration Camps USA*; Nelson, "Heart Mountain"; and Okihiro, "Japanese Resistance." Three others are unpublished studies: James Minoru Sakoda, "Minidoka: An Analysis of Changing Patterns of Social Interaction" (PhD diss., University of California, Berkeley,

1949); Toshio Yatsushiro, "Political and Socio-Cultural Issues at Poston and Manzanar Relocation Centers: A Themal Analysis" (PhD diss., Cornell University, 1953); and Matthew Richard Speier, "Japanese American Relocation Camp Colonization and Resistance to Resettlement: A Study in the Social Psychology of Ethnic Identity under Stress" (master's thesis, University of California, Berkeley, 1965). A final work is Jerome Charyn's *American Scrapbook* (New York: Viking, 1969), a fictionalized account of the events that has deepened our appreciation for Gene Wise's insight that historians could profit by adopting the novelist's multifaceted view of experience.

34. In their study of the social psychology of the Manzanar Riot's membership, "Riot and Rioters," *Western Political Quarterly* 10 (December 1957): 864, George Wada and James C. Davies provide a definition from which ours is extrapolated.

35. This dynamic conception of collective behavior stems from Speier, "Japanese American Relocation Camp Colonization," 7–8.

36. Yatsushiro, "Political and Socio-Cultural Issues at Poston and Manzanar."

37. Yatsushiro, "Political and Socio-Cultural Issues at Poston and Manzanar," 40.

38. Yatsushiro, "Political and Socio-Cultural Issues at Poston and Manzanar," 41.

39. Yatsushiro, "Political and Socio-Cultural Issues at Poston and Manzanar," 41.

40. Yatsushiro, "Political and Socio-Cultural Issues at Poston and Manzanar," 209–95.

41. Yatsushiro, "Political and Socio-Cultural Issues at Poston and Manzanar," 183.

42. "Social distance" means the degree of sympathetic understanding that operates between any two persons. See Robert Howard Ross, "Social Distance as It Exists between the First and Second Generation Japanese in the City of Los Angeles and Vicinity" (master's thesis, University of California, 1939).

43. Sue Kunitomi Embrey, interview by Arthur A. Hansen and David A. Hacker, November 30, 1973, 10, CSUF-COPH O.H. 1366a.

44. Ross, "Social Distance," 113–14. Tamotsu Shibutani, in "Rumors in a Crisis Situation" (master's thesis, University of Chicago, 1944), 36, while emphasizing the cultural schism between Issei and Nisei, still acknowledges that as "the Nisei came of age in large numbers, they did not go out into the American community. Rather they developed a society of their own." Tanaka encapsulates the Nisei's prewar plight: "From 1936 [upon graduating summa cum laude from UCLA] to 1942, I immersed myself behind the walls of Little Tokyo, venturing forth into the wider community only as an advocate of equal rights or civil liberty and of the proposition that, although we may look Japanese, look harder and you'll find a good American." Togo Tanaka, "How to Survive Racism in America's Free Society," in *Voices Long Silent*, edited by Arthur A. Hansen and Betty E. Mitson, 89 (Fullerton: Oral History Program, California State University, Fullerton, 1974).

45. WRA, Community Analysis Section, "Japanese Americans Educated in Japan," Community Analysis Report No. 8, January 28, 1944, 2, MWRCR, box 16, folder 1.

46. WRA, "Japanese Americans Educated in Japan," 8.

47. Sue Kunitomi Embrey, interview by Arthur A. Hansen and David A. Hacker, November 30, 1973, 10, CSUF-COPH O.H. 1366a. On the other hand, another Nisei interviewee maintained that "Kibei more or less looked down on us because they enjoyed the privilege of American citizenship plus they were fluent in the Japanese language; so they could wear both hats and be comfortable in both societies, where many of us were just Americans, period." George Fukasawa, interview by Arthur A. Hansen, August 12, 1974, 16, CSUF-COPH O.H. 1336.

48. WRA, "Japanese Americans Educated in Japan," 7. Although the data are drawn from this source, we have placed an entirely different construction on them than that intended. To our knowledge, there exists no "sympathetic" study of Kibei; in fact, there seem to be very few Kibei studies of whatever persuasion.

49. John H. Burma, "Current Leadership Problems among Japanese Americans," *Sociology and Social Research* 37 (January 1953): 158.

50. Speier, "Japanese American Relocation Camp Colonization," 4, 43. A Hawai'i Nisei, Koji Ariyoshi, explains that Nisei in Hawai'i "disapproved of Mainland Niseis' obsession, particularly among middle-class and college-educated ones, to be like a middle or upper-class Caucasian." "They wanted," writes Ariyoshi, "to crash the white community and be accepted. Failing this, they were frustrated." Ariyoshi, "Memories of Manzanar," 1.

51. For an amplification of the prewar JACL and its relationship to the larger Japanese American community, see Togo Tanaka, "JACL," JAER, folder O10.16.

52. See, for example, the case study of one family during the period prior to their incarceration at Manzanar in Leonard Broom and John I. Kitsuse, *The Managed Casualty: The Japanese-American Family in World War II* (Berkeley: University of California Press, 1974), 64.

53. Shibutani, "Rumors," 114.

54. Daniels, *Concentration Camps USA*, 26.

55. Daniels, *Concentration Camps USA*, 27.

56. Daniels, *Concentration Camps USA*, 26.

57. See Shiho Imai, "Mike Masaoka," *Densho Encyclopedia*, https://encyclopedia.densho.org/Mike_Masaoka/ (accessed March 13, 2021).

58. Hosokawa, *Nisei*, 223–41. For Tanaka's arrest, see Tanaka, "How to Survive Racism," 93.

59. On December 13, 1941, Chairman Fred Tayama of the Anti-Axis Committee issued the following statement: "The United States is at war with the Axis. We

shall do all in our power to help wipe out vicious totalitarian enemies. Every man is either friend or foe. We shall investigate and turn over to authorities all who by word or act consort with the enemies." (From an Anti-Axis Committee circular given to the authors by Karl Yoneda.)

Tokie Slocum's anti-subversive activities were pursued with such vigor that even his JACL allies were offended. See Togo Tanaka, interview by Betty E. Mitson and David A. Hacker, May 19, 1973, CSUF-COPH O.H. 1271a, 46–47, and 1271b, 2–7.

One interviewee, who served simultaneously as the vice president of the Santa Monica JACL chapter and a member of the Santa Monica auxiliary police during the pre-exclusion period, maintained that the two roles of assisting the community and aiding the FBI and the military intelligence agencies were not mutually exclusive but compatible. Indeed, in the latter role he averred that he was able to exonerate many Issei from flagrantly irresponsible charges and spare them from being apprehended and sent to detention centers. Fukasawa, CSUF-COPH O.H. 1336.

60. *Nichibei Times*, February 15 and 20, 1942; Shibutani, "Rumors," 109–10. For information about Kibei chapters of the JACL and their policy differences relative to the pre-eviction and detention period, see Fukasawa, CSUF-COPH O.H. 1336; and Yoneda, CSUF-COPH O.H. 1376b.

61. Shibutani, "Rumors," 114–15.

62. Goldberg, "The Manzanar 'Incident,'" 2. Both the unrepresentativeness and the unpopularity of the JACL in Los Angeles are apparent in the following remarks of one Nisei: "The record of the Los Angeles Citizens League is such that your stomach would turn when looking into it. To say it represented the Nisei would be silly; out of thousands of eligible citizens the LA branch could number about one hundred members. . . . Among the Nisei in Los Angeles the League was considered a malignant cancer; if the evacuation had not taken place it should surely have been cut out and a truly representative group would have taken its place. To most Nisei the League is as distasteful as the pro-axis label." Sachio Saito, Block 33-4-5, Manzanar, California, to Ralph P. Merritt, Project Director, Manzanar War Relocation Center, December 20, 1942, MWRCR, box 7. For an analysis and overview of anti-JACL sentiment in prewar Los Angeles, see Togo Tanaka, "A Report on the Manzanar Riot of Sunday, December 6, 1942," folder O10.12, JAER, Bancroft, 13–15l, "Addenda," 40–49.

63. All of the rumors derive from Shibutani, "Rumors," 115–16.

64. Shibutani, "Rumors," 162–66.

65. Kai T. Erikson, *Wayward Puritans: A Study in the Sociology of Deviance* (New York: Wiley, 1966), 3–29.

66. Shibutani, "Rumors," 66. The collective indictment of the Kibei and the reasons behind it are implicit in the following remark by one JACL official: "We had

most of our opposition [to the JACL strategy of cooperating with the government officials in the exclusion and detention] from a group who called themselves Kibei, that were educated in Japanese propaganda and culture through their formative years over there [in Japan]." Fukasawa, CSUF-COPH O.H. 1336, 15.

67. The preceding four rumors are drawn from Shibutani, "Rumors," 66–67. Shibutani does not attribute these rumors specifically to JACLer sources, though internal evidence strongly suggests that the rumors did indeed originate there. Our imputation here, therefore, represents merely historical inference, not factual information.

68. Morton Grodzins describes Manzanar's WCCA leadership as "a generally unfriendly staff." Grodzins, "Making Un-Americans," 577. For a sharply contrasting estimate, see Robert L. Brown's observations in CSUF-COPH O.H. 1375. Brown's recollection is confirmed by his diary entries during his March–June 1942 tenure at Manzanar. Brown's 1942 diary is available in the Arthur A. Hansen Papers, box 1, Lawrence de Graaf Center for Oral and Public History, California State University, Fullerton.

69. The residents of these two communities expressed considerable hostility toward the inmates, thereby compounding the problem of camp administration and inmate morale. David J. Bertagnoli and Arthur A. Hansen have interviewed extensively among the residents of the Owens Valley communities and attempted to assess their reactions to the camp and its inmate population. See CSUF-COPH O.H. 1343, 1344, 1345, 1346, 1347, 1378, 1384, 1385, 1393, 1396, 1398, 1399, 1401 (which is reproduced in its entirety in Hansen and Mitson, eds., *Voices Long Silent*, 143–60), and 1402. In addition, a local businessman and politician, Rudie Henderson, described the reaction of his fellow Owens Valley residents as one of "almost unanimous reaction was keen resentment and open hostility." Henderson also described a "vituperative petition," signed by 500 local merchants and citizens, designed to prevent inmates from shopping in nearby Lone Pine. See Robert L. Brown, comp., "Final Report: Manzanar Relocation Center," vol. 1, Project Director's Report, appendix 26, MWRCR.

70. Rice, "Manzanar," 25–28. Yatsushiro, "Themal Analysis," 342–43; Ariyoshi, "Memories of Manzanar"; and Kiyotoshi Iwamoto, "Economic Aspects of the Japanese Relocation Centers in the United States" (master's thesis, Stanford University, 1946), 13.

71. Broom and Kitsuse, *Managed Casualty*, 40, is explicit on the favored role accorded JACLers in all of the camps: "One of the first administrative policies was to assign preferential status to the Nisei. The Administration systematically encouraged the emancipation of the Nisei from Issei control. Special recognition was accorded to the leadership of the JACL, which was committed to cooperation

with the Administration. The preferential treatment toward the Nisei extended into all aspects of center life: community organization, employment, leisure, and relocation."

Whereas a few scholars, such as Daniels, *Concentration Camps USA*, 79, have alluded to the role of the Japanese American left within the JAI experience, this subject has yet to be pursued in a systematic or comprehensive way. John Modell, ed., *The Kikuchi Diary: Chronicle from an American Concentration Camp* (Urbana: University of Illinois Press, 1973), provides a starting point for such an inquiry. Additional understanding of this topic can be gleaned from an examination of the newspaper *Doho*, JARP, UCLA; and two studies focused on the policies and personalities of this Los Angeles–based "progressive" journal: Tanaka, "Report on the Manzanar Riot: Addenda," 8–18, and Ronald C. Larson and Arthur A. Hansen, "*Doho*: The Japanese American 'Communist' Press, 1938–42," in part 1 of this book.

While, for the purpose of convenient analysis, this study treats the JACL leadership and the left-wing intellectuals at Manzanar under the generic label of "JACLers," it should be noted that there were marked differences in overall background and philosophy between these two groups. Indeed, the contrast, in spite of shared views on exclusion and detention, camp objectives, and the war, was so extreme that Togo Tanaka designated leftists like Karl Yoneda, Koji Ariyoshi, Chiye Mori, James Oda, Joe Blamey, and Tom Yamazaki as the "Anti-JACL" group. "It should be recalled," writes Tanaka, "that members of Group II [left-wingers] arrived at Manzanar as inmates before Group I [JACL]. This was true almost without exception. Group II members established themselves at the relocation center first. When Group I members arrived a month or so later, they generally discovered that Group II 'had laid the mines and torpedoes in advance of our coming; they prepared the Administration—and volunteer inmates—for a hostile reception to us; they kept up the vicious rumors to perpetuate themselves in their petty little jobs, continuing jealousies and friction of pre-war and pre-evacuation days.'" Tanaka, "An Analysis of the Manzanar Incident," 94. See also Tanaka, CSUF-COPH O.H. 1271b, 14–20. Group II's influence was particularly notable both in the English and Japanese editions of the *Manzanar Free Press*, which was heavily staffed by its members.

Unlike the JACL, which supported the exclusion and detention program primarily for patriotic reasons—to uphold American principles and to safeguard citizenship rights—leftist support stemmed from international convictions: "We were," reflects Karl Yoneda, "at war with the most vicious, brutal racists—Hitler's fascist butchers, Mussolini's musclemen, and the Japanese imperial rapists of Nanking. We had no choice but to accept the U.S. as it was at that time, and fight on the side of the Allies. Although we were guilty in not speaking out against the Evacuation

Order and acquiesced fully, we have NO GUILT OR SHAME regarding our efforts to defeat the fascist Axis. We were sure there would be ovens in Manzanar and other camps if the Mein Kamp[f]ers won the war and that all of us, including all non-white and white anti-fascists would end up in those ovens." Karl Yoneda, "Manzanar: Another View," *Rafu Shimpo*, December 19, 1973 (supplement). A similar outlook is expressed by Ariyoshi in "Memories of Manzanar."

72. *Manzanar Free Press*, April 11, 1942, emphasis added. Robert L. Brown said that this editorial was a gambit designed to circumvent possible resistance by DeWitt to a camp newspaper. According to Brown, "Larry Benedict [a public relations man employed by the WCCA] said [to Brown], 'I don't want to ask, because I know the old general won't let us do a newspaper, so why don't you just print a newspaper anyway? And on the front page, in a little editorial, why don't you put a little thing thanking the general for allowing you to do it, and he won't remember whether he allowed you to do it or not, and that will make him feel good.' So, we did that. We put a little box and thanked General DeWitt for permission to print the paper, because it was such a necessary item. And I remember the old general was tickled to death. He said, 'That's fine. That's fine. That's what they need to do over there; they have to have communication.'" Brown, CSUF-COPH O.H. 1375, 19–20. While this anecdote explains the origin of the item, it must nonetheless have rankled the Issei and Kibei—and no doubt many Nisei—who read it.

73. Yatsushiro, "Themal Analysis," 310, 356.

74. The growing Japanization of Manzanar's Nisei population occasioned particular concern among JACLers, who communicated this development to the administration. See Tom Yamazaki's personal and confidential report dated August 1, 1942, MWRCR, box 9, and Togo Tanaka and Joe Masaoka, "Historical Documentation: Project Report No. 35," August 11, 1942, and "Project Report No. 87," December 1, 1942, MWRCR, box 9. The steady evolution of this trend is best grasped through reading the complete collection of project reports submitted by Tanaka and Masaoka between June and December 1942. See JAER, folders O10.06 and O10.08.

75. See Yamazaki, "Report: August 1, 1942," 10.

76. Morris E. Opler, "A History of Internal Government at Manzanar, March 1942 to December 6, 1942," MWRCR, box 12, folder 1, 4–30. Although this report issued from a WRA source, it was consistently critical of the WRA-JACL perspective and adopted a line of analysis closely conforming to what we have termed the ethnic perspective. This situation did not endear Opler to the Manzanar administration. When a copy of the report was forwarded to the head of the Community Management Division in Washington by the Manzanar representative of this division, she felt obliged to append the following message:

Mr. Merritt [the project director] has read it and has some question in his mind about the material. He feels that the presentation is one-sided in that it criticizes but does not attempt to explain the WRA policies and the action of the WRA personnel, while, at all points, it attempts to vindicate evacuee attitudes and actions. He feels that some of the events are capable of interpretations which are not suggested by Dr. Opler. . . . I don't have the same questions . . . but I realize, after talking with Mr. Merritt, that the impression given to an outsider might be very one-sided. Mr. Merritt has asked Mr. [Dillon] Myer [WRA director] to look over the material and let us know whether he thinks it is desirable to continue with this type of interpretive, historical study. (Lucy Adams [for Ralph P. Merritt] to Dr. John Provinse, July 26, 1944, box 12, folder 1)

77. Opler, "History of Internal Government," 30.

78. Ned Campbell, Assistant Project Director, to Ted Akahoshi, July 4, 1942, memorandum regarding meetings conducted in the Manzanar Relocation Area, MWRCR, box 9.

79. Karl G. Yoneda, Block 4 Leader, 4-2-2, Manzanar, California, to Roy Nash, Project Director, and Ned Campbell, Assistant Project Director, Manzanar Relocation Center, Manzanar, California, July 10, 1942, MWRCR, box 9.

80. For confirmation of Akahoshi's cooperative stance, see "Board of Review Reports, Dec.–Jan. 1942–43: Ted Ichiji Akahoshi," MWRCR, box 16, and J. Y. Kurihara, "Murder in Manzanar," JAER, folder O8.10, 17.

81. All of the subsequent statements relative to the block leaders' debate over the Japanese language ban are drawn from Yoneda to Nash and Campbell, July 10, 1942.

82. In an earlier version of this essay, in Hansen and Mitson, *Voices Long Silent*, 66–67, the phrase "Karl Yoneda, a Kibei Communist who aligned himself with the JACLers, outdoing them in his chauvinism" was used. In a letter dated October 1974 to Arthur A. Hansen, Yoneda objected: "This characterization as a blind patriot hardly jibes with my activities, in Japan as a youth, and [in the] U.S. since 1926 to date. My life has been an open struggle against imperialism, exploitation, fascism, racism and for decent working conditions and peace in the world." Our intention was certainly not to discount or depreciate Yoneda's acknowledged lifelong achievements as a champion of human rights and dignity. Perhaps "chauvinism" was an unhappy term for us to have used in this connection, but it was intended to convey that in the context of the camp Yoneda assumed a higher profile than JACL leaders (with the exception of Tokie Slocum) in regard to American patriotism. We

believe this was the case for two reasons: (1) JACL leaders were so stigmatized that they had to muffle their patriotism during the early months at Manzanar; and (2) Yoneda's ideological strategy encompassed the use of aggressive pro-Americanism as a tactical weapon to mobilize sentiment and manpower against the Axis forces. Possibly a third reason is suggested by Yoneda's fellow leftist, Tom Yamazaki, who asserted that "Karl Yoneda and myself are only ones [in the Block Leaders Council] who hold pro-democratic convictions and are working . . . to support the government war efforts." Yamazaki, "Report: August 1, 1942," 10. No doubt Yoneda's patriotism was shrilly pitched in part because of his involvement in a body where pro-Japan attitudes were particularly evident and dominant.

83. Yoneda to Nash and Campbell, July 10, 1942.

84. Yoneda to Nash and Campbell, July 10, 1942.

85. Tanaka and Masaoka, "Project Report No. 36," July 29, 1942, MWRCR, box 9.

86. Ralph P. Merritt, Project Director, Manzanar War Relocation Center, Manzanar, California, to M. M. Tozier, Chief, Reports Division, WERA, Barr Bldg., Washington, DC, January 7, 1946, MWRCR, box 16, folder 8. Since the JACLers were not "electable" as block leaders because of their general unpopularity among the inmates, the Citizens Federation was conceived as a counter organization to mobilize support for their objectives. For a comprehensive analysis of this group's aims and organizational development, see Tanaka, "Report on the Manzanar Riot: Addenda," JAER, folder O10, 10–27.

87. Tanaka and Masaoka, "Project Report No. 36." For a description of this meeting by a principal participant, see Yoneda, CSUF-COPH O.H. 1336. Another account is offered by George Fukasawa, a second-ranking member of the inmate police force who attended the meeting to provide internal security. Because Tokie Slocum was "targeted for elimination," Fukasawa accompanied him to his quarters after the gathering. Fukasawa describes Slocum, a special officer in the inmate intelligence agency, as "a super-patriot type of person. . . . He was very vocal . . . he'd get up at these meetings and he was quite an orator. I think he was the type of person that would engender a lot of hatred from anybody who would be opposed to his views." Fukasawa, CSUF-COPH O.H. 1336, 27.

88. Merritt to Tozier.

89. Opler, "History of Internal Government," 40.

90. See Greg Robinson, "Koji Ariyoshi," *Densho Encyclopedia*, https://encyclopedia.densho.org/Koji%20Ariyoshi/ (accessed February 16, 2021).

91. Yoneda, CSUF-COPH O.H. 1376b. For a copy of the second-front petition alluded to by Yoneda, see box 152, folder 4, JARP, which also includes other important documents bearing on Yoneda's activities at Manzanar. Ariyoshi's role in and attitude toward the Citizens Federation is discussed by him in "Memories of Manzanar."

92. Tanaka and Masaoka, "Project Report No. 35," includes the following cautionary note: "A large proportion of the English-speaking, American-educated population, composed largely of younger persons, appear to be confused, bewildered, in many cases bitter; they listen readily to pro-Japan elders and Japan-educated & indoctrinated citizens."

93. WRA, "Information Regarding Kibeis taken from Block Reports, Activities of Town Hall, and Special Meetings," August 4–8, 1942, MWRCR, box 16, folder 8.

94. WRA, "Information Regarding Kibeis."

95. Fred Tayama, "Brief Report of the Kibei Meetings Held at Mess Hall 15, Manzanar Relocation Center, August 8, 1942," MWRCR, box 17, folder 1, emphasis added. A copy of this report, which was sent to the FBI, was apparently given to Joe Kurihara. Since it recounted his part in the meeting, Kurihara was determined to kill Tayama. See Emily Brown, "Story of Joe Kurihara," 30, JAER, folder E2.332; and Merritt to Tozier. Ironically, Tayama's report seems to have been passed along to Kurihara by Tokie Slocum, who aimed to distract attention away from his own reputed "stool-pigeoning" activities and concentrate all the blame on Tayama. Brown, "Story of Joe Kurihara," 29–30.

96. Brown, "Story of Joe Kurihara," 29–30.

97. Brown, "Story of Joe Kurihara," 29–30. Karl Yoneda in a 1974 oral history interview provided Arthur A. Hansen with a graphic profile of Ben Kishi:

> *Hansen:* Who was Ben Kishi exactly?
>
> *Yoneda:* I describe him as a Meiji samurai type . . . he says something very exciting that the people go for. For instance, when he opened the Kibei meeting, he didn't say, "Men are dying in Asia," but "Men are dying, let's stand up and have a one minute of silence." He put it in such a way that everybody, even myself, wondered, "My god, what the hell's this guy trying to prove?" Later I figure out, my gosh, this guy is really pulling this pro-Japan stunt.
>
> *Hansen:* Did you think of him as pretty intelligent?
>
> *Yoneda:* No, he isn't; he's one of those "ghetto-boss" type guys. Oh yeah, he knows how to maneuver: "You follow me. You listen to me. I'll take care of you."
>
> *Hansen:* Did you see him as the major leader of any pro-Japan sentiment within the camp? Did you think that Kishi was the leader?
>
> *Yoneda:* Oh yes, definitely, the leading "open" spokesman from the start. (Yoneda, CSUF-COPH O.H. 1376b)

This portrait of Kishi needs to be set alongside another one offered by John Sonoda, also identified with the JACLer group at Manzanar. Explaining a beating delivered to him in June 1942 by Kishi and five other Kibei for allegedly discriminating against Kibei in his capacity with the Personnel and Employment Division, Sonoda said that "Ben Kishi was very emotional about it all. When he was telling me about my wrong attitude towards a lot of things, tears were streaming down his face. He said we were all Japanese and we all owed our allegiance to the Emperor of Japan, and all that." Quoted in Tanaka, "Report on the Manzanar Riot," 19.

98. Roy Nash, Project Director, War Relocation Authority, Manzanar, California, Official Bulletin, August 10, 1942, MWRCR, box 16, folder 1.

99. In addition, this month saw the wholesale resignation from foremanship jobs and the refusal of administrative cooperationists to accept any positions whatsoever. "With the growth of disillusionment over relocation camp conditions, and the rise of the Issei to dominant positions within the Japanese community," explains Morton Grodzins in "The Manzanar Shooting," JAER, folder O10.04, 9, "a prestige job became a marked liability rather than an asset. It subjected its holder to threats of violence or to violence itself." See also Opler, "History of Internal Government," 51–52.

100. Karl G. Yoneda, 4-2-2, Manzanar, to Roy Nash, Project Director, Manzanar, August 24, 1942, report on block leader's election in Block 4, MWRCR, box 9, folder 3.

101. The point here is not to contradict Yoneda's assertion that while in Manzanar he had "the future of Japanese in America always at heart." Yoneda, CSUF-COPH O.H. 1376b. Rather, it is merely to suggest that most inmates, at least by the summer of 1942, were inclined to believe the very opposite.

102. Opler, "History of Internal Government," 56–57.

103. Opler, "History of Internal Government," 58.

104. Opler, "History of Internal Government," 71–72.

105. Robert Throckmorton [Project Attorney], "Biographies of Riot Participants in the Lone Pine Jail: Harry Ueno," [January 1943], MWRCR, box 17; Opler, "History of Internal Government," 72–73; Rice, "Manzanar Center," 36–37.

On the other hand, Kazuo Suzukawa, a member of the union, claimed that between the time of its organization in September to the time of the Manzanar Revolt its membership grew to consist of the chef and two representatives from each of the thirty-six kitchens. See Throckmorton, "Biographies: Kazuo Suzukawa."

106. Iwasmoto, "Economic Aspects," 28. According to Togo Tanaka, Ueno was alleged to have maintained that "the person who controls the mess halls of Manzanar controls the whole relocation center." Tanaka, "Report on the Manzanar Riot," 22.

107. Yoneda, O.H. 1376b.

108. Quoted in Opler, "History of Internal Government," 74–75.

109. Apparently, neither the camp's internal security nor the FBI, which frequently came into camp for investigations, was able to penetrate the organizational

structure of this group. See Fukasawa, CSUF-COPH O.H. 1336. The clearest insight into the membership of the Manzanar Underground emerges from Yoneda's "Manzanar: Another View." Herein he explains that the membership "consisted of between 25 and 30 members who constantly disrupted things by spreading false rumors and threatening the lives of evacuees, thus keeping the camp in constant turmoil." In Yoneda's opinion, most of the group were "kamikaze type supporters of fascist-militarism," not "truly 'genuine protesters' against evacuation." In his diary entries quoted in this article, there is mention of their pressure tactics as early as June 16, 1942: "Scavenger truck with Kibei crew, bearing Black Dragon flags (skull painted white on black cloth), appears in front of Block Leaders Council and Camouflage Net Garnishing Project telling everyone not to work on nets." An entry of July 22 indicates that pressure had given way to terrorism: "Very hot, 114 degrees. While Tokie Slocum (WWI vet) and I were talking in front of Block 4 office, a Black Dragon truck suddenly charged us at full speed. We managed to jump onto top step. Truck busts lower step and speeds away."

110. Rice, "Manzanar Center," 53.

111. Tanaka and Masaoka, "Project Report No. 87," emphasis added. This is the documentary source for all of the quoted commentary at this meeting.

112. Prefiguring the action that followed a few days later, the documentary historians, Tanaka and Masaoka, "Project Report No. 87," 388, observed that small group discussions transpired after the meeting: "Typical comment: 'Why don't the Nisei who think they are Americans get out of the camp. They are disturbing element. If they are willing to throw away their citizenship and become true Japanese, then that's different. We certainly don't need self-government.'" It is also suggestive that this meeting was conducted entirely in Japanese.

113. Quoted in Tanaka, "Report on the Manzanar Riot," 23.

114. Throckmorton, "Biographies: Harry Ueno," 3–10.

115. Grodzins, "Manzanar Shooting," 4.

116. Tanaka, "Report on the Manzanar Riot," 3.

117. Tanaka, "Report on the Manzanar Riot," 2.

118. Tanaka, "Report on the Manzanar Riot," 3–4. For *Doho*'s attacks on Tayama, see the issues of March 1, 1939, July 15, 1941, and August 15, 1941. Prefiguring the latter alliance between *Doho* staffers like Karl Yoneda and James Oda and JACL leaders like Fred Tayama and Tokie Slocum at Manzanar, one should note that Tayama, as chairman of the Anti-Axis Committee, appointed *Doho*'s editor, Shuji Fujii, to its subcommittee on publicity. For political reasons, Tayama reluctantly suspended Fujii, though when Slocum succeeded Tayama, he reactivated Fujii and expanded his activities to encompass the subcommittee on press control as well. See *Doho*, January 2, 1942, and February 6, 1942.

119. Quoted in Tanaka, "Report on the Manzanar Riot," 5.

120. Tanaka, "Report on the Manzanar Riot," 11.

121. Tanaka, "Report on the Manzanar Riot," 12–13; Grodzins, "Manzanar Shooting," 2–3. For more information about Terminal Island, see Naomi Hirahara and Geraldine Knatz, *Terminal Island: Lost Communities of Los Angeles Harbor* (Los Angeles: Angel City Press, 2014).

122. Tanaka, "Report on the Manzanar Riot," 8. See also the documentary attachments 8a and 8b.

123. Tanaka, "Report on the Manzanar Riot," 14.

124. Grodzins, "Manzanar Shooting," 3–4.

125. Opler, "History of Internal Government," 124.

126. Opler, "History of Internal Government," 125.

127. Even WRA official sources confirm this fact: "Not one person interviewed in camp following the riots had a good word to say for Tayama. One young Nisei, 24 years old, who holds a most responsible position in camp and knew Tayama prior to evacuation had this to say following December 5: 'Group hatred of Tayama was the general touch off as far as the population was concerned.'" Goldberg, "The Manzanar 'Incident,'" 1.

128. Grodzins, "Manzanar Shooting," 12.

129. See, for example, Lucy Adams, "Notes on Manzanar Disturbance," JAER, Bancroft, folder O10.00, D6.

130. See the near-daily project reports submitted by Tanaka and Masaoka between June and December of 1942. MWRCR, box 9.

131. Grodzins, "Manzanar Shooting," 13.

132. The names of the Committee of Five members, with their generation and age, are as follows: (1) Genji Yamaguchi, Issei, forty; (2) Sakichi Hashimoto, Issei, forty-two; (3) Kazuo Suzukawa, Issei/Kibei, thirty-eight; (4) Shigetoshi Tateishi, Kibei, thirty-five; and (5) Joe Kurihara, Nisei, forty-seven. Although their average age of slightly over forty years is some ten years younger than the average for the Issei generation in camp, nonetheless they were certainly not young men. It is also significant that the two college-educated members of the committee, Yamaguchi and Kurihara, took the leading roles in the negotiating proceedings. See the Board of Review reports for Yamaguchi, Hashimoto, Tateishi, Suzukawa, and Kurihara, December–January, 1942–43, WRAA, box 16. On Kurihara's counter organization, alternatively called the Manzanar Center Federation, see Henderson, in Brown, "Final Report: Manzanar," vol. 1, appendix 26, and Brown, "Story of Joe Kurihara," 24–25.

133. Tanaka, "Report on the Manzanar Riot," 88–89, 102.

134. Uyeno, "Point of No Return," 20.

135. See Ariyoshi, "Memories of Manzanar"; Yoneda, "Manzanar: Another View"; and Kurihara, "Murder in Manzanar," 25.

136. A good insight into the administrative style of Winchester and Brown can be ascertained from reading their comments in the Board of Review reports, WRAA, box 16. The reports suggest that Brown was later dismissed from his position when it was discovered that he had falsified his educational record on his employment application. See especially Ralph P. Merritt, Project Director, Manzanar War Relocation Center, Manzanar, California, to Charles Carr, US District Attorney, US Department of Justice, Los Angeles, California, July 14, 1943, WRAA, box 16.

137. Tanaka cites the eyewitness testimony of one inmate: "The mob was raising hell outside [the jail]; they first sang 'Kimigayo' (the Japanese National Anthem); they followed it up with '*Aikoku Koshin Kyoku*' (a Japanese patriotic march), then with '*Kaigun* March' (Navy marching hymn). They even started dancing the ondo. They would get close to the soldiers and taunt them." Tanaka, "Report on the Manzanar Riot," 105.

138. The restoration of Issei dominance and community ethnicity is a theme taken up in a number of studies dealing with America's concentration camps. The most notable examples include Yatsushiro, "Themal Analysis"; Sakoda, "Minidoka"; and Speier, "Japanese-American Relocation Camp Colonization." The first has special relevance for the Poston center, the second for the Mindoka center, and the third for all of the camps. For a discussion of the patterns of resistance used by the inmate populations in the various centers, see Okihiro, "Japanese Resistance."

Part 2
ORAL HISTORIES

This section of *Manzanar Mosaic* offers a medley of voiced perspectives from five notable inmates at the Manzanar concentration camp during its turbulent opening year of 1942. All of these oral histories, with the exception of that with Harry Ueno, were transacted prior to both the 1974 *Amerasia Journal* publication of the Manzanar "riot" essay coauthored by David Hacker and me and the completion of the 1975 essay on *Doho* by Ronald Larson and me that the *Amerasia Journal* declined for publication. Up until shortly before Sue Kunitomi Embrey and I interviewed Harry Ueno in 1976, we had falsely speculated that after World War II he had either moved to Japan or met with his death. Ten years later, we atoned for our misperception by coediting with Betty Mitson the book *Manzanar Martyr: An Interview with Harry Y. Ueno* (Fullerton: Oral History Program, California State University, Fullerton, 1986).

Whereas the four oral histories with Sue Kunitomi Embrey, Togo Tanaka, Karl Yoneda, and Elaine Black Yoneda all contain information relative to the subject matter of both of the essays featured in this volume, that with Harry

Ueno, the central figure in the Manzanar Revolt, offers pertinent information solely on the essay pertaining to that event.

In 1942 Sue Kunitomi Embrey (1923–2006) was a nineteen-year-old fledgling Nisei journalist on the *Manzanar Free Press* newspaper, whose staff included several former *Doho* personnel and individuals who shared their progressive ideological perspective. Although at Manzanar Embrey did not personally know any of the other four interviewees represented in *Manzanar Mosaic*, she was aware of their presence in camp and their association with the Manzanar Revolt and recalled vividly, and was later able to powerfully recount, the mayhem that ensued in the Manzanar camp on December 6, 1942.

As for Togo Tanaka (1916–2009), in 1942 this twenty-six-year-old Nisei, before coming to Manzanar with his wife and daughter, had been as the editor of the *Rafu Shimpo*, a luminary within the constellation of English-language Japanese American journalists in Los Angeles, a national officer in the Japanese American Citizens League, and an enterprising commercial investor. At Manzanar his position as the camp's co-documentary historian, with Joe Grant Masaoka, had permitted him to survey and write reports on a regular basis about the various people and activities transpiring in camp. In addition, he had played such a pivotal role in controversial camp politics that it landed him on the death list compiled by camp dissidents at the time of the Manzanar Revolt. His pre–World War II familiarity with *Doho* and its staff and his being nearly murdered as a perceived *inu* on December 6, 1942, sufficiently fortified him in January 1943 to compile an illuminating report for the University of California, Berkeley–based Japanese American Evacuation and Resettlement Study that encompassed both the prewar progressive newspaper and the wartime riot/revolt. He and his family resettled in Chicago after the war; he returned to Los Angeles in 1955.

Karl Yoneda (1906–99), a thirty-six-year-old Kibei, and his Jewish-American wife of the same age, Elaine Black Yoneda (1906–88), were dedicated Communist Party members in the pre–World War II years, and they had become well-known activists on behalf of a plenitude of political and social causes in both Los Angeles and San Francisco. As the Bay Area correspondent for *Doho*, Karl Yoneda was intimately familiar with its staff members, including those like James Oda and Tom Yamazaki, who became fellow inmates with the Yonedas at Manzanar as well as staff members of the *Manzanar Free Press*. Naturally, Elaine Black Yoneda knew these same people as well.

As for their knowledge of the developments that led up to and culminated in the Manzanar Revolt, both of the Yonedas were closely attuned to them in somewhat different ways. Whereas Karl Yoneda encountered them in his capacity as an outspoken block leader and a high-profile participant in public events, Elaine Black Yoneda did so through her employment as a superpatriotic US war industry worker at the camp's camouflage net factory. Both, too, became targets of reprisal actions against them by alleged members of the pro-Japan Black Dragons organization on the grounds of their presumed turncoat collaborative alliance with the US government, the WRA, and the FBI. While Karl left camp shortly before the riot/revolt on December 6, 1942, as a volunteer in the Military Intelligence Service, Elaine remained behind in camp with their infant son Tommy and, along with numerous other leftists and JACL family members, faced beatings and death threats, was assigned protective custody status, and was hastily transferred from Manzanar to the Cow Creek camp in Death Valley, California.

Harry Ueno (1907–2004), a thirty-five-year-old Hawai'i Kibei and the head of the Kitchen Workers Union, took a progressively major role in the resistance movement at Manzanar in the months that climaxed on the evening of December 6, 1942. Upon being accused as one of a several inmates who had administered a beating to unpopular JACL leader Fred Tayama in his barrack on the previous evening, Ueno became the first Manzanarian to be removed from camp and imprisoned in an outside jail. Convinced that the popular Ueno was innocent as to the assault on Tayama and that he was instead being punished unfairly for accusing select disliked camp administrators of corruption, thousands of irate inmates mobbed together in camp meetings on December 6 and demanded that their martyred hero be returned to camp and there be placed in jail before receiving a just trial as to his innocence or guilt. But after the camp leadership agreed to this demand by bringing Ueno back to Manzanar, with restrictive conditions, and placed in the camp's barrack jail, his throng of supporters now called for his immediate release. When Ralph Merritt, the camp director, refused this demand, the stage was set for an incendiary standoff between the massed inmates and the military police that Merritt had called into the camp to enforce his will. Accordingly, Ueno had a ringside seat that evening to witness the violent proceedings of that night, which ended in the shooting deaths of two young inmates and the gunshot wounding of nine or possibly still more additional inmates.

Progressive

An Interview with Sue Kunitomi Embrey

*A person who is open to or favors new ideas,
policies, or methods, especially in politics.*

Sueko "Sue" Kunitomi Embrey, a Nisei, was born in Los Angeles, California, on January 6, 1923.[1] Her Issei parents, Gonhichi and Komika Kunitomi, came from the same village in Okayama, which is in the southern part of Japan. They were distant cousins and shared the same surname.

Embrey's father emigrated to Hawai'i on a passport dated September 14, 1898, to work as a plantation laborer. Upon completing his three-year contract, he moved to the US mainland, arriving in San Francisco and, after a stint as an itinerant agricultural worker, settling down in Los Angeles. When working in Hollywood as a gardener or domestic employee, he asked Komika, ten years his junior, to join him in America and become his wife, which she did (as a picture bride) on January 24, 1910.

Embrey, the sixth child of eight, was born when the Kunitomi family was living in the Little Tokyo district of Los Angeles. There her father ran a small transfer and moving company until in late 1938, when he was killed in an automobile accident, which left the family in dire straits and forced Komika

FIGURE 15. Sue Kunitomi Embrey, founding chair of the Manzanar Committee, speaking at the 1972 Manzanar Pilgrimage, an annual event sponsored by her Los Angeles–based organization. Courtesy Manzanar Committee.

to enter into outside business activities to repay the outstanding debts left by her departed husband.

Before and after her father's death, Embrey attended the K-8 grammar school in her heavily Nikkei-populated east Little Tokyo neighborhood. In the Amelia Street School, 90 percent were of Japanese descent, while the rest of the students were Americans of Chinese and Mexican ancestry. The school—whose alumni included future California attorney general and governor and chief justice of the US Supreme Court Earl Warren[2]—was innovative, progressive, and multicultural in its curriculum and outlook, which reflected the orientation of the Los Angeles school board at that time.

Embrey also attended the nearby Japanese language school, which she, as opposed to most other Nisei students, greatly enjoyed and profoundly appreciated, both for its linguistic and its cultural activities.

Upon graduating from grammar school, Embrey enrolled in Lincoln High School, located in the Highland Park or Lincoln Heights area. Its student body included a small number of Asian Americans but consisted predominately of Italian Americans and Polish Americans. At the time that Embrey graduated from high school in January of 1941, a great deal of war talk was in the air.[3]

> *Hansen:* What did you do after you got out of high school?
>
> *Embrey:* Well, our next-door neighbors decided to go back to Japan, and they had a small grocery store. My mother said she had always been business-minded and she would like to take a chance and buy the store from them and run it. I just happened to be the person [in the family] that was not working. I'd finished high school, so she said, "Why don't we try it?" So we borrowed some money and bought the store, and my mother and I ran it until April of 1942, when we sold it to be evicted [and incarcerated in inland concentration camps along with the West Coast Japanese American population by the US government under Executive Order 9066 issued by President Franklin Roosevelt]. I sort of ran the store with my mother and so I didn't get back to school at all. Then we were sent to Manzanar, and then from Manzanar I went to Madison, Wisconsin, toward the end of 1943.
>
> *Hansen:* Let's back up a little bit. I want to cover what you've said in greater detail. Now, when you were running the store, this was just at the time of the eviction. Did the store act as something of a clearinghouse for information about the eviction? Didn't you have a lot of people coming into the store from the [Japanese American] community, thereby allowing you to feel the pulse of the community, so to speak?
>
> *Embrey:* Well, yes, I guess we did. I'm trying to think of who was around. All of the [Japanese language] schoolteachers were gone. They'd been arrested. There were a couple of [Issei] fathers around the neighborhood who also had been arrested. But for most of the families around then, the fathers were not active in community affairs, so they were not picked up. I guess toward the end we started giving credit because the people just didn't have any money, and we ended up never collecting for that. But I remember when they started to post the notices up, some people did come in and ask us to get information out to the community. And we had posters all

around the area. I guess they wanted to know what we had found out about different things, and we all sort of tried to get information out to everybody. I guess it was no real organized kind of thing, but it sort of became a place where people came to ask questions.

Hansen: Did you notice a lot of divisiveness within the [Japanese American] community itself, as to how they should respond to the kinds if policies that were being enacted relative to possible removal?

Embrey: Yes, the biggest feeling that I think came out was that the JACL was the only organization and that they had sold us out.

Hansen: Were you in the JACL at the time?

Embrey: No, I wasn't.

Hansen: Who were then prominent JACLers in Los Angeles that you can now recall?

Embrey: At that time? Well, Togo Tanaka. He was English-language editor of the *Rafu Shimpo*. Tokie Slocum was another one, although I don't know how active he was; he was Japanese [-born], but he had been adopted, I think, by a family named Slocum [in Minot, North Dakota].

Hansen: Did you know Slocum?

Embrey: No, I never met him.

Hansen: Did you later meet him at Manzanar?

Embrey: No. I understand he was beaten up in Manzanar, but I didn't know him at all. Let's see, who else? Well, the Suski family. Dr. [Sakai Peter] Suski was a doctor, an MD, and his children were older Nisei. I know his daughter Louise was quite active.[4] She also wrote for the *Rafu Shimpo*.

Hansen: What's the name of the woman who was the first editor of the *Manzanar Free Press*? I know her surname is Mori.

Embrey: Chiye Mori.[5] She was quite active in the Democratic Club before the war, I think. I don't know whether she was active in JACL or not.

Hansen: About how old was she at the time of the eviction? Was she a contemporary of yours?

Embrey: No. I would say she was older than I. I used to watch her, because to me she was a very unusual Nisei. I never had come across anyone who could talk about politics and who damned the leaders of our country like she did; I had never heard such talk before! And she had some very liberal ideas which I had never come across, and I used to listen to her a lot.

Hansen: I've heard it said that there were two factions that were so-called collaborators [with the US government] in the eviction. You mentioned one already—the JACL. But there was apparently another group of Nisei who, although they shared a similar ideological position with the JACL, were involved in a competitive way for positions at Manzanar. Apparently, this non-JACL group arrived earlier at Manzanar and gained most of the political positions before the rest of the inmates arrived. Also, I understand [that] the two groups were locked into a pre-"evacuation" squabble that carried itself into the camp. In camp, they shared the same ideological position—vociferously pro-American—but nonetheless remained aloof from one another. Does this make any sense to you at all? Can you think of a group which fits that description?

Embrey: I know of a group which was in Manzanar. I don't know how active they were before the war, because I think in Manzanar the pro-Americans did split off into two [groups]. I remember the one group wanted an increase in monthly wages. They fought to try to get some kind of citizens' council going, and they were all anti-JACL, as I remember. And it seemed to me [that] most of them were quite left of center in terms of the JACL.

Hansen: Can you think of specific individuals in this left-of-center group?

Embrey: Yes. There was Koji Ariyoshi, who lives in Honolulu now, and Karl Yoneda.

Hansen: Would they be part of the group you would have described as "Red" prior to the war?

Embrey: I guess the people considered them that way. I don't know how active they were. I know that both Karl and Koji were very active in labor unions before the war, trying to get labor unions opened up to minority groups. And I think their ideology was based on the thought that they had to fight fascism first, and they went along with the eviction as just one of the minor things that had to happen during a war.

Hansen: Would you say they were equally as detested by the Japanese [American] community at Manzanar as the JACL faction?

Embrey: I think so. Yes, because I think some of them were also victims of beatings as well as those who were connected with the JACL. But I think that they were not doing anything that was out of line with what they'd been doing before the war.

Hansen: Except that they weren't quite as pro-American before the war, were they? I think their vigorous patriotism in the camp was more or less expedient, wasn't it?

Embrey: I think they felt that they had to go along with the eviction because there was nothing really that they could do about it. There was no way we could really organize for resistance. It was better to go along with it and then from there go on. Both Koji and Karl volunteered for the military intelligence because they were bilingual. A lot of them did, maybe thirteen or fourteen of them from Manzanar. And they fought in the war, too. You know, they don't want to talk about it either, because they don't want that kind of thing to come out because they felt their first battle was to win against fascism, and whatever happened to them was not as important.

Hansen: They were committed ideologists at the time.

Embrey: Yes.

Hansen: Now I want to get into your removal to Manzanar. Did you go directly to Manzanar from Los Angeles?

Embrey: Yes. When we signed up, we were supposed to go to Santa Anita [Assembly Center in Arcadia, California] with everyone else in the Little Tokyo area, but a couple of days before we left, a notice came out that those who had relatives in Manzanar could apply to transfer to Manzanar. And a brother of mine had been one of the thousand volunteers that had gone to Manzanar in March 1942. So when we left in May—he had gone on March 23—we were supposed to go to Santa Anita first and then we thought we would be transferred to Manzanar. But since we weren't really sure, we decided we would all sign up and ask to go to Manzanar. So there was a whole trainload of people that did go to Manzanar. I don't know if they were all related to the volunteers that had gone, but we went because of that. It was May 9, 1942.

Hansen: When you got there, about how many blocks [of barracks] were already functioning?

Embrey: Well, we were assigned to Block 20, so I guess half of the camp was already filled. One whole block was filled with people from Bainbridge Island in [the state of] Washington. The other block was all the people from Terminal Island in San Pedro [Los Angeles County].

Hansen: I hear the Bainbridge Islanders left the camp because the climate was too bad.

Embrey: They later went to the Minidoka in Idaho, because they lived directly across [from] the block in Manzanar where the San Pedro people were, and the two groups of people—those from Bainbridge and San Pedro—were very different. You know, if anybody wanted to do a sociological study of life-styles—well, these two groups were so far apart!

Hansen: Where was the San Pedro group in the camp? Do you recall their blocks by any chance?

Embrey: Gee, I don't know. They were situated sort of diagonally from Block 20, so they must have been—let's see, how many blocks there from it? You know, because 13 was directly across from 20, so it must have been 6, 13, and 20 all in a row. So they may have been in like Block 5 in the other end of camp, and then the Bainbridge Island people were almost directly across from them. I didn't know too much about them, but I understood there was a lot of bickering going on between the two groups. You see, the San Pedro group spoke almost all Japanese, and the Bainbridge Islanders spoke almost all English. The Bainbridge Islanders included a lot of college graduates and college students. They were highly intellectual type people, very artistic and rather more interested in that kind of thing. And the San Pedro people were kind of rough. They were fishermen and they lived in their little ingrown community in San Pedro and Terminal Island, and they were almost like a Japanese village.

Hansen: Was it Japanesy because the culture was kept intact or because a lot of Kibei lived there, too?

Embrey: I don't think there were that many Kibei. I think it was because they were isolated from the rest of the Los Angeles community and the rest of the Japanese [Americans] in Los Angeles.

Hansen: How were the people living there looked upon by people in the Little Tokyo area?

Embrey: They were almost like a subgroup of Japanese [Americans].

Hansen: I heard there was a lot of fear of them at Manzanar.

Embrey: There was. Yes, I remember being at a baseball game between two teams, and one team happened to be the San Pedro group and someone in our block had just made a remark. There were some people from San Pedro standing behind her who resented the remark, and that night, after the game, a whole group of San Pedro kids—I guess they were from the San Pedro Yogores or the baseball team, I don't know—came through our block and went up to look for her barrack and specifically wanted an apology from her. And they said if she didn't give it, they really were going to go after her. "Well," she said, "what for? I don't recall that I said anything insulting." Well, to them it was insulting and to her it was nothing.

Hansen: Do you recall the activities of Terminal Islanders at the camp in terms of the jobs they had and whether they figured in the "evacuee" hierarchy of the camp?

Embrey: No, I don't. There were a few working on the paper, the *Manzanar Free Press*. I think they were younger Nisei. I guess they worked in various departments. Probably a lot of them worked in things like deliveries—driving the trucks. There were a few who were on the police department. I don't know if any of them were used for their bilingual ability.

Hansen: Were there some who didn't even speak English?

Embrey: There may have been, yes. But most of the ones I met were bilingual. They spoke English fairly well, and they could also speak Japanese.

Hansen: Do you know if the Kibei had anything to do with the San Pedro people because of the commonality, both being, as the Nisei would describe them, "Japanesy"?

Embrey: Japanesy, yes. I don't know. I think the San Pedro people were pretty much to themselves. I know they formed their own baseball teams.

Hansen: Did you find that there was within the camp, then, pretty clear cultural divisions within the subculture?

Embrey: Yes, I found that that was even more the case after I started doing a lot of reading and talking to people, too. But I could tell it even on the strength of my own observations of people that I saw in Manzanar. I had been pretty much within Little Tokyo. I didn't get out very much as a kid, and I was very curious about the different groups in Manzanar. I guess working on the paper [*Manzanar Free Press*] made me a little more aware, too, of some of the thinking of the people. So when I look back on it, I can see where the Bainbridge Islanders would have had a lot of problems with the San Pedro people because of the difference in cultural outlook. And I think this is probably one of the most tragic things of the "evacuation." You don't put groups of people together because they're one race, because each group, depending on where they come from, has a very different life-style. I think that in Manzanar the biggest difference was between Bainbridge Island and San Pedro, and even San Pedro from the rest of Los Angeles. The people were so different. My mother said when I asked her one time, "Well, even in Japan, fishermen are considered an entirely different group. They're rough. They have to have a lot of courage; they're fighting the seas all the time. You know, their living is very precarious. And their attitude becomes quite different from the attitude of people who work the land."

Hansen: Were there any other groups at Manzanar? I know that at Manzanar about 85 percent of the people were from Los Angeles County and about 70 percent were from Los Angeles city proper. You mentioned Bainbridge Island. Can you think of any other areas that were included at Manzanar outside of Los Angeles, people from places other than Los Angeles?

Embrey: I think possibly there were a few people from central California. I don't know how they got there, unless they had relatives in the city who they moved in with.

Hansen: I'm thinking of people like Karl Yoneda. Where was he from at the time? Wasn't he from San Francisco?

Embrey: Karl was from Los Angeles, although he had lived in San Francisco. And I think Koji Ariyoshi was in San Francisco at the time, although I think, originally, he came from Hawai'i. There was a small group of Hawai'i Japanese Americans who were stranded here because they were going to school. I met about three nurses that were in nurses' training, and the fellows I met were doing various kinds of drafting work and going to school. And their life-style was quite different. I guess for them, you know, their families were back in Honolulu or different islands, and they knew that they would be able to go back, and there was no real concern about what would happen to them. Most of the Hawai'i Japanese Americans I knew volunteered for the service.

Hansen: Something should be said, too, about residential areas within Manzanar. A lot of times people refer to it as a "camp" in toto, and I think we've already established that there were radically different groups there, culturally and otherwise. I've heard, too, that there tended to be considerable in-group solidarity among blocks, that it was almost a real community that grew up around each block. Did you find this true of, say, Block 20?

Embrey: I found it true in Block 20.

Hansen: What about meetings with respect to problems as they came up in the camp? Did you meet, say, at the mess hall to discuss certain things? Did you have block meetings?

Embrey: They had block meetings, which were, I guess, part of the administration's way of getting messages to the people and the community and getting messages or complaints to the administration. I don't know how often the block meetings were held, but we did have a block manager. One of them was an Issei who spoke English, and the other one was a young Kibei who was married to my brother's sister-in-law. He spoke both English and Japanese quite well, and he had also been to college.

Hansen: What sort of major problems were there in your block?

Embrey: I left in October 1943. There was a lot of pressure put on by the block people for their sons not to go into the service. It wasn't just the parents telling the kids, but the community and the block people saying, "After what they did to us, you don't want to go into the service in the army." So there was a lot of pressure from that angle, too.

Hansen: Who would you say had the power in the block with respect to leadership: Issei, Kibei, or Nisei? You've indicated that the block managers were Issei and Kibei.

Embrey: The two in our block were. In the beginning they wouldn't allow the Issei to take any kind of office because of the fact that they were classified as enemy aliens, and the United States government was not supposed to have them do anything that might put them in jeopardy with their own country. But when the Issei began to feel they were not doing anything, the administration, the WRA, began to change some of its policies and give some of the leadership to the Issei. But I think generally the camp itself, outside of the administration, was pretty much controlled by Issei.

Hansen: So unofficially, in any event, Issei held the real power.

Embrey: I think they still did. People talk a lot about the Issei not being able to keep family control and all that, but I think when you come down to it the co-op was run more by Issei than Nisei, and most of the block leaders eventually became Issei, partly because the young ones were leaving. In the first year, I think, there was a lot of control by the Nisei and a lot of policy making going on behind the scenes. But when furlough time came and the young men left to go work in the fields and some to enlist in the army, then there wasn't anyone left to take over except the Issei.

Hansen: In what capacity were you originally employed at the camp?

Embrey: Well, I had volunteered to help a couple of Catholic nuns who had come into camp and were going to live there and start a school because the school had not been organized. I guess I must have worked a couple of weeks without pay when I found out they were setting up this camouflage net factory and they were looking for workers. So I went and applied, and I worked there.

Hansen: You had to be a Nisei to work there, didn't you?

Embrey: Yes, you had to be a citizen to work there because we would be making camouflage nets for the United States Army and the administration had evidently signed some kind of contract. There was a lot of bickering about how much we were going to get paid and were we going to get paid, and we eventually did get paid. Then there was a lot of competition about which crew was going to make the most nets and win the watermelon or whatever they were giving away for prizes. Then the first group of furlough workers left, which meant that a lot of the staff people from the *Manzanar Free Press* were leaving, and so I thought it might be a good time for me to apply for a job there. So I applied at the *Manzanar Free Press*, and they told me that I could probably get a job there.

Hansen: About when was that?

Embrey: Let's see, we got there in May, so this must have been maybe June or July. It might even have been later than that, I'm not sure. But I know I didn't work very long at the camouflage net factory. I started out as a cub reporter on the *Free Press*.[6]

FIGURE 16. *Manzanar Free Press* editorial staff, 1943. Seated: Roy Takeno (second from left), reports officer, and Sue Kunitomi, managing editor. By this time, the camp newspaper's staff was no longer dominated by political leftists, as it had been in 1942. Courtesy Manzanar Committee.

Hansen: After your stint as a cub reporter, what did you do then?

Embrey: Well, I learned all the routine that went on in the newspaper field. One of the things we had to do was have it already laid out, and then the layout was picked up by someone like Bob Brown, the reports officer, or whoever was making a special trip into Lone Pine to deliver our final copy. It was printed in Lone Pine by the Chalfant Press. So none of us ever really got to see the print shop because we were in a military area and we couldn't get out of camp.

Hansen: Were you working on the paper before it became printed, when it was still a mimeographed newspaper?

Embrey: I guess I was because I remember that there was a mimeograph machine around with a couple of operators. And then we got two additional typists to do the final draft.

Hansen: Now, the editor of the paper when you first started working was Chiye Mori, right?

Embrey: It was Chiye Mori, yes. She was the first editor, and there were a couple of other people on the staff: James Oda, who was a Kibei, and there was a fellow who was partly Japanese. He didn't have a Japanese name. I'm trying to think of it. Now I remember, his name was Joe Blamey.

Hansen: It was a small staff, then?

Embrey: It was fairly small. We did have, of course, a separate sports staff, and then we had the business office part, the ones who collected advertising and took care of the money that came in for the advertising. We had a whole Japanese section, and they did theirs on the mimeograph machine because there was no way to get Japanese type. Rather than photographs they had sketches that one of the artists would do on a stencil. Then they would run it off so it would go inside the English section. We delivered the paper to everybody in camp.

Hansen: Now, when you first started working on the paper, Bob Brown was the reports officer.

Embrey: He was reports officer and directly under him was a man named Roy Takeno, who is now with the *Denver Post*, and Chiye Mori was the editor. Joe Blamey was one of those who was beaten up. And that was sad, because he was a "cripple." He had one leg which was shorter, and he always carried a cane with him. But he was quite outspoken, and I would say he was one of those on the progressive side.

Hansen: You said Chiye Mori was also on that side.

Embrey: Chiye Mori was also called an *Aka* ["Red]," and she was very liberal in her views and very outspoken for a woman. They were all threatened, so they left camp early. I think Joe Blamey was beaten a couple of times. Then, of course, Jimmy Oda was also on the staff, and he was considered a radical for a Kibei. Then Jimmy volunteered for military intelligence and served in the army.

Hansen: Maybe you weren't conscious of this since you were young at the time, but did you find yourself in sympathy with the editorial policy of the *Manzanar Free Press*? For instance, sometime in April 1942, prior to your being on the staff, they had publicly printed a thank-you note to General DeWitt for his efficient handling of the "evacuation" and also commended Karl Bendetsen and others associated with the "evacuation" itself, and thereafter followed a very pro-administration position, which I think explains a lot of the retaliatory beatings and things. Did you find yourself at odds with this policy?

Embrey: No, most of the time I found myself agreeing with it because I guess that was the feeling I had, although I'm not so sure about that editorial on

General DeWitt because I think that personally I had a very deep grudge against him and others who had pressured for the "evacuation."

Hansen: Did you feel that the name *Free Press* was an accurate or an ironic name?

Embrey: Well, when I think about it now, I think it was pretty silly, but at the time I guess I agreed.

Hansen: What control was there over what appeared in the paper with respect to administrative censorship?

Embrey: Well, they didn't want us to write about things like—well, once there was a strike going on at Lockheed or somewhere, and somebody commented on it. I don't remember whether I wrote the story or somebody else wrote it, but a crack was made about, "Why are they on strike? Our government is having a war." After it was printed, we got the feedback, "We don't want things like that in the paper." I don't recall that there was any actual censorship of the articles. The editorials, I think, were checked before they were run pretty much.

Hansen: Who wrote most of the editorials?

Embrey: I guess all of the editorials were written at the beginning by Chiye Mori. Later, when Roy Takeno came in as editor, he wrote a lot of them. And I know that he consulted very often with Bob Brown. I don't know whether they were just consulting over official things, but I think a lot of the editorial statements probably were checked. I'm not so sure about censorship of informational material. A lot of the material was about community activities, this group doing that and the school having this. I think in terms of official reports that were coming in from the project director, or the Washington WRA office, were already sent out as a press release, so there wouldn't be too much we could do with them.

Hansen: Who do you recall from the community being around the *Free Press* office? People who might have been in, say, close social contact with the staff and editors of the paper.

Embrey: I can't think of any, although I think when the original staff was still there, people were coming in often to talk to them, you know, like Chiye Mori's friends and people like that. I know we had a lot of visitors also, but I don't recall that there were any special people who used to come in.

Hansen: Well, you know, Togo Tanaka, as you mentioned earlier, was the English-language editor of the *Rafu Shimpo* before the war. By the time he was "evacuated," when he went to get employment at the camp, the only thing that was available for him with respect to journalism was to deliver the paper. And he delivered it with Joe [Grant] Masaoka. I was just wondering if, for instance, Tanaka was considered by the staff as something of a rival or a person not to allow to have a position on the paper, that he was excluded by design?

Embrey: That's possible, because I remember that both Togo Tanaka and Joe Grant Masaoka were there on the camp staff, and I don't know whether they were there for collecting information for the administration, keeping records, or what.

Hansen: They had a job as War Relocation Authority documentary historians.

Embrey: That's what I thought.

Hansen: Did you ever see them around?

Embrey: I used to see them around, but I guess, you know, just coming in as a cub reporter and all, I was sort of in awe of all of these people. They were a lot older than I, and I felt, with their college degrees and whatever their background, they were people to look up to.

Hansen: That's what I was wondering, whether that impressionable sort of mood carried over to the people you came in contact with in the community? Who seemed important to you at that time?

Embrey: I suppose people like Koji, Karl, and Tokie Slocum may have walked in and out of the *Free Press* office all the time and I wasn't aware of them, you know. I didn't even know who they were.

Hansen: Didn't you know Karl Yoneda at the time?

Embrey: I had heard of him, I had seen him, but I had never met him. And I guess that again is that Nisei generation. You know, you have possibly ten or twelve years in between, and all of the older Nisei had gone to college and had experiences outside that I wasn't aware of.

Hansen: Did you know Togo Tanaka at camp?

Embrey: Well, my family knew his family, and my brothers knew him. I had met him, but I don't think he knew me from the next person because I was a lot younger.

Hansen: Yes, he was probably twenty-six or -seven at that time. And did you know Joe Grant Masaoka or not?

Embrey: No. So a lot of these people were, I guess in my eyes, sort of leaders. I wasn't too aware of any kind of division that was going on. Now, I heard when I was in camp that Togo Tanaka was considered a stool pigeon or a spy for the US government and that he was seen opening mail from the FBI.

Hansen: You heard that in camp?

Embrey: Yes, I heard that in camp. I remember that he was pointed out to me. And they said, "He's that *inu*." *Inu* means "spy."

Hansen: And that was well before the riot in December of 1942?

Embrey: That was before the riot.

Hansen: Like back in, say, September of 1942?

Embrey: Yes, and at that time several people were pointed out as being very cooperative with the administration, so that there was no other excuse except that they were spies, you know.

Hansen: Can you think of anybody else that was branded as such?

Embrey: Well, Tokie Slocum was another one, and I guess Joe Grant Masaoka. But I didn't hear anything about Joe Grant.

Hansen: I read that the beatings didn't necessarily have anything to do with politics. For instance, there was the beating of Chiye Mori. Do you recall what the circumstances were surrounding her beating?

Embrey: No. I thought it was because of being pro-administration. But I didn't hear anything at the time. And she was very outspoken.

Hansen: Do you remember her beating? Were you on the staff then?

Embrey: I thought that she was threatened, but I didn't know that she was beaten. Oh, they did come into the *Free Press* office, I guess, one time when they were —I don't know who it was that did it, whether it was a gang or just individuals.

Hansen: So you were on the staff as a reporter throughout the time after you left the camouflage net factory.

Embrey: Then after the Manzanar Riot, a lot of the staff people like Chiye and Joe Blamey were taken out of camp and sent to [Cow Creek camp in] Death Valley. I think Roy Takeno became the editor. A lot of the ones who were left behind were promoted along the way. So I guess when Roy took over, I sort of got into the feature section of the *Free Press*.

Hansen: You worked for Bob Brown for a long time. What did you think of him as an administrator?

Embrey: Well, he was pretty low-key, as I remember him, and he was well-liked by the staff. I don't think we got into any kind of problem or any controversy with him. I remember that he seemed to be very sensitive to other people's feelings.

Hansen: What was his background?

Embrey: I understand he came from the Owens Valley, and he was raised there, either at Independence or at Lone Pine.

Hansen: He was reasonably well-respected at camp, though?

Embrey: Yes, I think he was. I don't think there was any negative kind of reactions toward him.

Hansen: How about the camp's assistant director, Ned Campbell? He comes in for a lot of abusive commentary by former "internees" at Manzanar.

He figured very prominently during the time of the riot and was ousted thereafter from his administrative position. Did you have any contact with Campbell? Were you privy to any rumors about him?

Embrey: I didn't know him. The only thing I heard was that part of the possible cause of the riot was that Campbell had some kind of black-market deal going on in camp. That was all I heard.

Hansen: Did you get any substantiation on that or not? Or was that just a rumor?

Embrey: No, that was only rumor. I think it was a rumor going around at the time when the riot occurred. It was a rumor that was going around at the time in camp. I had heard it before the riot actually. But there were so many rumors going around. I don't know whether people, you know, actually believed all of them or just believed half of them and figured there wasn't anything they could do about it.

Hansen: What do you think caused the so-called Manzanar Riot on December 6, 1942, when two "internees" were killed and nine others wounded? Looking back, did it come to you as an utter shock that it happened or did things seem to be building toward some sort of showdown in camp?

Embrey: Well, I was feeling the tension, but I don't know if other people were. I think that all of these things were piling up after almost a year of camp living, and the people were complaining constantly about lack of privacy and the poor food and the weather. I think it was a culmination of all these things. I think that the fact that the man who was arrested for the beatings, Harry Ueno—you know, Fred Tayama was beaten—was a very popular man really triggered the whole thing. People really just felt there was nothing they could do except have some kind of protest. I don't really think that either the administration or the camp people themselves realized how serious it was, because in the afternoon the protesters were having—I think they had a mass meeting in what they called the fire breaks between blocks, and there were a lot of people there.

Hansen: Were you there at the meeting?

Embrey: We sort of walked around to look, you know. We weren't involved, so— And then nothing really happened until after supper. I was in our room with my mother. I heard voices and a lot of footsteps. And a man, an Issei, told me about a year ago, "I'll never forget the sound of marching feet." And I said, "When was that?" And he said, "The night of the riot." He said, "I remember it so well, even today." It was everybody wearing these big boots and just walking on this loose gravel and dirt, and there is a particular sound it makes. And I remember that it was very cold that night, and I recall my mother, my sister, and I were standing around that Coleman stove in our barrack when we heard all this noise. And we saw all these people walk by, and it looked like a couple of hundred people in the crowd.

Hansen: I believe most of this meeting was outside of Block 22 and you were in Block 20, right?

Embrey: Yes.

Hansen: And which is closer to the jail at the entrance to Manzanar?

Embrey: Block 20.

Hansen: Block 20, so they came past it.

Embrey: They came past our block, and I understand they came from the hospital, which was way inland beyond 22. They came past our block, and they were going to Block 19, and later I heard they were looking for someone in Block 19 that they were going to beat up, that they thought was pro-administration. Whether he was with the pro-American group I don't know, and I don't even know who he was.

Hansen: I think it was Tokie Slocum.

Embrey: In Block 19?

Hansen: I think they were looking for him there. Or perhaps they had already spirited him off and put him in the military police compound or something.

Embrey: I heard that they couldn't find him, that they just ransacked the place. Was he one of the house parents at the YWCA dorm that was in Block 19? Because I understand that they went through there and went through everything, trunks and closets, looking for someone. Then from Block 19, which is right along the edge of the camp, and along a road and beyond that there's a strip of land and then the barbed wire fence and Highway 395. So they evidently went down that road toward the police station and met the other groups that were coming from the other areas. The next thing I heard, my older brother Kinya ran into the room and said that people had been shot. He had thrown his [internal security] badge and his cap away in the trash can along the way and run home because he didn't want to get involved. He had heard some shots and was very worried that some people had been either wounded or killed. I remember that my mother said that we'll all get shot now because people had protested. And then my younger sister's boyfriend, who had been observing, came running into the apartment saying some people had been killed. He was shaking from fear. We were saying, "Oh, what's going to happen?" You know, "What's going to happen next?" I don't know how soon after that, but all the kitchen gongs began to ring, and they rang all night. I don't know what the purpose was, whether they were trying to get everybody to assemble or tell everybody to go inside and stay indoors or what.

Hansen: I think they tried to have some meetings, and they kept forming in certain areas, and the military patrolled around and broke up the meetings and kept moving them around.

Embrey: The military came inside the camp?

Hansen: They were circling around the camp breaking up the various meetings to make sure the Japanese didn't take retaliatory action.

Embrey: I recall that jeeps were going up and down in camp. I wasn't sure whether they were just patrolling or were trying to break up the groups that were trying to meet or what, because my mother was so frightened that she wouldn't let any of us out. She said, "You just can't go out there because they may just shoot at you." By that time, I guess, it was just my two brothers, myself, my younger sister, my younger brother, and my mother. My oldest brother, who was married, was in a room across the next barrack, and my mother was even afraid to go out and see whether he was inside or not and safe! I guess, you know, if she thought that way, I probably figured all the Issei were thinking the same thing. You know, "The military is going to come in and shoot us all." That's all I remember of that night. You knew that somebody had been shot, and then days later different people told me different things about what happened if they were down there, and what they had seen.

Hansen: I noticed looking through the files on the *Free Press* that no issues appeared between the time of the riot in early December and the Christmas edition.

Embrey: No.

Hansen: I read somewhere that they did put out a paper for the next day, although—

Embrey: It was impounded.

Hansen: What happened? Can you tell us a little bit about that issue and why it was impounded?

Embrey: Well, I remember that we had an issue that was sent into Lone Pine on Friday, I think, or Saturday, and it was supposed to come out Monday. The riot happened Saturday night and all day Sunday, I guess, and the military police came in Sunday, so they impounded that issue. We never saw it. And I don't know whatever happened to it. I understood that the US Army just impounded it. The thing I remember about that issue was that it was an anniversary issue, and the staff put "Remember Pearl Harbor" on the first page. I think that was the thing they didn't want distributed. Then there was a suspension of all work until Christmas just about, because the whole camp went into a state of mourning. I guess no one worked except the work crews that were delivering the oil for the stoves and the kitchen crews cooking the food. It was just those two things and the hospital, I guess, because I remember that no one would go to work. And we were told, "If you go to work, you're really going to get in trouble." Then they had the funeral for the two boys outside of camp, and nobody was invited except for possibly the representatives of the blocks and the family. One boy was seventeen. He was just a bystander. He got pushed by the crowd when the tear gas was thrown, and he died there on the spot.

Hansen: This was James Ito.

Embrey: Yes, James Ito. His brother was in the US Army somewhere back East. They had to call for him to get back, so the funeral was postponed until he came. My brothers knew the brother in the army and also knew the young boy himself. My brothers told my mother, but when she tried to remember who he was, she said she didn't remember him, "He's the one who came and laid the linoleum on our floor. He was on the work crew when they came, the one who died." And I think his brother came to see us when he came to camp, because my brothers knew him. I don't know who the other boy was. I don't know whether he was involved in the riot. I don't know whether he was also another bystander.

Hansen: Both of them were apparently innocent bystanders, from all accounts of it.

Embrey: Yes. And evidently they got pushed by the crowd and then were shot.

Hansen: Let me ask you a little bit about some of the personalities who are usually identified with the Manzanar Riot. One, the major cause célèbre of the riot, I guess, since he was the person that they were demonstrating to get released from the Independence jail and brought back to Manzanar, was a man by the name of Harry Ueno.

Embrey: That's right.

Hansen: He was the head of the Kitchen Workers Union, and he was from Block 22, which wasn't too far removed from yours. Did you ever hear of Harry Ueno prior to that time? Did he figure as a name in your life at all, or as a person?

Embrey: No, not until he was arrested. I knew that they were trying to organize a kitchen union, the Kitchen Workers Union. Now, I'm not sure whether they were doing this as opposition to the group that was trying to form a Manzanar Citizens Federation or whatever.

Hansen: They formed it, I believe, in opposition to the Manzanar Works Corps, which included many of the same people who were in the Citizens Federation.

Embrey: Yes, a work corps group. Evidently, he had a lot of support, because he was the one that they [the inmates] wanted returned [to camp], claiming that he was not the one who beat Fred Tayama up. I don't know whatever happened to the case or what was resolved from it. Did he spend time in jail after?

Hansen: He was then sent to Moab, to a temporary isolation center there.

Embrey: To Moab, Utah?

Hansen: Right. And then I know he went to a permanent isolation center in Leupp, Arizona.[7] From there we don't know what happened to him.[8]

Embrey: Was he a Nisei or a Kibei?

Hansen: A Kibei. But he hadn't figured at all in camp as a personality?

Embrey: I don't think he was even known among the people in the camp except among kitchen workers. But from what I heard, he was very popular, and he had a lot of support compared to the support the others were getting, those who were beaten up. No one was giving them any sympathy.

Hansen: David Hacker, who is doing some research on the Manzanar Riot, wants to ask you a question, so let's now hear from him.

Hacker: When you say Ueno was popular, do you know exactly why he was popular or how he got his popularity?

Embrey: No. That's all I heard, that someone had been arrested for beating up these people, and he was the prime suspect. They had sent him to jail in Independence, and the purpose of the protest was to get him back to Manzanar, which had a jail located behind the police department building, and that the reason that he was getting so much support was that he was very popular. Now, where that popularity came from, I don't know, but they attracted something like two thousand people to that afternoon meeting alone.

Hansen: Had you heard of Joe Kurihara?

Embrey: The only mention of Joe is through Karl Yoneda and a couple of books, I think Allen Bosworth's book, *America's Concentration Camps* [New York: W. W. Norton, 1967].

Hansen: But he wasn't somebody that you knew about?

Embrey: I didn't know him at all. I don't even think his name was in the paper at all, in the *Free Press*. If it were, I probably would have known it.

Hansen: So these people emerged out of relative obscurity with respect to the camp—at least as prominent personalities—at the time of the riot?

Embrey: I think so, yes. I don't think they were known outside of their own group, possibly their own block even, but they managed to get a lot of support because people had a lot of complaints and grievances that they wanted to be brought out. Possibly they thought that they would be able to do it this way.

Hansen: Returning to the question of causation, when you think back upon the riot now, do you think that perhaps maybe a lot of the cause had to do with just the fact that a certain number in the camp were discriminated against, weren't eligible for work or didn't have jobs made available to them because they were noncitizens or sometimes Kibei? Although they were citizens, Kibei weren't allowed to participate in leave clearance so that they could relocate, and they were shunted into undesirable jobs, like on kitchen crews or as janitors and so on. Do you think that part of the cause was a protest against those kinds of conditions?

Embrey: I think so, although I think that a lot of it has to do with how people felt toward that demonstration as a way out.

Hansen: You yourself wouldn't have participated at that time?

Embrey: I doubt it very much. (laughter) Maybe later, but not then, I don't think.

Hansen: And most of the people who you came into contact with at that time, do you think they would have, either? I mean, the people that you worked with?

Embrey: No, I don't think the majority of the people would have. I think the riot involved just a very small number of people.

Hansen: Except that it struck some sort of responsive chord in the camp at large?

Embrey: I think it did, because people were just—well, they were still making adjustments from living by themselves in the city to being very crowded, living with strangers, having no privacy of any kind. And they had a lot of grievances about the food and about whether they were going to get paid. Some people hadn't even gotten paid, you know. Then there was the fact that the Issei weren't really recognized as adult leaders. I think there were so many grievances that they just sort of erupted at that time, and I guess, you know, the arrest of Ueno was just the straw that really broke the camel's back. And I think everyone sympathized with this group.

Hansen: Did you ever experience any resentment toward you of the kind we've been talking about?

Embrey: Well, if there was, I wasn't aware of it, although I know that one girl said to me, "If I were you, I wouldn't talk to those *hakujin* [Caucasians]. You know, the administrators." And I said, "Well, they're not any different from other people." And she said, "Yeah—." She wasn't so sure. And she said to me, "I will never talk to a Caucasian as long as I'm in this camp." And she didn't!

Hansen: What sort of contact did you have with the administrators? Very little?

Embrey: I didn't have that much, actually, outside of possibly talking to Bob Brown. I met Mrs. [Margaret] D'Ille, who was the social welfare department head. I think she had also lived in Japan. She was a very friendly person. I got to know her pretty well. She started to conduct some kind of seminar, and a bunch of us would go. We did talk a lot to the teachers. There were three or four high school teachers who were Quakers, and they lived right in the barrack next to the school. They didn't live outside the area like some of the administrative people did, but they lived inside. There was one woman who was—I'm not sure whether she was a teletype operator or a Western Union operator there, but I think she was from either Independence or Bishop, and her husband had gone into the US Navy. Well, she was looking for work and had been working as a teletypist, I think, so she came to Manzanar. She was very friendly, and we talked a lot. I stopped by and talked with her and visited with her. I don't recall her name. I don't know what happened to her. She was the one who encouraged me to leave and get out of there, saying, "Look, you know, you're young. You don't need to spend your life here."

Hansen: Did you have mixed feelings about leaving.

Embrey: Yes, very much so.

Hansen: Did you feel you were abandoning your family?

Embrey: Yes, you know, it's funny how the different restrictions placed on you as a child and the social customs have a very strong influence. I felt guilty, although a lot of people were leaving camp at the time. A lot of my friends had left and had written to me saying, "Come out here, things are not that bad. At least you'll make a decent living." I still had a lot of mixed feelings. A lot of things were happening, and I just felt I couldn't spend another year there.

Hansen: What kind of things were happening?

Embrey: Well, I was finding myself, you know, being left behind when people were leaving from Manzanar, from the *Free Press* staff.

Hansen: I want now to turn the interview back over to David Hacker, who has a final question to ask you.

Hacker: Earlier you used the term *Aka* in connection with certain people. I wonder if you could interpret that term. I mean, when you think of a "Red," you think of a Communist. Did *Aka* mean something special in the Japanese American community?

Embrey: Well, I think in the Japanese American community, the term *Aka* or "Red" indicated anybody who sort of didn't really fit into the community thinking. Their thinking was maybe a couple of steps ahead of the Japanese. Some of them, I think, were active in the Communist Party. I don't know which ones. I had heard there were some before the war, and they were just called "Reds." It was a general term, I think, that was used to include anybody who was sort of left of center. I don't think that they even differentiated between leftist or progressive or anything like that.

Hansen: Okay, Mrs. Embrey, we'll wrap up today's session, and next time we get together we'll pick it up from there and take you from your [resettlement] experiences in Madison, Wisconsin, and Chicago, Illinois, down to the present.

NOTES

1. Biographical information is from the following sources: Sue Kunitomi Embrey, interview by Arthur A. Hansen and David A. Hacker, August 24, 1973, Oral History 1366a, and by Arthur A. Hansen and David J. Bertagnoli, November 15, 1973, Oral History 1366b, CSUF-COPH, O.H.

2. See "Earl Warren," *Wikipedia*, https://en.wikipedia.org/wiki/Earl_Warren (accessed February 18, 2021).

3. The interview transcript reproduced below is from Embrey, CSUF-COPH, O.H. 1366a.

4. See Patricia Wakida, "Louise Suski," *Densho Encyclopedia*, https://encyclopedia.densho.org/Louise%20Suski/ (accessed February 16, 2021).

5. See Patricia Wakida, "Chiye Mori," *Densho Encyclopedia*, https://encyclopedia.densho.org/Chiye%20Mori (accessed February 16, 2021).

6. In 1943 Sue Embrey became the newspaper's managing editor.

7. See Hansen, "Moab/Leupp Isolation Centers."

8. Ueno was imprisoned at the Tule Lake Segregation Center. See Barbara Takei, "Tule Lake," *Densho Encyclopedia*, https://encyclopedia.densho.org/Tule_Lake/ (accessed on March 14, 2021).

Thinker

An Interview with Togo W. Tanaka

A person with highly developed intellectual powers.

Togo W. Tanaka, unofficially, was born on January 7, 1916, in Portland, Oregon, as the fifth of six children of Issei parents originating from the Yamaguchi prefecture of Japan.[1] Originally they worked as domestic servants in a large Portland household but moved to Los Angeles when Togo was only three months old. His father there gained a job as a gardener and moved the Tanaka family to Hollywood. Afterward, he and his wife operated a vegetable market, and this allowed them to live in a largely white middle-class area of the city. At age sixteen, Togo, an exceptionally bright student, graduated from Hollywood High School, after which he matriculated at the University of California, Los Angeles.

At UCLA Tanaka majored in political science and was on the staff of the school's *Daily Bruin* newspaper, while concurrently serving as the associate editor on the English-language staff of Los Angeles's Little Tokyo–based *Kashu Mainichi* (bilingual paper). After graduating as a Phi Beta Kappa from UCLA in 1936, Tanaka gained the position of English-language coeditor (with Louise Suski) of still another, and more prominent, Little Tokyo bilingual

FIGURE 17. Togo Tanaka, Los Angeles, ca. 1960. Courtesy Lawrence de Graaf Center for Oral and Public History, California State University, Fullerton.

newspaper, the *Rafu Shimpo* [Los Angeles Japanese Daily News]. In this capacity he wrote editorials promoting the role of his Nisei generation to serve as a bridge of understanding between Japan and the United States and also promoted the Japanese position in its raging conflict with China, while claiming that the American support was due to Chinese propaganda. When this perspective became increasingly untenable, Tanaka and the English-language *Rafu Shimpo* staff split from the Japanese-section's viewpoint and adopted a 100 percent position of pro-Americanism. In addition, Tanaka became a member of the chauvinistic Japanese American Citizens League, for which he came to hold the national position as the person in charge of publicity.

In October 1941 the *Rafu Shimpo*'s Issei publisher, H. T. Komai, sent Tanaka to Washington, DC, to seek US governmental authority for the paper to continue publication should hostilities between Japan and the United States commence. Tanaka had the pleasure of meeting First Lady Eleanor Roosevelt, but he also had the misfortune to arouse the suspicion of War Department officials who, after interrogating him, challenged his allegiance to the United States. The upshot of this situation was that, on December 8, 1941, a day after Japan's attack on the US naval base of Pearl Harbor in Hawai'i, Tanaka became one of the handful of US-citizen Nisei who were arrested as so-called "enemy alien" suspects along with some 5,000 plus Japanese American community leaders of the Issei immigrant generation. After being held incommunicado for eleven days, Tanaka was released without any charges.

After Tanaka's release from jail, he continued to edit the *Rafu Shimpo*, notwithstanding that the Issei members of the Japanese-language section of the newspaper remained in custody and more the 1,000 of the paper's subscribers had cancelled their subscriptions to deflect any accusation that they were pro-Japan in their national allegiance. On the same day that President Franklin Roosevelt signed Executive Order 9066, which served as the basis for the mass eviction of the West Coast Japanese American population and their incarceration in concentration camps, Tanaka mobilized the United Citizens Federation. It brought together twenty-one Nisei organizations. In addition, he investigated the possibilities of "voluntary evacuation" for his racial-ethnic community. But when forced mass removal became operational, Tanaka edited the last issue of the *Rafu Shimpo* and thereafter readied his family for becoming inmates at the Owens Valley Reception Center, which occurred on April 23, 1942.[2]

> Hansen: Mr. Tanaka, during your earlier interview for our project,[3] you spoke a considerable amount about the so-called Manzanar Riot, of which you were both a principal in and an historian thereof. Prior to this interviewing session, you had the opportunity to review an account of the riot which was written by you, shortly after the episode, in your capacity as Manzanar's documentary historian for the WRA. Herein you analyze the roles relevant to the disturbance of three "internee" factions: Group I—the JACL group; group II—the anti-JACL group; and group III—the anti-administration, anti-JACL group. I would like for you today to discuss the Manzanar Riot in still greater depth than last time, and to begin by examining the personalities and policy orientations of each of the three groups you cite in your analysis.
>
> Could you begin, therefore, by addressing yourself to the JACL group? Now, in addition to yourself and your fellow documentary historian at Man-

zanar, Joe Grant Masaoka, there were several others in this group. I'd like to find out a bit more about each of these people. Can you tell me about Tokie Slocum?

Tanaka: Tokie Slocum was a man I had met and knew as a member of the editorial advisory board of the English-language section of the *Rafu Shimpo*. He had been a friend of George Nakamoto, who had been my predecessor as an English editor. George was, in age, more a contemporary of Slocum and had invited him to serve on the editorial board. I don't think it would be too accurate to identify Slocum as JACL. Although he was sympathetic to the JACL and had served as a lobbyist for them, he stood out pretty much as a loner, as I recall. He was more an "extremist" in the direction of his so-called pro-Americanism, which he wore on his sleeve and demonstrated to everyone, even to the extent of offending most Issei and Nisei by his loud and outspoken manner. As things got a little bit tighter and there was the threat of war breaking out, he simply said it was his duty and everybody else's to not only inform on but "turn in" people. He was a very conspicuous target at Manzanar, and anyone who identified himself with him immediately became suspect in the eyes of most people.

Tad Uyeno [a prewar columnist for the *Rafu Shimpo*], another of the so-called JACL group which I referred to in my analysis of the riot, is writing a series of articles for the *Rafu Shimpo*—being published now in the English section under the title "Point of No Return"—recalling what happened at [Cow Creek camp in] Death Valley, which is where the JACL group was removed after the riot.[4] In "Point of No Return," Tad reminded me that when we were being held in [protective] custody by the soldiers at Manzanar—immediately after the riot and before our removal to Death Valley—clusters of us got together to help in the kitchen, and we tried to figure out what had happened in the riot. Whenever Slocum appeared on the scene, the conversation died. He was not taken to Death Valley with the rest of us; if he was, he stayed a very short time. He was removed elsewhere simply because he didn't fit in with the group, even though in the riot most of the people in Manzanar identified him with us.

Hansen: I was looking through some documents concerning those people removed to Death Valley as well as those of the alleged "pro-Japan group," who [eventually were] taken to Moab, Utah, and conspicuous by his absence at either of those places was Tokie Slocum. I later discovered from the Girdner and Loftis book, *The Great Betrayal*,[5] that he was taken to New Mexico. Would you say, then, that he was almost persona non grata among the JACL people?

Tanaka: Personally, I had neither any feeling of affection, warmth, or trust for the guy. You know, it's funny; I remember many years later after I had returned to Los Angeles, somebody had written a book about concentration camps—I can't remember the name of it—and there was a full-page photograph in the book where my face was pictured along with Slocum and a few others. We were appearing before the Tolan congressional committee, and after the book was published, a letter somehow came to me from Tokie Slocum. For old times' sake, generally you would respond, but I couldn't get myself to acknowledge that letter. So I have never been in touch with him. Even when he was on the [prewar] editorial advisory board of the English section [of the *Rafu Shimpo*], and he said things which I was writing in the English section and I agreed with him in principle, still there was something about his style that repelled me. Inevitably, he would say that in the event of war he wanted us to turn our parents in. I had parents, and he didn't. He set himself apart by this. I think that was the crux of the whole thing. All of us had parents who were "aliens ineligible for US citizenship," who were technically "enemies of this country"—in wartime—and they were our parents. He was raised by a [Caucasian] farm family in the Midwest, the Slocums. His wife was a girl from Texas, and she was different too—that is, his second wife, Sally. See, he didn't have too much in common with us to begin with.

Hansen: Was his wife Caucasian?

Tanaka: His first wife was Caucasian. He was married to her for about ten years. Then he married a girl named Sally Yabumoto, of Japanese descent. They had their circle of friends, but I never regarded myself as belonging to it. I used to feel uncomfortable about being identified with him. But this is the way it goes.

Hansen: Slocum achieved a certain reputation from being a lobbyist for the JACL, and I suppose it grew out of his lobbying for one thing in particular—the granting of the citizenship rights for the World War I veterans of "Oriental" ancestry [the Lea-Nye Act of 1935].

Tanaka: Yes, he had done some very good work, and there were some old-time JACL people—perhaps Saburo Kido[6] or Tom Yatabe or one of the early leaders had engaged his services—and they recognized his contributions. He was JACL in that sense. I think in terms of their feeling and affinity for him personally, I always figured they felt they had a bull by the tail; you couldn't control him, and he was a self-styled spokesman for everybody—in his own estimation—but really only for himself.

Hansen: Is there any truth to the reputed selling of names by Slocum to the FBI? Certain reports indicated he boasted of being in the service of the FBI

FIGURE 18. This March 7, 1942, photo depicts a somewhat embarrassed Toga Tanaka (second from left) as his fellow JACL leader, Tokie Slocum (gesturing) tells the Tolan Committee that he and other patriotic Americans of Japanese ancestry were gladly relinquishing their family homes as their sacrifice in the war effort. Courtesy Lawrence de Graaf Center for Oral and Public History, California State University, Fullerton.

and receiving twenty-five dollars a head for informing on "disloyal" members of the Japanese American community.

Tanaka: In my contacts with him, I have never heard him say that, and it would seem unlikely to me, but it's possible. I never heard him say he got twenty-five dollars a name. I did hear him say in several of our rather heated discussions at the *Rafu Shimpo* editorial meetings that we had an obligation, that the meaning of being loyal to the American flag included taking action against subversives, and if that included turning in your own parents, then it was necessary. To give him his due, he was consistent. As far as selling names for the fee, I never heard of that, and I would attribute the rumor to people who were malicious. It seems out of character, because to him patriotism wasn't mainly in terms of economics; he was not a mercenary selling his services. He would do whatever he felt he had to do out of a sense of duty.

Hansen: There is another story linked to Slocum which perhaps deserves a certain amount of exploration. Ralph Merritt, the project director of Manzanar, went up to the Tule Lake [Segregation] Center[7] in 1945 and interviewed Joe Kurihara, a leader of the "pro-Japan" group at Manzanar, who was there. Kurihara told Merritt that Slocum—in order to find out what was going on in the camp prior to the riot—had gotten himself employed by the police department and worked on the graveyard shift, and had access to the administrative records. Kurihara claimed that because Slocum was afraid of him, Kurihara, he relayed all of the information he had culled from the records and gave copies of this to Kurihara, so Kurihara was privy to everything that was going on in Manzanar. As proof of this—when Merritt questioned the story's credibility—Kurihara produced a document concerning the Kibei meeting of August 8, 1942, in which Kurihara was a participant. The document was a brief report of the meeting's proceedings, which had been written by Fred Tayama from memory on the following day. This report was in the form of a confidential memorandum to the Manzanar administration, with a copy sent to the FBI. Now, he produced this document for Merritt right at Tule Lake. Do you know anything about this particular story?

Tanaka: No, this is the first time I've heard it. It's curious because I lunched with Ralph Merritt frequently before he died; he used to live in Los Angeles on Westmoreland Avenue. He was active with the Southern California Rapid Transit District here and was doing an oral history for the University of California on his early days in California. We used to recall the things that happened at Manzanar, and I got very distinct impressions from him. I never asked him about Kurihara or Slocum, so this is news to me. The likelihood of Slocum as a double agent (laughter)—I didn't like him personally, but I can't imagine him doing that. It would seem more likely that Kurihara had access and was able to get the documents out of the administrative files. It was no great trick; anybody could do it. Kurihara had the contacts, the organization, and the influence to do pretty much anything in camp. But I'm in no position to know.

Hansen: So he didn't have to be dependent on this kind of connection?

Tanaka: No, "evacuees" were on the staff personnel. From what I understood from Jo Hawes about procedures in the hospital, it wasn't a big trick to get such records. Miss [L. Josephine] Hawes was a nurse at the hospital and was assigned to the group at Death Valley.

Hansen: Do you think Kurihara was pulling Merritt's leg?

Tanaka: I would be inclined to think so, but I'm only guessing. Had I known something like this before Merritt died, I'm certain he would have shared it with me.

Hansen: Now, I'd like to move to another member of the JACL group, Fred Tayama. All I know about Tayama is that he apparently owned some restaurants prior to the war, that he was about thirty-seven at the time of the "evacuation," and president of the Southern District Council of the JACL. Maybe you could tell us a little bit about his character and what connection you had with him prior to the war.

Tanaka: Well, I knew him as the president of the Los Angeles chapter of the JACL as well as chairman of the Southern District Council. He was also a member of our editorial advisory board of the English section of the *Rafu Shimpo*.

I found myself meeting with him frequently both in connection with the work of the JACL and in writing about him and the JACL in the English-language section of the *Rafu Shimpo*. Personally, I liked him very much and agreed with many of the things he was advocating at our English section editorial board meetings. While they coincided in substance with what Slocum was saying, Tayama seemed to have a better grasp of how you communicated certain principles to people so they would accept it. He was also very close to his father and mother, who were Issei; I knew his parents. He had many brothers and sisters; they were a very close family and successful in business. I looked up to him because of his leadership in the community. I regretted very much what happened to him—his beating on the night prior to the riot—in Manzanar; he was a decent person in my book.

Hansen: So he was one of the few Nisei in the community who you would have regarded as a leader?

Tanaka: Yes, before [the attack on] Pearl Harbor. I think all of us who thought we were in a position of influence in Los Angeles discovered we didn't have much of a following at Manzanar.

Hansen: How do you account for the suspicions floated in Tayama's direction prior to the [Japanese American] Incarceration, during the period of "evacuation?" Did he, for instance, testify at the Tolan hearings?

Tanaka: Yes, I believe he did. But all of us who testified at the Tolan hearings—depending on whether you were reading the [William Randolph] Hearst papers or the *Los Angeles Times*—were quoted out of context, misquoted, and misrepresented. Any effort to rectify impressions—no matter what we wrote for our own readers in the *Rafu Shimpo*—didn't improve our image. My own opinion is that Tayama, along with those of us in lesser roles, suffered from the group's frustration. We, as a community, were having things done to us that none of us really liked, and we had to find a scapegoat somewhere.

I think Fred was among those of us who were summoned to Governor Culbert Olson's [office in Sacramento, California] after Pearl Harbor.[8] I recall we came back [to Los Angeles] and reported on it. The governor said, in effect, that we must cooperate and go into detention camps. In other words, it would be our contribution to the war effort. Since we were not successful in changing his mind, the presumption was that we had all caved in and yielded—we were being the nice, docile Nisei. If we had any other choice, none of us were able to find it. This was part of Tayama's problem; he was the number one JACL figure, so naturally he was going to be the target of most of the animosity. I think that's what happened to him.

Hansen: What about rumors concerning Tayama's economic activities?

Tanaka: He and his brothers ran a chain of restaurants on Main Street. There was this local bilingual Japanese [American] paper, the *Doho*, edited by Shuji Fujii.[9] It was a small paper, and Communist. I say so now because a staff member was a man I subsequently met and came to know. This man was a double agent, a member of the Communist Party and trained in Moscow. He came over here and got his US citizenship by working in our Office of War Information during the war.

Hansen: I don't think you would like to identify him, would you?

Tanaka: I don't think he objects, but then I would want to get his permission. After the war he taught out here at UCLA, where I have some friends, and I regard him as a good guy. He's also writing a book. His brother in Japan is very prominent, the president of International Christian University, and this one says he was regarded as the black sheep of the family. His son, a business administration graduate from a California institution, I know very well and see very often. The father told me that they used to say, "[Shuji] Fujii [a Kibei]—who was proficient in two languages [English and Japanese]—nailed you all over when you went to Washington DC right before Pearl Harbor. He said you were an agent of the Imperial Japanese government because you accepted some money from the Central Japanese Association to defray part of your expenses."

I wasn't aware of it if this were so because the *Rafu Shimpo* made all of the arrangements. My publisher [H. T. Komai] sent me, and I believe[d] that I was going only for our newspaper. But I was described in *Doho* by Fujii as an agent of the Japanese government. However, I used to get nice personal letters from Shuji Fujii and his wife [Kikue].

If you refer to Tayama's economic posture, he was fighting a labor union. There was an effort to organize his workers and he said: "The hell with it!" And he fired them. The *Doho* took up the cudgel for the workers, and Fred was identified as "a goddamned, dirty, stinking capitalist who exploited his workers." I think this had some carryover into the camp. Anything he did do or he didn't do, he drew attacks in *Doho's* columns.

Hansen: So it was a combination of that reputation as an "exploitive capitalist" and his visibility as a JACL leader?

Tanaka: Right. Also [there was] the fact that we consorted with members of the United States Naval Intelligence at dinners before Pearl Harbor in an effort to secure the JACL's position with the federal government agency. This didn't help our image once we were behind barbed wire. I think this led to the accusation that we were a bunch of dogs or *inu*, informers.

Hansen: I'd like to know more about Roy Takeno. Did you know Roy before Manzanar?

Tanaka: Yes, I did. We worked together at the *Kashu Mainichi*. He subsequently became the editor of it after I left to go the *Rafu Shimpo*. I was very friendly with Roy, but I never knew him too well.

Hansen: Was he a reporter on the *Rafu Shimpo* for a while?

Tanaka: No, I think he was just on the *Kashu Mainichi* staff.

Hansen: Was he an active JACL member?

Tanaka: I always remember Roy as quiet, rather bland, and very proper. I thought then that he was the kind of person you would find in government civil service, because he wouldn't have to get himself hung up. That's my recollection of Roy.

Hansen: So he kept a rather low profile.

Tanaka: Yes, he did. He was later editor of the *Manzanar Free Press*.

You know, Joe Masaoka and I took a dislike to Bob Brown, who as the reports officer at Manzanar supervised the *Free Press*. We fought with him, and he was a pain in the neck to us. We probably were to him. I never did make the staff up there. I was relegated to delivering the papers; that was about the size of it. While Roy fitted in more neatly because he had the sense to keep his mouth shut and do what he was told to do.

Hansen: What about the other JACL members at camp? Wasn't Joe Blamey on the staff of the *Manzanar Free Press*? I believe he was threatened or maybe physically assaulted a couple of times prior to the December 6 riot. Did you know Joe Blamey?

Tanaka: Joe Blamey is someone I never knew before Manzanar, and I don't remember where he came from or how he turned up in camp. I have only faint recollections of him, and they're not too impressive. I don't identify him as JACL, but he could've been.

Hansen: What other names pop into your mind when you think back upon this designated group—the JACL group—at Manzanar, besides Joe Masaoka, Tokie Slocum, Fred Tayama, and yourself?

Tanaka: Tad Uyeno was definitely JACL. Apparently he kept better records than any of us. Tad operated and owned a plant nursery in the San Gabriel area before the war. He wrote a column called "The Lancer" for the *Rafu Shimpo* regularly. I often didn't write editorials simply because Tad's column was expressing a JACL point of view—in terms of our citizenship obligations. He was rather forthright and very clear-cut in the position he took. When he landed at Manzanar, Joe Masaoka, Tad, and I spent much time together. As a consequence, I felt rather badly that in the riot, while Tad wasn't a "troublemaker," he was linked to us. Well, maybe he did get himself into hot water with some of the administrators.

I took a dislike to Bob Brown and didn't think much of Ned Campbell, the assistant project director. Joe and I used to say we were probably on the "shit list" of a lot of these administrators because we were saying things we probably shouldn't have said. But we didn't actually do very much to deliberately stir up trouble. We tried to reach out of the camp to either Washington or somewhere else. Local people regarded this as troublemaking. Tad never did that, but he encouraged us. The three of us shared a great deal in the seven months we were in there. As a result, when Joe and I were on the death list, Tad was also on the death list. He had to be removed from camp to Death Valley like us.

Hansen: What about Hiro Neeno?

Tanaka: I don't remember him too well. I know he worked in the post office before the war, and I think he was JACL at the camp. He didn't have to be removed, as I recall. He wasn't a close associate.

There was Kiyoshi Higashi, who was active in JACL but who belonged to the Terminal Islanders. They were a group unto themselves, and even though Higashi was JACL and threatened, their in-group loyalty protected him. I think he was the [inmate] chief of police at Manzanar. He was definitely JACL and, I think, very, very close to Fred Tayama.

Hansen: So he was from Terminal Island. I have heard that on the night of the riot there were attempts to get Higashi, but he was protected by Terminal Island judoists.

Tanaka: He was from Terminal Island, and they had a big judo group there. As I remember, the military police were saying they would be bringing him to join us at Death Valley. Word later came through, though, that he would stick it out [in Manzanar].

Hansen: Now, let's move to the second group, the one that you describe as the "anti-JACL" group. There is only a cursory description of the group in your analysis, however. I'm interested in the membership of it—what positions the various people included held and so on. Since you don't cite particular individuals as being in this group, who did you have in mind?

Tanaka: I understand. I describe this group as anti-JACL, which may not be an altogether accurate description, but they were people who were critical of the JACL, although to Kibei "pro-Japan" elements, they were lumped together as JACLers. It was a more liberal, left-of-center political group.

At Death Valley there was a woman named Chiye Mori, the editor of the *Manzanar Free Press*. Before the war, in Little Tokyo, she was married to the son of a very famous actor, Sojin Kamiyama. Chiye, while she may not have identified herself with Shuji Fujii of *Doho*, had an affinity for many of the things he was writing about.

Two others in this "anti-JACL" group were Tomomasa Yamazaki and his wife, Ruth Kurata Yamazaki. If you read Tad Uyeno's "Point of No Return," an account of our days at Death Valley, he points out how we gravitated into our own groups, even in our work assignments. We were given jobs to go out and dig ditches and to work for the park rangers, and Tad's recollection was that people like Tomomasa Yamazaki and Chiye Mori did a lot of talking. They were articulate intellectuals. However, they weren't conspicuously present when we had to go out on the trucks to dig ditches. I can't recall all the names, but those two come to mind.

Hansen: What about Karl Yoneda?

Tanaka: Karl Yoneda would be in this group, and yet he was not anti-JACL in the same sense as the rioters. He was certainly supporting the JACL effort to get us to volunteer to go to the camps, but I think he would be identified with the liberal Left, anti-JACL group.

Hansen: I'm going to return to your analysis for a moment. You say in it that you use the designation of "anti-JACL" to indicate this group "only for want of a better name." From what I can gather from analyzing relevant documentary materials, this designation does indeed seem to be unsatisfactory. For example, when the Manzanar Citizens Federation was established in camp to carry out the work done in the prewar years by the Japanese American Citizens League, the person you selected to head this group was Koji

Ariyoshi, a close associate of Karl Yoneda's and others in the reputed anti-JACL group. And there are many other examples of cooperation between the members of the JACL and the anti-JACL groups. In what sense, then, were those in Group II actually anti-JACL?

Tanaka: So long as the adversary was the "pro-Japan" rioters in the camp, the JACLers were one—the prewar JACL leadership group and the liberal Left group that I refer to as "anti-JACL." Once removed from the ideological and physical battleground of Manzanar, the so-called "pro-American" coalition came apart at Death Valley. The JACLers, like the Tayamas, Masaokas, Tanakas, and Uyenos, looked to the JACL organization headquarters in Salt Lake City for leadership. The "anti-JACL" group like Mori, Yamazaki, and Yoneda looked elsewhere. There was close cooperation within Manzanar. I'm not aware that it survived at all outside of that camp.

You mentioned Koji Ariyoshi. I didn't know him too well. I remember him as an articulate spokesman at some of the meetings and that he was JACL. I think he would be closer to Karl Yoneda than to Fred Tayama. That's just my observation.

Hansen: How did this group function prior to the war? You call them something of an *aka* [Red] group. Could you describe what *aka* means? Does it mean precisely Communist or what?

Tanaka: In the prewar establishment press, the *Rafu Shimpo* being an example, the so-called anti-JACL group was referred to as being sympathetic to the Communist Party and its ideals. *Aka* was a term used loosely. It was also a broad brush used to smear the liberal Left.

Hansen: The label might apply to Karl Yoneda, for example?

Tanaka: Right. Karl and Koji Ariyoshi—I understood they were both labor organizers. Labels, like designating colors, mean all things to all people; at that time, it was an easy way to describe them.

Hansen: Do you remember if in JACL discussions at Manzanar, you ever explored the fact that this coalition was at best a rather unstable one—insofar as many of the people in this so-called *aka* group were rather new converts to pro-Americanism? Prior to this time, their positions weren't exactly what you would call filiopietistic.

Tanaka: It was really a reflection of what was happening in the United States—the Soviet-American Friendship Society suddenly became popular with a movie, *Mission to Moscow* [1943], depicting Stalin as our great friend.

What we must keep in mind about any activity we engaged in at Manzanar was that it was all very ephemeral, very transitory. We had one objective: we wanted to get the hell out of there. In the meantime, we were dying of anxiety neurosis and frustration from seeing the barbed wire and watchtowers. There wasn't a day when I didn't try to figure out some way to get out of there. I think this was the overriding concern of the people—particularly of the "JACL group." I can't remember a single day where I could really say, "I want to stay here another day." I'm sure that was true of Joe Masaoka, Tad Uyeno, Fred Tayama, and of just about all of us who were eventually driven out of there in the wake of the riot.

Hansen: There is something else which comes across in your report. While there was a preoccupying concern to get out and work during the war, there was also a certain amount of in-fighting over what you described as "petty positions." You indicated that almost without exception the second group—the *aka* or anti-JACL group—came and took over most of the camp's [prime] positions. You used Chiye Mori as an example. She took over the position as the editor of the *Manzanar Free Press* newspaper, and when you arrived, you took over the position of the paperboy.

Tanaka: Right. Well, we gave up early. We knew we weren't in our element, and it seemed that this was poetic justice. Hell, we wouldn't print her [Chiye Mori's] stuff before the war, and I didn't think she was much of a writer. Also, it seemed like a useless battle to seek a position in camp; we weren't going to toady to somebody we didn't care for. Just let us out.

Joe Blamey was in that group, too. The world had turned upside down in the camp. There was this in-fighting, but not for very long. I think that the people rose to their proper levels in that setting, and the rest of us just wanted to get the hell out of there. That's what we were concerned with.

Hansen: Other than simply commingling with this so-called anti-JACL group for political reasons, did you have much to do with them at Manzanar, or was it a clear sort of expedient cooperation?

Tanaka: There was probably none at all, except that we might pass each other along the so-called streets of Manzanar or at some meeting. We greeted one another and recognized each other, but beyond that I can't remember ever socializing with them or spending any time with them at all. There was no closeness.

Hansen: What were the affiliations of this anti-JACL group prior to the war? A name that appears from time to time in the accounts of the Japanese American prewar community is the Young Democrats. Did they have a Los Angeles chapter or was this just a San Francisco–based group?

Tanaka: I really can't remember. There may have been. I belonged to a group called the Democratic Luncheon Club, which I was invited to join, but this was not Japanese.

Hansen: The Young Democrats were purported to be a [Japanese American] group of somewhat leftist or radical elements centered in the San Francisco area. They had certain grievances against the JACL, which later dissolved in the wake of the "evacuation."

Tanaka: Tomomasa Yamazaki was from the San Francisco area, but I don't have any clear recollection of that.

Hansen: Now, let's move to Group III, the group that you indicated manipulated the factionalism—seized the opportunity to utilize the in-fighting between what you call the JACL group and the anti-JACL group—and which eventually had a much broader-based support in the camp than either of the other two groups.

Tanaka: Yes, I didn't have much opportunity to observe that. It must have been a conclusion I reached after we were out of Manzanar and at Death Valley. Obviously, there were individuals who were influential, who remained and spoke for a large number of "evacuees." They were people who fitted in. Names of individuals don't come to me.

In the reporting [Joe] Masaoka and I did, we went from block to block throughout the camp, and we must have met, talked, and encountered many of these people there. If you use the term low-profile to mean that they were not conspicuous—well, in each block they were there and they did exercise influence as spokesmen for the residents in dealing with the administration. Did Frank Chuman's name appear at all in your research?[10]

Hansen: Yes, wasn't he at the hospital?

Tanaka: Yes, he was the administrator. Chuman was JACL [after the war], but somehow he managed to stay out of trouble. There was a young man named [Tom] Ozamoto, who I would include in Group III because he was bilingual and a citizen—a Kibei. In the period after the riot many of the people regarded him as a leader in the camp.

Hansen: Maybe I've followed your analysis wrong, but it seems to me your reference to Group III is to an incendiary group rather than an ameliorating group.

Tanaka: Well, you're talking about [Joe] Kurihara and [Harry] Ueno. The group I'm talking about ultimately took over after the removal of the so-called incendiary group to Tule Lake. They inherited the Manzanar Relocation Center.

Hansen: What about the people who had to leave to go to Moab [Utah], people not really charged with any specific acts, but regarded as potential troublemakers or who had records before leaving Manzanar? I'm talking of people like Ben Kishi.

Tanaka: I knew of him, but I never met or recall him at all.

Hansen: Some people claim in reports that Kishi—during the time the crowd was looking for you on the night of the riot and you were standing with the crowd outside the door of your [family] apartment—was the one who led the crowd that sought to murder you. But these reports also maintain that he was the one who directed the crowd away from any beating of your family.

Tanaka: Yes, I heard that, too. I really wouldn't know if he was the person who said, "Leave them alone." I didn't know him at all in camp.

Hansen: Who do you think of as leaders in the third group? Kurihara doesn't seem to emerge as much of a leader—precisely speaking, with a following. In fact, he's rather atypical in that he was the only Nisei sent to Moab. All the rest were Issei and Kibei.

Tanaka: A man named Shigetoshi Tateishi [a Kibei] was outspoken. After one of my appearances at a mess hall to explain the desirability of joining the armed services, he was rather conspicuous by saying, in Japanese, what a stupid idea this was. There was also Genji Yamaguchi [an Issei]. But Kurihara stands out mostly because I could have a dialogue with him. With the others, it was Japanese coming out of their mouths and English out of mine, so we never met.

Hansen: Did most of the Kibei speak in Japanese while "interned" at Manzanar—at least during the time you were there?

Tanaka: Japanese was easier to speak for most Kibei. They felt more at ease and could communicate better. I remember one incident at the camouflage net factory in camp. Joe Masaoka conducted our interviews with Kibei workers, with these young men, almost entirely in our poor Japanese. Before the outbreak of war, at the *Rafu Shimpo*, I felt very close to Kibei friends. I did at Manzanar. I probably owe my life to Kibei relatives.

Hansen: Did you have any opinion of the Kibei in the camp at all? Could you provide a general assessment of how they stood and relate something of their organizational framework within the camp?

Tanaka: If I did have any opinion of the Kibei, Art, I can't recall it. I may have indicated one in some of the documentary reports I wrote, but I don't have a copy of those reports now. I haven't read the reports in thirty years, so I'd have to search my memory. I have some individual friends of mine who were Kibei.

Hansen: So you didn't know too many Kibei in the camp?

Tanaka: No. Well, Karl Yoneda's a Kibei. My older brother [Minji] was born in Japan, so he would be like a Kibei.[11] My father-in-law's cousin, who is also a Kibei, was at Manzanar. I stayed with him and my brother before the riot because some neighbors had told me to get the hell out of my quarters.

Hansen: You had a brother who worked in the mess hall, didn't you?

Tanaka: My older brother, the one who was born in Japan, did.

Hansen: One of the groups that frequently appear in accounts of the Manzanar Riot is the reputed Kitchen Workers Union, headed by Harry Ueno. Was your brother affiliated with that group? Was that possibly how you got information of the aggressive action planned against you?

Tanaka: I was told to keep away from my barrack that evening by a neighbor, an Issei named Motooka, who lived in Block 35. We lived in a barrack in Block 36. He told me about four hours before the attack that I was on the death list. I don't recall my brother giving me any warning. I don't think he knew about it.

Hansen: This group actually didn't appear on your horizon, then, until the time of the riot, right?

Tanaka: That's correct. Except for a few of their leaders, most of that mob hardly knew me by sight. It was a cold night and all of us, it seemed, were wearing these heavy navy-issue pea coats.

Hansen: Karl Yoneda and Koji Ariyoshi were people who volunteered for the armed forces prior to the riot, weren't they?

Tanaka: Yes, that's right. It might have been because they felt the JACL had closer ties with the FBI and other investigative agencies. In other words, they were regarded as informers, while these others were just people who volunteered.

Hansen: I think you indicated in your report that the second group wasn't as affluent as the JACL group in the prewar period, that they had worked mainly in labor organizational positions. Do you think this might have had something to do with it?

Tanaka: I think it would be more likely that you could obtain the answer from people who were on the other end, those who were drawing up the death list. I really have no way of giving a valid opinion. I really haven't given any thought to this.

Hansen: What about the popularity of Harry Ueno? Did you know Ueno prior to the "evacuation?"

Tanaka: I don't ever remember meeting him in camp. I might have heard him speak once. I don't know. During the riot, I wouldn't have been able to identify him. He was just a name.

Hansen: Was he somebody who became an important figure just because he was placed in jail and because of all the meetings that were held concerned with getting him removed from the jail and back in Manzanar?

Tanaka: Yes, that's about the size of it.

Hansen: Did it surprise you that so many thousands of people would appear at these meetings—either out of popularity, curiosity, or whatever? People have described Ueno as having popularity within the camp. How do you account for his following?

Tanaka: Well, first, I never attended any meeting where there were thousands. I can't remember attending a meeting where there were even a few hundred.

Hansen: I'm talking about the meetings on the day of the riot.

Tanaka: I didn't attend any of those. I didn't see any of them.

Hansen: There were numerous eyewitness accounts at the time which place the attendance at these meeting in the thousands. There must have been some reason why they were willing to protest Ueno's arrest. How do you explain Ueno's appeal for the "internee" population at large?

Tanaka: I didn't attend any of those. I did not see these gatherings. But I can understand how the long-pent-up feeling of the entire camp, suffering under all the grievances of confinement behind barbed wire and watchtowers, could rally behind some incident like this. Take the matter of food, our daily meals. There was the racist policy of serving steaks, in a separate administrative dining hall, to Caucasian staff members. The "evacuees," in the other section, were having wieners and apple butter. This stuck in the craw of every "evacuee"; it certainly did in mine. There were widespread rumors about the administrative personnel stealing beef—our food going into the pocket of people who shouldn't have it. If Ueno was made to look like a hero, it was because he was expressing the frustrations and the grievances of the people of Manzanar. The vermin they wanted to get rid of had betrayed them by serving those who were exploiting the "evacuees." This is what I think he was saying.

Hansen: Do you think that his leadership of the Kitchen Workers Union—keeping in mind that the kitchen workers made up a sizeable portion of the entire work force at Manzanar—had something to do with his influence?

Tanaka: Right. It was important—this was our food—and I think he was strategically placed.

Hansen: Now, about some of the administrators. They don't figure as a group in your report, but I'm sure they figure as factors at the camp. Now, you mentioned a dislike you had for Ned Campbell, a dislike that was apparently widespread. What was Ned Campbell like, and why was he so summarily dismissed at the time of the riot and kicked upstairs to the WRA regional office in San Francisco and replaced by Bob Brown?

Tanaka: I don't know the real reasons why. My contact with Campbell was peripheral. My impression of him was that he was what Joe Masaoka uncharitably labeled as "a loudmouth" who probably was in the habit of claiming more credit than he was entitled to. We thought he was a braggart. We were tempted once to write a footnote in our documentary report:

"Ned Campbell says he gave up a twenty-thousand-dollars-a-year income to render a patriotic service by helping in the 'relocation' camp. Our evaluation: bullshit."

Then we heard these rumors about how he helped himself to the provisions in the warehouse and the mess hall. I don't know if those were true or not, but he impressed me as the kind of guy who would. This is prejudice, so again my feelings are indeed subjective. I imagine he must have impressed a lot of people as if he was making such a great and noble sacrifice in his condescending way. "Who in the hell needs that!" This was my reaction to it, and so I didn't like him.

Hansen: Did you tend to think of him as the project director because there was such a turnover of project directors and acting project directors?

Tanaka: He had a high profile, he was conspicuous, he was everywhere, and he gave a lot of orders. If I may use a modern expression young people use today, he gave a lot of bullshit. That was my impression of him.

Hansen: Harry Ueno was reported at the time as saying every time Ned Campbell talks to you, it's as though you were a slave. Does that seem rather strong?

Tanaka: Maybe that was the way Ueno reacted. I just thought Campbell was a loud, obnoxious someone who, in another setting, I wouldn't hire, period! But he was a big shot.

Hansen: How about Bob Brown? You started to talk of him in a cursory way earlier in the interview, and you indicated an initial dislike for him. What was it that annoyed you about Bob Brown?

Tanaka: I can't put my finger on it. When you think back, certain people give you either a warm feeling or a cold feeling. I'm sure that he meant to be fair. I think my reaction to him may have been more my sense of frustration. I arrived late at Manzanar, and the positions were all filled—he had made that very plain. So maybe I resented him because I was delivering papers. I really don't know. If you're talking about before the riot, he was the project's reports officer or something.

Hansen: So he worked closely with the *Manzanar Free Press*?

Tanaka: Oh, yes, he set the *Free Press* up. That strikes me as being so funny, to call it the *Free Press*, but that's the way it was. I wish I knew more. I think if I had taken the trouble to look back into the notes and all—but I haven't, so I'm just trying to recall details over the span of thirty years.

Hansen: I know it's rather difficult after three decades to remember events which probably played a very small part in your life. Obviously, events at Manzanar occupied only a period of months and were probably only peripherally related to your concerns. But I do want to get into your position, as a documentary historian, who you reported to directly and exactly what you did.

Tanaka: Our job was loosely defined so as to cover anything that was happening throughout the camp. This was to give the WRA administration in Washington an idea of daily activities. We never had a manual that said what we should or shouldn't write about anything. We simply wrote about anything that was occurring of interest. If there was a triangle murder—an old man with a young wife who had a young lover, and the husband murdered the wife, leaving two young girls as orphans—we covered them in a report. The camouflage net factory work going up in the camp, we covered that. We wrote about the camp farm; we went into mess halls and interviewed the people who were there eating. My recollection is that we just trooped around the whole camp and wrote things and quoted people—I don't know whether or not we were very meticulous about getting their permission or not.

Hansen: Were your reports daily ones or were they only done occasionally?

Tanaka: They were daily, turned in to the Reports Office, as I remember. I'm just sorry I didn't have carbon papers to make copies of the whole thing. I kept some, but others we didn't. Joe and I took turns, and we established a particular format. It was typed up and turned in.

Hansen: Did you encounter abrasiveness or recalcitrance on the part of the "internees" when you were circulating among them?

Tanaka: No, we were very well received, as I remember. Joe was very friendly, and I don't have any trouble meeting people. We talked with both Issei and Nisei; maybe we just didn't meet the right people.

Hansen: Since you were pivotally involved in writing the reports, did the two of you start to sense that something was building up as various things came about?

Tanaka: I'm sure we did. I'm sure we sensed it. I think if I had an opportunity to reread the reports Joe and I wrote, I could pretty well trace the genesis of the tensions that began to mount. I think it must have been reflected in my own correspondence with friends on the outside. I was getting very, very desperate to get out of that place.

Hansen: You were a speaker at a meeting—and this will take you back a while, too—on November 30, 1942, of the charter committee which had drawn up a camp government, in line with a WRA directive, to lodge all voting privileges with the Nisei. At that point, it was agreed by all those at the meeting that you shouldn't go ahead with the charter vote, owing to widespread "internee" dissatisfaction with the charter.

Tanaka: We shouldn't?

Hansen: You shouldn't. They had earlier attempted to have the vote on November 9, but there was a singular disinterest on the part of the "internees" in registering for the vote, so they postponed it to November 30. At that meeting, everybody there agreed—with the single exception of yourself—to drop the issue. Since you were in this isolated position, do you recall it pretty vividly as your being the one who stood out? I know you were the acting chairman of the committee, which meant that you had some commitment to the charter.

Tanaka: You know, Art, I can't remember that. When you tell me that's what I did, I have to acknowledge that it must be so, but I have no recollection of it. I don't recall the meeting. In a vague way I remember we were meeting at that time, but no, that doesn't come back to me. Maybe with longer reflection and reexamining the record, it may come back. But I do know this: it was a part of my own experience not to hesitate whether I was outnumbered ten to one, thirty to one, or whatever. I grew up in schools where there were no Japanese [American] students, where I might be a minority of one, so that didn't bother me. And if I was a minority of one at that time, then I must have simply been expressing what my convictions were.

Hansen: Do you recall the frustration of putting in many weeks of work on the charter and then having it torpedoed?

Tanaka: Well, no, not specifically. I just remember the overall frustration of everything in that camp life. The sooner we could somehow find a way out of there, then this would be the beginning of turning it right.

Hansen: You indicated earlier that you testified before the Tolan Committee. Did you receive a lot of community opposition as a result of your testifying?

Tanaka: At this stage, my recollection is that I felt I was misquoted in the wire services and in the Hearst papers. They had some idiot named Ray Richards who was working for the *Los Angeles Examiner*, a Hearst paper.

Hansen: Did you testify in Los Angeles, San Francisco, or both?

Tanaka: Los Angeles. What I said—and I can't even remember specifically what I said—was misrepresented in terms of what I intended it to mean, and it made me look like a jackass. That's my recollection of it.

Hansen: I know there was a lot of misquotation. In fact, they even reported on a meeting on a day when they didn't have any sessions.

Tanaka: Oh, yes. This was set up by the Hearst papers in the worst tradition of journalism.

Hansen: Do you recall a proposed Kibei survey which was going to be given? This was prior to the war, and publicity about it incensed a lot of Kibei, causing agitation since it was identified with JACL sponsorship. Many Kibei felt as though they were being relegated to a noncitizenship capacity. Apparently, the Kibei survey was never realized, only announced and then dropped. Do you recall anything about the Kibei survey?

Tanaka: No, I don't. Was that carried in the paper down here [Los Angeles], too?

Hansen: I think it was in the San Francisco paper. I just thought you might have heard of it because frequently Kibei trace some of their later anguish at the camps back to that incident. From there Kibei resentment built as a result of other things, like the fact that they were excluded from resettlement.

Tanaka: Oh, I see.

Hansen: Getting back to the JACL, it is reported that the JACL had—out of the total Japanese American population in Los Angeles of 20,000—about 650 members. This is prior to February 1942. Does that sound right?

Tanaka: In Los Angeles? I don't think there were that many. Do you mean actual members?

Hansen: Yes, actual members in the Los Angeles chapter.

Tanaka: They called it the Southern District Council, and I can't remember how many chapters there were. If you included Orange County, Long Beach, West Los Angeles, and Culver City, it would be more than that, but if it were just the Los Angeles area, I think we have to define what—

Hansen: Jurisdictional boundaries we are talking about?

Tanaka: Yes, right. But even then, I would be a poor source for that.

Hansen: Well, the JACL had a group in Los Angeles called the Anti-Axis Committee, and I think you were involved with that. What exactly was the Anti-Axis Committee, and how did it interface with the JACL group as a whole?

Tanaka: I think when you mention that—what was the word you used up at Manzanar when Group I and Group II got together?

Hansen: Coalition?

Tanaka: Coalition. I think it was a coalition because it was formed right after Pearl Harbor and there were people in it who had not been so close to JACL. There were those who were JACL people, and they got together and said, "Let's make common cause to save our skins."

Hansen: Were Karl Yoneda and Chiye Mori among the group's members?

Tanaka: Yes, I'm sure. The leading individual, as I remember, the one who gave it that name, was Kay Sugahara. He had a rather early presence in the Los Angeles JACL. He was an early president of the Los Angeles JACL. He was a customs broker here, and shortly before the war—with the last trip of the *Tatsuta Maru*, a Japanese ship—his business went under. I was in partnership with him and two others in a commission brokerage house called Osage Produce Company. Kay named and organized what was called the United Citizens Federation. I think there were one, two, or three meetings held.

Hansen: Okay, one final question. You mentioned in your last report as a documentary historian—the one which you wrote from Death Valley—that Group I, the JACL people, almost without exception arrived later at Manzanar than the Group II personalities. Do you recall why that was?

Tanaka: I think we had less mobility because most of the people in Group I owned their own homes and had businesses, so it took longer to wind up. Maybe the people in Group II—I don't really know why; some of us were also trying not to go; so, we did arrive later.

Hansen: Well, I think that's my last question. I want to thank you very much, Mr. Tanaka, on behalf of the Japanese American Oral History Project of the Oral History Program at California State University, Fullerton. Your cooperation and candor are both greatly appreciated.

NOTES

1. Biographical information is from the following sources: Tanaka, CSUF-COPH, O.H 1271a and 1271b; Togo W. Tanaka, interview by Arthur A. Hansen, September 26, 1994, CSUF-COPH, O.H 1271c.

2. The interview transcript reproduced below is from Tanaka, CSUF-COPH, O.H. 1271b.

3. Tanaka, CSUF-COPH, O.H. 1271a.

4. Tad Uyeno, "Point of No Return," *Rafu Shimpo*, August 20–October 22, 1973.

5. Audrie Girdner and Anne Loftis, *The Great Betrayal: The Evacuation of the Japanese-Americans during World War II* (New York: Macmillan, 1969).

6. See Brian Niiya, "Saburo Kido," *Densho Encyclopedia*, https://encyclopedia.densho.org/Saburo_Kido/ (accessed March 24, 2021).

7. See Barbara Takei, "Tule Lake," *Densho Encyclopedia*, https://encyclopedia.densho.org/Saburo_Kido/ (accessed March 24, 2021).

8. For a biography of Governor Olson, see Esther Newman, "Culbert Olson," *Densho Encyclopedia*, https://encyclopedia.densho.org/Culbert%20Olson/ (accessed February 18, 2021).

9. See Jonathan van Harmelen, "Shuji Fujii and the Hidden Lives of Japanese American Communists," *Discover Nikkei*, http://www.discovernikkei.org/en/journal/2021/7/27/shuji-fujii/#:~:text=The%20result%20of%20Fujii%E2%80%99s%20work%20was%20the%20newspaper,in%20establishing%20a%20new%20paper%20in%20Los%20Angeles (accessed January 20, 2022).

10. See Frank Chuman, interview by Arthur A. Hansen, January 6 and 13, 1975, CSUF-COPH O.H. 1475a, and by Carol J. Bielmeier, May 20, 1975, CSUF-COPH O.H. 1475b; see also Greg Robinson, "Frank Chuman," *Densho Encyclopedia*, https://encyclopedia.densho.org/Frank_Chuman/ (accessed pm February 19, 2021), and Frank Chuman *Manzanar and Beyond: Memoirs of Frank F. Chuman, Nisei Attorney* (San Mateo, CA: Asian American Curriculum Project, 2011).

11. This does not fit with the definition of a Kibei, but rather a Yobiyose.

Advocate

An Interview with Karl G. Yoneda

One who speaks or writes in defense of a cause.

Born in 1906 as Goso Yoneda, the son of Hideo and Kazu Yoneda, Karl Yoneda (as he would later be called) spent the first seven years of his life on his family's small farm in Glendale, California.[1] Both of his parents were from the same village, Anamura, in Japan's Hiroshima prefecture. In 1895 Hideo went to work as a contract laborer on a sugar plantation on the Hawaiian island of Kaua'i. There he became a heavy drinker until he contracted tuberculosis, which led him to become a Christian and then promotion from a fieldworker to an overseer, a post usually reserved for those of Portuguese, Hawaiian, Spanish, or Italian ancestry. This new status prompted Hideo to return to Japan to marry Kazu, the first girl in Anamura to attend a private school, the Buddhist temple for ministers, where previously only male students were allowed to enroll. Later she fell in love with a neighbor and had a child out of wedlock. This did not deter Hideo from marrying her, for she was both beautiful and intelligent. After Hideo returned to Kaua'i with Kazu, he decided that Hawai'i was no place for them to live, so they ran away from their plantation to Honolulu, and from there, in 1903, they sailed to Los

FIGURE 19. Karl Yoneda speaking at the Manzanar Pilgrimage, April 28, 1984. Photo by Betty Mitson. Courtesy Lawrence de Graaf Center for Oral and Public History, California State University, Fullerton.

Angeles, where in nearby Glendale he farmed vegetables as a sharecropper and started a laundry business on the side. While in Glendale, Karl enrolled in grammar school at age six, one of only two Japanese Americans in the institution. The very next year, his father decided to take the family, then consisting of Karl and two sisters, aged four and five, permanently back to Japan to live in Hideo and Kazu's home village of Anamura. Two years later, however, Hideo's death forced Kazu to raise their three children by herself and maintain the modest-sized family farm.

During his tenure within Anamura's grammar school, Karl was an honors student who consistently placed at the top of his class. Nonetheless, he did not graduate with honors due to his receiving a failing grade in moral character, being very aggressive and getting into lots of fights with classmates. He also talked back to the school principal and made many negative remarks, such as questioning the Japanese emperor's status as a god. Karl was close to his mother, but lacked affection for his father, who beat him with a stick and never displayed any love for him like his mother. But neither Karl's father nor his mother influenced him, because he followed the dictates of his own mind.

Dropping out of high school in Hiroshima at age sixteen because of its emphasis on the *bushidō* code, samurai morality, and emperor worship, he spent several months hitchhiking around Japan and started reading Russian literature: Fyodor Dostoyevsky, Maxim Gorki, and Peter Kropotkin. But he was most impressed by the blind Russian poet Vasily Eroshenko, who after being kicked out of Japan for being an anarchist had sought refuge in China. Having fallen in love with Eroshenko's writings, Yoneda made up his mind to go to Peking University, where Eroshenko was teaching the Esperanto language, and meet him. Yoneda ended up living with Eroshenko for six months, during which time he not only served as his secretary and mastered Esperanto but also encountered the many revolutionaries from different countries who visited Eroshenko. When Eroshenko left China in 1923 to go back to Russia, Yoneda returned to Japan.

Leaving Hiroshima to study in Tokyo, Yoneda was forced to leave that city because of the great earthquake of September 1923 and to take up residence in Osaka. There he joined an anarchist group called the Tenant's League and became an apprentice in a union-affiliated printing shop made up of anarchists. When the union went on strike, Yoneda joined the picket line, but it soon became apparent that this union was more interested in destruction than negotiation, largely because the Public Police Peace Law that had been enacted in Japan in 1900 was the most vicious anti-labor, anti-democratic law ever enacted, giving the police the right to suppress any gathering on the streets, any speech, or any strike. Yoneda's participation in this strike led to his first arrest, after which he was sentenced to ten days in a detention house; confined to a small room crowded with some fifteen other detainees; fed rice, small radishes, pickles, and tea twice a day; and forced to sleep on lice-infested straw mats.

After a year in Osaka, Yoneda returned to Tokyo, where he became a typesetter, but only for a week or so before his employers found out that he was an agitator, a "hothead," and a labor organizer. He next moved back to Hiroshima, where in 1925 he organized the Hiroshima Printers Union and initiated a strike among workers of the Hiroshima Rubber Company. As a result, he was expelled from the Hiroshima city limits. Thereafter, he retreated to the countryside and published a liberal magazine, *Tsuchi* (Earth), but he did so without getting a government permit and thus was placed under house arrest at his parental home. He was later tried in court and fined for violating the law. Due to be drafted into the Japanese Imperial Army on January 10, 1927, Yoneda, an antiwar activist, felt a need to get out of Japan. His mother, not wanting him to go to China, told him that she had saved up enough money for him to go to the United States, where he held citizenship. Walking all ten miles from his village to Hiroshima, he there boarded a ship that, eighty days later, landed in San Francisco. Because his cousin, who was scheduled to meet him at the dock, had told the officials that he didn't want a person like Karl to be in the country, Yoneda was sent to Angel Island Immigration Station, a detention center. There he remained until his cousin changed his mind, which allowed Yoneda to accompany him to his home in Los Angeles. Feeling uncomfortable, he left in short order and began using the name Kiyoshi Hama. Then, through the intervention of the Japanese Laborers Association of Los Angeles in Little Tokyo, he ended up living in one of its sponsored boarding houses in Hollywood and working for various affluent Caucasian families, mostly connected to the movie industry. For doing dishwashing, gardening, housecleaning, and other odd jobs Yoneda received the comparatively well-remunerated wage of five dollars per day. Becoming a member of a new union for agricultural workers, he got interested in organizing farmworkers, which he found easy to do among Mexican Americans and Filipino Americans but less so among Japanese Americans. Ironically, all twelve of the union organizers were Japanese Americans, some Kibei and others Issei. They were also all devoted members of the Communist Party, to which Yoneda became affiliated in May 1927 as Karl Hama (the Karl in tribute to Karl Marx). As organizers, they did not push hard for workers to become Communist Party members but instead concentrated on achieving three demands for them: wages of twenty to thirty cents an hour; an eight-hour workday; and daily lunches.

Two years later, in 1929, Yoneda was arrested for distributing leaflets in Los Angeles that denounced imperialist Japan and asked residents of Japanese ancestry not to welcome Japanese ships to the city's harbor, since they were being readied for an aggressive war against China. Under the direction of William Hynes, acclaimed for hunting so-called "left-wing Reds," a special Los Angeles Police Department intelligence unit, called the "Red Squad," raided the meeting rooms of Yoneda and his cohort organizers, confiscated their leaflets, threw them in jail, and charged them with violating the Criminal-Syndicalism Act. Three days later, they were released, and the ships had departed. However, the arrest of the organizers made headlines in the Los Angeles vernacular newspapers, one of which, the *Sen Sakai*, identified Karl by his birth name of Goso Yoneda. Reading this, his two apolitical sisters, who then lived in Los Angeles, were mortified, declaring that he had dishonored them.

In 1931 Karl was involved on February 10 with the Los Angeles Hunger March, spearheaded by the Communist Party leadership. This event, which attracted some 10,000 people amassed between First and Third Street, featured marchers who hoisted placards with various slogans, such as that of Yoneda's, which read "Children Need Food." As soon as he raised it, he was assaulted with a nightstick by a member of the Red Squad and was knocked unconscious. Taken to the hospital, he was charged with disturbing the peace, which carried with it a ninety-day jail sentence. Thankfully, he was bailed out of jail by Elaine Black, later to be his wife, who was then very active in the International Labor Defense (ILD), an organization working for political prisoners and strikers. Elaine was at the time married to Eddie Black, and both of them were members of the Communist Party. Elaine and Karl worked together daily in the ILD office, she as a secretary/spokesperson and he as a literature agent charged with distributing literature and magazines to various branches' newsstands. By 1933, Elaine, now separated from Eddie, had transferred to the ILD's San Francisco office to serve as district secretary for the northern California area, and Karl was made editor of the San Francisco–based *Rodo Shimbun* (Labor News), the official organ of the Japanese-language section of the Community Party. Over the next two years, Elaine and Karl lived together as unmarried partners since California disallowed marriages between Caucasians and people of color. In 1935 they went to Washington, one of only sixteen states allowing interracial marriages, and in Seattle tied the knot.

The year prior to the Yonedas' marriage, 1934, Karl had run as the Communist candidate for a state assembly seat for San Francisco's Fillmore

District. Even though he lost the election, Karl received 1,017 votes, carrying the Issei vote, but not that of the Nisei, who voted for the Democratic Party candidate.

In 1935, while still the editor of the *Rodo Shimbun*, Karl became involved in organizing Alaskan cannery workers under the aegis of the Alaska Cannery Workers Union, Local 20185. Karl and his allied organizers were successful in organizing cannery workers of Chinese, Filipino, and Mexican ancestry but not those of Japanese ancestry.[2]

> *Larson:* Mr. Yoneda, I'm interested in finding out about your activities with the newspaper *Doho*. Perhaps it would be easier if you went back to the *Rodo Shimbun*, an earlier Japanese American newspaper, and tell me how you became involved with that paper.
>
> *Yoneda:* Well, when I took over the *Rodo Shimbun* in 1933, it was the organ of the Japanese-language section of the Communist Party USA. The paper was published on a monthly basis, and sometimes we used a special edition on a strike that took place in the Sacramento or Fresno areas. The paper continued until 1936, and we couldn't make any headway. We discussed among ourselves, and we decided that our paper, in the progressive nature, would have to change its format as well as its aim.
>
> We decided to have a new paper based in a place where most of the Japanese were situated; in this case, Los Angeles. So we decided to move our office to Los Angeles, and we published under the coalition of Communists, progressives, and whoever was to support our paper. I relinquished my editorship of the paper. When the paper started publishing in Los Angeles, the first issue was published on January 1, 1937, under the name *Zenshin*. *Zenshin* means "the march forward." It was under the editorship of Henry Sugimura. Incidentally, we didn't decide whether we should use his true name, which was Shuji Fujii. Fujii also had the responsibility to publish the paper.
>
> In the first issue, the paper asked the readers to submit names for this paper. Besides *Zenshin*, other names suggested were *Toso*, which means "the struggle"; *Zensen*, which means "the front line"; and *Doho*, which means "the brotherhood," et cetera. We eventually picked the name *Doho* because it had more support than the other names submitted by our readers.
>
> First, they published on a monthly basis. The editorial policy was to cover Japanese political news on the front page as well as page two. That's the kind of editorial policy that language newspapers published in this country followed. Then pages three and four would be filled with the local

news—some of it from farms and canneries—and also the paper had a space for readers.

Larson: For letters?

Yoneda: Yes. The paper was well-received among Japanese, particularly among working people, the farmworkers, and the others who worked in the shops and stores.

Larson: What approximately do you think the circulation was? What would be an estimate?

Yoneda: I think they published 2,000 copies, same as the *Rodo Shimbun*. *Rodo Shimbun* had a circulation of 2,000. Actual subscribers were anywhere from 200 to 300. And the rest of the copies were handled by the paper's agents in various places in Stockton, Sacramento, Lodi, Fresno, Los Angeles, Seattle, and New York. They would either sell them or give them away.

But in the case of the *Rodo Shimbun*, because of the fact that people knew that it was an organ of the Communist Party, it was very hard to push the paper. Some people shied away, you know, "I don't want the Communist paper." Well, they were antagonistic toward the Communist Party. Then also the position of the Communist Party means that they were subject to deportation, so there was a fear among some of them. Generally speaking, our group was very small, and we didn't have a strong mass base among the Japanese [American] communities.

But with *Doho*, it's a non-Communist paper. They tried to push the paper on the coalition basis, and wherever the paper found a place where it could be sold publicly, such as a drugstore or grocery store, these places were willing to generally keep them on the news rack. Whereas the *Rodo Shimbun* never got this kind of a chance. Then Fujii—the name of Fujii is a sort of, what do you say, regency among the Japanese community because of the fact that his father is a well-known newspaperman, especially in the San Francisco area. His father used to publish a paper back at the beginning of the 1900s. And his father was quite a newspaperman, a pretty good writer.

Larson: What was his father's paper like?

Yoneda: Well, the same as the other Japanese-language papers: mostly news of Japan. That's what the Japanese [American] people wanted to read. But the writing style is what many people like.

Larson: Oh, it can be easily read.

Yoneda: Many people said, "His son is editing; he's just as good as his father." So that sort of feeling existed among certain circles, especially among our newspapermen and among some intellectuals.

Larson: Several of the *Doho* copies advertised that *Doho* was the only Japanese-language progressive newspaper in the United States. Was that true at that time?

Yoneda: Oh, yes, that's the only one. We carried news of political and social interest and also news for the working people.

Larson: The *Rodo Shimbun* had a predecessor, too, didn't it, the *Kaikyu Sen*?

Yoneda: Yes, the *Kaikyu Sen*. The first issue of the *Kaikyu Sen* was published by the Japanese Language Association of Los Angeles in 1925. This group's members were mostly gardeners, farmworkers, restaurant workers, as well as domestic workers. Some of them belonged to the Communist Party, but the others didn't.

Half of the members were Okinawans. Okinawan people were subject to oppression and exploitation by Japanese interests while they were in Okinawa. They had this experience of being exploited so they are more socially conscience [sic] of what's taking place than other Japanese. You find more progressive people among Okinawans; their group membership numbered, I think, about forty to fifty.

Kaikyu Sen lasted, I think, three months, then later moved to Berkeley. Then the group of Japanese Communists in Berkeley and Oakland, as well as San Francisco, got together and continued to publish *Kaikyu Sen* under the editorship of Teiichi Kenmotsu, a university graduate.

After several issues, the publishing offices were moved to San Francisco, and they changed its name to *Zeibei Rodo Shimbun*. *Zeibei* means "in the United States." It became an organ of the Japanese Laborers Association of America, and the editor was [Sadaichi] Kenmotsu. This occurred in 1928. Then in 1930 the name changed to *Rodo Shimbun* and began publishing in Japanese and English, with Kenmotsu remaining as editor. The number of copies published were 2,000, and it became the organ of the Communist Party Japanese-language section on November 10, 1930.

About this time Kenmotsu was arrested and ordered to be deported as an undesirable alien Communist. And when he was deported in 1931, I think, someone else took over the editing until I came to San Francisco in 1933 and took over the editorship.

Larson: I see. So apparently you took his place because he was deported.

Yoneda: Yes. I stayed with the paper until 1936. As a matter of fact, the last issue of *Rodo Shimbun* was issued on December 1, 1936, issue number 172. So it had a long history. Of course, it was edited by different persons, but the policies and the programs were generally the same as in 1925. The only change was that it was made into a mass paper instead of a sectarian, small-group paper.

Larson: Going back, could you tell me a little bit more about Shuji Fujii? His background as far as the movement went, his dealings with *Doho*, his responsibilities, and what exactly he accomplished with the paper, and his activities after *Doho* ceased publication.

Yoneda: Well, I don't know his background too well. He is a Kibei. He returned to the United States after 1930. Among the Kibei you will find many of them under the influence of Japanese militarism, because when Japan invaded Manchuria in 1931, this was the beginning of an upsurge of a strong, pro-war, nationalist movement in Japan. And the government began to suppress free speech and assemblage—and began suppressing many trade unions as well as arresting union leaders and Communist Party leaders. One of the most famous suppressions was, I think, in 1932 or 1933, when the government arrested 7,000 to 8,000 activists throughout Japan.

So Japan has a long history of peoples' struggles. Shuji Fujii was the product of that period, but for some reason—I don't know how he became a Communist Party member. I have no way to know. When I met him, he was already a member of the Communist Party.

Larson: He was pretty much the backbone of *Doho*, wasn't he? He wrote both sections—the Japanese section and the English section. Isn't that correct?

Yoneda: Yes. You talk about the collective leadership, but you have to have a figure or figures [in charge] when you publish a paper. You know, this is so-and-so's paper. And Fujii was well-liked by many people. And many people were willing to supply all sorts of news that the other Japanese press refused to carry.

Larson: In the very first English edition of *Doho*, dated June 10, 1938, in the John Kitahara column, there is mention of Sei Fujii,[3] the editor and publisher of the *Kashu Mainichi*, a Los Angeles–based Japanese language newspaper. And from this point on, all the way through the paper's history, Sei Fujii is attacked as being pro-militarist Japan and pro-Axis. Could you expand on this? Who exactly was Sei Fujii and what type of things did he do?

Yoneda: Well, Sei Fujii was well-liked by Japanese leaders in the community because he acted as an interpreter as well as legal advisor. I think he was a lawyer in Japan, so he had a background. And because of the language difficulty, the Japanese had to depend on an interpreter with a knowledge of American law. That's why he had so many supporters among Japanese, not only leaders but businessmen as well.

Larson: But was he really pro-militarist Japan?

Yoneda: Oh, yes, definitely. He was for the emperor system. He was for the Japanese military clique. He was for Asia for Asians.

Larson: Since I mentioned John Kitahara, could you tell me a little about him? His byline appears quite often in the earlier years, and so does that of Fumio Tanaka. Could you tell me more about Tanaka, also?

Yoneda: John Kitahara, he must be Joe Koide.[4] He is the son of a Christian minister. He was born in Tokyo and graduated from one of the universities in Japan. Then he came to the United States and enrolled at the University of Colorado [Denver] in 1925. His background is an intellectual one. And he must have had some experience with the student movement.

Larson: In Colorado?

Yoneda: No, in Japan.

Larson: Oh, is he a Kibei?

Yoneda: No, he is an Issei.

Larson: Oh, he's an Issei?

Yoneda: Yes. I don't know how he joined the Communist Party, but during the process of studying he joined the Communist Party in New York. And for some reason the party saw that he was cadre material, so the party sent him to Moscow, where he attended the Lenin School in 1928. When he came back here, he took over the leadership of the Japanese section of the Communist Party USA. But most of the members among us didn't trust him because of his background and because he doesn't look like he's a worker, you see. You can see right away that he came from a nice family, and he talks different than us. He is a very refined one, although he knows quite a bit about the Communist Party policies as well as the war of politics. So maybe it was thought that this guy must be a somebody, but they don't know whether he is a genuine Communist or not, because we are always afraid of a government agent. He joined the party and posed as a very active member, and in the meantime he supplied names and other information to the government agencies.

Larson: There was a lot of that sort of activity, right?

Yoneda: Oh, yes. But Joe Koide later turned out to be a government agent.

Larson: He did?

Yoneda: Yes.

Larson: After going to Moscow and everything?

Yoneda: Yes, so I don't know when he became a spy. To this day, we just couldn't pin this down. He could have been an agent from the beginning.

Or he could have been coerced into supplying information on Communist activities because of the fact that he overstayed his student visa.

Larson: Oh, I see. As an Issei, he could have been deported.

Yoneda: Maybe the government brought the pressure on him, saying, "If you don't supply information, we will deport you."

Larson: What about the other writer I mentioned, Fumio Tanaka? Was there a Fumio Tanaka, or was this too a pseudonym?

Yoneda: Fumio Tanaka, he had written many articles for the Communist international publication. So it must be—oh. (reading from an edition of *Doho*) Fumio Tanaka's "Views and Reviews." It could be that Joe Koide used the two names.

Larson: I noticed he had the same column.

Yoneda: He was a very fast typist on the typewriter.

Larson: Both of their columns are called "Views and Reviews." And they never had both of them on the same page, so I was kind of wondering whether they were the same person. I noticed, too, this might be because of the idea of a coalition—that *Doho* always supported the Democratic Party. This was in 1938, during the New Deal.

Yoneda: Yes.

Larson: I have a copy here of *Doho* for November 1, 1938, and the headline says, "Vote Straight Liberal."

Yoneda: Yes.

Larson: Did *Doho* ever support any Communist Party candidates, or was all its support given to the Democratic Party then?

Yoneda: Oh, wherever there was a Communist candidate the *Doho* supported him.

Larson: It seems as though *Doho*'s candidates were usually what they called liberal candidates: Democrats, New Dealers, or the like. During this time was that pretty much party policy, too? Wasn't the Popular Front a move toward supporting Roosevelt's New Deal?

Yoneda: Yes, that's more or less the Communist Party policy, to work within not only the Democratic Party but any mass organization where workers belong.

Larson: Unions?

Yoneda: Yes, unions and the other mass organizations, the women's organizations, and even churches.

Larson: In the November 1, 1938, edition of *Doho*, there is an article with the caption, "Nisei Elected to Offices in Alaska Cannery Union." And throughout the paper they refer to you as vice president of the Alaska Cannery

Union. Could you tell me something about this union, your role in it, and a little background about it during the *Doho* period of, say, 1938 to the end of 1941?

Yoneda: Well, *Doho* supported the CIO organizing drive, and one of the organizing drives was among cannery workers used in Alaska. So in 1937 I was asked to come up to Seattle to organize the cannery workers, which resulted in the forming of the Cannery and Field Laborers Union, Local 7, CIO. The union was mostly composed of Filipino [Americans], about 3,000 of them, and also included some 700 to 800 Japanese [Americans]. The rest of the union members were blacks, whites, and others. It was quite a big union. Usually the president was a Filipino, and the vice president was George Takigawa, a student at the University of Washington at that time. And the publicity chairman, Dyke Miyagawa, was another university graduate and a very capable writer.

Larson: Yes.

Yoneda: So that union functioned until 1941. After Pearl Harbor, Japanese [Americans] were excluded from the Pacific Coast so they were not able to go to Alaska. But the union operated without the Japanese members until after the war. When the Japanese came back from the camps and the other areas, they were allowed to go to Alaska, but not too many went there; I'll say maybe 100 or 200.

Larson: Not nearly the number that were in it before. What was your role within *Doho*? What was your assignment? What did you do?

Yoneda: Well, my function in the *Doho* was to act as the San Francisco agent, so I used to take care of the correspondence, collecting money, and also getting ads, as well as getting subscriptions. And also we had the *Doho* readers circle here, monthly meetings. This group of Japanese readers got together once a month and discussed ways and means of how to get new subscriptions or how to raise money, and also made suggestions as to what sort of articles should appear in the paper. I also had my own column in each issue of the Japanese section.

Larson: I noticed that periodically you had Friday columns in the English edition as well.

Yoneda: Yes, now and then I thought that maybe it would be interesting for Nisei or descendants in English, but otherwise they were all in Japanese.

Larson: Are you more comfortable writing in Japanese than in English?

Yoneda: Well, definitely. You know, I think in Japanese first.

Larson: Oh, I see. In the March 1, 1939, edition of *Doho*, Shuji Fujii had a column entitled "Fred Tayama, Hypocrite." And from this point on, the paper seems militantly opposed to Fred Tayama and his dealings with his restaurant employees. Could you tell me a little bit about Fred Tayama and why *Doho* opposed him?

Yoneda: Well, Fred Tayama was a successful Nisei businessman. He and his brothers used to run a chain of restaurants in Los Angeles. I don't know how many; they must have had four or five. The name of the restaurant chain was the U.S. Café. There were other restaurants run by Japanese, but Fred Tayama's restaurants had the worst working conditions. And when the employees complained, they got fired. It was very hard to organize his shop because he fired anyone who made a move toward the union. He would spot him right away and kick him out. The working conditions in the restaurants was, I think, the worse than in other fields.

For instance, in those days, men used to work twelve hours a day at the split shift, seven days a week—with just two days off per month, and pay was one dollar per day. So in many instances they didn't even have cigarette money after paying for their rooms. Of course, the employers said, "Well, we feed these men three times, even four times a day, and give them as much as they can eat." That's their excuse. At the same time, the number of unemployed people was so great, not only among the Japanese but among others throughout the United States. So through the eyes of the employer men were plenty available. These men were looking for any kind of a job. So for even one dollar a day they were willing to work as long as they had something to eat.

So Fred Tayama and others took advantage of this situation. In the case of Fred Tayama, he took a very strong anti-union stand, which he told to union organizers and other people. So that's why he was hated by many restaurant workers, "By gosh, I don't care how much he pays me, I don't want to work for him!"

Larson: It's also mentioned in the same issue of *Doho* that Fred Tayama at this time was the first vice president of the Japanese American Citizens League.

Yoneda: Yes. In the meantime he promoted himself within the Japanese business community, and a certain segment of the people in the community looked up to him as one of the leaders.

Larson: Because of his success in business?

Yoneda: Yes.

Larson: In the March 15, 1939, edition of *Doho*, there is a letter written in response to a Fumio Tanaka article, which refers to Buddy Uno.[5] It's very derogatory. Tanaka describes him as being a "fence sitter," one willing to go whichever way fortune takes him. In later editions of the paper Uno is reported as having spoken at JACL meetings, and *Doho* attacks the JACL for allowing such a Fascist speaker.

Yoneda: Yes. Buddy Uno was the news reporter for, I think, the *Hokubei Asahi* [New World Sun, a San Francisco–based newspaper]. During the Manchurian occupation he went to Japan, and he also went to Manchuria. And he was convinced that what Japan was doing was just cause. So when he returned to the United States, he made a lecture tour of the Japanese community wearing a Japanese officer's uniform with a sword. Really! (laughs) In the Japanese military fashion. And the Japanese community loved it. Because here he made such a strong pitch for the cause of Japan. "Someday Japan will be the king over Asia, and Japan will be the emancipator of all Asian people." Naturally, Japanese people swallowed his propaganda talk.

Larson: So he had a big effect on Japanese Americans then?

Yoneda: Well, in some sections they looked at it as sort of a comic thing; they didn't pay much attention. But most of the people thought it was great. I don't know what happened to him. He is a Nisei. Incidentally, he is the brother of Edison Uno, who you hear so much about.

Larson: Tell me something about Edison Uno.[6]

Yoneda: Well, he is a liberal, a quite outspoken liberal among the Nisei. He served on the grand jury here in San Francisco. He exposed the grand jury system to the press and to a television audience. He made a big name [for himself], and some people think he will make a good member for the Board of Supervisors. He's a very eloquent speaker, and he teaches at San Francisco [State University].

Larson: Is Kasimuro Uno the same person as Buddy Uno?

Yoneda: Yes.

Larson: Okay. I just wanted to clear that up since both names are used by *Doho* at different times. Buddy Uno's father was a very noteworthy figure, wasn't he?

Yoneda: Oh, I don't know too much about his father. His father was interned, suspected as an enemy alien Asian. I think he stayed in camp for the duration of the war. I take that back. I think the second year the government allowed internees to send for their families. That's how Edison Uno and others lived with their fathers in detention camp [in Crystal City, Texas]. Then later he was released, so he took his family and they went to the relocation center. I don't know which one.

Larson: Do you think *Doho*'s main interest, editorially, was labor? Or was it primarily political, in the sense that it was anti-Japanese militarism and pro-progressive toward American issues? What would you call it, a labor paper, a political paper, or what?

Yoneda: Well, I would say it was a political paper as well as a labor paper. But I would also say that community paper would much more fit in this case. Because *Doho* carried a slogan at the top of the front page in its Japanese section, "For Peace and Prosperity for the Japanese in the United States." We kept that slogan all the way through *Doho*'s history.

Larson: In every issue of the Japanese section?

Yoneda: Yes. Not in the English section. Was there any heading in the English section? I forget.

Larson: Yes, "Equality, Peace and Progress."

Yoneda: Yes, but in the Japanese section it clearly says, "For the Japanese in the United States." And this was a pretty good slogan, so that most of the Japanese would support us. They'd say, I go for it. There was no argument about it, but only a question as to how to go about it. Then there would be arguments. Our paper not only appealed to the working class but to professional people and business people.

Larson: The May 20, 1939, issue announced that *Doho* would sponsor a huge rally on June 3 to protest Japanese fascism. They said that they expected a turnout of thousands of people. Two issues later, I think, they declared the rally a great success. Do you remember anything about that rally? What was it like?

Yoneda: You know, Japan began invading North China in 1937. That was the beginning of the Sino-Japan War. This unjust war was going on at full scale, so naturally *Doho* was the only paper among the Japanese press which attacked the action of the Japanese government. And the *Doho* had quite strong support among Japanese as well as Caucasians. Because of the English section, quite a few Caucasians subscribed to *Doho*. And its name was well-known among progressive circles, particularly in California. So this meeting, I gather—I wasn't there—was attended by not only Japanese but Caucasians, too. That's why the rally was such a success. That was the kind of unity that the Japanese needed.

Larson: In *Doho*'s "Letter Box" for June 15, 1939, a letter appears over your signature as vice president of the Alaska Cannery Workers Union.

Yoneda: Yes.

Larson: Was this your official title? Did you usually sign your name in this fashion?

Yoneda: That's right. Well, usually, whatever I wrote or any other office wrote, reflected the policy of the union.

Larson: I see.

Yoneda: Of course, in other unions they do it differently. You know, the head of the union writes whatever he wants, and he doesn't give a damn about what the members have to say. Our union was one of the few militant unions in the Bay Area at that time. We took a strong anti-Japanese militarist stand. We were also against the Nazis as well as the Fascist tendencies that existed in the United States.

Larson: In *Doho* there were many critical references to the *Kashu Mainichi*. I was just wondering what reaction the *Kashu Mainichi* and the other vernacular papers had toward *Doho*. Do you remember that?

Yoneda: There were four dailies in Los Angeles at that time: the *Kashu Mainichi*, the *Rafu Shimpo*, *Rafu Nichibei*, and I forgot the other one. The Japanese sections of these papers were more or less pro-Japan. Most of the items they carried were from the Domei dispatch, which sugarcoated the imperial headquarters' announcements. Well, that's what most of the Japanese people want to read. But in the English section, it depended on the editors. Some of them took a mild approach toward the Sino-Japan War. In some issues they might take a strong stand, but not too strong, just strong enough not to antagonize the editors of the Japanese sections—because they are the bosses. All the publishers were Issei. But in the case of *Kashu Mainichi*, Sei Fujii was one of the outspoken publishers for the cause of the Japanese military government. So that's why *Doho* picked on *Kashu Mainichi* more than the other papers. Incidentally, the publisher of *Rafu Shimpo*, H. T. Komai, approached some issues with more or less of a liberal mind.

Larson: This is Togo Tanaka?

Yoneda: No, he was the editor of the *Rafu Shimpo*'s English section. But the publisher was H. T. Komai. So maybe *Doho* didn't pick on the *Rafu Shimpo* so much, even though the front-page articles were the same as the *Kashu Mainichi* or the other Japanese papers, because they all carried the Domei dispatch.

Larson: Did *Doho* also carry the Domei dispatch?

Yoneda: No, because everyone read the Japanese dailies. So [it was] no use to carry duplicate information.

Larson: So *Doho* provided an alternative then, right?

Yoneda: Yes. Besides there is not enough space there. But some of the items that *Doho* carried explained what the news meant to us and to the future of Japan.

Larson: Since I mentioned Togo Tanaka, was there a pretty good relationship at that time between *Doho*'s staff and Tanaka?

Yoneda: Well, I don't know too much about their personal relationships. But most likely, Shuji Fujii, being a full-time editor, must have known all of the English-section editors of the Japanese press. And among the English editors there weren't any anti-labor or anti-Communist editors at that time. So Shuji Fujii must have gotten along with all of them.

Larson: Another prominent feature of *Doho* that I noted was its coverage of what they call fifth-column activists within Little Tokyo and their criticism of other papers for not mentioning them, as if trying to hide the fact of their existence.

Yoneda: Yes.

Larson: Exactly what sort of fifth-column activities were going on then? And were they as considerable as *Doho* appears to point out?

Yoneda: Well, one example was that the overseas ex-servicemen, of those who served in the Japanese army, organized the Overseas Ex-Servicemen League [Japanese Military Servicemen's League] in San Francisco in 1937, right after the outbreak of the Sino-Japan War. And they began collecting a war relief fund, which is understandable, for wounded soldiers and families.

But later they began handling Japanese government war bonds. Naturally, in these drives there must have been some fifth-column activists among the organizers. And I'm sure that the Japanese government was pushing this campaign through some channel that those in the organization were not able to see. And once you start to push the Japanese government war bonds, suddenly it's a violation of the American democratic principle. Or when you buy bonds, you are supporting the Japanese invasion of China, which is unjust. And practically everyone in the American public knew it.

There was great support for Chiang Kai-shek at the—that time. He is a hero and you welcome him. And then you can't help these fifth-column activities. Even the government stepped in, and I think it stopped the handling of war bonds because they didn't register with the government under the—what do you call it? The security—the handling of foreign countries through stocks [US Security and Exchange Commission?]. You must have registered with the government. So later they withdrew the war bond drive. Oh, yes, the organizational step calls for —— [inaudible]. They had as high as 8,000 members throughout the United States. And many Nisei don't want to talk about it.

Larson: They like to pretend that it wasn't there.

Yoneda: Then they'll say, "Why wash dirty linen in public? Let's keep quiet." But the facts are facts, you know. It was there, and the record shows that 8,000 supported it. And most of the Nisei who kept quiet knew what was going on in their families. The Nisei kept quiet because of the Japanese family system: the father is the master of the family and whatever he does—why, the rest of the family members don't say. So most of the Nisei keep quiet. And I'm sure that no writing by Nisei mentioned this fact. They must've raised a couple of million dollars.

But in 1941 Roosevelt froze the foreign assets as well as the sending of money. And this organization decided to disband. Not only [fund-]raising for war chest fund, but also they had a big drive among Nisei students who attended the Japanese language schools. You know, in California alone 20,000 Nisei attended Japanese language schools. And in each classroom there were two boxes. One to put in a penny. They said, "Don't eat candy. Save that money for the war relief fund." It was clearly stated. And the other one for scrap metal, or chewing gum wrapping paper, or anything. That was for the war chest fund to be sent to Japan.

Larson: Little pieces of metal?

Yoneda: Yes, or anything. It comes in handy. Particularly they stressed very strongly that when your father or someone used the cigarette—you know, they used to have this tinfoil—be sure to bring them to the classroom and put it in the box. To see which school raised more, that kind of a campaign went on. Then the school instructors instructed the students to write the so-called comfort letter to the Japanese soldiers in North China. And several Buddhist churches organized the comfort mission to be sent to North China to visit wounded soldiers. Of course, that's in name only, "wounded soldiers." They wanted to say brave, courageous, Japanese soldiers fighting in China—they didn't say killing off Chinese indiscriminately.

The most common phrase the Japanese army used was the "Communist bandit." They would arrest anyone and say he was a Communist bandit—so just chop off his head. They must have killed off thousands under the guise of people being Communist bandits. But this wasn't reported in any English section of the Japanese press.

Larson: Talking about language schools and the fifth-columnist activities, in the August 15, 1939, edition, *Doho* exposed a recruitment plan from Japan: to recruit twenty promising students to come back for training and then come back as information agents. Can you tell me more about that? Later *Doho* printed names of the people who went. Do you remember that?

Yoneda: They sent some from here, too. It was, I think, in 1940. Was it in 1940?

Larson: This was 1939.

Yoneda: Oh, this was arranged by Japanese generals in the consulate here.

Larson: In the October 15 edition of 1939, it gives names: Kay Tateishi from the *Rafu Shimpo*. Another person they cite is Isamu Masuda, who won a *Rafu Shimpo* award for patriotic oratory. I was just wondering, since they gave names, if you knew anything about that recruitment?

Yoneda: I don't know any details, but usually they picked them from Japanese language schools, to see which one is good material for the Japanese government. Not only Japanese language schools but also Buddhist youth associations, Christian youth associations, and women associations of various churches. All these groups cooperated with the Overseas Ex-servicemen Association to raise the war relief and the war chest fund during the Sino-Japan War. This continued until 1940. Everybody pitched in practically, including Nisei language school students.

Larson: And newspapers were pretty big on it?

Yoneda: Of course, some of the Nisei you ask about it today are apparently unaware of these facts. For instance, —— [inaudible] the martial arts association that mostly teaches you Japanese fencing, their head was Mitsuru Tōyama, head of the Japanese Black Dragons in Japan. And one of the Nisei who took this fencing said, "Well, I joined this just for the sports purpose. I never thought of this organization being controlled by Japanese militarists." But just the same, there they were asked to contribute for the cause of war in Japan.

Larson: I'd like to introduce Arthur Hansen, who will continue with the interview.

Hansen: Mr. Yoneda, during the period in the late 1930s when *Doho* was spending most of its time directing its attacks against the Japanese nationalism coming out of the *Kashu Mainichi*, they had a rather ambivalent attitude toward the *Rafu Shimpo*. What was the basic philosophical difference between the *Kashu Mainichi* and the *Rafu Shimpo* at that time?

Yoneda: Well, as I gather, the policy of the Doho was to work with whoever agreed on a certain issue—not all issues. And in this case, some of the Japanese press, particularly in the English section, cooperated with the Doho. That's because of Shuji Fujii. He was well-known among the Japanese community as a well-liked, progressive guy.

Hansen: Who in the English section cooperated with Shuji Fujii?

Yoneda: Oh, I don't know their names.

Hansen: Did Togo Tanaka, the [English-language] editor?

Yoneda: I don't know when he took over the editorship of *Rafu Shimpo*.

Hansen: About 1936, I think it was.

Yoneda: So most likely he [Shuji Fujii] had a friendly relationship with Togo, I gather, but I don't know these personal relationships with these Nisei newspaper people.

Hansen: One of the things that happened was during the crisis, just prior to the announcement of Executive Order 9066, Togo Tanaka went back to Washington several times. And one of his trips was partially financed by the Japanese Association, and *Doho* took him to task for that.

Yoneda: Oh.

Hansen: And he claimed later on that he had no knowledge that the tab was being paid for by the Japanese Association. He felt that the publishers paid it, and he didn't realize the source of the money.

Yoneda: Well, Togo went to Washington with [Katsuma] Mukaeda.[7] He was, I'm not sure, the secretary or president of the Central California Japanese Association, and I think the Japanese Association coughed up the expense. I don't think *Rafu Shimpo* had that much money for sending Togo to Washington, DC. This was mainly to try to ease the relationship between the United States and Japan. At the same time, I don't know what Togo told you about it. I think his assignment was to see that this crisis would not affect the Japanese in the United States, particularly Nisei.

Hansen: What was the attitude of *Doho* toward the JACL?

Yoneda: Well, the JACL was controlled by a very conservative element, so *Doho* criticized certain policies. On the other hand, *Doho* had many friends within the organization. So they didn't have a frontal attack on the JACL. They thought it was one organization that they had to work with very closely.

Hansen: So there was an overlapping relationship between *Doho* and JACL.

Yoneda: That's right, yes.

Hansen: What about the repeated attacks by *Doho* on the Kibei group within the JACL? There was a Kibei chapter, wasn't there?

Yoneda: Oh, yes.

Hansen: And was that only in Los Angeles, or was there one in San Francisco also?

Yoneda: Yes, in San Francisco, too.

Hansen: And what was the nature of that organization that set it apart from the mainstream of the JACL?

Yoneda: Well, the Kibei group—you see, the Japanese American Citizens League didn't take any stand on the Sino-Japan War when the war broke out in 1937. They finally took a stand on the war issue—no, they didn't say anything whatsoever when the crisis became so acute in 1941. Finally,

Saburo Kido issued a statement stating that we are loyal Americans, our place is in the United States, we have to uphold the Constitution of the United States, et cetera. But they didn't touch on what's going on in the Far East or the Japanese community.

I said before that the Overseas Ex-servicemen Association, composed of mainly Japanese servicemen who lived here, organized to raise the war relief and the war chest funds, and they had as high as 8,000 members throughout the United States, with more than eighty branches. And certainly *Doho* was the only one to expose this pro-Japan activity, and no one else. So the Kibei group within the JACL usually sided with these pro-Japan groups. And James Oda was one of the Kibei section members. Oda criticized, and in some cases, attacked the Kibei leadership headed by Dave Itami, a vice president of the Kibei. "Why don't you take a stand on the upsurge of fascism in the United States?"

Hansen: Was the JACL also a little bit uneasy about the Kibei wing of the organization?

Yoneda: Well, yes. On the one hand, they more or less treated them as their stepson.

Hansen: As an unwanted stepson?

Yoneda: Yes. Actually, they didn't like to have a Kibei section. They'd much rather have them under the general overall organization instead of a Kibei section as such.

Hansen: So JACL was pretty conservative itself, but the Kibei section was even more conservative?

Yoneda: Yes.

Hansen: If you measure it against Japanese nationalism as a standard?

Yoneda: The Kibei section, without consent of the JACL headquarters, carried on many cultural activities, which turned out to be nothing but the praising of Japan's war effort in China. They put on this play praising the courageous Japanese soldiers—three soldiers who carried the dynamite with them and broke through the barricade in Shanghai, a famous story.

Hansen: The Kibei put on a play?

Yoneda: Yes. That's true in San Francisco, too. They put out their own publication in the Japanese language, so that the JACL headquarters didn't know what the contents of that were. But every item praised Hitler and Mussolini as well as the Japanese military government.

Hansen: Did you ever go to any Kibei meetings?

Yoneda: No, but I had access to their publications.

Hansen: Do you recall the name of it?

Yoneda: Well, I don't know exactly. I don't have a copy with me. I should have kept those copies.

Hansen: Did this magazine parallel the *Pacific Citizen*, only separately run by the Kibei group within the JACL?[8]

Yoneda: Well, mostly. Usually, no news item appeared in the magazine, only what some member thought and his attitude toward a certain subject, or his reminiscences of his life in Japan.

Hansen: Did that come out of San Francisco or Los Angeles?

Yoneda: Both places.

Hansen: Do you recall who was the editor or the moving force within that publication?

Yoneda: Well, in Los Angeles, most likely Dave Itami. He was very capable of writing in both Japanese and English. And the San Francisco editor was [a man named] Akai, who later joined the Communist Party. He broke away from the Kibei group.

Hansen: Now, *Doho* was taking a very strong stand against Japanese nationalism, and all of a sudden Pearl Harbor comes along and you were arrested, weren't you?

Yoneda: Yes.

Hansen: And what was the rationale for that?

Yoneda: Well, I guess that sort of shows that the US government doesn't even trust a person like me, making sure that he's really for the United States and against Japan.

Hansen: A person like you, meaning because of your left-wing ideology or because of the fact that you're [of] Japanese [ancestry], or both?

Yoneda: Well, I guess this has much to do with the anti-Japanese [and anti–Japanese American] racism that exists in this country. Whether he is Fascist or nationalist or Communist, they just don't want to trust him. The best way to find out is to put him in the can and see whether what the guy says is true or not.

Hansen: Was it exceptional to have Nisei rounded up and put in jail after Pearl Harbor?

Yoneda: Well, besides myself, there were three others that were picked up here.

Hansen: In San Francisco?

Yoneda: In San Francisco.

Hansen: Who were they?

Yoneda: One is Yasuo Abiko,[9] the son of Kyutaro Abiko, a well-known pioneer. Abiko was the English editor of *Nichibei*. Another is George—I forgot his last name, but a proprietor of a Japanese tea garden in Golden Gate Park.

Hansen: He was a Nisei, too?

Yoneda: Yes. Then the other one I didn't know what his connection was.

Hansen: Koji Ariyoshi wasn't picked up?

Yoneda: No. The reason they picked up the others was because of their ties with the tea garden and newspapers—especially newspapers, because all newspapers were pro-Japan.

Hansen: Well, your situation was probably most unusual, then?

Yoneda: Yes.

Hansen: They didn't have a real ground for it in the same sense that—well, they probably didn't have a real ground in the other cases either, but they at least had a sense that the person was the head of an organ of opinion or something of that nature.

Yoneda: As a matter of fact, the FBI told me many times, "We know where you stand, but we want to make sure if what you say is the truth."

Hansen: So how long did they keep you?

Yoneda: Two nights.

Hansen: Two nights? How did you get released?

Yoneda: The third day one of the inspectors came around, "I'm sorry we kept you so long. We have to check and double-check to make sure. We don't know, a person like you may play as the double agent and do damage during time of war."

Hansen: I guess there were double agents even within *Doho*, as you've indicated. So there was a possibility.

Yoneda: Well, I didn't get mad too much, you know. Anyway, I said, "I don't have my car, so you better take me home." So one of the agents said, "Well, we'll get you a car and they'll take you home." That's the only time that the government agency chauffeured me.

Hansen: You must have been pretty uncomfortable—after you were picked up, being put into jail—more than likely with Issei, who perhaps had some strong affiliations with Japanese nationalism. And you had been playing a role over the past number of years, bringing attention to their nationalism and calling them to task for it. You must have been spending a couple of uneasy days and nights in that cell.

Yoneda: No, I had a grand time with these pro-Japanese groups. Let me tell you the incident. As soon as I was brought in in the morning to Immigration Detention house on Silver Avenue, I noticed about fifty or sixty Japanese [American] community leaders there, most of whom I knew. And as soon as I came in, the principal of a Japanese language school, Suzuki—he is for Japan, but he is a very kind, sort of a nice guy that likes to talk to me.

He said, "Mr. Yoneda, you must have come to the wrong place!" (laughs) So I said, "Yes, I think so." "Well, sit down, and don't worry about the others."

Well, of course, others there were the strong anti-Communist bunch. As a matter of fact, one of them said, "If this wasn't under the control of the US government, you would be a machine gun target." And they are loudly talking about—through the window you can see the Golden Gate Bridge. Especially Kondo, that's the one who raised the three daughters that were university graduates and ran a pro-Japan weekly. And Kondo said loudly, "Wait and see, in another couple of days there will be a Japanese Navy that will come into the bay and free us." (laughs)

Hansen: They were fully anticipating that?

Yoneda: Oh, yes. They truly believed it. And there was no use to argue with these people. But there were a few that were very friendly toward me. One was Kenji Asai. His brother was a graduate of Columbia [University] and elected to the Diet [of Japan]. He made lecture tours of the United States many times on behalf of the Japanese government. His brother had an office on Fourth Street to handle stocks. He was also a University of California graduate. But he was constantly with me: "At a time like this, we need a person like you." He said this to me many times because these people didn't pay attention to him; they were really fanatics. "But now I realize," he said, "that Japan is wrong. At a time like this we have to be quiet and not raise any issue like other people do."

Hansen: So your experience there wasn't really that tense?

Yoneda: No. As a matter of fact, as soon as I was released, I sent him cigarettes and fruit, and I have a nice letter from him. I still have that letter with me. He repeatedly said, "I'll depend on a person like you to meet a crisis like this that the Japanese—particularly the Japanese—are facing."

Hansen: Could you be so kind as to read the letter he sent you into the tape?

Yoneda: Yes. This is a letter from Kenji Asai for detainment at the immigration house. (reads from letter)

Dear Mr. Yoneda, December 11, 1941, 8:00 a.m. I express my deepest appreciation for your kind present, from the bottom of my heart. Please imagine how I have been deeply impressed how it came to me so unexpectedly. I was called to the letter office just atop the step at 7:30 last night, and found a large bag containing the most delicious fruits and the cigarettes. I was quite astonished to find your name and choked with appreciation. I shall endeavor to conserve them to enjoy your kindness as long as I can stretch. I confess to you that I gave up my smoking habits fourteen years ago, so I gave the cigarettes to my friend, who enjoyed your kindness the same as I do. At first, I wished to take the package as a treasure of this incident, but I realize it is selfishness, so I decided to share it with my friend, who appreciates it most. Please appreciate this with me. After you left here, our number is increasing day and night, as you will see in the paper. Now it is almost 100 from San Francisco, Sonoma, Stockton, Hollister, San Jose, Watsonville, Salinas, Monterey and others. Mr. Yoneda, please do your best at this most crucial moment in our Japanese American history, by realizing your duty as a Japanese American citizen, and do your utmost efforts to lead and counsel our helpless Issei and their children on the outside by utilizing your privileges as an American citizen. Please give my best regards to Mrs. Yoneda, to whom I have no privilege of meeting yet. Most sincerely yours, Kenji Asai. P.S. Many thanks for your weekly. I shall sure enjoy it. I wrote a letter this morning to express my feelings as best I can by my limited English, but I was puzzled where it should be sent. Fortunately, the paper reached me in time. With appreciation, Kenji Asai.

That was the *Doho* that I sent him.

Hansen: Oh, you sent him a copy of *Doho*?

Yoneda: Yes.

Hansen: So he could read the situation, and he thought that it would be better to take an attitude like yours than some hysterical, pro-Japanese position, then?

Yoneda: Well, the school teachers, they didn't get excited like the other community leaders.

Hansen: You mean the language school teachers?

Yoneda: Yes. I became friends with these teachers while I was gathering the news for *Doho*. I would usually stop by language schools and sometimes would use their libraries as a reference place.

Hansen: So you had known them in the past, then, and just the human contact dissolved some of the ideological differences, right?

Yoneda: Yes. So I had enemies, and at the same time I had friends among them. The restaurant called the Eagle Café, its proprietor was a real pro-Japan type. You know, "For the emperor I will die anytime." That kind of a type. And every time I came up, "Here comes Mr. Communist Party boss. Come on in. I admire your principles. I admire your guts. Have a coffee on me." Free coffee every morning I go there. "I want to pay." "No, no, no, I respect you as a person, not as a Japanese [American], who has the guts to stick to the idea and the principle."

Hansen: So you were a respected adversary for him.

Yoneda: Yes. He returned to Japan. He died. His son took over the Eagle Café.

Hansen: There is no doubt in your mind during this period that, as you've documented other places, there was a very concerted pro-Japan movement within the Japanese American communities on the West Coast.

Yoneda: Oh, definitely. We just couldn't pin down who were the fifth columnists. But at the same time, you know, the US government really played a dirty trick on the Japanese [Americans]. The number arrested among Italian and German aliens nowhere near approached the number of Japanese aliens. I remember the Thursday when the list of all the arrested enemy aliens was announced, more than 1,100 Japanese aliens were arrested. Whereas in the case of German or Italian aliens, only 1,000. And I knew very well at that time that we had more vicious, open, fascistic activities among the [alien] Japanese Americans. So certainly, to my way of thinking, this anti-Japanese racism played a great part in this rounding up of an unnecessary number of Japanese [aliens]. For instance, Terminal Island. I'm sure there were a few outspoken, pro-Japanese [alien] leaders, but not all 500 fishermen.

Hansen: Terminal Island has sometimes been talked about as a particularly Japanized area. What explains the fact that their assimilation was less than, say, among the Japanese in West Los Angeles or in parts of San Francisco?

Yoneda: Well, first of all, the place was isolated from other parts. And their lifestyle and their daily life was similar among 500 families. They were a family of fishermen, and during the cannery season, their wives worked in a cannery. So in everyone's daily conversation the subject was whether my husband brought in more fish or less fish than last catch, or made more money or less money. Naturally, there was a close tie, a close kinship among them.

Hansen: So they were very much more contained and homogenous as people, then?

Yoneda: Yes. So there was a close tie among them. So when the councils were raising the questions of money for certain events, they always met the quota that the Japanese Association used to assign them. They had their own Japanese Association besides the Japanese Fishermen Association.

Hansen: Well, pro-Japan sentiment then was more pronounced in, say, that area, too?

Yoneda: Yes. In a place like that it is understandable, you see. Just like in a country area there is more pro-Japan feeling as well as pro-Japan customs. For instance, January first, they have a New Year's celebration. Usually residents get together at the language school auditorium and sing the national anthem, and then they'll have the opening of the pictures of our emperor and empress, which you're supposed to not look at. The principal takes the pictures out of a box and bows three times. And then they put them back again and put the box away. This is one of the ceremonial customs. Then the representatives of various groups, associations, and youth groups—in some cases Boy Scout leaders and student leaders—will make short speeches praising Japan's greatness.

Hansen: Is it fair to say that the strength of the pro-Japan sentiment was not in the cities like Los Angeles and San Francisco but in the rural areas?

Yoneda: Well, in comparison to the population, let's say, in the Sacramento area; there practically all of them attended ceremonies. But in San Francisco, with, say, a population of 20,000, how many will attend New Year's ceremony or founding day or the birthday of the emperor, or other holidays or ceremonies? Maybe 400 or 500 or more.

Hansen: So it's sort of like today, when we speak about Mid-America being the heart of super-patriotism, you might say the same thing prevailed then for the Japanese [American] population on the coast.

Yoneda: Yes.

Hansen: Although the organs of opinion were in the cities. And there were movements that gathered strength from these rural areas because it was just a more conservative way of life, and they were all together in this large, sort of family, and they didn't interact with other influences like those in the larger American culture. So they almost had preserved for them a Japanese way [of life], right?

Yoneda: Especially among the fishermen. They made very good money. Among the Japanese [Americans], I think, occupation-wise, fishermen did far better than the other occupations. For instance, every time you see a new Buick—it used to be a fancy car in Japantown—it was usually owned by a fisherman.[10] So we used to say, "Well, here comes a fisherman. He must have a good catch; he's driving a new Buick."

Hansen: So their standard of living was a little bit higher?

Yoneda: No, they invested in additional boats and other supplies. I don't think so. They lived the same as they had before because of the living quarters, you know, you can't make them any bigger. The small, individual houses were just like barracks. It's the same style of building.

Hansen: So their housing and their outward style of life was pretty much the same, but they were able to make a little bit more money than the average person who worked in a restaurant or had a small business in Little Tokyo.

Yoneda: It is very common that among them their annual earnings were from $7,000 to $15,000. This is according to a Japanese history book edited by the

Japanese Association, published in 1940. So, naturally, among them they had kind of a feeling of pride in doing better than others. So that added to their feeling of kinship and closeness. Of course, if they were poor, I'm sure that their ties of kinship were much stronger, too.

Hansen: There was at least a third Los Angeles vernacular newspaper. I think it's called the *Sangyo Nippo*. They largely had a readership within the rural areas. It would be interesting to me to know whether they pursued a strong pro-Japan stand, or did they mostly concern themselves—

Yoneda: In Los Angeles?

Hansen: Yes.

Yoneda: Hold it, I'm going to find it. Los Angeles had the three Japanese dailies in 1940: *Rafu Shimpo*, *Kashu Mainichi*, and *Beikoku Sangyo Nippo*. The last one was mainly supported by the growers and the businessmen. So their editorial policies were geared toward the thinking and wishes of businessmen and growers. And, naturally, it was very conservative, and in many cases, very pro-Japan oriented.

Incidentally, the editor of this paper was Shin'ichi Katō. I think he is another one that you ought to interview. He wrote the book called *A History of One Hundred Years of the Japanese and the Japanese Americans in the United States*. He is retired now. He is an Issei born in Hiroshima. And he is an intellectual. In 1928, when a group of intellectuals organized the Friday Association to study Marxism, he attended this group. We were on talking terms, but their stand was anti–Communist Party. They were for Marxism but against the Communist Party.

Hansen: When he edited the paper, he wasn't a Marxist, was he?

Yoneda: No. At the time that he was in the Friday Association, he was a news reporter for *Rafu Nichibei*. And when the *Rafu Nichibei* bankrupted, I think these people started organizing this *Sangyo Nippo*. And during the strikes, which took place in various Southern California farms, Katō also became the secretary of the Southern California Japanese Growers Association. And he led the immigration officers to various campuses, pointing out, "He is a Red, he is a Red, he is a Communist." They were all Japanese [Americans]. He led anti-labor scab activities. But otherwise the guy was well liked by many people, particularly businessmen, because he was the spokesman for them.

Hansen: I want to ask you about the term *aka*. It was used in the Japanese American community prior to the war. And *Doho*, of course, was sometimes smeared by the accusation that it was run by *aka*. What connotation did this term carry to people within the [Japanese American] community?

Yoneda: Well, I think it's the same as in English. You know, he is a Red. It would mean that he or she was a traitor. In many cases, they would be isolated by a community. And it made life difficult in getting a job and a place to live.

Hansen: Did it mean specifically Communist or just progressive?

Yoneda: Well, anyone contrary to the established customs or traditions within the community, they call him *aka*.

Hansen: Was it used with pride by people who were self-consciously Communist or left-wing?

Yoneda: No, but it's funny, you know. If someone starts to argue and you don't agree with him, he figures that you must be an *aka*, although he is apolitical and has nothing to do with politics.

Hansen: So it means troublemaker in that context, right?

Yoneda: So it's widely used. I think in English we don't use that so widely as among the Japanese.

Hansen: It's a term, then, that has a lot of different applications, but it usually means that somehow or other you're being hard to get along with.

What was the general opinion in the Japanese community of *Doho*? Did the community resent *Doho* because of its activities? Because of its exposures? Because of its attacks on restaurant owners, et cetera? Did you ever have your office, say, visited by people who wanted to shut it down? Was there any form of intimidation? Was it something you had to do surreptitiously, behind the scenes? Or was it something you could do quite openly?

Yoneda: Well, generally we were well received within the community. They read the Japanese press every day, nothing but the Domei dispatch because they liked to read the one showing the imperial headquarters announced that the Japanese Army captured this town, that town, killed so many enemies. That kind of news they like to read, but sometimes you get fed up with the same news. You would like to read something contrary to what the Domei dispatch carries. So some of them were curious. Some of them just wanted to read some other items. But among working people, they welcomed the *Doho*.

Hansen: Was the readership largely among young Nisei?

Yoneda: No, mostly among young Issei and the Kibei.

Hansen: So you had very few Nisei readers then. Who financed *Doho*?

Yoneda: Oh, the average working people like myself and others. Each city, like New York, Seattle, Los Angeles, San Francisco, Stockton, Sacramento, had *Doho* readers' circles. They met once a month, sometimes once in two months, and raised the money. They found the ways and means to get more subscriptions.

Hansen: You mean it had extended that far?

Yoneda: Oh, yes. It was a national paper, not only a Los Angeles paper.

Hansen: But most of your news had to do with Los Angeles, right?

Yoneda: Yes, because it's easier to get it, and most of the news that the outlying districts would send in would become old news by the time it got to Los Angeles. Besides, there was not enough space anyway. Then sometime or another we would have a Japan night. There would be served chop suey and coffee and donuts to raise money.

Hansen: What was *Doho*'s attitude toward Pearl Harbor? What did that event signal to them as a policy? Did they, at that point, decide that they would have to try to further expose, to flush out people who would have made it tough upon Japanese Americans by their identification with the Japanese government? Or how did they react to that?

Yoneda: Right after Pearl Harbor, *Doho* issued a statement—not only a statement, they issued many statements urging the Japanese [American community] to support the United States war effort. And also *Doho* followed the same line that the Anti-Axis Committee issued: buy war bonds and inform on any fifth-column activities among the Japanese [American] community to the authorities. That's really why most of the Japanese Americans turned against, not so much the Anti-Axis Committee, but Fred Tayama. Of course, some of them worked in his restaurants, so there already existed some antagonism toward him. Then here's Fred Tayama telling us to inform on our own brothers, and even sisters, to the FBI. In other words, he is becoming an FBI *inu*, an FBI spy.

Hansen: Tayama was the head of the Anti-Axis Committee.

Yoneda: He felt very uncomfortable. That's why he resigned and Tokie Slocum took over.

Hansen: What did you think of Tokie Slocum? Did you know him at that time, before the war?

Yoneda: Yes.

Hansen: Had you had contact with Slocum then in some connection or another? Or did you just know him casually?

Yoneda: Well, I encountered him during his activity on behalf of getting citizenship for those Japanese [Americans] who served in the First World War.

Hansen: In what connection exactly did you run across him?

Yoneda: Well, I attended some of the meetings that were run by the JACL. He was quite an outspoken guy. He was a real flag-waver, especially at the time of World War II. The guy came in handy; nobody ever thought to attack his record. And I'm sure that Joe Kurihara would have played the same role if he had wanted to, or if he had happened to be there.

Hansen: So Slocum was a super-patriot then.

Yoneda: Yes.

Hansen: Well, I'd like to now move into the period in which *Doho* gets phased out and you go off to Manzanar. Prior to the time that you went to Manzanar, I guess about the time you went to Manzanar, *Doho* sent a group of representatives to Manzanar to survey what was happening there. And they wrote a little piece about their findings in one of their final editions. Do you recall when the *Doho* people went to Manzanar?

Yoneda: Yes, I remember.

Hansen: At this time, what was the general strategy of *Doho* and people of that persuasion toward the "internment" camps?

Yoneda: Well, we discussed the many things among ourselves. One of the things was that we must have our own paper and maybe raise enough money to move it to Salt Lake City, like *Pacific Citizen* did later. We continued to stress our point of view, and also that by all means we must cooperate with the "evacuation" order and there shouldn't be any hitch whatsoever in completing the "evacuation."

Hansen: In what ways, then, did you cooperate?

Yoneda: Well, first of all, we asked people to volunteer to go to camp. And we helped build a camp that would be livable for "evacuees." Of course, when the first "evacuees" went to Manzanar on March 23, 1942, the government stopped the volunteering altogether.

Hansen: Did you succeed in being able to establish a newspaper outside of the strategic area, like in Salt Lake City or someplace else?

Yoneda: No. It was a question of finance. We looked around, and we couldn't find anyone with the money. Most of our so-called sympathizers—we had a few—their assets were frozen so they couldn't take any money out of the bank.

Hansen: Did you make any attempt, therefore, to take over the existing newspapers that were in the camps, like the *Manzanar Free Press*? Was there an attempt to move public opinion through somehow having a shaping voice in the media at Manzanar and the other camps?

Yoneda: We had no intention of taking over. In the first place, our force was scattered all over the camps. But in the case of the *Manzanar Free Press*, we had James Oda on the Japanese section, so he was able to carry [out] our wishes or thinking. At the same time in the English section we had Tom

Yamazaki, a capable Issei writer. He worked for *Shin Sekai Asahi* [New World], and also later he edited the organ of the Japanese trade union, which was composed of 2,000 members.[11]

Hansen: What about Chiye Mori, who was the editor of the *Manzanar Free Press*?

Yoneda: Yes, she was part of the *Free Press*. I didn't have too much connection with Chiye and the others on the staff.

Hansen: You didn't know Joe Blamey?

Yoneda: No. The first time I met him was in camp.

Hansen: I have here a report that was written by Togo Tanaka, January 25, 1943. And this was written in his role as the documentary historian at Manzanar, and it was after the Manzanar Riot of December 6, 1942. And he, along with many others, a party of about sixty, were sent to Death Valley for protective custody purposes. And he wrote back to the Manzanar administration an analysis of the riot, his final report as a documentary historian. In the course of this analysis, he claims that there were, roughly speaking, three groups at Manzanar. One of which was a JACL group; another which was what he calls, for want of a better name, an anti-JACL group; and then the third group that was anti-JACL and anti-administration and perhaps pro-Japan.

But in describing the second group, which I suppose would encompass *Doho* and your own position, he writes, "Group II, an anti-JACL group, a term used only for want of a better name, this faction in pre-war days held a reputation among the Japanese population generally as being *aka*, Red, meaning Communist. In a community where economic control or dominance was held largely by a Japanese-speaking, non-citizen element, to be labeled *aka* was synonymous with ostracism. It was a complete and utter brush-off. You just didn't belong. It should be mentioned here that individual, political thinking was neither characteristic nor conspicuous. Among the so-called anti-JACL group, however, it was. Some individuals who shied away from this group for personal, economic, or social reasons considered it more as a left wing, liberal, or progressive group, rather than the *aka* label more generally recognized."[12]

Anyway, he later on claims in his analysis that, during the riot, Group I individuals, who were JACLers, found themselves on the death list. Group II individuals usually found themselves only on the black list. He says that "it should be recalled that members of Group II, this *aka* group, arrived at Manzanar as evacuees before Group I. This was true almost without exception. Group II members established themselves at the relocation centers first. When Group I, JACL members, arrived a month or so later, they generally discovered that Group II had laid the mines and torpedoes in advance of our coming. They prepared the administration and the volunteer evacuees for a hostile reception for us. They kept up the vicious rumors to perpetuate themselves in their petty, little jobs, continuing jealousies and frictions of pre-war and evacuation days. On the other hand, Group II members felt justified in their attitude toward the late-comers. Troublemakers and would-be big shots, the whole lot, the JACL should have sense enough to know that the people are fed up and sick of its name. They were so used to grabbing self-control on everything. When they discovered that they couldn't do it at Manzanar, they began agitation. They should have kept their trap shut and minded their own business."[13]

Okay, so he sets down two groups, the main point being that he claims people like James Oda, yourself, Tom Yamazaki, and Koji Ariyoshi came to Manzanar first, took control basically of positions, and then more or less jockeyed the JACL crowd out of those positions. And I imagine he's talking about the newspaper and perhaps other jobs that were available to "evacuees." Do you have any comment on that analysis?

Yoneda: Well, I think he stresses this number two group a little too much. Because it was true that—I'll say this much about JACL. You have to give the JACL people credit for staying as the last persons in the communities so that all Japanese [Americans] were properly attended [to], such as filling out records and making arrangements for the "evacuees" as much as they could under the circumstances. Without them, the people, particularly Issei, would be left without leaders. So they did serve the people.

However, when they arrived—particularly in the case of Manzanar—they began establishing the post office and the other administrative sections. And they grabbed all this clerical work and administrative work, naturally, because of their knowledge and skill, such as typing. Among the Kibei and Issei, we didn't have those kinds of skills. So it's natural that they got that kind of a job.

On the other hand, as far as I'm concerned, I never had any anti-JACL feeling or antagonism toward the JACL people. Myself and our group, we didn't have organized meetings, but in the camp you meet every day, so we talked and so forth. One of our main aims was to try and work together, get along with everybody, because the "evacuation" would last long years. That's what we estimated. And we were going to be there for a long time.

In the meantime, we were, more or less, you know, the dreamers on the council [Block Leaders Council] there. We thought that we were going to establish sort of a model camp for the rest of the "relocation" camps. We were going to start a democratic constitution, with bylaws, a copy of the US Constitution, as well as Bill of Rights. So we talked about these things with the camp administrator. "Okay, we'll appoint you on the Constitution Committee to draw up the bylaws of the camp." So they appointed Ted Akahoshi, an Issei and a Stanford graduate, a very capable guy. Then Tommy Yamazaki and me. Three of us. You can imagine three of us. All three of us, more or less, when it comes to operation camp, had about the same ideas. We tried to establish the kind of camp that the rest of America would look up to, a really nice camp, so that maybe we wouldn't need to stay there too long. We thought that maybe we could win the confidence of the American public.

So we sat down, and naturally when the JACL group began coming in, they started to raise hell. They don't like a bunch of *aka* sitting on that committee trying to run the camp. And naturally this talk spread all over camp, and it made it very difficult for us to operate. But, on the other hand, we did many things that influenced the administration to improve camp conditions.

My wife, Elaine, took a very active part, too. She's an outspoken woman. Anything that was wrong with camp, particularly matters concerning women, she barged into the administration office and pounded the table, saying, "You have to do this or that, otherwise the camp will be in turmoil." She complained about such things as the conditions of the women's toilets. A noble person—especially Japanese [ancestry] women, they don't dare do that. It's not for them. It's not the way they are trained. A Japanese woman's part is to be in the kitchen.

Hansen: Did it create some hostility toward you because your wife was acting in a non-Japanese way? Did that make it tougher on you to operate within the camp with respect to the rest of the community? Because if you already had one strike against you, in the same sense that you were labeled an *aka*, and then all of a sudden you had this additional one of having an untypically Japanese type of wife—

Yoneda: Well, camp people resented, too, that I brought a Caucasian wife into camp. Some of them said, "Well, you know, she has the right to stay outside of camp. Why does she have to come into camp and become sort of a sore thumb?" It was easy for some to point out the ways that she didn't fit into the Japanese [American] community. Naturally, in the camp you didn't have anything to do, so camp became really a rumor factory. You can't imagine every day some of the rumors I noted in my diary. It will really blow your

FIGURE 20. Karl And Elaine Black Yoneda at their San Francisco home, March 1974. Photo by Betty Mitson. Courtesy Lawrence de Graaf Center for Oral and Public History, California State University, Fullerton.

mind. I mean, these people figured out that tomorrow morning they're going to cut people in on this story or that story. They were cooking up stories because they had nothing else to do.

For instance, we arrived in camp and a couple of days later somebody spread a rumor saying that the army killed about five or six Japanese [Americans]. Nobody asked how or what. One tells one, another tells another, and the rumor spreads throughout the camp. And another time they said, "Japan is winning the war so they won't keep us here too long. They're going to ship us to an isolated island someplace, so be prepared."

Hansen: So you became a block leader, and you were in Block 4. When they formed the Block Leaders Council, the procedure, initially, was to have the block nominate three candidates, and then the administration would have final determination over which of the candidates was appointed block leader. So you apparently were one of three, then later were appointed by the administration. Do you think your appointment was a popular one with the people in Block 4?

Yoneda: Well, at the beginning, three or four names were submitted. But under my name it stated that I had the support of the majority in my block, that's Block 4. They considered, "This guy is an outspoken man; maybe he'll do whatever we want, and he's able to meet face-to-face with the administration."

Hansen: Did it help because you were a Kibei in being able to speak both languages, too, so that you could meet with the needs of the Nisei on the one hand and the Issei on the other?

Yoneda: Not so much Kibei as my past record being known as an *aka*. At that time there wasn't such a strong antagonism toward the so-called *aka* group.

Hansen: They just wanted someone who would be forthright and able to present their grievances to the administration.

Yoneda: Right.

Hansen: What about the Block Leaders Council once it coalesced? What did you think of that organization, or what was its composition? Was it basically Issei, basically Nisei, what? What was it to begin with?

Yoneda: Let me see. At the beginning there were very few Nisei, [it was] mostly Issei and Kibei.

Hansen: So they appointed people who were previously leaders in the community?

Yoneda: Yes.

Hansen: Who were some of the leading figures within the Block Leaders Council? Ted Akahoshi was the block leader—

Yoneda: No, he was not the block leader. He was the chairman of the Block Leaders Council. Most of the other people I didn't know, because they came from the Los Angeles area. Most of the people who lived in a certain block knew this particular person—that they chose as their block leader—from prewar days.

Hansen: Did you find yourself somewhat isolated on the council by the fact that you were, for one thing, from San Francisco and, secondly, because of your political background?

Yoneda: Not at the beginning. They took the attitude of "Wait and see what he has to say." They had the idea, "Well, here is a guy who did a lot of organizing in unions and was also active in politics, we'll see what he says." Whatever I said, therefore, they listened to it.

Hansen: Did you speak quite a bit at the council meetings?

Yoneda: Oh, yes. Oh, yes.

Hansen: Who else on the council—on the early council—were outspoken individuals?

Yoneda: Well, Ted Akahoshi, and also Tom Yamazaki took an active part in it.
Hansen: They shared most of your positions, didn't they?
Yoneda: Yes.
Hansen: What about some of the Issei that were on the council?
Yoneda: Issei didn't say much.
Hansen: Were the meetings originally, then, conducted in English, Japanese, or both?
Yoneda: English. And the Issei spoke in Japanese. Usually Tom Yamazaki or someone acted as their interpreter. The Issei spoke very seldom. I guess they were just feeling around. And at the same time they never faced this kind of situation.
Hansen: What about the Kibei?
Yoneda: The Kibei, too.
Hansen: They were pretty silent as well?
Yoneda: Except one or two, like this guy Shigetoshi Tateishi.[14] Let me see, is he a Kibei or an Issei? I forgot, but he took the floor quite often.
Hansen: Did he have any position that was in opposition to your own?
Yoneda: No.
Hansen: It was just that he happened to speak out within the council.
Yoneda: Well, at a council meeting, usually—you know, the policies are laid down by the administration already, so we can't say much. Actually, the council is not the camp policy-deciding body. Whatever instructions came down from the administration offices; we simply discussed how to carry it out. You can't say no.
Hansen: So what you could do was to decide on ways to either carry out a measure more effectively or not. In other words, by cooperating, you could implement programs and help facilitate WRA policies.
Yoneda: Yes. Well, in many cases we were the first ones to speak in favor of a policy decision. If it is against our wishes, we will speak against it. I didn't come across any instances where camp policies were not in our favor except, you know, when the instruction came from Washington, DC, that all Block Council Leaders meeting[s] will be conducted in English. That's where we made a mistake. We should have allowed Issei to speak in Japanese. So that really added another item to the fire. They spread the story right away, "Well, these guys won't even let us speak Japanese in the camp."
Hansen: Why did you not want them to speak Japanese?
Yoneda: Well, at that time we felt that these Issei began to take the floor, and sometimes they spoke in such a way as to hint the pro-Japan sentiment. Their oratory sometimes became strong, "You don't belong here." Or some

Issei would end a speech with *bonsai*, you know, which usually we say at a Japanese national holiday. When we get together, we end up with *tenno heika, bonzai, emperor bonzai* [Long Live His Majesty the Emperor], you know. In other instances, we don't use that.

Hansen: You mean that you were getting some pro-Japan sentiment at the Block Leaders Council meetings?

Yoneda: Yes, it began to show, so we sort of limited discussions to English only so that we wouldn't hear these pro-Japan phrases being thrown up. These people were more or less—that was their way to protest, I guess.

Hansen: What about the Manzanar Citizens Federation? What was the rationale behind starting that, and when did it first emerge?

Yoneda: Manzanar Citizens Federation, the first meeting I did not attend. I was not invited. Koji Ariyoshi, Togo Tanaka, and others got together and thought that since the JACL leaders couldn't express their real feelings or their ideas, then maybe they ought to have an organization that is mutual to, more or less, the larger organization.

Hansen: You mean they didn't have much of an input into the Block Leaders Council so they set up an alternative organization that would be able to have some policy statements voiced at camp?

Yoneda: That's why, I guess, they started. But when James Oda and myself came in, we turned it around and made it into an entirely different organization altogether, which they didn't like, because as soon as we got in, we took over the leadership. Koji Ariyoshi, myself, and James Oda became the new leaders, and Togo Tanaka, Joe Grant Masaoka, and Fred Tayama didn't say boo when we decided to have a mass meeting. They said, "Well, Karl, you speak." I said, "Okay, I'll speak on the war efforts of the 'evacuees.'" And even Mrs. Miyo Kikuchi,[15] a social worker, was supposed to speak on camp conditions. She declined at the last minute. So this fellow from Hawai'i, Hiro Neeno, spoke. Togo Tanaka and Joe Grant Masaoka also spoke at the first mass meeting, so there were four speakers.

Hansen: This was on July 28, 1942, then. What were the differences in philosophy with respect to the Citizens Federation? How did the JACL look at its purpose, and how did the people in your group look at its purpose differently?

Yoneda: One of the purposes was to push this petition drive. This was not done in the name of the federation. But through the Citizens Federation, we saw that we had more support among "evacuees."

Hansen: Which petition drive was this, to establish a second front?

Yoneda: Yes, open a second front and utilize manpower of Japanese Americans within the camps. I think we obtained only about 214 signatures. Among them, I think, were about forty women. Even we were surprised. These women said, "I'll join if they allowed Japanese Americans to serve in the American Army service."

Hansen: And what was the JACL's philosophy? How did that differ? What do you think they wanted out of the organization?

Yoneda: Well, the JACL people—actually, they don't know what to do, you see. Many times, they asked us, you know, "What do you think?" Because we were really the driving force within the Manzanar Citizens Federation. Although opening the second front, that's the Communist Party line. There is no such physical condition existing in the United States. The United States is just building up its armed strength. It is impossible to open a second front in 1942. So they have to open it later, in 1944, two years later, you see. You need preparation. But they took it slow on this. Why don't they open a second front—in our way of thinking, this was a way to help the Russian front, because the Russian front is being beaten by Nazis, and the Russians keep on retreating. And if we open a second front, why, Hitler will divert most of the force toward the European front. This way, this will help the Soviet Union. That's our thinking. And that's also the party line, too.

Hansen: So you, in a sense, maneuvered the JACL into certain policies through the Citizens Federation. In a sense, they didn't know what they were doing at this period.

Yoneda: No, not even Togo Tanaka or Joe Grant Masaoka. They signed our petition. "Oh, it's a good idea." Of course, one of the driving forces was Koji Ariyoshi.

Hansen: He was made president as a strategic device, I imagine, because he really was not connected with JACL, and he was from Hawai'i. He wasn't even so much connected with any left-wing activities in the States, is that right? So he was a strategic choice, acceptable to all parties.

Yoneda: Right.

Hansen: But, by in large, the Citizens Federation somewhat backfired as a device in camp, didn't it?

Yoneda: Well, naturally the formation of this organization created opposition, mainly from Joe Kurihara and Ben Kishi. They didn't come from any organization. But in one meeting—my Manzanar diary shows—they came to a group meeting, and Joe Kurihara questioned the name of the Manzanar Citizens Federation. He suggested that it be changed to the Manzanar Welfare

Federation. And when a vote was taken, we narrowly won. Let's see, the vote was about 214 to 210 or something.

Hansen: Do you think this Manzanar Citizens Federation excited a lot of resentment on the part of Issei?

Yoneda: Among the Issei we had many supporters. At least the Manzanar Citizens Federation was also asking that the manpower in camp be used to save the crops in the Idaho and Wyoming areas. And the first group came back from Idaho—Koji Ariyoshi and his men. I think about six or seven hundred went to Idaho. They made a good impression in Idaho. In the meantime, they earned quite a sum of money. They came back, and many in the camp said, "We will ask for a follow-through, and then we'll go out to where they need us to."

Hansen: So this won some favor with the Issei, then?

Yoneda: Yes. Well, not only Issei. Nisei, too.

Hansen: What was the big resentment against the Manzanar Citizens Federation?

Yoneda: Well, it mainly came from Ben Kishi and his group.

Hansen: Who is this Ben Kishi exactly? I know he was a young fellow about twenty-two years old.

Yoneda: I describe him as a Meiji-Samurai type. He says something very exciting that people go for. I forgot some of the things he said. But for instance, when he opened the Kibei meeting, he didn't say, "Men are dying in Asia," but "Men are dying; let's stand up and have a one-minute silence." He put it in such a way that everybody, even myself, wondered, "My god, what the hell's this guy trying to prove?" Later I figured out, my gosh, this guy is really pulling this pro-Japan stunt.

Hansen: Did you think of him as intelligent?

Yoneda: No, he isn't. He's one of those ghetto-boss type of guys.

Hansen: He knew how to pull the right strings.

Yoneda: Oh, yes. He knows how to maneuver: "You follow me; you listen to me; I'll take care of you."

Hansen: Did you see him as the major leader of any pro-Japan sentiment within the camp? Did you think that Kishi was the leader?

Yoneda: Oh, yes, definitely, the leading "open" spokesman from the start.

Hansen: Much more so than, say, somebody like Harry Ueno?

Yoneda: Ueno is such an unknown figure. He talks about organizing the kitchen workers union. To me, through my experience of organizing, he just had a handful of followers, mostly in his kitchen and among the strong pro-Japan kitchen crew members in my block, Block 4. So he and his group used to come to Kitchen 4, and after supper they used to have a meeting in the kitchen. They used to tell the waitresses, "You people go home; this is a men's affair." And it would turn out to be a meeting that they had. Actually, they don't have an organization such as the Kitchen Workers Union. They merely named themselves.

Hansen: So they didn't really have much of a following either. The kitchen workers constituted about a third of the workforce at Manzanar.

Yoneda: Yes.

Hansen: But of this group, very few of them identified in any real strong sense with the Kitchen Workers Union.

Yoneda: No, I don't think so, because I was there. If they had such a strong force, I'm sure I would detect it right away.

Hansen: Well, what kind of an organization did exist at Manzanar around pro-Japan sentiment that coalesced? Was there an organization, or was it a series of groupings here, there, and elsewhere that had common indignation over specific causes?

Yoneda: Well, I'll say that loose bodies such as the Blood Brothers would get together, and they'd call themselves by various names. In the case of the Manzanar Citizens Federation, we met and had a secretary there who took minutes of each committee meeting as well as mass meetings. I don't know what happened to our minutes. At the first Manzanar Citizens Federation meeting, we elected three secretaries to take the minutes—only Nisei university students. In fact, they volunteered. "Does anybody want to take minutes?" And three of them said okay. But we should have kept the minutes. I have kept most of the documents that were issued or made in Manzanar camp.

Hansen: They have a folder on the Manzanar Citizens Federation in the Manzanar collection at UCLA, and I'm pretty sure that they have those minutes from the first couple of meetings there. I don't recall seeing them right offhand, but they might be there. They do have a folder which deals only with the Manzanar Citizens Federation material.

Yoneda: We had many committee meetings at Togo Tanaka's apartment, so-called apartment. It's only one room. And I think Joe Masaoka acted as secretary. And he took down all the things that we said, but that too, I guess, was lost someplace. In my diary I just put down who attended and what they discussed.

Hansen: Getting back for a second to Ben Kishi, you said that he was definitely the number one leader of pro-Japan sentiment. What did his organization or following consist of exactly? Who was he appealing to?

Yoneda: Well, this group that he had—I figured this was a way to express their dissatisfaction, create turmoil, or to protest. Whatever comes along, they just go after somebody, whether it's me or Tokie Slocum or anybody else.

For instance, Ben Kishi and his scavenger crewmembers had access to a truck, so they used to drive around in the truck every day and pick up garbage cans. So they'd meet more camp people than us. The weather is sometimes unbearable, going as high as 114, 115 degrees. And if you walked from one block to the next block, you get tired. You can't go from one end of the camp to Togo Tanaka's place in Block 36. It's about a mile, mile-and-a-half walk. Even in the evening the sun is way up, and by the time you get there, you'd be pretty tired. So it's very hard to find out actually what is taking place in the camp. The only way to find out is through the grapevine. Naturally, through the grapevine many untrue stories and rumors get mixed with fact.

Hansen: Were you aware of Ben Kishi fairly early?

Yoneda: No, I encountered him in camp.

Hansen: I mean, within the time you were in camp, did you know of his hostility?

Yoneda: Oh, yes, practically every day. Because his scavenger crew members passed by Block 4, and we had the Block 4 office located in one of the apartments. So we sat there, and Kishi's scavenger trucks would pass by shouting out some name, such as "you damn Korean *inu*" or "FBI spy."

Hansen: Were they shouting this at you in Japanese?

Yoneda: Yes.

Hansen: Were they mostly Kibei in the scavenger crew?

Yoneda: Oh, yes. Some of them came from Terminal Island. Some of them belonged to a judoist club.

Hansen: On August 8, 1942, at the Kibei meeting that you talked about earlier, there was a lot of hostility directed against Nisei and against the JACL and against the Manzanar Citizens Federation. There was a lot of pro-Japan sentiment aired there. And one of the things that the meeting [was] called to protest was the fact that the Kibei were disallowed to be available for relocation, to take off [from camp and settle in the free area of the country]. But I read in the documents, subsequently, that both you and Ben Kishi, both of whom were Kibei, went off to Idaho. How did that come about?

Yoneda: Let me tell you the incident. Ben Kishi came to me and said, "We'll have a meeting. I want you to be a speaker." I said, "Who is organizing the meeting?" "One of my group." "What do you mean, your group?" "Well, you know, us. The several of us get together and we want to organize for this meeting, and I want you to be a speaker." So I said, "No, I won't speak at your meeting. You go ahead and have your own meeting."

Then he went to the administration office and told the administrators, "Karl Yoneda is one of the speakers. Give us permission to have a meeting." On that basis he got the permission, you see. For any gathering you have to get permission. So I must be a very important person. Later the administration asked me, you see, "You sure you gave the consent for this kind of meeting?" "No, no, I refused to be a speaker."

But at the Kibei meeting they asked anyone to speak, to take the mic. And of course, in my case, they shouted me down. (laughs) They called me all kinds of names. But I was stubborn enough, and I decided not to budge a step but to stay put. I wasn't going to speak my piece until the crown quieted down. I said a few things, but I'm sure the crowd didn't listen. They didn't know what I said.

Then Jimmy Oda, he spoke. He spoke in such a fashion that the crowd listened to him. He appealed toward them all being Japanese: "Why do you have to fight each other?" That's how he got the crowd to listen to him. Then he started to go into what we're supposed to do, and then the crowd started shouting at him that he was a spy and an *inu*. And he couldn't continue either.

Hansen: Now, I read the minutes of that particular meeting, and they were recorded from memory the next morning by Fred Tayama. What was he, a Nisei, doing at a Kibei meeting?

Yoneda: He was, I guess, a bystander. Inside there were about two hundred people. It was very hot, you see, so all the windows were open. And outside there were easily about three hundred or four hundred people. So most likely he and others maybe went over there among the crowd. When you have about five hundred to six hundred people, you know, it's pretty hard to notice who is there.

Hansen: That means that to a large extent the Kibei were rapidly reaching the point of becoming outrightly pro-Japan, right?

Yoneda: Not only Kibei. Many high-school-age boys participated. And this is understandable. They have nothing to do, and here comes someone telling them, "Your citizenship paper is nothing but a scrap of paper, and what you've learned about US democracy is phony." And they buy it. "Here you are in concentration camps the same as us, the same as your parents." And so they'll buy it. But that's all there is. They don't know what to do.

Hansen: Were there any intellectuals among the pro-Japan group?

Yoneda: There weren't any.

Hansen: So by and large it was people like Ben Kishi.

Yoneda: The muscle type and all, I guess. You know, I don't see any intellectualism in Hitler. How come people follow him? Ben Kishi is that kind of type. He doesn't have any big figure. I don't know why some of them admire him. Whatever he says, everybody agreed with him, followed him. It is very hard to describe what kind of a guy he is.

Hansen: What about Joe Kurihara? How does he fit into this? Would you describe him as a leader or a person who was just used? Or as somebody who was bitter for personal reasons and all of a sudden then turned out to make statements that were helpful to the pro-Japan cause? I mean, here was a guy who was a citizen, had fought in World War I, and had also earned a good livelihood. He made quite a bit of money before the war.

Yoneda: Oh, yes.

Hansen: He tried to volunteer to get into the service, the Merchant Marines. He was turned down there. He gets into camp and then finds the situation there not very much to his liking either. Then he becomes outrightly, like he says in this one speech, "I'm one hundred percent Jap, and that's how I'm going to act from now on." What was his role in relationship to people like Kishi?

Yoneda: Well, at least with Joe Kurihara, I could talk to that guy. You see, Ben Kishi, you couldn't talk to that guy. Right away an argument starts, and you call each other names, so I didn't like to talk to him. But this Joe Kurihara, you can sit down and talk to this guy. You see, he listens to reason. I'll say he spoke for himself, not that he wants to take over the leadership. He outrightly expressed his feelings. Rightly so, on many occasions, most of the people want, "Well, Joe, you take over the leadership; you lead us and we'll follow." He's not that kind of a guy. Whereas with Ben Kishi, they said, "You are right, you spoke your piece; you take over and lead us. We'll follow you wherever you go."

Hansen: Did he have any following among the Issei?

Yoneda: Not so many, maybe a handful.

Hansen: How would you characterize the Issei sentiment in camp during the time that you were there? Would you say that it was increasingly becoming, although still silent, more pro-Japan than when they first came to the camp?

Yoneda: Well, I would say so. If they don't become more pro-Japan, there's something wrong with them, you know.

Hansen: You mean, because of the experience they had in camp?

Yoneda: Yes.

Hansen: So it's justifiable in a sense. You felt the growing pro-Japan feeling then, while you were there?

Yoneda: Yes.

Hansen: And it was registered by hostility directed against you for your pro-American stand?

Yoneda: Yes. For instance, when I volunteered for the Military Intelligence Service, James Oda asked me, "What about the camp people? If we leave here, they will be in the hands of these terrorists. Who will protect them?" So I told Jimmy that we had better things to do than dealing with ten thousand people, which was true. And after we talked it over, Jimmy agreed with me: "Yes, I'll volunteer, and I'll go with you."

Hansen: So you had some kind of strategic choice to make?

Yoneda: Yes. And when I left camp, I felt sorry for the people that were left behind.

Hansen: I bet you also felt frightened about what might happen to your wife and child,[16] too, didn't you? Hadn't you been attacked earlier?

Yoneda: Yes, that's what I expected. You know, I was in the movement for many years, and this was expected. I thought, If anything happens, I'll not be surprised. But I really felt sorry for those who were left behind, especially for those who supported our cause and our opinion.

Hansen: Would you say that your main reason for your pro-American position in camp was because you wanted to defeat the Fascists or because you wanted to uphold the democratic way of life? Or were you phrasing the one in terms of the other?

Yoneda: No, upholding the democratic way of life was secondary. Well, you had to say so. We were trying to get the confidence of the US government. (laughs) But I never paid much attention to so-called American democracy.

Hansen: So that would almost be a difference between your group and the JACL group.

Yoneda: Yes.

Hansen: Whereas you were really concerned with defeating somebody, they were concerned with preserving a particular way of life that was really objectionable to you to begin with, wasn't it?

Yoneda: Yes.

Hansen: I mean, American capitalism wasn't something that you were really fighting to uphold.

Yoneda: I had the future of the Japanese [Americans] in my heart always. I figured out what is the best for us is to survive this war. And when the war is over—I told many of them, "Suppose we resist en masse. What will happen to us after the war? We will be called all kinds of names. You know, you bunch of slackers, you bunch of SOBs. Here we shed our blood to defeat Hitler, Mussolini, and Tojo. You guys sat on your asses and didn't do a damn thing." But, on the other hand, those who resisted being drafted in 1943, 1944, for this I certainly condemn the actions of the government. They have no business drafting those that were kept in camps. That's really one of the greatest mistakes that the government made.[17]

Hansen: Did you feel uncomfortable, psychologically, in camp? All of a sudden becoming a flag-waver when your past was basically concerned with exposing certain kinds of injustices under the name of patriotism? I mean, here suddenly the people you're linked with are Tokie Slocum, who is a super-patriot wearing his flag on his sleeve, and Fred Tayama, who is an exploitive capitalist, who you had been attacking right along the line with *Doho*, as almost the number one enemy of the Japanese American community, because of his policies and wage scale. And now these are the people that you're in shop with, that you're doing business with.

Yoneda: Well, I wasn't too closely associated with them. But we talked these things over, and sometimes we have to do these kinds of thing[s], you know, to achieve your aim. Just like the Soviet Union had to make a pact with Hitler, which astonished thousands of Soviet supporters as well as liberals, too. "How could you shake hands with the bloody hand of Hitler?" Here Hitler is killing left and right, not only Communists, but trade union activists and also many Jews, in the camps. And here the Soviet Union was supposed to be a defender of freedom. But sometimes you have to do that.

Hansen: So it was a question, then, of maintaining a higher morality, keeping that in mind while in the meantime you might resort to more expedient devices or coalitions?

Yoneda: Well, this we told to Togo Tanaka, Fred Tayama, and others, "If you want to survive this war, you should not only give your lip service, but support the US government through actually participating in fighting, maybe shedding your blood." And they all agreed that they were not aggressive enough. That's why Fred and Togo and Joe Grant Masaoka didn't volunteer. You hear a story about the Masaoka brothers all volunteering, but Joe Grant stayed behind.

Hansen: And Togo Tanaka worked for the Quakers in Chicago, didn't he?

Yoneda: Yes. So they were really forced to adopt this resolution asking the US government to draft the Nisei at the JACL convention in November 1942.

Hansen: The Salt Lake [City] convention.

Yoneda: Yes.

Hansen: I have a few more questions about camp which I would like to ask you before concluding the interview. I had thought that the Manzanar Charter Commission—which was formed to draw up a revised camp governmental structure—was headed by Togo Tanaka. But in the reports that I have read, it merely states that a Mr. T. was head of it. Was it Togo Tanaka who was adamantly holding out for the constitution, whereby only citizens could serve on the council that they were going to implement? Or were you gone from camp at the time that this issue surfaced?

Yoneda: Yes, I think Togo participated in that. He is not an aggressive type, you know. You have to coax him into something. He'll say, "Yes, that's right, that's right," but that's it. In the case of Fred Tayama, he won't agree with something that he doesn't like to hear. But in the end, in most of the cases, he agreed with us: "Yes, you are right." What else can they say, you know? Because they are not the ones who first proposed that the government utilize the manpower of the Japanese Americans in the camp. We were the ones who proposed it first, as soon as we landed in Manzanar. And they realized that was the only way. That's why Mike Masaoka, executive secretary of the JACL, and others got our message.

Hansen: The policy came out that way.

Yoneda: Yes, that's right. In fact, I have a letter from Mike Masaoka, written, I think, in July or August of 1942, asking [for] my cooperation.

Hansen: I understood that at one point about fourteen individuals came to your block and spent about an hour or so in your apartment, with the intention of either maiming you or in some other way doing harm to you. But they refrained because your wife and your child were both there in the apartment. Do you recall that situation?

Yoneda: Yes.

Hansen: What exactly was the nature of the episode, and who was involved in that?

Yoneda: Well, Ben Kishi was the spokesman, and I recognized the rest of them. I had a hunch right away that they really came to get me, either beat up or cripple me. And I decided, well, even one against fourteen, I'll fight them. So I stood near the wall by the window so in case I had to get out, I could get out through the window. But I noticed that outside the window were about ten or fifteen guys marching back and forth, and all of them belonged to the judoist club headed by Seigoro Murakami. Incidentally, Murakami was given a nice black belt, which is more or less an honorary procedure on the part of the Kodokan [school of judo]. There was a big ceremony in Los Angeles a couple years ago. It was about seven or eight years ago. Very smooth operator, never says anything, just directs, do this and do that. He lived in our block. That's how I knew him pretty well.

Hansen: Did Kishi have that group at his disposal to use for intimidation purposes?

Yoneda: Yes. What led to that incident was that at the Block Leaders Council meeting I had made a report of what transpired at the Kibei mass meeting. Kishi and his group asked me to retract what I had said at the previous block meeting at the forthcoming block council meeting. And I refused. "Whatever I said is the truth, and I'm not going to change it."

So this kept them going back and forth, back and forth. And of course I'm ready to jump on or take on any one of them, so they didn't dare move. I sensed it right away. If anyone moved, I was ready to get up and start to fight.

So this continued for about two hours until somebody said, "Well, don't you have a mother that lives in Hiroshima? All I have to do is inform the Japanese government that her son is anti-Japan and speaks against the Japanese emperor and the Japanese government. We'll fix up your mother." When I heard this, I realized that, wow, he meant what he said. This really made me madder than anything. And when they get down to this kind of situation, it becomes personalized, and it's either you or me. And especially you felt that very strongly in the camp. So I have no place to go and they have no place to go. I guess they were willing to give a life to get rid of me. But because of my stubbornness—and you know, I shouted back and forth. I shouted louder than them, you see. Finally, they retreated. I thought they'd really get me and that I'd be a goner. (laughs)

Hansen: They left peacefully, then?

Yoneda: Oh, yes.

Hansen: And what about the fact that sometimes these salvage trucks used to try to run you over. Was that a repeated thing, or was that just once?

Yoneda: Well, I got wise to them. When a salvage truck came down to Block 4, then I stayed away or just stayed inside so I wouldn't be bothered by them.

Hansen: So the last couple of months that you were in Manzanar, you were pretty much on alert all the time for any sort of foul play.

Yoneda: Well, fortunately, I had Jimmy Oda and several others who supported me physically. Just two nights before we left for Minnesota, Jimmy and the others stayed with me in the apartment.

Hansen: Oh, they stayed within your apartment? To give you some kind of protection?

Yoneda: Yes.

Hansen: Well, I don't have any further questions, so I'd just like to thank you very much, Mr. Yoneda, for all your cooperation. Your interview has been most informative and interesting.

NOTES

1. Biographical information is from the following sources: Yoneda, CSUF-COPH O.H. 1376a and 1376b.

2. The interview transcript reproduced below is from CSUF-COPH O.H. 1376b.

3. See "Sei Fujii," *Wikipedia*, https://en.wikipedia.org/wiki/Sei_Fujii (accessed February 17, 2021).

4. According to Karl Yoneda's autobiography, *Ganbatte: Sixty-Year Struggle of a Kibei Worker* (Los Angeles: Asian American Studies Center, UCLA, 1983), Koide's true name was Nobumichi Ukai.

5. See Brian Niiya, "Buddy Uno," *Densho Encyclopedia*, https://encyclopedia.densho.org/Buddy_Uno/ (accessed February 17, 2021).

6. See Alice Yang, "Edison Uno," *Densho Encyclopedia*, https://encyclopedia.densho.org/Edison_Uno/ (accessed February 17, 2021).

7. See Jonathan van Harmelen, "An Activist's Dilemma: The Life of Katsuma Mukaeda," *Discover Nikkei*, August 29, 2019, http://www.discovernikkei.org/en/journal/2019/8/29/katsuma-mukaeda/ (accessed February 17, 2021).

8. See *"Pacific Citizen," Wikipedia*, https://en.wikipedia.org/wiki/Pacific_Citizen (accessed February 17, 2021). For a biography of Larry Tajiri, the newspaper's principal World War II editor, see Greg Robinson, *Pacific Citizens: Larry and Guyo Tajiri and Japanese American Journalism in the World War II Era* (Urbana: University Press of Illinois, 2012), as well as Robinson, "Larry Tajiri," *Densho Encyclopedia*, https://encyclopedia.densho.org/Larry_Tajiri/ (accessed February 17, 2021).

9. See Brian Niiya, "Yasuo Abiko," *Densho Encyclopedia*, https://encyclopedia.densho.org/Yasuo%20Abiko/ (accessed February 17, 2021).

10. For more information about this ethnic enclave, see "Japantown, San Francisco," *Wikipedia*, https://en.wikipedia.org/wiki/Japantown,_San_Francisco (accessed February 28, 2021).

11. See Brian Niiya's entry for this newspaper (*Sekai Asahi*) in the *Densho Encyclopedia*, https://encyclopedia.densho.org/Shin%20Sekai%20(newspaper)/ (accessed November 21, 2022).

12. Togo Tanaka, "A Report on the Manzanar Riot of Sunday, December 6, 1942," 409–10, Bancroft Library, UCB, JERS, O10.12.

13. Togo Tanaka, "A Report on the Manzanar Riot of Sunday, December 6, 1942," 413, Bancroft Library, UCB, JERS, O10.12.

14. Born in 1907, at Manzanar Shigetoshi Tateishi was the Kibei block leader of Block 23, and at the time of the Manzanar Revolt he was a member of the five-person inmate negotiating committee.

15. See Brian Niiya, "Miya Sannomiya Kikuchi," *Densho Encyclopedia*, https://encyclopedia.densho.org/Miya%20Sannomiya%20Kikuchi/ (accessed February 17, 2021).

16. Tommy Yoneda's experience at Manzanar is described in more detail in the interview with Elaine Black Yoneda later in part 2.

17. For information on the World War II draft resisters, see Eric L. Muller, *Free to Die for Their Country: The Story of the Japanese American Draft Resisters in World War II* (Chicago: University of Chicago Press, 2001), and Muller, "Draft Resistance," *Densho Encyclopedia*, https://encyclopedia.densho.org/Draft_resistance/#:~:text=The%20phrase%20%22draft%20resistance%22%20refers%20to%20resistance%20by,largest%20numbers%20coming%20from%20Poston%20and%20Heart%20Mountain (accessed February 17, 2021).

Partisan

An Interview with Elaine Black Yoneda

*A fervent supporter or proponent of a party, cause,
faction, person, or idea.*

Elaine Black Yoneda was born as Rose Elaine Buchman on September 4, 1906, in Manhattan, New York.[1] Her Russian Jewish immigrant parents, Nathan and Mollie Buchman, were raised in the Russian village of Kimberoffka, Mozyr, in the state of Minsk. There both of them had worked in a match factory, starting as children, and as they matured they became active in the underground Bund, fighting against the terrorism and the horrors of the czar's regime. In 1904 Nathan fled to the tenement area of Manhattan to avoid conscription into the czar's army, and later sent for Mollie. Having apprenticed as a barber in Russia, Nathan found work in Manhattan as a barber, whereas Mollie, who had a beautiful figure, found employment as a shirtwaist factory model.

When Elaine was nine months old, the family moved to Pennsylvania, where her father continued his barbering but also found work in the mines to supplement his income. But working in a damp place was too trying for him, so he moved the family to Waterbury, Connecticut, where Elaine's brother was born in 1909. Very shortly thereafter, the family moved once

FIGURE 21. Elaine Black Yoneda at the Yonedas' San Francisco home, March 1974. Photo by Betty Mitson. Courtesy Lawrence de Graaf Center for Oral and Public History, California State University, Fullerton.

again, this time to Brooklyn, New York, where they remained until 1920, when they relocated still once more to Lemon Grove, California, now a suburb of San Diego, where Nathan had two sisters. Having gotten out of barbering in Brooklyn, Nathan, along with Mollie, operated a small department store. Then in 1923 the Buchman family moved north to Los Angeles, where Nathan and Mollie bought a neighborhood store that sold primarily dry goods and shoes. It also included a county library section, which was maintained by Elaine.

After attending business college, Elaine found work in a hotel office doing bookkeeping, which she hated. So much, in fact, that she quit her job and, in 1925, married a man named Ed Black, who worked as a machinist and who had pragmatically changed his surname, Russell, to Black in order to not lose his job because of his alleged association with the Communist Party's International Labor Defense (ILD) organization. At the same time, Elaine started identifying herself as Elaine Black. In 1927 Ed and Elaine had a daughter, Joyce. In 1930 Elaine joined the ILD, while Ed affiliated himself with the left-wing Trade Union Unity League. In 1931, in her capacity as an ILD representative, she bailed out of jail her future husband, Karl Yoneda, then a Communist Party member going by the name of Karl Hama, who had been beaten and arrested by the Los Angeles police for his activities as a demonstrator. At the end of that same year, both Elaine and Ed joined the Communist Party. Not too long after that action, in 1932 they separated, and Elaine started dating Karl.

In April of 1933, Elaine moved to San Francisco, where she was employed as a district secretary for the ILD. A month later, Karl also relocated to San Francisco. There they both continued their activities in the civil rights, labor, and union movements. Unable to get married because anti-miscegenation laws in California made it illegal for them to get married in the state, they "lived in sin" together until November 5, 1935, when they got married in Seattle, Washington. Together they maintained their political activism, both before and after their marriage. Elaine was arrested in March 1935 for participating in a rally, held in San Francisco's Delores Park, against the Criminal Syndicalism laws. By this time, she had become widely known as the "Red Angel" for her work in defending union members and labor defenders on the San Francisco waterfront and in the city's 1934 general strike, for which she was the sole woman on the strike's steering committee. She also was a militant participant in many other labor and civil rights activities, including the Salinas Lettuce Strike, National Scottsboro Week, and Spanish Civil War relief. In 1939, Elaine Black Yoneda ran, unsuccessfully, for the San Francisco Board of Supervisors on a platform of free day care, low-cost housing, and civil rights. Then, following Japan's attack on Pearl Harbor in Hawai'i on December 7, 1941, Karl and Elaine, along with their three-year-old son, Tommy, were evicted from their San Francisco home and incarcerated at the Manzanar concentration camp in eastern California's Owens Valley.[2]

> *Hansen:* When did you and your husband, Karl, first have some sense that an "evacuation" was imminent, or at least forthcoming?
>
> *Yoneda:* From the time of December 7, the hour it [the attack on Pearl Harbor] started, we were aware of it. Karl and I sat and looked at each other and asked, what was going to be the fate of the Japanese Americans? What was going to be the fate of a vast number of people here in San Francisco?
>
> We were residing at a place in the Fillmore area close to Japantown. I stayed home with our son [Tommy Yoneda], who was not quite three yet. I didn't go out into the streets, so I didn't get the reflections of what was going on.
>
> *Hansen:* What did you get from Karl in the way of the general tenor of J-Town at that particular time?
>
> *Yoneda:* Well, bewilderment. What I gathered from Karl was that they really didn't know what was happening or what was going on.
>
> The next day Karl went to work. He was a longshoreman since 1936—the only Japanese American longshoreman on the mainland of the Pacific Coast here in the San Francisco port. Koji Ariyoshi, a Hawai'i longshoreman, was here in San Francisco on his way back from getting his master's degree in journalism, I believe, at the University of Georgia. So he was the only other one in the longshore labor force on the West Coast who was of Japanese ancestry. The harassment began against them the next day. It started at our home with someone knocking at our door. In came three men, identifying themselves as FBI agents, wanting to know if this is where Karl Yoneda lived. I said, "Yes." They asked, "And where is he?" So I was going to cooperate with the FBI at that point if it was to help expose any Fascists that might do damage to this country. So I let them come in. They entered the house and wanted to know where Karl was. I said, "He's at work on the docks. He's pursuing his work." "What do you mean, he's working on the docks? He's a 'Jap'; he can't be," they said. I just looked at them. I was sort of bewildered at their attitude.
>
> *Hansen:* This is already on the morning of December 8?
>
> *Yoneda:* Yes. I said, "You must be looking for the wrong person. Karl is anti-Fascist. He has been clubbed, beaten, and jailed for being an anti-Fascist, and now you come looking for him instead of looking for the Fascists that might be among us?"

They went and searched the house. I had been in the process of sending out our 300 Christmas cards, which that year we purchased for Chinese war relief. In some of them we were enclosing a picture of our son with Tom Mooney, our son's godfather.[3]

Hansen: Is that who your son is named after?

Yoneda: Yes. And they said, "Oh, what a front, what a front. Look, Chinese war relief in a 'Jap' house!" I said, "You must have your papers wrong. Somebody must have given you the wrong address. We have been supporting the Chinese fight against the Japanese imperialists, so don't say this is a front. Your papers must be all wrong." And they said, "Where did you say Karl is working?" I said, "I believe it's the army dock today." They said, "Well, he couldn't be." I said, "Karl is working with Copenhagen Hansen's gang." They didn't believe me. I said, "Well, I can call the hiring hall, but they are not supposed to give that information over the phone. I'll try, if you don't believe me." I dialed the dispatcher's office. I identified myself—and one of the FBI men put his hand over the receiver—and I said, "Someone wants to know where Karl is. It is very important." I didn't know at the time that there were other FBI agents on the roofs of the houses surrounding ours with machine guns.

Hansen: Who do you think fingered Karl?

Yoneda: Well, Karl does have a dossier, and so have I, because of our activities, which were considered "Red," quote, unquote.

Hansen: But shouldn't they have known, as you tried to point out to them?

Yoneda: But they didn't care. They also knew that Karl was known as Hama. That was, perhaps, one of their ways of continuing their harassment of anyone who was politically aware. It was a name that Karl assumed when he returned from Japan in order to protect his mother and his two sisters.

Karl had been arrested on the waterfront for picketing. He was a picket captain for the union, picketing scrap going to Japan. The San Francisco Police Intelligence Squad had dragged him into the captain's quarters of a Japanese ship. The captain asked him what he thought would happen to his mother in Hiroshima if he kept on with his activities? This was in 1938. So I'm sure they had his whole dossier there.

Hansen: It was just a good example of very sloppy stereotyping.

Yoneda: Of course, and not knowing who the real enemy was! So that was sort of a forerunner of what they might do to a whole people. We were also aware of American history, United States history, and what they [the US government] had done to the Indians, the Native Americans, in the 1830

Removal Act and broken treaties. They could take a whole people at the points of guns and drag them away from their homes.

Hansen: Was Karl pretty unpopular then in Japantown as a result of his activities?

Yoneda: Yes. But there was also a group of people who knew of the role he had played in helping to get better conditions, not only just in Japantown but also in Chinatown and other areas where he was involved as an organizer for the Alaska Cannery Workers Union, as a spokesman for all races, not just the people of the Orient. He was internationalist in his outlook. He was for all people.

Hansen: What about the traditional kind of aversion to what was then called *aka* or "Red" among the Japanese-ancestry people in the community?

Yoneda: Well, some of them were very hostile, while others were friendly. We had a number of progressive friends in all three of the Asian communities: the Filipino [American], the Chinese [American], and the Japanese [American]. We had a number of friends, close friends, that we socialized with, too. But, of course, there was a majority that wouldn't have anything to do with us.

Hansen: Karl was assailed then by certain elements within the Japanese [American] community?

Yoneda: Well, I imagine in the Japanese [American] press, but not after December 7, I don't think.

Hansen: But what about prior to that? How would you say the *Nichi Bei Shimbun* would view his activities?

Yoneda: Well, the Japanese section, no doubt there was an attack, not just on him personally, but on anyone connected with the *Doho* and the *Rodo Shimbun* and anyone who had run on the Communist ticket. Karl was the first Asian on the Pacific Coast to run for public office. In 1934 he ran on the Communist ticket in California for an assembly seat.

Hansen: How big and how thriving was the progressive element among the Japanese [Americans] in San Francisco?

Yoneda: Well, I imagine there were about a hundred men and women who were sympathizers.

Hansen: Can you think of some of the leaders who would have been identified along with Karl as leaders?

Yoneda: Well, I believe Tom Yamazaki—although he was Issei—in his writings and things. He was a journalist who was anti-Japan militarism. There were some agricultural workers who were out in the field and would perhaps come into San Francisco when the peak season was over. And I must say that quite a number of them did use assumed names. And some of them perhaps were the offspring of men who were very reactionary and didn't want to be associated with that particular person, even though that was his father or mother, to protect families.

Hansen: Which element in the progressive community do you think dominated: the socialist or the Communist?

Yoneda: Oh, there were very few socialists in the thirties. There were Communists and sympathizers. Not all Communists, but some who sympathized with the ultimate aims, or some who just sympathized with the civil liberties actions, like the International Labor Defense.

We had a branch, the Nagura Branch, here of about fifty men and women who held affairs to raise money for the defense of those who were arrested, not just those of Japanese ancestry, [such as] the Scottsboro Nine, Angelo Herndon, Tom Mooney, and others. We had quite a branch going. At that time, the International Labor Defense had language branches, so they spoke in their native tongue. But I wouldn't know who was an alien or who wasn't. To be an alien and be a member of the Communist Party in the thirties, and even before that, there were deportations and threats of such actions. But there had been a full swoop because the registration of aliens came into being, I think, in 1938. So, once you registered as an alien and were associated with any so-called progressive force, you were putting your life on the line.

Hansen: Did you have connections with elements within the Los Angeles Japanese [American] community at that time? I know that Karl worked as a northern California correspondent for *Doho*, which was a Los Angeles-based progressive newspaper.

Yoneda: Well, Karl, when he came up to San Francisco in 1933, came up here to become the editor of the *Rodo Shimbun*, which was the official Communist Party Japanese press in the United States.

Hansen: He came from Los Angeles?

Yoneda: Yes, I met him in Los Angeles.

Hansen: I see, you're from Los Angeles as well.

Yoneda: I'm not originally. But we met in Los Angeles, and Karl came up here in 1933, a month after I had come up here to become the district secretary of the International Labor Defense for Northern California. I had been that in Southern California for a while and then came up here. Then Karl came to the *Rodo Shimbun* and was editor of that.

Hansen: Was that in the English language or just purely Japanese?

Yoneda: It was in Japanese.

Hansen: Let me get back for a second to December 8 [1941]. You have the FBI harassing you at this particular time.

Yoneda: Yes, and I didn't know what had happened, of course. I finally found out afterward that they went down to the dock with their guns, pulled Karl off the job, and took him to the immigration center up here on Silver Avenue, where he was put in a cell with about thirty other Japanese, most of them aliens, most viciously pro-militarist.

Hansen: They jailed him right along with them.

Yoneda: Yes. The International Labor Defense, through its attorney, George Andersen, announced their intention to assist Karl by applying for a writ of habeas corpus, which would be issued by a court. Karl was being illegally held. He was not an enemy. If anything, he foresaw what fascism-militarism might bring and had been fighting against it.

So this was a Monday morning when Karl was arrested. Late Tuesday night, about ten o'clock, he was released. And he said that was the most frightening period in his lifetime up to that point. Being in that jail, with some of them saying, "You're in here as a spy; you're spying on us. Wait until the submarines come in here; you'll be the first one machine-gunned." Most of these men were Issei. But among those who were picked up, some of them were pretty vicious and had been very vocal in their papers or whatever else they had control of, being pro-Japan. Especially with what Japan had been doing in China.

Hansen: Did he know some of the people in the jail?

Yoneda: He knew them all.

Hansen: So the big problem was actually with the pro-Japan element?

Yoneda: Yes.

Hansen: How powerful was the pro-Japan sentiment within the Japanese [American] community in San Francisco?

Yoneda: It was varied. It was a small group. Just like when we got down to Manzanar. I don't think out of the ten thousand there were really more than thirty men who were dedicated to the imperialists. But they were the wealthiest. They had the media at their command, so they could control some of it.

Hansen: Did they control J-Town in San Francisco at the time?

Yoneda: Well, I don't know whether they controlled it, because up to that point I wasn't that connected with J-Town. I knew a few families, those that were in the International Labor Defense. I did not associate or go to other affairs that some of the other forces might have held. I had never been to a JACL affair up to the point.

Hansen: Did you feel hostility directed toward you as a result of your being a Caucasian married to a leftist in the community?

Yoneda: Well, not too much, frankly. I must say that, within the community I associated with, most were primarily of the same persuasion I was.

Hansen: They were internationalistic.

Yoneda: Yes!

Hansen: Would you say that your frame of reference, both of you, would be more ideological than ethnic?

Yoneda: Yes. Until the "evacuation" period, where it affected just that one segment of the population. Then it became something we paid more attention to. Karl went to meetings with JACL leaders who, up to that time, perhaps wouldn't even pass the time of day with him.

Hansen: He wasn't in the JACL, was he?

Yoneda: No, no, before the war we were never members of the JACL. We never joined the JACL while we were in camp.

Hansen: Did you know JACL people in San Francisco?

Yoneda: No, I didn't. Karl knew some of them, but I didn't.

Hansen: So then what happened following Karl's release from jail?

Yoneda: Well, he went back to work whenever he could. I continued with whatever activity I could. Then the Tolan [Committee] hearings came in February.

Hansen: Where did they hold them in San Francisco?

Yoneda: Above what was then the main post office on Seventh Street in one of the courtrooms.

Hansen: Did Karl testify?

Yoneda: He submitted, I believe, a letter because they'd had so many others speak there.

Hansen: Well, then, the thinking must have been rather ambivalent on the part of both yourself and Karl at this time, in the sense that it became increasingly clear that you were going to have an "evacuation." Here you have an allegiance to, on the one hand, the Japanese [American] people and, on the other hand, an allegiance to, say, an anti-Fascist commitment.

Yoneda: Well, it became apparent that we couldn't possibly fight it. We couldn't possibly fight it knowing the forces that the United States had at its command, knowing that the powers that be would think nothing of dispatching a battalion or two with their guns to "evacuate" the Japanese, should there be resistance.

Hansen: When did you then shift into a frankly cooperationist stance?

Yoneda: Well, from the minute we felt it would become imminent, from the minute we knew that Karl and Koji would not be able to have anything to do to make a livelihood and that if they became vassals in the welfare struggle, certainly something would happen to them anyway. It was during the Tolan hearings that we had a sense that "evacuation" was an accomplished fact and that this was just window dressing.

Hansen: So did you stay in San Francisco?

Yoneda: We stayed in San Francisco. But when Karl heard that there was going to be a camp set up in Manzanar, he volunteered, because most of the people in Manzanar were not from Northern California. He volunteered for a two-fold purpose. My parents lived in Los Angeles. They had offered my son and daughter and I a home. So that would be the best place for us to go. And if he had to leave, it would be closer if he went to Manzanar from Los Angeles, where my dad could drive me to visit him. I had no intentions of going into camp.

Hansen: You had no intentions of going into camp at that time?

Yoneda: At that time, of going into camp, no! What for? I wanted to do war work. I wanted to do whatever I could, even learn to make a bolt so that they could go quicker into the airplane or the ship.

Hansen: And you thought you'd have visitation privileges?

Yoneda: Privileges, yes, that was what we thought. All through this thing there was also this harassment of those who had backgrounds of being anti-Fascist.

Hansen: You went down to Los Angeles. About when was that?

Yoneda: We went on March 14 [1942].

Hansen: And then later he [Karl Yoneda] goes to Manzanar on March 23?

Yoneda: Yes, we [Karl and I and Tommy and Joyce] went first to my parents' home. They were living in Boyle Heights in Los Angeles.

Hansen: Then they were living pretty close to other Japanese [American] families?

Yoneda: Yes, on the fringe. Then we went down to San Diego to visit one of Karl's sisters, down near San Diego.

Hansen: When you were in Los Angeles, did you have any contact with the Japanese [American] community during that week or so prior to going to Manzanar?

Yoneda: Well, not so much with the community. We had communications with those who were in the progressive movement and discussed what was going to happen.

Hansen: Do you remember seeing the editor of *Doho* at that time, Shuji Fujii?

Yoneda: Shuji Fujii, yes. Karl went to say good-bye to him.
Hansen: Do you recall a woman by the name of Chiye Mori at that time?
Yoneda: I met her in Manzanar.
Hansen: You didn't know her before then?
Yoneda: No, I didn't know her.
Hansen: Was your daughter Joyce with you then?
Yoneda: Yes, but we left her with my parents when I finally went into Manzanar.
Hansen: Now, Karl went to Manzanar on March 23.
Yoneda: With a group on a train. He went with the large contingent who went by train. I saw a picture of the big caravan of cars that started out that day also. They went from a 1927 Model T to a 1942 Buick convertible in that procession of about 120 or 130 cars.
Hansen: So you saw him off. And where did they depart from?
Yoneda: From the Santa Fe depot in Los Angeles.
Hansen: At the time that he left, the assumption was that you'd just be visiting Manzanar.
Yoneda: I wasn't going to stay there. And in fact, I wasn't going to visit until he told me to come there. Our son happened to be asthmatic, as well as having eczema, and had quite a problem from the time he was five weeks old. He was under very strict medical care, trying to really pinpoint what it was that was making him so sick. So I wasn't even going to go there until Karl told me what the physical being was. Oh, no, it was the furthest from my thought.

When he left, I didn't know whether I was going to see him in a month or see him in six months. There was a picture taken of Karl kissing Tommy and a comment made—I have forgotten which paper—and it was sort of a snide remark, "Well, here's a 'Jap' kissing a child." Just as if they have no emotions or feelings.
Hansen: Were you one of the few Caucasians married to a person of Japanese ancestry?
Yoneda: Yes. I got no mail from Karl until, I think, the thirtieth [of March].

On Sunday, March 29, there came this blast over the radios: "Attention, attention! All those of Japanese ancestry whose breadwinners are at Manzanar are to leave Military Area 1 by noon,[4] April 2, or be in violation of this-and-this." Of course, I realized it didn't mean me, but would it also mean a child who had just turned three, who was "Eurasian," to whatever degree it might be, and what degree did they put on it?

I immediately ran to the phone and called up the closest army post listed in the phone book. I said I wanted to talk to someone who could tell me what the edict for "evacuation" meant, under army order. I was told that since the captain of the day was going to be so busy tomorrow morning, I should report to a federal building at Ninth and Spring [Streets], for filling out the proper papers, getting inoculations, and instructions to start the trek to Manzanar. So since he was going to be busy that morning, he wasn't returning to the army post, and perhaps I could get information from the Maryknoll fathers.[5]

I proceeded to call the Maryknoll fathers, and they put a priest on the line. I asked the question, did it mean that our son, whose father is in Manzanar, has to go? The voice answered, "It doesn't mean you." I said, "That was not my question. My question was, does it mean this three-year-old, two months and X number of days, who is 50 percent of Japanese ancestry, whose father *is* in Manzanar, one of the volunteers—does it mean him?" And again, he said, "It doesn't mean you." Again, I said, "That is not my question, Father." He said, "Well, we are going to go by international law." "Well, what is international law?" "The father's ancestry is what counts." I said, "But the father was born right here in the state! If anyone is an alien, it is *I*. I was born in Manhattan. I wasn't born in California, so I'm an alien to this state, and it's occurring in this state." "Oh, but it doesn't mean you!" Again I asked. "It does mean anyone with more than one-sixteenth Japanese blood," this voice answered. I said, "Well, my child is not going to go without me." He said, "Oh, you don't have to go; you don't have to go." And that ended the discourse that night.

I had made up my mind that I'd try to be bright and early down there at the seven o'clock lineup. Of course, when I got there, there were quite a number already in line. So many of the Japanese people were living in downtown Los Angeles, having been brought in from Terminal Island, and were "evacuated" on twenty-five- and fifty-five-hour notice. They were centered downtown so there was quite a number there. I took my place in line. Suddenly an army officer and a priest came running to me, shouting, "Not here; not here!" Then they escorted Tommy and I inside the building. Well, I felt that if that was the line and I came there at the correct time [then I was in the correct place]—oh, no, no. It was just as though a red carpet had suddenly been placed in front of me, which I didn't appreciate. But there I was with a white face and a small child in line.

So when I got in there, they started to try to tell me the facts of life, that it "didn't mean me." I turned around to this Maryknoll father and said, in no uncertain, loud words: "Father, for all you know, I may be an atheist, but I took a vow to love, honor, and cherish, for better or for worse. And if this is what the men in my life have to face, I am facing it with them! I give credence to that oath I have taken." And this Maryknoll father's face started to get purple above his collar. He just couldn't visualize that, I suppose. I'd seen a lot of injustice from the church, so his demeanor didn't impress me any.

The captain started telling me that I wouldn't have to go. Then the Maryknoll father injected, "Well, I've told you there's going to be a Children's Village there.[6] It will be 'manned' by nuns well versed in childcare, and they would give him a very beautiful upbringing." I repeated my thing about how I had taken a vow. They kept saying, "Well, it doesn't mean you." And then they turned around and handed me a blank form to fill out for Tommy.

Hansen: Did you feel that they didn't want you there at Manzanar?

Yoneda: Well, the whole "evacuation" was on a racial basis! This was a racial thing. The whole thing had racism behind it. You scratched that surface a little bit, and you see the hands of Hearst and all those "yellow peril" forces that we've had in this state coming out of the woodwork. They've been silent for a couple of years. In fact, some of them had become partners with Japan in their venture with China.

Hansen: Why do you think they didn't want you there? Why were they so insistent?

Yoneda: Well, they didn't know me. They didn't know me from Eve at that time.

Hansen: It was just that you were Caucasian.

Yoneda: Caucasian. It turned out afterward there was one other Caucasian who went the same day that I did. Now, there may have been more, but I didn't meet any of them, except one woman who went the same day I did. And that is something else again. They just went and classified the two of us in the same bag again, because she also had a white face. They handed me the one application [for Tommy], and I refused to accept it. I said, "If he goes, I go!" They tried to tell me how hard it would be, and it wouldn't be an easy life. I said, "Is it going to be easy for these people? None of us know what the future holds. In fact, just as I left for here, I was handed a special delivery letter," which was the first letter I'd had from Karl. I hadn't had time to read it. I thought I'd stand in line and read it, but I was whisked right in there, so I hadn't had time to read what Karl had even written about the camp.

Hansen: You were carrying the letter in your hand.

Yoneda: Yes, without knowing what was in there, what he had said about camp life, good, bad, or indifferent, you know? So, I said, "I haven't had a chance to read this, but I am going to go! You are not taking this child and putting him in an orphanage. I am not abandoning him on the steps of a church or some other building. He has a home where he'll be cherished and well taken care of. I don't understand this madness. A child who had just turned three and whose father, before many moons pass, will be in the service of the United States Army!" I was very positive on that point. I just knew that that was going to be our fate, that Karl would go into the army.

And finally they handed me two applications. They said there would be a train leaving on April 1, which was Wednesday—this was Monday—and one leaving on Thursday before noon. When would I want to go? I said, "Well, I may as well pick April Fool's Day." And I signed up to leave.

Then they started up the questions of inoculations. They weren't going to inoculate me. They were just going to inoculate Tommy. I said, "Look, you're not playing that on me. First of all, you haven't inquired as to the condition of his health, or my health, as far as shots are concerned. You're just not going to give shots per se. You're going to have to find out something about our medical conditions. As far as I know, I'm not allergic, and you can give me the shot right now. But this child has been allergic since he was five weeks old. And before you shoot him with *anything*, you better have someone here in a higher capacity than someone who can just push a needle with serum in it." So they did inoculate me that Monday, but they held off from inoculating Tommy.

You've also got to remember that these men and women who volunteered to go to Manzanar were in several groupings. There was a small handful who were progressive, whose livelihood had been taken away from them because they couldn't continue on their jobs, who felt that if they went into the camp, perhaps they could get union conditions, better conditions, livable conditions. At the same time, fighting to get into the army, fighting to work in war work. Then there were those who had handicaps and could never be accepted into the army because of their health but felt that they could do other things. Also, there was another small group who felt that they would be one step ahead of the FBI if they volunteered to go to Manzanar.

Hansen: What do you mean, "one step ahead of the FBI?"
Yoneda: By going into Manzanar as a volunteer.
Hansen: They wouldn't be picked up and sent—
Yoneda: —someplace else.
Hansen: Issei, for instance?

Yoneda: Issei, or—there weren't too many Issei, I don't think, in that first group. There were a number of Kibei and Nisei.

Hansen: Where were they thinking they might be sent?

Yoneda: Well, to Missoula [Internment Center] in Montana.[7]

Hansen: But you would have to be an Issei, an alien, to be sent to Missoula.

Yoneda: You could be a Nisei and be a potentially dangerous enemy! Just like when Karl was picked up. They knew he was American-born. But he was picked up December 8 as a potentially dangerous enemy. That was the classification. So some of those who were volunteering to go to Manzanar felt that they would be a step ahead of any derogatory reports that might come up of their affiliation with Japanese militarist groups.

Hansen: They volunteered, then, as a badge of their commitment to democracy.

Yoneda: Yes, to democracy and cooperation with the powers that be. So there was a sprinkling of those groups among the eight hundred or nine hundred men and women who volunteered to go to Manzanar. There were only about eight women, who were primarily nurses, and a couple of doctors in the first group. They were told that their families would be the last ones ordered out of Military Area 1—because it was such a rushed thing, they didn't have to worry about their properties or their personal wealth. Their families were remaining behind and would be able to amply take care of it. No doubt by that time the government would have set up warehouses—which they didn't have—and storage for the first group.

Hansen: So this was the promissory note?

Yoneda: A promissory note that they would be the last ones out. As a result, doctors left behind medical instruments, even some x-ray machines, I'm sure, and dentists left behind their wherewithal. Other lab equipment was left behind, buildings, business, whatever one might have had, because the wife was staying behind, or the brother was staying behind and would take care of the business. Then comes this edict a week later that they have to be out within seventy-two hours. You know, it was mind-blowing.

Those who drove cars to Manzanar were told to park in a certain area of that desert, inside the barbed wire encampment, and were not allowed to take their things out. When we approached Manzanar, the first thing I was aware of—after we got off the train at Lone Pine and took buses for Manzanar—was this group of cars parked out there in the camp that were just laden with dust. Of course, after I had read Karl's letter, I was aware that they had been told to park there. His letter said, "Don't come to visit me for at least another month. Conditions here are terrible. We don't have windowpanes in our barracks. If you bring Tommy here, I'm sure the dust will kill him," and along that vein. He also said, "Yes, there are white workers here getting union wages, but it doesn't look like *we'll* ever get into that stream, although I'll keep fighting for it. I will keep on fighting, but please do not come. And, above all, do not bring Tommy."

And here I'd already signed up and was going to bring Tommy there on April 1 without any further fight—except that if he had to go, I was too. There was no thought in my mind of tying up the army in federal court and maybe filing an injunction. It was a time of hysteria. It was a time of not knowing where to turn, feeling that none of my friends would turn away from me. But others, who might be able to give me a logical answer as to what to do, were afraid to be seen talking to anyone, so where do you turn? Certainly, the Catholic Church wasn't giving any guidance! They were telling you to sign up and go, and if you couldn't go, to send your child anyway. That was no guidance.

Hansen: So almost all your connections, then, were persona non grata, either because they were identified with the Left or identified with the Japanese [Americans].

Yoneda: Yes. We got into the camp, and there was a group of men standing there—I think we were the second bus. Tommy stuck his head out and said, "Daddy!" Karl came running to the bus, ashen-faced. I've never seen him look as ashen, before or since, as he did at that particular moment. He yelled at me. He used a few waterfront words and then asked, "What are you doing here? Are you bringing our son to be killed?" Look, he wrote that letter. It was special delivery—but I think it took four days to get to me. I pulled out the order I had received and said, pointing to Tommy, "This is the reason I'm here. Because he has to be here." Karl just stomped away. He was really upset. Karl had written so fully about what was going on there. He had written about the dust and the cold and everything, which were things that Tommy was susceptible to.

We got off the bus and he helped us. The other white woman was there and was put in the same room that we were put in. To this day, I don't know the other white woman's real name. She gave the name of one of the old Issei there. She turned out to have been a madam who ran a house that Japanese men frequented. Perhaps she had been living with this old man. We don't know. But she was a very loose character—not that I condemn anyone, but that was her background. About four weeks later she had to be escorted at gunpoint out of camp for some of her actions. There she was, a white person, who was going to be in the same room with us.

Nine of us were put in the same room, and that was going to be where we slept, and there were nine army cots there. I immediately complained about the straw mattresses. I said, "Tommy is allergic to straw. He can't sleep on straw. You're going to have to get something else for us." Well, that first night we couldn't get anything better.

The next day they began wanting to know who were family groups, and they were going to put us together. So right away they insisted that this woman and her spouse—the five of us would be in one room because if you were less than a family of four, you had to share with somebody else. We were just three, so we'd have to share. The logical thing would be to share with the other white woman. I said no because I did not like some of the things she said. I didn't care that she was living with anyone. It was what else she intended to do with her life that I was concerned with, you know, and the reflection of what would happen there. Her old clientele was there, and she probably saw a way for a fast buck, the men having been so many years deprived of having women of their choice.

Hansen: So there was going to be a little red-light district right in your apartment, right?

Yoneda: Yes. The reason she had to be led out afterward was because she made a play for the Caucasian workers, not because of what she was doing to further demoralize the camp, but what she was doing with some of the local men who were there in a crew. As a result, we were put in 4-2-2 with a fifteen-year-old boy and a blind seventy-five-year-old man, who were the overflow of the family in 4-2-1. The barracks were divided into so-called apartments, four of them.

Hansen: But the 4-2-2 refers to what?

Yoneda: Block 4, Building 2, Apartment 2. So 4-2-1 had the Nakamura family, and we shared the apartment with their overflow. There were five army cots put in there. Our three were close together. The other two were put at the other end of the room. There was nothing provided to have partitions, just the cots. But we were given—because of Tommy's allergic condition—extra army comforters to use as mattresses. But there were only two comforters and therefore wasn't much of a mattress. You just doubled it up, you know. So that's what we had for our mattresses, for our own beds. But the other two had straw, which resulted in Tommy becoming quite ill over the period and in and out of the hospital. Then, too, from the time he was five weeks old, the child was allergic to milk. Imagine a five-week-old not being able to have milk! They didn't have the soy milk or anything similar at that time. It was quite a horrendous task to try to keep him alive. There were times there we didn't think, personally, that he'd make it.

Hansen: So you were sensitized to a lot of things that concerned his health.

Yoneda: Yes, yes. What he could and couldn't eat. He wasn't allergic to rice, fortunately. There were cereals he couldn't eat. It was really quite a difficult time trying to keep his diet going. We tried in our own way, but that wasn't paid for by the government. We were paying for special foods from San Francisco out of our own pocket, and that was one of the reasons I later went to work in the camp library, having had some previous library experience. The pay, of course, turned out to be the starting sum of twelve dollars a month for semi-professional work. Karl, as a block leader, was getting sixteen. So we had twenty-eight extra dollars monthly with just one child to keep in shoes, and two adults, so our money went a little further. But what about those who had several children?

Yoneda: My parents did send us sheets. So we did have that bit of privacy early in the game. But many other families never were able to afford—I call it luxury in camp—to have a screen between them or anybody else, even in their own family, if they wanted privacy in bed. (laughs) You weren't able to really fulfill your love, or whatever, you know, in any fashion, even after you got a room of your own.

Hansen: So this was creating psychological tension?

Yoneda: Oh, yes. The first I was aware of psychological tension—which I really raised quite a to-do about—was the fact that when the families got there, there were no toilets, no running water, except one pipe outside each barrack. The laundries weren't ready. You couldn't wash clothes. You couldn't do anything. What if you have a baby who's in diapers? How are you going to wash your diapers? Or what if you have a child who eats something that doesn't agree with him and suddenly, out of the blue, starts throwing up, like Tommy did very many times?

Hansen: Was he sickly during the whole time you were at Manzanar?

Yoneda: Yes, so that the people, I'm sure, whether friend or foe, were aware of Tommy's condition, and there wasn't any jealousy because of that.

When they opened up the toilets, there were big knotholes in the walls because of the green lumber. It hadn't been covered with tarpaper yet. There were five bowls, back to back, in two rows with no partitions in between them. They were segregated by sex. There were knotholes in both. But you didn't find peeping gals or girls, but you did find peeping toms, which created some dissatisfaction and upheaval. Having those five toilets, bowls back to back, without any partition, fore or aft—I'd be in there with

Tommy. I had been in jails before, in solitary as well as in the main prison tank, so I wasn't so appalled by it. But I could see a young girl opening up the door who perhaps—and this is unladylike—was menstruating for the first time, and there I am with Tommy. Or she's having the "Manzanar runs," which we all had, and would run out with this look of distress and fear and panic on her face. This happened especially often among the young teenagers who were used to more privacy and had never been exposed to anything like this. They would see, time after time, the peeping eye looking at them. I finally couldn't contain myself any longer and I told Karl, "I'm going to raise hell if I have to!"

Hansen: Where did you raise hell?

Yoneda: At the administration. I went and pounded a desk and said, "If you don't do something about it and get partitions in there, not only are you going to have mass hysteria, you're going to have mass suicides among the young girls!"

Hansen: For the purposes of the tape, I'd like to say that Mrs. Yoneda is now consulting the diary that she kept while at Manzanar. She's going to backtrack to the early portion of April 1942, and she'll be picking it up there and expanding on some of the entries that she inserted in her diary from that point on during her stay at the center.

Yoneda: As I have already indicated, we arrived at Manzanar April 1. That day began with a 6:45 a.m. start at the depot, surrounded by soldiers with guns. The train pulled out at 9:30 a.m. When we arrived at Manzanar it was 7:00 p.m. There were 413 of us from the Los Angeles area that arrived that evening. About 230 from Bainbridge Island had preceded us by a couple of hours, we found out afterward.

On April 2 we experienced our first dust storm, and by 4:00 p.m. it was impossible to keep our eyes open. Tommy was beginning to have an asthma attack. Another group of 800 arrived. The wind raged all night. We found that among the new arrivals were our friends, Ruth and Tom Yamazaki from San Francisco. I have a little footnote: "How the dust bowlers must have felt!" You'd stand in line and not be able to recognize the person in front of you or in back. You would just get coated. It seemed to adhere. It was thick and rocky sand. It wasn't fine sand. It's hard for me to describe it, not being anyone who had been on land or known the different types of soil.

Hansen: You didn't have any foliage to hold down the dust, then?

Yoneda: No, no, no, no. Afterward, there were some lawns put in front of some of the barracks, but not at the beginning. On April 10 I complained about the fast-driving cars and trucks through camp, because there were small children running around.

Hansen: Who was driving the trucks?

Yoneda: Well, some of them were Kibei and Nisei who became the ground crews or were hauling material. Some of them were the outside workers coming in, the carpenters, who were all white and received union wages. Those of Japanese ancestry were helpers.

Hansen: They were just tearing around the camp in the cars and trucks.

Yoneda: Yes, and there was no speed limit. It was hazardous because by then there was quite a number of small children who hadn't been exposed to outside roads, so that was part of it.

On April 11 we found the first issue of the *Manzanar Free Press* at our doors. Also, some of the apple trees were beginning to blossom—they were beautiful. On Easter Sunday we found that the mountains on both sides of us were covered with snow.

Hansen: So it was still pretty cold in April.

Yoneda: It was cold in March, and it was cold in April, very cold in April. It didn't get warm there until about May. On April 1, we found rumors flying all around. One of them was that sixty patients were in the hospital; another one was that Hawai'i had fallen, but the United States hadn't announced it. What trash!

Hansen: What sources of information did you have outside to help diffuse these rumors?

Yoneda: Well, we got the *San Francisco Chronicle* and the *San Francisco News*. We got the union paper. We had correspondence coming in from all over, and we read a great deal and tried to keep up. We didn't have a radio. Also, my parents and other friends would clip some things they would think we'd be interested in from the newspapers in their area. I believe we were also getting the *People's World*. It was a daily then. So we had that slant on what was going on, finding that a vast number of progressives were enlisting and attempting to enlist into the military service.

On April 13 there were elections for block leaders. Here is what I wrote in my diary: "First lesson in democratic procedure for many. Block 4 dominated by Issei. Applause indicating vote. Non-Japanese-speaking [inmates] didn't realize this [that the applause meant the vote]. About fifty-three present, six women. Karl and I don't have the names of the other two men nominated for block leader. I helped Karl prepare a brief biography for the administration."

Hansen: This was just a nominating meeting then? This wasn't the election as such?

Yoneda: Yes, this was the nominating meeting. Then they submitted biographies to the administration. And from the three nominated in each block, the administration had the final say on which one would be the block leader. On this same day we also suggested to the administration official that United States flags should be displayed on post office and administrative buildings. Also, that they should have a campaign to save newspapers, rags, tin, et cetera. "It's a sin to waste tin."

Hansen: Who's "we," Elaine? Karl and you?

Yoneda: Karl and I. Or I may have suggested it. [reading from diary] "Heard in some blocks secret ballots used for election. That's as it should be." I didn't feel that the applause was a lesson in democracy. I felt that a secret ballot would be the best way to express our wishes.

On April 16 I noted the birth of the first child, a baby boy, in Manzanar. There was dust again. On April 17, although there was dust still raging, there was a ceremony when the flag-raising took place at 3:00 p.m. So they [the administration] did raise a flag. In other words, we felt that people had to remember that they were part of the United States. It wasn't our first fight against injustice, the injustice of the hunger that went on in this country, the low pay, and the exploitation hadn't just started. It had been there So, the struggle was a long one to adhere to what our Bill of Rights and Constitution stood for.

Hansen: So the administration apparently followed up on your suggestion.

Yoneda: Maybe they had it in the back of their minds earlier, but there it was. I'm not taking the credit for that one. On April 21 I write that I began doing some volunteer work for the [*Manzanar*] *Free Press* on certain days.

Hansen: What kind of work were you doing for the *Free Press*, Elaine?

Yoneda: Typing primarily. I'm not a writer.

Hansen: Do you remember any people on the staff?

Yoneda: I remember Joe Blamey. His grandfather was a general in the British army or something, and he himself had been born in Japan, and that made him suspect. Although he was terribly crippled by polio, had to walk with crutches and canes. I'd never heard the name until I met him at Manzanar.

Hansen: So you just volunteered to work at the newspaper office.

Yoneda: To do typing and whatever I could. On April 24 I worked for seven hours on the *Free Press*. I then went to work in the library for the first day on May 8. I worked there until the camouflage net factory was opened; then I quit the library and went to work on the camouflage nets. Because if I was going to be honest to what I was advocating for others, I also had to—I was a citizen and I wanted to do war work. That was the only war work open for me.

Hansen: When did they open the net factory?

Yoneda: I think it was in July. I haven't gotten to it yet in the diary.

Hansen: How were you accepted there at Manzanar, Elaine, within your block, et cetera?

Yoneda: Well, I was accepted by the young adults—the women primarily—very well, I thought. I didn't find any hostility. The hostility came where someone was a rabid Republican—who was even against Roosevelt, because he was a Democrat, not because of anything else. I was already in my thirties. I was the same age as Karl. So we were no spring chickens when we went to Manzanar. We were accepted by these nineteen-, twenty-, and twenty-one-year-olds. They were constantly streaming in and out of our place when we were home.

We had people that we didn't know, who were not progressive, but who felt that, "Yes, we do have to have democracy, and how are we going to go about it?" Not a big group, but it was a vocal group. The others were still too young, and the older ones were more set in their ways.

Hansen: Were these the people, then, who gave support to Karl as block leader—to get him on the nomination list?

Yoneda: Well, some of them weren't even able to vote yet if they were under a certain age.

Hansen: Well, what was the force behind nominating Karl among the three that were recommended to the project director?

Yoneda: Well, perhaps the fact that he was bilingual. Perhaps some of the people didn't know that "Karl Yoneda" was "Karl Hama," who they'd hated for all these years. Although he began using the name Karl Yoneda in 1936.

Hansen: So it was because he was a Kibei and could intermediate between the Nisei and the Issei.

Yoneda: Yes. In fact, he knew Japanese better than he knew English. So there was that affinity there among the Issei.

Hansen: They didn't know he was Karl Hama, and they *did* know he spoke Japanese.

Yoneda: So that probably was it. And, of course, they did know he belonged to a union because he never made bones about that. He said, "Now in my union we would have done it this way, and we wouldn't let them get away with that." Well, perhaps they thought he was all on their side when he made remarks like that. Sure, we acquiesced to going into camps, but we were not going into camps per se. We had principles about going in there, too, and seeing that conditions were good, if possible.

Hansen: And to look beyond the camps, too.

Yoneda: Of course, yes, to that day when there would be no camps.

Hansen: What resistance, within the block, did you meet with?

Yoneda: I didn't meet with too much. The stumbling block was the fact that if some of the Issei wanted to befriend me, I wouldn't know how to answer them if they only spoke in Japanese. I had a language gap more than I think I had a person-to-person gap.

Hansen: Well, what about Karl? Did he get along with the block?

Yoneda: Well, there were different people who came to him with their problems. When a husband beat up a wife, the wife would come and complain, or vice versa.

When it would be laundry day, Karl would make arrangements to have the same day off that I would have so that we'd go to the laundry together. Not only would he carry Tommy on his shoulders, but he would help me carry the laundry. Where most of the scenes that we saw of the older men, even those who had younger wives, was of the wife carrying the child, the wife carrying the soap, the wife carrying the laundry, and the father maybe not even going with her. He's sitting playing Go [Japanese board game] or just talking. So our practices were a reverse of what they considered their custom. Karl was breaking down their custom by going with me, and, of course, he got me a little bit uptight, too, a couple of times. He would take the tub where my personal underwear was and begin washing that instead of maybe washing Tommy's clothes—to make the point that you can, and it doesn't make less of a man out of you if you're helping equally.

Hansen: So he was actually undermining some of the traditional Japanese roles.

Yoneda: Yes.

Hansen: Your marriage stood somewhat in contrast to most of the marriages within the block because of the sense of equality.

Yoneda: Yes, yes. I note that my parents wanted to come and visit me, and I still hadn't written to them to tell them not to come yet.

Hansen: Why didn't you want them to come, Elaine?

Yoneda: Well, because, first of all, it wasn't clear to us whether they could come in. And it was such a long, hard road for them to come. If I was in my thirties, my parents were in their fifties. They were very much into the Russian war relief thing, working day and night, gathering tons of things for war relief for the Allies, primarily for the Russians because that was their background; going to affairs for defense and everything else; housing friends' sons who were coming to them, perhaps who had leave in the city. So they kept busy. It was a hard trek, and I felt it would be sort of physically hard on them. So I thought it was an imposition on them—if they were to come there only to have to turn around, which in the end is what happened the first time they came. They were allowed into just the guard house, you know. I wanted to have more freedom for them to be able to come in and, if necessary, spend the night inside and so on.

Hansen: So it was just the wrong time.

Yoneda: Yes, it was the wrong time. On June 8 I note in my diary that Karl voted as an absentee. A San Francisco vote. So all that time we were there, we never lost sight of some of our rights as United States citizens.

There was a farewell party for four, who were going from Kitchen 4 to Idaho, so they left with the first bunch—with Koji Ariyoshi. He was in a different block.

Hansen: Where were they going in Idaho, and what were they going to do?

Yoneda: Well, they were going to try and help save the sugar beet crop. They needed people who could do that stoop labor and would volunteer to do it. It was a necessity in the war effort to have the sugar. They asked at the different camps for volunteers. I know that Koji led the first group out in June. They did have trouble on the different farms, which he, being of a labor and union background from the time he was a small boy, helped fight against. So when the next group went later on, they didn't meet such bad conditions.

Hansen: What kind of problems and conditions are you talking about?

Yoneda: Well, housing, food, freedom to go out for entertainment or something, rather than being in another camp again while they are saving something inland. Of course, this was in Idaho and so on. Karl did go with the next group to Idaho.

Hansen: Elaine, who were your best friends within the camp, as you recall? What social group did you usually meet with?

Yoneda: Well, there was a young [woman]—I believe she was only about twenty-one at that time or not even quite twenty, Yo Ukita, who was in Block 4, Barrack 8 or 9. She and a younger brother and a married brother, his wife and two children, were close friends, and their mother and father.

One of the things, too, that I didn't realize, as far as the culture and things like that, is the administration said if there was an elder father, he became the head [of the family], even if there were married sons. The elder male was the one who had the say-so, keeping on that backward tradition—which I had never been exposed to since Karl did not have a father who was living and his mother was in Japan. I wasn't quite aware. I'd heard rumors, but I'd never really seen it in practice, where the head of the house was the father, if he was alive. He was the one who cracked the whip, and this is the way it was. Now I saw it.

Hansen: I was asking you about the friendship circle you had.

Yoneda: Well, Yo Ukita was one of those who became very friendly with us. There was another family in Block 6. One of them [Mary Oda], who is a [medical] doctor now and is married to James [Jimmy] Oda. The Yamazakis [Tom and Ruth] were close friends, of course. And Koji Ariyoshi, who we had known in San Francisco. Several other unmarried Kibei were of the same persuasion as Karl.

Hansen: Was Jimmy Oda, too, out of the same type of background?

Yoneda: Yes, yes. He had also been a union organizer down south. We had known him when we were in Southern California. Altogether it was a very small group. But each one of them developed other groups so that when we circulated a petition to open up the second front and get signatures on it—this was after several battles at the camouflage net factory—we were able to get over two hundred names. Because they had to be citizens and of an age where they could go into service. And getting that petition was something. Several people were circulating it, not just Karl and Koji, although they were the ones who drew it up. So that was the circle.

Hansen: Were you vocal within the camp, too, in putting forth a position like this?

Yoneda: Well, I helped with the petition. I immediately quit my library job when the camouflage net factory was established. The net factory work was harder. And, as I found out later, it was also physically impossible for me because of my reaction to the dyes that were used.

Hansen: Did you speak up?

Yoneda: At times, yes.

Hansen: Did you speak up to the point that you think it might have been resented?

Yoneda: What I spoke up about was certain conditions. They all knew about my scene at the administration building over the toilets.

Hansen: But that's a local concern. Did you speak up about anything that was a broader ideological concern?

Yoneda: Well, I always spoke up saying that I hoped the United States and the Allies won. Most of them who spoke the reverse would speak in Japanese because they knew I didn't speak Japanese.

Hansen: Do you think many of the people there knew you were a political figure?

Yoneda: Well, I think some of them became aware, because I had also run for public office. And if anyone started, you know, scratching the surface, they began to realize that I was the Elaine Black they had heard about—and that he was Karl Hama. You could feel the tenseness. But I felt uncomfortable just among certain ones. The ones that I felt most uncomfortable about turned out to be members of the Black Dragons. There were others on the periphery of that society. I felt they were able to do a lot of damage because of the inactivity on the part of the administration to achieve good conditions. Some of them, I had a feeling, were completely dominated by their dedication to the emperor and the emperor's system, which included the militarist aspects of that regime. They were anti-US, in fact, from way back.

Among the Kibei there were various groupings. You have a group of Kibei who went to Japan during the period of growing unionism, of growing revolutionary activities. Especially after the 1917 Russian Revolution, and Japan wasn't doing so much militarily in that period. So they had a different atmosphere in which they were growing into maturity. You find a lot of Kibei who came back here in the twenties an entirely different people from those who came back in the thirties. Because, in the thirties, Japan was again asserting its military power, was attacking China, had taken over Manchuria, and that is what they believed in. The emperor could do no wrong, and "Look what he's doing. He's freeing the Chinese people"—by having his army go through with the Rape of Nanking and things like that. So they had a different outlook. Their training was pro-military.

Hansen: Which Kibei group dominated at Manzanar?

Yoneda: The latter, but they didn't actually dominate.

Hansen: But didn't you get a sense that there were Kibei in the camp who more or less were in a similar situation linguistically, by virtue of the fact that they were in Japan during a similar period? And wasn't there a certain amount of suspicion of Kibei, as a group, on the part of the administration and the American public?

Yoneda: There may have been on the part of the administration. I never did have too much rapport with the administrators. I made friends with some teachers, but I didn't make friends with any of those on the administrative staff. Also, all this time I was trying to talk to those that I could talk to about the need to maintain their voting rights. They would ask me, "Why did Karl send away for an absentee ballot? Look, he's locked up here, he's no longer a citizen." "Well," I replied, "we are going to maintain that right." When we were in jail [before the war] and it was time for an election, we also demanded our absentee ballots, and therefore we are not going to lose it here. While we feel the war, as it is now being conducted, is a war against fascism, we have to take our side, yes. We have to line up either pro-Fascist or anti-Fascist. We can't be sitting in the middle.

Hansen: You said you felt uncomfortable around those Kibei who had been more recently in Japan in the thirties?

Yoneda: Yes, their being a little older than most of the young, average-aged Kibei, and not yet fitting in with the Issei group because they were so much older. I was in that very small group that helped bring up the average age, because there weren't too many of us in our thirties.

Hansen: The in-betweeners.

Yoneda: Yes. There weren't too many of us at that time.

Hansen: Because that's the so-called missing generation within the Japanese [American] community.

Yoneda: So we were among the missing in more ways than one because we didn't have our peers there with us to be able to communicate and carry on with.

Hansen: Plus, you didn't even have your San Francisco friends.

Yoneda: No, I didn't have my San Francisco friends. Also, an awful lot of our Los Angeles friends that we had known in the early thirties had dispersed into various areas over the years.

Hansen: Then in some ways you were strangers in Manzanar.

Yoneda: Yes, we were. We were among just a handful of those that we could call friends. Even some of those had become afraid, you know, because of threats that had been made to them—physical threats, which were being carried out with physical attacks.

Hansen: Did you have any friends among the JACL people in camp?

Yoneda: No. In fact, I didn't know any of them, but Karl knew some of them. I didn't go to any of the meetings of the Manzanar Citizens Federation because I was working on the net project. Tommy wasn't well, and I wasn't either because it was a physical strain to work on the camouflage nets—but I was determined to do so. As long as the doctor said I could do it, I was going to do it. And I did. I found it very strenuous in more ways than one because there were physical attacks on me with rocks and things like that when I was working on camouflage.

I'm trying to find the exact day I went to work at the camouflage net factory. I notice here on June 19 I write, "Signed up for camouflage work to begin Monday," and this was on a Friday. That same day I wrote, "Books came to the library, which we'll be able to circulate."

Hansen: So you're phasing out your library responsibilities and preparing for work on the camouflage nets.

Yoneda: Yes. At this time, there were all kinds of rumors flying around. There were rumors about what was going to happen to those who were going to work on camouflage. There were Black Dragon posters beginning to appear. Some of them joined garbage crews so they could have a truck at their command, adorned with Black Dragon flags.

Hansen: Was this before the camouflage net factory opened?

Yoneda: Oh, yes, yes. So, when they began talking about camouflage nets, the Black Dragons began threatening and putting up signs saying, "Don't let your children work on the nets," because only citizens could do this work. So on Monday, June 22, I started to work at the camouflage net factory. I write in my diary: "Haven't got the exact hang of it yet. Many are laying down on the job."

Hansen: It wasn't any kind of passive resistance, was it?

Yoneda: I don't think so.

Hansen: Because these were people who volunteered for this work.

Yoneda: Volunteered, yes. I was one of those who felt if I didn't know what I was going to do next, I was going to ask somebody who did. And, actually, some of these people had never worked before. They had just come out of school. So they didn't know what was required. I had worked in yardage and in offices, so I knew certain things. But often they didn't know what to do next or what color to take next—and patterns were slow in coming. So it looked like they were loafing.

Hansen: Were the camouflage workers all women?

Yoneda: No, there were some men, but primarily young women. The work wasn't very hard. It was just tedious, and it got very hot. At times, I think, it was about 120 degrees in the shade. So you can imagine. We had to start taking salt pills every hour or so. We had to wear a nose mask of gauze to keep the fumes out. The strips of burlap we were working with had been doctored with certain dyes.

On Monday, June 29, we found more workers signing up for camouflage work, despite the warnings that had been given by word of mouth and by certain posters, in Japanese, that had been posted around.

Hansen: Were they threatening some kind of dire consequences?

Yoneda: Oh, yes. Dire consequences to any of those who had families in Japan. There would be dire consequences for their family there and so on. On June 30 I was made a "key girl." And I put down, "Don't know how the new crew will take to it." Then, July 1, I write, "A couple quit, but others took their places very soon." Then, on July 6, I have a notation: "I made only three nets. Time was wasted changing patterns." Perhaps I was too fast a worker; I would resent time wasted. There were all sorts of problems. Perhaps the army would send in the wrong pattern, but then in the end they weren't getting the amounts of nets they needed.

Hansen: Do you remember who was in charge of running the camouflage net factories?

Yoneda: No. They weren't very visible. They would bring patterns in and say, "Listen, the next batch we're going to make is desert." And they would leave a pattern. But I was at that point quite happy because I was doing something that I felt was going to help beat that damn enemy that I wanted to see eradicated and never able to raise its head again among people.

Hansen: Would you say that it would be accurate to characterize the general temperament that you had while at Manzanar as one of doing everything possible to uphold the American way of life?

Yoneda: I think it was a mixture of both—the feeling that democracy, as it could be, was possible.

Hansen: You were separating democracy and capitalism, weren't you?

Yoneda: Yes. The principles of what democracy is supposed to be, if carried out in full, might not mean doing away with everything that is here, but certainly equalizing it among people so that all of us could live in dignity, regardless of what we had in our pocketbooks.

Hansen: So you were carrying on a battle on two fronts. One front was against fascism, and one was against exploitative capitalism—although you were putting one on the shelf temporarily?

Yoneda: Temporarily. But I brought it up whenever it was germane to what was going on.

Hansen: So it wasn't that you repressed all your criticism of "capitalist exploitation."

Yoneda: No! Oh, no! Or profiteering and things like that.

Hansen: Would it be fair to say that perhaps inside of yourself, there might have been an uneasiness about being thrust into a supportive position for a culture which, in fact, you had been spending a good portion of your life more or less fighting?

Yoneda: Well, I wouldn't call it culture. I've fought against war profiteering and the harassment of those who have nothing, or are unemployed, or have to apply for welfare. I don't call that culture. I hope it isn't considered culture by anyone! (laughs)

Hansen: I just meant a way of life.

Yoneda: I just wanted to make it clear that I didn't consider capitalism as culture of any kind. (laughs) We had to put aside, perhaps, the inner battle that had to be waged in this nation to maintain and enhance democracy as it is intended and can be practiced, given the right set of circumstances. Yes, that took a secondary position. The prime position, at that time, was one of anti-fascism, knowing what had gone on in China, knowing what had gone on in Manchuria, knowing what had gone on in the European countries that the Nazis had taken over, knowing what had gone on in Spain, and collecting money for the Spanish Loyalists. It was a background of long struggle. And some of it was not easy, including jail time and so on. But the fight went on. The secondary position [enhancing democracy] had to take second place during the heat of that battle.

Hansen: You didn't get any sidelong glances? After all, there was Karl Hama and Elaine Black becoming flag-wavers, demanding that an American flag be put up.

Yoneda: Because we weren't on the side of the Fascists. We weren't for the rising sun or the swastika.

Hansen: So it became one symbol against another.

Yoneda: One symbol, yes. I would have liked to have seen the United Nations flag or the flags of the Allies there. Although when we spoke, we spoke about the second front relieving the hardships of the Soviet people and bringing peace more quickly to the forces of democracy. We didn't say that the Soviet system should overtake the United States, because that certainly wasn't in the offing then.

Hansen: The perspective then was to relieve people who were under pressure from fascism?

Yoneda: Yes. And there were American Fascists, such as the Hearsts. When I'd see the Hearst press come into camp, I'd get uptight. Whoever I could talk to, I'd ask, "How can you read that rag and say this is what you're basing your opinions on? At least get something that is neutral!"

At this time I was also asking the administration if my folks, when they came [to visit], could stay within the camp. But on July 7 Ned Campbell, the assistant project director, told me that my request for a permit was refused. He said, "No, they can't stay here."

Hansen: What did you think of Ned Campbell?

Yoneda: I didn't like him. I felt he was a racist from Texas. And, of course, he was particularly down on me. I could feel his hostility because here I was, a white woman married to someone of a different race. I felt that hostility from him the first time I met him.

Hansen: What was his personal style like?

Yoneda: We didn't socialize with him, but I had a feeling that the man was not telling the truth about certain things, was shutting his ears and his eyes to some of the things that were happening—like the attempt of the Black Dragons to kill Karl and Tokie Slocum with a truck flying a Black Dragon flag right in front of the Block 4 office. When Karl came back [to our apartment], he was physically shaken. He went and reported it, but they didn't take any action.

Hansen: Campbell just ignored it.

Yoneda: Ignored it, and other things that were reported. Because maybe he didn't give a darn whether we killed one another.

Hansen: Okay. Where are we now in your diary?

Yoneda: On July 7. We are dealing with the refusal to allow my folks to spend the night. When the permit was turned down, I immediately wrote to the folks. Tommy was taken to the hospital that day with measles. We discovered afterward that children were brought into Manzanar with measles on April 1, and then it spread to all the children there.

Hansen: What were some other epidemics there in those early months?

Yoneda: Well, the only ones I have listed in my diary were whooping cough and measles.

Hansen: Were you pleased with the hospital conditions in Manzanar?

Yoneda: Well, I thought they worked awfully hard, under a handicap, with so many people there and so few doctors.

Hansen: You were satisfied with the personnel, but less satisfied with the facilities.

Yoneda: The physical facilities, yes. The hospital building itself got improved. On July 23 I note that the temperature in our apartment was 114 degrees. That was when I was typing a resolution to FDR on a stencil.

Hansen: That's the resolution asking the US to open the second front in Europe?

Yoneda: Yes, to open the second front and to admit those of Japanese ancestry into the ranks of the service.

Hansen: To open up admission on the same basis as for any other US citizen?

Yoneda: Yes, any citizen. Then, on July 27, I mention that a rash began to appear near my elbows. That same day the *Manzanar Free Press* wrote that I had set the record of net production: 133 percent efficiency.

Hansen: You had broken the record in terms of productivity in making camouflage nets.

Yoneda: Yes. I sure wanted to get that war over with! (laughs) That day I had the doctor look at my rash. I was given a lotion to put on to see if it would help. I kept making four nets, and my rash was getting worse. The doctor, on July 31, said they believed it was the camouflage nets that caused my rash. And there seemed to be a couple of others who were affected. That's the same day I made five nets, and the week after I produced twenty-two.

On August 1, at two o'clock in the morning, I had to send Karl to the hospital because I was very feverish and sick. He came back by 3:00 a.m. with a nurse, who gave me a morphine shot, which made me worse. I tried to tell her not to give me morphine because I was allergic to it. But that's all she had with her, and she thought it would ease my pain. But it never does, and it never did. I got worse and my arms were swollen, feverish and itching. On August 2 the new hospital was opened up. Although I was so feverish and itched, I took a ride in the truck to the new hospital.

Hansen: This was the hospital they built way in the back of the camp?

Yoneda: Yes. On August 6 they had the second federation meeting, but I couldn't go because Tommy was restless.

Hansen: Was that the Manzanar Citizens Federation?

Yoneda: Yes. As I said, I didn't get to any of their sessions. If Tommy would have been able to go, we could have all gone and perhaps participated. I say in my diary: "Heard organized opposition was ready."

Hansen: What date was that again?

Yoneda: August 6. This was the second meeting.

Hansen: Right, the first was held in late July, wasn't it?

Yoneda: So maybe I missed the day of the first meeting of the Manzanar Citizens Federation.

Hansen: I think it was July 28.

Yoneda: Let's see. That's the day I went to the hospital with Tommy and got the lotion for my hands, so that's probably what kept me from going.

Hansen: Of course, you were preoccupied at this time with your own problems, too.

Yoneda: Oh, yes. The doctor, on August 7, told me that I couldn't go to work until August 17. And things were happening. (reading from diary) "There are rumblings at the camouflage [net factory]." I wrote: "The Kibei held lousy meetings. Karl was threatened. How long will this be?" This is August 8: "Strike talk at camouflage net factory."

Hansen: What was the camouflage net factory strike about?

Yoneda: They wanted better conditions. They wanted going wages. Someone was pushing them [the workers] to start a strike, I'm sure.

Hansen: What was your attitude toward that?

Yoneda: Well, at the time this started I was off sick.

Hansen: I mean, here you were a victim of bad conditions, and yet you also wanted to promote the work that they were doing.

Yoneda: Yes, but at the same time, when we wrote to the camp administration or to Washington, we said that things would be better if they *did* get proper working conditions. "Let us work and produce at the going wage, so that we won't be wards of the government, and can help, in more ways than one, in hastening the close of the war."

Hansen: To do everything possible to facilitate the war effort, then, was your intention.

Yoneda: Yes. On August 14, I got a letter from my folks telling me that my daughter Joyce had disappeared. They didn't know how, when, or where. They said that I might have to ask for a leave for a week or ten days. That would be the first time that I had asked for anything special, any privilege. If I asked for a privilege, it would have to be for something that would be whole and sound rather than just asking for a privilege for the sake of asking.

Hansen: Well, it seems to me that you would be a little sensitive, being one of the few Caucasians in camp.

Yoneda: I was the only one on my side of the barbed wire, outside of the administration.

Hansen: It would be only human for you to try and make every attempt not to look as though you were getting special privileges.

Yoneda: Well, I never did ask them for any job that I applied for. I had to show, the same as anybody else, that I was capable. Perhaps at the camouflage net factory I outdid myself. I worked hard. Although the conditions were bad, I felt the need. Perhaps I had an extra drive to do more because I felt the need to get the nets done, because we had to do away with the Axis so we could go on to better things.

Hansen: You tried to set an example at the same time?

Yoneda: Yes, because that was really what I wanted to do: something for the war effort. On August 20 I note that "Karl had things thrown at him today." Also, four Kibeis "playfully" threw rocks at me. Then I have the word "bruised" in my diary entry because I got bruised on my head and legs.

Hansen: Did they throw the rocks very hard?

Yoneda: That time it was harder than the first time, yes.

Hansen: Did you feel that you were a specially picked target?

Yoneda: No, because I heard from others that they also had objects thrown at them, but I don't know whether it was as hard. I was in a position where they could do it more readily, without having been noticed by anybody else.

Hansen: Would you have interpreted the rock throwing, then, as being aimed at you because you were a camouflage net worker?

Yoneda: No, because I was, as they called it, pro-American.

Hansen: Well, that would have been established by your employment at the net factory, wouldn't it?

Yoneda: Also, I was outspoken and one who had circulated petitions for the war effort.

Hansen: Had you circulated a petition?

Yoneda: I had run some off for Karl, went with him, talked with some of the women, and told them that they mustn't be backward about saying what they felt. I was one of those that had signed the petition. So I figured it was because of the fact that I was Karl's wife. Karl being who he is, and the fact that I had the same ideas as he did—that already put three more stripes on me than anybody else working on the camouflage nets.

    On August 21 there were elections for block leaders held in Block 4. Thirteen votes for Karl. What a mobilization! In the block they went from door to door and told people that they should be there, and that they've got to do away with that "Korean dog," as they called Karl, as the block leader.

Hansen: Who's "they"?

Yoneda: A few of the Black Dragons. One of them was the kitchen help, the person that was the most vocal in our block and the head of the kitchen. Some of the others were not even from Block 4, but they went around from apartment to apartment, mobilizing and telling people to go and vote—and be sure not to vote for that "dog." Yet there were thirteen votes for Karl among the 163 who were there that voted.

Hansen: So this was an intimidation against anybody who had voted for Karl?

Yoneda: Yes, against Karl. If they voted for Karl, they were voting for a Communist, for someone who was against the Japanese people, and someone who would like to see them all get killed and all that. Smear.

    On Sunday, August 23, another hot day. (reading from diary) "Started typing letters about 7:30 p.m. Halfway through the second letter, someone knocked on the door. I said come in. The voice said, 'Yoneda-*san*? May I come in?'" Karl said yes. Fourteen Kibei trooped in and started talking in loud voices. I looked out the window and saw more of them staked out all around. They were here for over an hour. I don't know Japanese, but there are a few words that you hear enough. They were talking about his mother. They were saying, "What do you think is going to happen to your mother if we report this?" And "You're going to be the first one to be machine-gunned down when the Japanese land here." That was their attack. Not that we wanted it better there in camp. But "You're going to be the guy we're going to get because you're anti-Japanese and we are one hundred percent for Japan."

Hansen: So the meeting itself—

Yoneda: It wasn't a meeting; it was a confrontation. Actually, if they had found Karl alone, they would have really beaten him to a pulp. Well, they thought I had gone.

Hansen: If he were alone, they would have killed him then?

Yoneda: Well, they would have maimed him. They didn't care.

Hansen: So, in other words, you being there with Tommy—

Yoneda: It deterred them at that particular moment. On the next day, Monday, there were Kibei all around the camouflage net factory.

Hansen: You started to see these same people showing up, and there was either tacit or direct intimidation all the time, right?

Yoneda: I saw them in their trucks with their Black Dragon flags—three and four on their trucks—racing down the roads. You got to know them just like you got to know some of the other people.

Hansen: So during this time, whether you committed it to your diary or not, you probably were able to put together some kind of membership list for the Black Dragons. You knew who made up the core of that group.

Yoneda: That core was about thirty, if they had that many.

Hansen: How do you think they were able to be so successful in intimidating such a large population?

Yoneda: Because of the "do-nothing" policy of the camp administration: not giving the "internees" proper work, proper recompense, and an understanding of what this war was all about. As I said, these were all young people. How many of us were mature enough to know what the Axis meant? Those who were pro-Japan military, thinking that Japan had done such a wonderful thing in Manchuria and China, would say, "Look, they were liberating the people. They were bringing in more people to think the way the Japanese were thinking." Well, you take an Issei who has been removed from his fatherland for twenty or thirty years, reads only the Japanese press, and would hear people who were born in this country say things like that, he or she would think there might be something to it. Some had strong ties with their homes. They had feelings—that they should rightfully have—for their fatherland. We didn't permit them to become attached to this country.

Hansen: The context was favorable, then, for manipulations?

Yoneda: They *were* manipulated.

Hansen: Would it be a fair evaluation of the camp situation to say that there was probably a reasonably small group of committed pro-Americans and a reasonably small group who were pro-Axis, while the large population itself was just confused in going about everyday things, concerned about problems of diet, or problems of health, or problems of housing?

Yoneda: Yes. Also, there was the JACL group, who had always professed that they were more American than most Americans. They did not have a sound or vocal program to give the people. So the people were sort of in a vacuum. I can very well see why people were swayed. "Look, you've been eating slop; that's because they don't care for you." If you had a block where the chief chef was part of the Black Dragons or could be influenced by someone in there, you had slop. And I mean, it was slop!

Hansen: So they took an already undesirable situation and made it as undesirable as possible.

Yoneda: Of course. They blew it up and blew it up so that you could be at the pit of despair, unless you were determined and strong, as perhaps Karl and I were. We were a little more mature and sophisticated in our knowledge of what can be done in an attempt to break you down when you're taken into a prison cell.

Hansen: How much political sophistication do you think the hardcore, pro-Japan person had?

Yoneda: They had a lot of sophistication in things military because they had it drummed into them in Japan.

Hansen: What about political sophistication? You know a lot about that because you've seen it at work. In terms of the Manzanar situation, what kind of organizational setup did they have, and what kinds of techniques? What did they use to manipulate the population?

Yoneda: A lot of it was intimidation. If they found out that you had any relatives in Japan, they would play that to the hilt. To the Issei, who couldn't become citizens, they would say, "Are you going to allow your daughter, who is a citizen, to go and work for the camouflage net factory? That camouflage net might be put on a gun that'll kill your relative." Thus, they played on that sympathetic note. "You don't want your kinspeople to be killed."

Hansen: You thought they might be in contact with people who could do Japanese relatives harm?

Yoneda: Yes, who could do it. Who knows? They may have even indicated that, some way or another, they had secret ways of communicating. They knew submarines were on the way, and they knew that they would be liberated. They would be heroes in the eyes of the Japanese people. "Do you want to be a hero like I'm going to be, or do you want to be a dog?"

Hansen: How strong of an argument was it to brand somebody a Communist in that context?

Yoneda: There was much branding of Communists in that context. They were dogs, you know, government agents. Korean *inu*. You see, Karl was tall for his age group. Now, the Nisei, Sansei, and Yonsei are much taller. But at that time, standing five foot eight and being thirty-six years old, he was quite tall. So they immediately said, "Oh, he's really not Japanese. He must be a Korean *inu*." They said this because some of the Koreans are taller.

Hansen: There's no doubt in your mind that the Black Dragons was a real organization and not a symbolic one? I mean, it wasn't just a few people putting out leaflets; you think there was a disciplined organization behind the leaflets.

Yoneda: At first they may have been unknown to one another, but later they became, I think, a well-organized core who were out to destroy in whichever way they could.

Hansen: Do you think that was true at the time that you're talking about in your diary, in August?

Yoneda: By August they were highly organized, yes. Because they would appear almost in toto, you know, the whole group.

Hansen: What percentage, roughly, were Kibei?

Yoneda: Most of them were. There may have been a couple of Issei among them, and there may have been just a couple of Nisei who had never been to Japan but had close ties there.

Hansen: Do you think Karl was picked out as a special object of abuse because, in part, he was a Kibei?

Yoneda: He was picked out not so much because he was a Kibei but because he, along with others, was vocal in his stand. He was anti-emperor.

Hansen: I mean, because he was not only a pro-American but he was also a Kibei pro-American. Plus, he could speak fluently in either Japanese or English.

Yoneda: Yes, if it was in Japanese, he could answer them in kind.

Hansen: Where are we now in your diary, Elaine?

Yoneda: I'm leaving Manzanar, to be gone for about three weeks, to try and help locate my daughter Joyce who had disappeared. I left Manzanar on August 25.

Hansen: Where was she living at the time? Los Angeles?

Yoneda: Yes, she was living with my parents. She asked to go to camp with us, and I told her I didn't think it was the place for her, that she had better stay with Grandma and Grandpa. The school was close by. I didn't know what conditions were going to be like at Manzanar, and I felt I would probably have my hands full taking care of Tommy and his needs because of his health. That was perhaps an error, I don't know. I don't know whether it would have been better for her to go to camp or not. But she did disappear, and we didn't know where she was.

I was granted permission to go, and I went with a couple of the administrators who were going to Los Angeles. From there, I took the train up to San Francisco, where my mother had already gone to try to find her. We looked for her for about three weeks. In the meantime, I visited with various friends in the area. I also indicate in my diary that I spoke to the National Lawyers Guild and was questioned as to how could I say that the camps weren't too bad. I said I hoped there would be more war work so that we could finish the war in a hurry and do away with the Axis. I also told them that we couldn't equate these camps to the Hitler camps and their ovens. They weren't anything like that. There was restriction. So I said, "We can't condemn them altogether." What would have been the end result if there had been a lot of resistance? Our fight for civil rights would have to come after the war was over.

Hansen: You preferred certain inconveniences to being annihilated?

Yoneda: Yes. I also spoke to the CIO council and different organizations here in San Francisco. I was given some records, *Ballads for America*, with Paul Robeson singing them. I brought them back to camp. I remember playing them, and a lot of people bit their lips, you know, when he sang out in those Chinese ballads for victory and things like that, against the Fascists and against the Spanish generals. It was a joy for us to be able to hear that powerful voice again and have it right there with us. Also, on September 6, I visited the Tanforan [Assembly Center] and saw a lot of our prewar acquaintances incarcerated there, some of them in the horse stalls.[8]

I was welcomed by friends in the Bay area and was taken around in my search for my daughter. Fortunately, we found our daughter. She had to be put into juvenile hall for evaluation and so on. I couldn't stay any longer. My mother stayed there and took care of that problem. So that was going on at the same time. On September 15 I left for Manzanar. Karl and Tommy were happy to see me, and that, of course, destroyed the rumor that I had left him.

Hansen: I'll bet you were really torn about going on this trip, because your daughter was perhaps in danger and your husband was, too.

Yoneda: Yes. Really it was a mixed thing. When I got back to Manzanar, I found that it was 101 degrees. It was that hot! Koji and Taeko Ariyoshi came over in the evening. They had just been married while I was gone. Karl was best man. I had missed that. I went back to work at the camouflage net factory. On September 19 my mother wrote to me telling me that there was still nothing definite about Joyce.

Yoneda: On September 26 Koji Ariyoshi and a group left again for Idaho. That same day, my mother wired me and said that she and Joyce were going back to Los Angeles, so that problem was settled for a while.

On September 30 still another group left for Idaho and Montana. A few days later, Karl got a wire from Koji to help about recruiting, and for the first time, he thought that maybe he ought to go, too. But he wanted to be around camp just in case they ever came around to recruit for the army or the navy. So he was torn between leaving and staying. But he decided that he would go, so he signed up on October 3. The last day that I worked at the camouflage net factory was October 5 because Karl was going to leave the next day.

Hansen: So you had to stay home.

Yoneda: I had to stay home with Tommy. Karl left and, I write, "Tommy had quite a crying spell and misbehaved." Then I went to a nursery that was in 1-14, and Tommy seemed to like it. It was in the area, the same barracks, where I then made arrangements to go to work as a kindergarten helper.

Hansen: You were getting a little more income now that Karl was up in Idaho, I suppose.

Yoneda: He hadn't gotten paid yet. He had the lump sum when he came back, and he didn't fulfill his full contract.

On November 9 I got a letter from my folks saying that my daughter Joyce disappeared again. On this day, too, I note that somebody from Terminal Island brought back whiskey to the camp. Whether he was returning from Idaho or from one of the other work projects, I don't know. He was caught, and a mob threatened the Japanese [American] policeman who reported it. In other words, a citizen of Japanese ancestry reported him. And on November 10 I have a notation that the Japanese [American] policeman who reported it was badly beaten by a mob of twenty-five men who were staked around his barrack at night. (reading from diary) "All were dressed in black."

November 11 was Armistice Day. Then the next day I got a letter from Karl with five dollars. He wanted to know about the colonel. That meant the recruiter, because earlier in the year someone said that there was going to be recruiting [for the army] and that they'd be coming back to Manzanar soon.

A wire from Karl on November 16 said that he was coming home. Karl finally did get back to Manzanar on November 18. Then we had word that the colonel and his party would be here on the November 27. On November 26, I note in my diary: "Had Thanksgiving dinner at 4:00 p.m. A Manzanar Black Dragon poster appeared." And, of course, since I didn't read Japanese, I wasn't quite aware of what it said, so Karl translated it. Then, on November 27, I have a note here, "Someone tried to set fire to the dry goods store. Things are popping, but what?" I am questioning, "What are the aims?" On November 28 I was informed that my daughter had gotten married. She was just fifteen. Also, the major had come to Manzanar and Karl was inducted into the army as a buck private, and "will leave about Tuesday. We had a gathering [at our apartment], and Taeko and Koji Ariyoshi stayed until 10:00 p.m." That was the day that the fourteen men were inducted into the army for military intelligence training.

Hansen: Had they taken a battery of exams prior to this?

Yoneda: They had been called in and were tested—to what extent I don't know. All I knew was that they had to be proficient in the Japanese and English languages, had to more than understand both of them. Of course, if they had any military training, it would have been a little better. But I don't know how many of the fourteen even had ROTC. I know Karl never had any military training since he had run away from serving in the Imperial Army in Japan.

Hansen: Were most of the fourteen Kibei?

Yoneda: I believe they were. I knew some of them, but the others I didn't know. There were quite a number that attempted to join, but they lacked the Japanese language qualification. But being the scholar and having the masterful mind that he had, when he graduated from training at the military intelligence school, he was at the top and got awards for being the top student.

I was *not* going to follow Karl to the army camp. My feeling was that he probably wouldn't have to receive quite as much training as some of the others. Being very efficient in both languages and having the background in writing and organizing, he might be sent on a mission quicker than some of the others. I wanted to go back to San Francisco. I didn't want to go to Minnesota [site of the army language school]. I didn't know anyone there. I had applied for permission to return to Military Area 1 with our son. The permit I was requesting for the two of us. I was asked by Ned Campbell, "Why don't you go to Minnesota? Why are you making all these maneuvers, trying to put stumbling blocks up?" I said, "Look, Tommy and I weren't going to come to this place. Those were not our plans. My plans do not include following my husband into army camp! I want to do war work! I want out! I want a place where I know my son can have adequate housing and care. I don't know what our fate would be in Minnesota. My request is to return to Los Angeles or San Francisco, wherever I can get a job."

On November 30 I write: "Campbell said the [travel] permit would take about thirty days." I make this notation: "About ten to twelve guys are sulking around our barrack. They followed us for a couple of hours. Karl notified [Chief Internal Security Officer John W.] Gilkey." From then on, we had to have people posted around our barrack, because the others appeared every night around our barrack after Karl enlisted. They were always talking in Japanese around our place, so I didn't know what they were saying.

On December 2 the fourteen recruits left Manzanar, and Tommy cried miserably. The parents, the wives, and the sweethearts of the men who were leaving were not allowed to go with them to the bus, which was parked right outside the barbed wire gate. We had to stay on the other side of the barbed wire, so our last farewells to each other were through barbed wire. And here they were, members of the US Army! It was a heartbreaking scene because most of us didn't know if we'd ever see them again. And, of course, some of them didn't return. (reading from diary) "That night Tommy took very sick." He was very distraught about his daddy leaving him behind. He wanted to go. In fact, his last words were screamed through that barbed wire fence, "I want to go with you and help you kill the Fascists!"

One of the rumors at that time said that Karl had walked out on me because he was scared of the Kibei, and that was why he went into the army!

Hansen: So they thought he was running from them to save his own skin. So virtually everything being done was misconstrued in rumors.

Yoneda: I think it was deliberately misconstrued to arouse hostility.

Hansen: I have heard that they made attempts to prevent the fourteen enlistees from leaving Manzanar.

Yoneda: Well, that's why we had the gang around our place after Karl enlisted. You see, when he went to Gilkey, we had been followed and harassed by ten to twelve guys that were sulking around our barrack.

Hansen: They were just shadowing every move he made.

Yoneda: Yes, and circling the barrack, you see, trying to intimidate us.

Hansen: Did you find out from the others who were going at the same time what happened to them? Koji Ariyoshi, James Oda, and the rest?

Yoneda: I really don't know. On Sunday, December 6, I received a wire from Karl saying that they had arrived at Fort Snelling in Minnesota. At noon that day I heard that Fred Tayama had been badly beaten [on December 5]. (reading from diary) "One suspect was arrested. About 2:00 p.m. [on December 6] a mob led by J. K. [Joe Kurihara] and [Genji] Yamaguchi went to the administration building, demanding the return to camp from the Independence jail of Harry Ueno, who had been arrested at Block 22. The MPs were called in to camp. Joe Kurihara, in a speech, said, 'If Karl Yoneda was here, we would kill him.' I asked for protection, but it seems I am not able to get any." In my diary entry for that day, it says: "Judo guy threatened Yo Ukita for associating with me."

Actually, I was walking toward the administration building to see whether or not they'd gotten something about Tommy, and I got into part of that demonstration where they were speaking Japanese to the crowd, and the crowd was getting bigger. Mr. [Edward] Chester [secondary teacher and assistant procurement officer] came over to me. And I heard the name Yoneda, so I knew that they were saying something about Yoneda. Joe Kurihara said it about four or five times.

Hansen: You could hear him on the loudspeaker.

Yoneda: Yes, I could hear him speak. And Tommy was there. We couldn't get into the administration building to see if I had a wire. I thought maybe there was a wire from Washington saying that I could take Tommy out. I didn't know how they were going to send that. Mr. Chester came over and said that the crowd was saying that since Karl got away from them, they'd better get after his son. You know, the oldest son becomes the one that they go after if they can't get to the father.

Hansen: Even though the oldest son is a little boy.

Yoneda: Well, he wasn't quite four yet. So that's why I asked for protection from the inmate police, but there wasn't any. Yo was threatened. Her mother and father, both Mr. and Mrs. Ukita, were told to have their children, all mature, watch their steps.

Hansen: Do you have anything there [in the diary] indicating the approximate number of people in the crowd?

Yoneda: No. It was a very big crowd. I did not put that down. As you can see, my handwriting was sort of shaky and much bigger than it is in other entries.

Hansen: Yes. So this was definitely a panic situation.

Yoneda: Yes, I could feel the tenseness. Then, "About 9:30 p.m. Kitchen 4 started banging on their bells, and it was taken up by others." You know, you could hear the echo. Then I think it was Yo Ukita who came over and said, "Johnny Sonoda was almost killed, and two were shot by MPs." "Kitchen 4 says 'Strike!' I stayed home. Yo came and said she could not come over anymore." There were just too many threats against her family, and she just didn't know what to do. She wanted to come in there and stay with me but thought that I'd better keep the door locked. I had come back from the administration building and locked myself in the apartment. I didn't go out for the evening meal or anything. The commotion didn't seem to stop until about 11:30 p.m.

Hansen: Was the kitchen crew at Block 4 closely connected with the activities of Harry Ueno, since he was the head of the Kitchen Workers Union?

Yoneda: Well, I think the head of our kitchen crew was one of the Black Dragons from the start, never mind the Kitchen Workers Union.

Hansen: You don't remember his name, do you?

Yoneda: No. At 1:00 a.m. [December 7], and an ambulance came to the Ito apartment in Block 4. At that time, I heard crying. When I heard all that, I opened the door and ran across to the Itos and found that young James Ito had been killed. His sister, Martha, said to me, "Elaine, please leave. Some of the people here are saying it's Karl's and your fault that this happened to my brother." The Itos were in a barrack, directly across from our 4-2-2, so our doors faced one another. Mrs. Ito, the mother of the boy killed, and I embraced and we cried. I ran back and locked the door to my apartment. There were some dark figures all around. Tommy was awakened by all that ruckus, and crying. Finally, about 4:00 a.m., I just couldn't take it anymore. I dressed Tommy. It was dark. I started running toward the administration building. I had heard about the beatings of Fred Tayama and John Sonoda, and I didn't know how bad they were. I'd heard why the administration demonstration was going on. I hadn't been to Block 22, so I didn't know about that, but I had been right in the midst of what had gone on there.

Then I found out that a group of people commandeered a truck and started to run down the MPs who were guarding the police station. And that's when fire opened. That's when they shot. [James] Ito and the other fatal victim [Jim Kanagawa] were on their way to their night jobs at the administration building. They were not part of this. In fact, they had been among those who signed our petition in August, asking for them to be allowed to serve our country. So, you see, young men were killed because of the actions of a few who did not have the well-being of the "evacuees" at heart.

Hansen: Well, what happened to you?

Yoneda: As I got past Block 4, at the firebreak, I was suddenly stopped, "Who goes there?" Then a soldier came at me with a gun, turned a flashlight on me, and said, "What are you doing here? You belong over there." And he pointed over to the other side of the barbed wire when he saw my white face. I said, "No, I'm married to a soldier, but not to anyone stationed here. He's in Minnesota. I want to go to the administration building. I want protection for our son. He's been threatened all day, and there have been men gathering around our barrack. I want protection, and I'm not getting it. I asked for police protection, but I haven't gotten it. Now perhaps the army will protect me. I want to get to the administration building!" Tommy said, "Yes, my daddy's a soldier! My daddy's a soldier!"

He took us down to the next block. There was another soldier there. He gave the proper password, and this was the way I was passed down to the administration building.

When I got there the building was surrounded by MPs. There were two or three around a machine gun. And then a few feet away there was another. When I got inside, lo and behold, I found quite a number of people on cots. There were about fifty-eight cots. All the desks had been shoved back, you know, and cots were put there. Then Campbell came over to me and said, "Oh, I forgot to send you protection." I said, "You forgot. Thanks."

Not too long after we had gotten there, reveille sounded, and we were taken by truck over to the dispensary of the MP section and were fed there. And then brought back at night to sleep on the cots in the administration building, because there was just no room in the MP area.

Hansen: So all the kids were there, too, right?

Yoneda: Yes, babes and everyone else. There were old people as well. Fred Tayama was there with his head bandaged.

Hansen: Was he well enough to be able to walk around?

Yoneda: I don't recall him walking around. All I remember is that bandage was on his head. It was quite a big bandage. But he did come back to the administration building to sleep, as far as I know. Whether he was laying on a bed, I don't know, but I recall seeing that big bandage on his head. And, of course, Tommy wasn't too well. He had just gotten out of the hospital. So I was more concerned in seeing that he didn't go into any "wing-ding," because dust was raging and it was very cold! So shall I say that I wasn't paying too much attention to the others?

Hansen: Can you characterize the general mood of the group that was in the administration building at night and over at the MP barracks during the day?

Yoneda: Well, some of us were discussing what's what. We thought of ourselves as a clan. Those of us, like the Yamazakis and a few others, would sort of get together and say, "Well, what's going to happen to us? What are we going to do?" Tom, as you know, was an alien.

Hansen: Tom Yamazaki?

Yoneda: Yes. Therefore, his enlistment hadn't been accepted. We wondered what was going to happen to him. So it was a confused situation. I noted in my diary: "The whole Ukita family was brought in at 5:00 p.m. Yo whispered to me that it would be okay if only she was taken out, but they weren't just going to take her." So they all went back to their barracks. Here was my account on December 8: "It was reported that no one in camp was working except for the kitchen and hospital crews. John Sonoda was moved from the hospital because guys were still looking for him. More troops arrived from Reno. Some soldiers on duty for forty-six hours already. Slept at the administration building. I asked Mr. Chester to send a wire to my folks telling them that I was okay."

Hansen: Because they had been reading in the papers about this trouble?

Yoneda: Of course, they had.

Hansen: Was Karl frightened when he left Manzanar about the possibility of any kind of vindictive action against you and your son?

Yoneda: Well, he said to be careful. He didn't know to what extent some of these Fascist Black Dragons, or Blood Brothers, or whatever else they wanted to call themselves, would go. He told me to demand and re-demand protection if anything happened. He said that he hoped it wouldn't take the thirty days, like Ned Campbell said, before Tommy and I could get out.

Those who left families behind were making arrangements to go to either Minnesota or other places. I wasn't the only one who was demanding that our son be allowed to go back to Military Area 1. All of us were involved in trying to see where we were headed.

On Wednesday [December 9], under escort, we were all taken to our different barracks to try to gather as much stuff as we could, because they said

FIGURE 22. Elaine, Karl, and Tommy Yoneda, Fort Snelling, Minnesota, 1943. Karl was enrolled as a volunteer in the US Military Intelligence Language School. Courtesy International Publishers.

that we were going to be leaving. Crowds formed around our barrack, but I don't know whether that was true with the other barracks. (reading from diary) "The sergeant in charge was told to hurry, and he told *me* to hurry, too. He didn't like that way it looked out there. When I was inside packing a bag, he told me to hurry up. And I, in the excitement, forgot my purse, trying to get the proper clothing that I thought Tommy and I would need. I could take only what I could carry, because Tommy couldn't carry anything. He could carry a toy, but nothing else. So, on the way back, I discovered I had forgotten my purse, and we had to go back to our so-called apartment. We turned around. When we got there, we found two men trying to break the lock."

Hansen: They were trying to get into your apartment then, right?

Yoneda: Yes. I became aware of a lot of men wearing a black band. I thought it was a mourning symbol but found out afterward that the Blood Brothers started it and were forcing almost everyone to wear it. All the progressives left in camp were being called *inu*, "dogs," et cetera.

I had no mail [from Karl] by December 10. Then about 2:30 we left for Death Valley under heavy army escort. I didn't know why we required that heavy of an escort in the truck outside of the drivers, because we were going to Death Valley and the Slocum family was going to New Mexico.

Hansen: Some people have mentioned, in particular Tad Uyeno, that during the time that you were at the MP quarters, there was an avoidance of Tokie Slocum. He seemed to be viewed as objectionable, even to those people who were supportive of a pro-American position. Do you recall that Tokie Slocum was somewhat on the fringe of that group?

Yoneda: What I recall is, through the years, Karl and Tokie Slocum were bitter enemies. With Tokie Slocum being what I would call one thousand percent patriotic, thinking, "My country, right or wrong. My country could do no wrong. Even though you see it's wrong, don't tell me about it; I won't listen to you." So here we find ourselves in the same camp, being allied in a fight to destroy a vicious enemy—a mutual vicious enemy, the Fascist Axis. I don't know how much Tokie had in his mind about fascism. So it was strange to find ourselves allied. I didn't have much to do with him. I would only see him occasionally, but Karl saw him constantly because of the block leader thing and the Manzanar Citizens Federation and so on.

Hansen: How about some of the other people there? Did you have any contact with Fred Tayama?

Yoneda: I didn't have too much to do with him. I would see him occasionally at some town meeting or something. Karl's association with him and the others [the JACL people] was through the Manzanar Citizens Federation.

Hansen: What did you think of Tayama, as a surface impression? How did he strike you?

Yoneda: Well, I had known of his background of being such an exploiter of labor for his own gains. I thought that, yes, maybe he's in this fight so he can preserve some of his—well, not so much for the betterment of humanity or whatever. We didn't associate with him socially or anything. As [Tad] Uyeno pointed out,[9] when we got to [Cow Creek] camp, there was this schism. I was quite surprised to find out how highly Uyeno thought of Tom

Yamazaki—for instance, in his article. I didn't find it there in the few days that I was there. But I wasn't in Death Valley as long as the others.

Hansen: Well, anyway, you were going out to Death Valley under heavy guard, perhaps even an inordinately heavy guard.

Yoneda: I found out that the permit had been rushed through for the Slocums to leave for New Mexico. As to Death Valley camp—now, Tad Uyeno says he found it well preserved. I found that it was broken down. A lot of the windows were down. We had to put up newspapers and blankets in the section where we went to stay. Just Tommy and I were in one of the rooms there, beside where the kitchen was. "It's broken, et cetera," I reported in my diary, "but we'll make a go of it." We cleaned up the place the next day—Friday, December 11—but there were no letters. I got a box of candy from Karl, but there was no letter. He had sent that much earlier. On December 12 I wrote to Karl and the folks, but I received no return mail. Then on December 15 [E. Reesman "Si"] Fryer came in from Utah, on his way to Manzanar.

Hansen: He was the regional director from San Francisco, right?

Yoneda: Yes, and he came to Death Valley. (reading from diary) "He says he'll send regards to Karl, and he'll try to rush Tommy's permit." On December 16 I got eighteen cards and letters from Karl, postmarked up to December 7. He didn't know yet about the riot, it seems, because the letters were dated up to December 7, and he didn't mention it. Of course, the news probably hadn't reached back there yet.

I wrote in my diary: "Campbell back from Manzanar at 7:30 and told me to pack. I am thrilled. He also said they had a long wire from Karl, which they answered. Campbell gave me the order, telling me I could leave with Tommy." He gave me this validated permit. There were some instructions. Tommy was always to be with his mother or Caucasian escort, and there was to be a report to General DeWitt once a month. He was going to be four on January 10, 1943, and this was already the middle of December 1942. I had to have very good instructions on how he was to play. So I asked a question. Because I felt that this might be important to somebody else later on, I asked Campbell [referring to the Caucasian escort], "What does this mean?" Campbell replied, "Why are you raising obstacles? Why don't you just take it and let it be?" I said, "I'm not raising obstacles. I don't want to get entrapped. I don't want to have Tommy taken away from me, and I don't like this word 'Caucasian.'" He said, "Well, anybody in Military Area 1 would do." That's the way he put it. I said, "All right, if that's what you say. But if I get into any trouble because of this, I'll certainly subpoena you as a witness." So you can see, Campbell and I did not like one another.

Then on December 17: "I left Death Valley at 10:20 a.m. I went to Lone Pine and bought shoes." "The bus didn't come until 4:00 p.m., and I couldn't get through to my folks until I reached Saugus [Los Angeles County]. And there they met us at the bus depot."

Hansen: Well, Mrs. Yoneda, on that note, I'd like to thank you very, very much for a wonderful interview. We are indebted to you for your wartime recollections of a very trying time in your life and that of the Japanese American community.

NOTES

1. Biographical information is from the following sources: Elaine Black Yoneda, interview by Betty E. Mitson, March 2, 1974, Oral History 1377a, and by Arthur A. Hansen, March 3, 1974, 1377b, CSUF-COPH.

2. The interview transcript reproduced below is from Yoneda, CSUF-COPH O.H. 1377b.

3. See "Thomas Mooney," *Wikipedia*, https://en.wikipedia.org/wiki/Thomas_Mooney (accessed February 28, 2021).

4. Military Area 1 included the western halves of Washington, Oregon, and California and the southern half of Arizona.

5. The multifaceted relationship between Maryknoll and Manzanar is articulated by Jonathan van Hamelen in his June 26, 2021, posting on *Discover Nikkei* titled "The Sisters of Maryknoll and Manzanar," http://www.discovernikkei.org/en/journal/2021/6/29/sisters-of-maryknoll/ (accessed November 30, 2022).

6. See Catherine Irwin, "Manzanar Children's Village," *Densho Encyclopedia*, https://encyclopedia.densho.org/Manzanar_Children%27s_Village/ (accessed March 24, 2021), and Irwin, *Twice Orphaned: Voices from the Children's Village of Manzanar* (Fullerton, CA: Center for Oral and Public History, California State University, Fullerton, 2008).

7. For more information about this penal facility, see Brian Niiya, "Fort Missoula (detention facility)," *Densho Encyclopedia*, https://encyclopedia.densho.org/Fort%20Missoula%20(detention%20facility)/ (accessed February 5, 2022).

8. The center was in San Bruno, south of San Francisco. See Konrad Linke, "Tanforan (detention facility)" *Densho Encyclopedia*, https://encyclopedia.densho.org/Tanforan_(detention_facility)/ (accessed March 24, 2021).

9. Uyeno, "Point of No Return," part 39, August 22–October 20, 1973.

Martyr

An Interview with Harry Y. Ueno

*Sacrificing one's life, station, or what is of great value
for the sake of principle or to sustain a cause.*

"Free Harry!" shouted Jimmy Nakamura in the riot scene of the 1976 television movie *Farewell to Manzanar*, the first full-length cinematic treatment of the World War II eviction and incarceration of Japanese Americans; it was based on Jeanne Wakatsuki Houston and James D. Houston's novel by the same name (Boston: Houghton Mifflin, 1973) and originally telecast by the National Broadcasting Company on March 11, 1976. The original riot on which the scene was based had occurred at the Manzanar camp in 1942 to protest what the inmates regarded as the unjust arrest of a dissident cook named Harry Ueno. Nakamura, at age eighteen, had participated in the actual riot. Now, thirty-three years later, he was an actor in its dramatization on location at a prison near Oakland. In the movie some of the names were changed, and Nakamura was supposed to chant "Free Joe!" But "with all the torches and the running of the mob," explained Nakamura, "I found myself shouting, 'Harry! Harry!' When the guns started firing, I felt the same terror. It really hit me the next morning when I woke up. I cried for hours; the tears wouldn't stop."[1]

FIGURE 23. Harry Ueno (right) reviews research material with Art Hansen at the Ueno home, San Jose, June 28, 1985. Courtesy Lawrence de Graaf Center for Oral and Public History, California State University, Fullerton.

On the evening of December 5, 1942, some masked inmates at the Manzanar Relocation Center assaulted Fred Tayama, a Nisei, severely enough to hospitalize him. Camp authorities arrested thirty-five-year-old Harry Ueno, a Kibei who was head of the camp's Kitchen Workers' Union. Ueno had formed this group a few months earlier to represent Manzanar's 1,500 Kibei-dominated mess hall workers more effectively than did the Japanese American Citizens League–inspired Manzanar Work Corps, chaired by Tayama. Without delay, authorities removed Ueno from the camp to the jail of the nearby town of Independence.

Ueno's arrest and jailing—he was the first Manzanarian to be jailed outside the camp—aroused hostility among the other inmates. They widely believed him innocent of any part in the beating of Tayama, who was reviled by many for his alleged role as a government informant and for his promotion of unpopular JACL policies regarding the management of Manzanar and the drafting of the Nisei into the military from behind barbed wire. Many inmates felt, too, that Ueno was being victimized because of his recent report to the FBI that certain WRA administrators were appropriating inmates' meat and sugar allotments and selling them on the black market. At least in part because of the pressure mounted by an inmate committee formed to protest Ueno's removal from Manzanar, Ralph P. Merritt, the camp's director, agreed to return Ueno to the camp on December 6 and have him placed in the jail there for further processing.

At 6:00 p.m., when the negotiating committee appeared at Mess Hall 22, where Ueno was employed as a cook, to report that Ueno had returned, the committee encountered a crush of some 2,000 to 4,000 inmates. When the committee attempted to disband, its objective having been accomplished, the move was shouted down by the crowd, which felt Ueno should be unconditionally released. If not, it would use force to free him. Moreover, some in the angry crowd yelled out that inmates like Tayama, who many considered the camp's number one *inu*, or "dog," should be murdered.

Next some of the crowd devised a hurried plan of action whereby one group set out to find Tayama in the camp hospital to finish the job begun the night before and the other moved to liberate Ueno from jail. Thwarting the first group, hospital personnel hid Tayama under his bed; the second group became involved in what came to be known as the Manzanar Riot. Eleven people were wounded, two of them mortally.

What follows is an excerpt from a 1976 interview with Harry Ueno at his home in San Jose about his key role in the Manzanar uprising.[2] Although by the time of this interview what preceded the riot had been well established, what transpired at the camp jail once the demonstrators arrived there had remained clouded. Ueno relates what he witnessed from his vantage point inside the Manzanar jail in the California desert that particular evening in 1942.

> *Hansen:* Did any of the inmates see you when you came back from Independence?
>
> *Ueno:* Only the people inside the jail. There were about five or six inmates in there. They told me, "A lot of people were rushing around here last night." They told me what was going on. Then pretty soon the Committee of Five, [Joe] Kurihara and the other four people [three Issei and one Kibei], came over and talked to me. They said, "Wait a little while. We are going to negotiate, and we might get you released or something. So just wait quietly in here." So I slept in the jail for a while, until another hour or so. Then, little

by little, people started coming by the police station and the administration building. A lot of them came over to the window and shook hands with me because the window was wide open. I could have walked out if I had wanted to. Some of them said, "Come on, let's go out." I said no.

Hansen: Michi Weglyn's book shows a picture of the jail at Manzanar.[3] It appears that it would be impossible for a prisoner to look out of a window. How could you have gone out a window?

Ueno: No, no. They had a great big window. I think there were two windows. The glass was wide open, so I could have walked out if I had wanted to.

Hansen: Would you describe the jail?

Ueno: The jail was just a regular barrack like those we lived in. I think that half or one-third was taken up by the police station, and the rest was for the jail purpose, see. So the window was wide open. I could have gotten out anytime I wanted to. But I didn't want to break my promise to the negotiating committee, so I stayed in there. Then by the evening—

Hansen: Had you seen your wife yet?

Ueno: No, she didn't come to the jail because they [the committee] told her, "Maybe by late tonight we might have good news."

Hansen: Oh, you might be released.

Ueno: Yeah, so that's why she didn't come over. She was waiting at home. About six o'clock, I guess, it started getting a little' darker, and a lot of people filled up the open space there [in front of the jail]. They were yelling and shouting, and the wind was blowing about thirty-five miles an hour. You know how Manzanar is when the wind is whipped up; it's dusty and pebbles fly. It was kind of a cold night. I think it was about a little after six that I noticed some of the MPs were shaking because so many people were out there—young fellows. Then the sergeant in charge went around and said, "Remember Pearl Harbor!" He was yelling, "Hold your ground!" Because they were scared, see. Two or three times he went around yelling, "Remember Pearl Harbor! Hold your ground!" In the meantime, I could see that Captain [Martyn L.] Hall was in the sentry box because the top of the sentry box was glass, and lights were right in there.[4] I could see that he was meeting with two or three people inside the sentry box. Then soon they [the military police] started putting on gas masks. So I told the people in the front, "You'd better back off, because they're going to [throw tear gas]."

Hansen: When did the guards come in? When did the soldiers come in?

Ueno: They were already there when they brought me back from Independence. Then they were putting on the gas masks. So I told the people,

"You'd better step back. Otherwise, they are going to throw the tear gas." I could see the tear gas canisters.

Hansen: You were talking to some of the people?

Ueno: Yes, in the front of the jail. I could yell because they were all nearby. So they started to back up a little bit. Then as soon as they put on the gas masks, they started throwing the canisters. I don't know how many—ten or twenty. You know, the smoke was so whipped up with the wind, and people started running. And you couldn't see anything; the smoke covered it up.

Then I heard five or six shots nearby and tommy guns or machine guns on the far eastside of the police station. When the smoke was clear, I saw one man lying on the ground. I was hoping that just—I heard the gunshot, but I hoped that it was just a dummy bullet. I was hoping it was just to scare off the people. But I saw one person lying flat in the front of the police station. As soon as everything cleared, I saw them carry in that boy [James Ito].

Hansen: Into the jail?

Ueno: Into the police station side of the building, and they put him right on top of the table. He had a bullet in his stomach, and he had a little bit of life left. Raymond Hirai [an inmate] was sitting there and another fellow [inmate]. You know, when this other fellow saw that the boy was shot, he yelled, "Is this a democracy? My gosh, I made a mistake!" A lot of people thought he was working for the FBI. A lot of Japanese had been stool-pigeoned by him. I haven't any proof, but that's what the people had talked about. But he said, "I made a mistake. How could I have known such a thing would happen?" He was yelling about himself. That was about 9:30 p.m.

Hansen: Mr. Ueno, just before, when you were in the jail and the crowd had gathered and you were talking to them, I've heard that the negotiating committee had lost control of the crowd, that the crowd was no longer listening to their suggestions. Is that pretty accurate?

Ueno: I think that the crowd was impatient. The committee was looking for Merritt. After the riot, I talked to Kurihara and others. They were looking for Merritt, up and down the administration building and all around. But they couldn't find Merritt, because Merritt was outside in the sentry box talking with Captain Hall and [John W.] Gilkey. He wasn't there. In the meantime, the crowd was getting impatient. So I think it was partly Merritt's fault. If he had stayed out and talked to the committee, they could have calmed down the people maybe.

Hansen: He let things get out of hand.

Ueno: Yeah. But I didn't see people carrying rocks or sticks or anything like that, as was shown in the *Farewell to Manzanar* television show. I never saw anybody doing that. I couldn't see on the other side of the administration building. But as far as I could see, nobody threw anything physically.

Hansen: How about singing patriotic Japanese songs?

Ueno: They sang the Japanese Navy march song and others, too. It was cold. They had to exercise to keep warm, so they were singing those kind of march songs, yes. But otherwise I didn't see any direct violence toward the MPs. I know the MPs were only a few, compared to the big crowd, so they were scared.

Hansen: Were the people shot in the front or the back?

Ueno: The one I saw that fell down, I saw the blood stain on the front. It's possible that he was hit at close range, so the bullet might have penetrated through his body. But the other people, every one—the way I heard, I never saw them—all got the bullet in the back. Every one.

Hansen: They were running from the tear gas.

Ueno: Yeah, they were running away. The bullet was a shotgun pellet, but, you see, the pellet was a big one. I think there are six or eight pellets in a shotgun. So if they are at close range, they could probably penetrate the body. I saw the boy named James Ito. His blood stain was in the stomach. I don't know, but it probably came from the back and came out in the front. Could be, I don't know for sure.

Hansen: There is some confusion about one point that I keep reading about in different reports. It is said one way one time and another way another time. There's a lot of talk that just prior to the shooting somebody released a driverless car in the direction of the jail and that it hit into the jail. And after it hit the jail, the firing followed. Some people say that this happened after the firing. Others say that it never even happened. Do you recall anything like that?

Ueno: No, nothing on the jail.

Embrey: No truck?

Ueno: No, no truck on the jail. But, you see, the line was long, you know, a lot of people were in the front there, and the other side curved in, so I couldn't see beyond that. But I saw nothing like that happen on the front of the jail or nearby the jail. The only thing, they were attacking the MPs verbally, and the young MPs were kind of shaking and scared. I don't blame them; there were so many people in front. Probably a lot of them had never seen Japanese people before in their lives until they were called into the service.

Embrey: Did you hear any order to shoot?

Ueno: No, no. Nothing.

Never charged or given a hearing, Harry Ueno was again removed from Manzanar after midnight following the riot and taken this time to the jail at Bishop, the largest town in Inyo County. A few days later he was transferred to the jail in Lone Pine along with a number of other suspected troublemakers. During the month that they were there, Ueno recalled, the military policemen guarding them sometimes got drunk in the night and peppered their cell door with rifle shots.

On January 9, 1943, this group of suspects was transported by bus and train to an abandoned CCC camp in the mountains outside of Moab, Utah. Most of the next four months of Ueno's time was spent in this temporary isolation center that the WRA authorities had established for dissidents from all of the ten camps. His last two weeks were passed in the county jail in downtown Moab after a disagreement with a guard. From there Ueno was trucked in a four-by-six-foot box with five or six other men across three states to the town of Leupp, Arizona, which the WRA had selected as the site of the permanent isolation center for inmates deemed recalcitrant. Prior to settling into the camp at Leupp, replete with guard towers, a high fence, and 150 military police assigned to guard about forty-five incarcerees, Ueno was jailed in nearby Winslow for two or three days where he was served adulterated food, housed in cramped quarters, and left inadequately protected from the oppressive weather. When finally taken to the camp at Leupp, he was jailed for about two weeks before being granted housing in a barrack. Ueno had not yet, in spite of repeated WRA promises and his persistent demands for their fulfillment, received a trial or hearing to determine his guilt or innocence to any charge that caused him to be removed from his family at Manzanar and detained at various jails and camps.

When the WRA closed its facilities at Leupp in December 1943, almost a year to the day after the riot at Manzanar, Ueno was transferred to the segregation center at Tule Lake. Again he spent an initial week in an army-supervised stockade before he was permitted to live in the compound. At last reunited with his wife and children, he promised the director of the center, Ray Best, that he would remain apart from all camp politics.[5] Although a distressed Ueno had renounced his citizenship while at Moab, he was ultimately persuaded in late December 1945 by his knowledge of the devastated condition of postwar Japan to remain in the United States and spare his family any further hardship. Three months later he was released from Tule Lake, one of the last to go.

FIGURE 24. Left to right: Betty Kulberg Mitson, Harry Ueno, Yaso Ueno, Art Hansen, and Sue Kunitomi Embrey, Monterey Park, California, December 1982. Harry Ueno was being honored at an event sponsored by the National Council for Japanese American Redress/Reparations. Photo provided by Betty Mitson. Courtesy Lawrence de Graaf Center for Oral and Public History, California State University, Fullerton.

In a September 8, 1994, letter to Arthur A. Hansen, Harry Ueno voluntarily confessed his role—along with that of a contingent of allied Kibei—in the December 5, 1942, beating of Fred Tayama.[6]

NOTES

1. Quoted in James D. Houston and Jeanne Wakatsuki Houston, "Other Days of Infamy," *Mother Jones* (February–March 1976), 66.

2. Harry Y. Ueno, interview by Sue Kunitomi Embrey and Arthur A. Hansen, October 30, 1976, transcribed and edited by Betty E. Mitson, Oral History 1518.1, CSUF-COPH. For an earlier version of this excerpted interview, see Arthur A. Hansen, Sue Kunitomi Embrey, and Betty E. Mitson, "Dissident Harry Ueno Remembers Manzanar," *California History* 64 (Winter 1985): 16–22. The full interview with Ueno was published by the same authors as *Manzanar Martyr: An Interview with Harry Y. Ueno* (Fullerton, CA: Oral History Program, California State University,

Fullerton, 1986). See also Harry Yoshio Ueno, interview by Arthur A. Hansen, June 17, 2000, Oral History 1518.3, CSUF-COPH.

3. Michi Weglyn, *Years of Infamy: The Untold Story of America's Concentration Camps* (New York: Morrow, 1976), 61.

4. Hall was commander of the military police, which had been called in to the Manzanar camp from their adjacent compound by Manzanar's project director, Ralph Merritt.

5. See Brian Niiya, "Raymond R. Best," *Densho Encyclopedia*, https://encyclopedia.densho.org/Raymond%20R.%20Best (accessed March 14, 2021).

6. For a full contextual discussion of this event, see appendixes A, B, and C in Arthur A. Hansen, "A Riot of Voices: Racial and Ethnic Variables in Interactive Oral History Interviewing," *Barbed Voices: Oral History, Resistance, and the World War II Japanese American Social Disaster* (Louisville: University Press of Colorado, 2018), 127–39. For a still more detailed and definitive depiction of the beating of Tayama by Ueno and his younger Kibei cohorts, see Ueno, CSUF-COPH O.H. 1518.3.

Coda

In the interest of transparency and credibility, readers of *Manzanar Mosaic* are invited to explore how exactly and to what extent the oral history interviews in part 2 with Sue Kunitomi Embrey, Togo Tanaka, Karl Yoneda, and Elaine Black Yoneda were exploited by the authors of the two essays in part 1 of this book. (Since the oral history interview with Harry Ueno was transacted after and not before these essays were concluded, it should be regarded as an exception to this blanket invitation.)

In addition to these five oral histories, six others were conducted in the 1970s by me alone or in concert with other members of the Japanese American Oral History Project at California State University, Fullerton, that relate just to the Manzanar "Riot" essay. (All six of these interviews, rendered in the same format as the five interviews that appear in *Manzanar Mosaic*, are available online to readers through the website for the Lawrence de Graaf Center for Oral and Public History: http://coph.fullerton.edu/collections/JAcollections.php.) Four of these interviews were tape-recorded prior to that essay's 1974 publication in the *Amerasia Journal*. The interviewees for these oral histories were Robert Brown, Ned Campbell, George Fukasawa, and

Yoriyuki Kikuchi. Brown was instrumental in the selection and early development of the Manzanar site and in 1942 served as its public relations officer and head of the Reports Office, overseeing both the *Manzanar Free Press* and the camp's two documentary historians, Togo Tanaka and Joe Grant Masaoka. Campbell was officially the assistant director for Manzanar after its conversion from an "assembly center" to a "relocation center," but unofficially he functioned as its "acting" director up to late November of 1942 and, in the run-up to the Manzanar Revolt was accused by Kibei dissident Harry Ueno of selling the camp's rationed provisions on the outside black market. Kikuchi, the Issei head of Manzanar's dental services, was threatened with retaliatory violence in advance of the Manzanar Revolt and in his interview provides testimony about a highly controversial aspect of that event. George Fukasawa, the Nisei prewar president of the Santa Monica, California, JACL chapter and that city's auxiliary police, became a member of Manzanar's inmate security force; he was among the very few of this unit who risked reporting for duty on the dangerous night of the December 6, 1942, revolt.

The other two oral histories, with Frank Chuman and Morris Opler, both tape-recorded after the Manzanar "Riot" article appeared in the *Amerasia Journal*, also offer significant information as to the content of that essay. Chuman, the Nisei supervisor of the Manzanar hospital, arrived in camp with the first group of inmates on March 21, 1942, and like, Yoriyuki Kikuchi, was targeted for violent inmate reprisal preceding the revolt; in its wake he was so positioned as to comment authoritatively to the fact that his friend and colleague, chief surgeon Dr. James Goto, had refused under pressure by officials to misrepresent the body location of the military police gunfire that killed and wounded inmates during the Manzanar revolt. As for Opler, an anthropologist who began his tenure as Manzanar's community analyst in early 1943, he made it a point to dedicate his first initial report to an in-depth historical account of the developments that preceded the climactic revolt of the previous year.

It is hoped that, taken collectively, the above-noted eleven oral histories—all but one of them (that with Frank Chuman) enacted with a now-deceased interviewee—will not only assist readers of *Manzanar Mosaic* to appreciate the strengths and shortcomings alike of the two essays in part 1 but also serve as a goad to future researchers to produce revisionist studies of these essays that greatly exceed them in terms of both source material and new modes of theory, method, and historical explanation.

Acknowledgments

In the 1970s decade I was privileged to direct and be a part of the pioneering Japanese American Oral History Project of the Oral History Program (now the Lawrence de Graaf Center for Oral and Public History) at California State University, Fullerton. Most of the project members, but not all of them, were undergraduate or graduate students in CSUF's Department of History. All of them, irrespective of their academic affiliation, were highly motivated to enrich the historical understanding of the Japanese American World War II exclusion and detention experience, through the generation of oral history interviews with those individuals, chiefly of Japanese American ancestry, connected with that experience—and most especially in the context of the Manzanar War Relocation Center.

The core members of the Japanese American Oral History Project included the following people: Betty Mitson, Dave Hacker, Ron Larson, Jessie Garrett Milano, Liz Stein, Reed Holderman, Mary Reando, Sue McNamara, Paul Clark, Dave Bertagnoli, Lannie Amigo, Janis Gennawey Logsden, Kristin Mitchell, and Duff Griffith. I am deeply indebted to all of these people for their abiding interest, scholarship, dedication, friendship, and profound commitment to human rights, civil liberties, and social justice. I think of all of them frequently—and always with deep admiration, great respect, and enduring love and appreciation.

History Department members who abetted the work of the Japanese American Oral History Project in the 1970s were Kinji Yada, Jack Elenbaas, Tom Reins, Larry de Graaf, Dave Pivar, Carmon Hardy, Mike Onorato, Gary Shumway (then director of the CSUF Oral History Program), and Tom Flickema (then chair of the CSUF Department of History).

Among the many people who have enhanced my work on Manzanar over the years are four current members of the staff at the Manzanar National Historic Site, Alisa Lynch Broch, Jeff Burton, Patricia Biggs, and Rose Masters, and three former staffers, Richard Potashin, Jane Wehrey, and Kristen Luetkemeier. In addition, each of the six superintendents for the Manzanar site—Ross Hopkins, the late Frank Hays, Tom Leatherman, Les Inafuku, Bernadette Lovato, and Brenda Ling—have taken the time and trouble to enfold me into their dedicated stewardship of Manzanar as an invaluable US government facility.

Others who have greatly assisted my work on Manzanar and the World War II Japanese American experience are Sojin Kim, Marie Masumoto, Martha Nakagawa, Carla Tengan, the late Cedric Shimo, Sharon Yamato, Naomi Hirahara, Jonathan von Harmelen, Chizu Omori, Emiko Omori, Barbara Takei, Hiroshi Shimizu, Kenji Taguma, Frank Abe, Frank Chin, the late Karen Higa, Nancy Araki, Allyson Nakamoto, John Esaki, Lisa Itagaki, Kristine Kim, and Yoko Nishimura.

Three people who deserve my thanks for all they have done and continue to do for me as a person and historical researcher-writer are my wife, Debra Gold Hansen, my closest friend, Kurtis Nakagawa, and Natalie Garcia, the archivist for the Lawrence de Graaf Center for Oral and Public History at California State University, Fullerton.

Lastly, I want to acknowledge my heartfelt appreciation to the two anonymous reviewers of the manuscript that led to this publication for their insightful and constructive critiques, as well as the following staff members of the University Press of Colorado for enacting their respective experet roles in making this book much, much more than a mere business transaction: Darrin Pratt, director; Laura Furney, assistant director and managing editor; Allegra Martschenko, acquisitions editor; Daniel Pratt, production manager; Beth Svinarich, marketing and sales director; Alison Tartt, copyeditor; and Lee Gable, indexer.

Selected Bibliography

The references below are restricted to those secondary publications that are devoted in a significant degree to the subjects of the Manzanar War Relocation Center, the Manzanar Revolt, the *Doho* newspaper, and the five Manzanar inmates whose oral histories constitute part 2 of *Manzanar Mosaic*.

MANZANAR

Alinder, Jasmine. *Moving Images: Photography and the Japanese American Incarceration.* Urbana: University of Illinois Press, 2009.
Armor, John, and Peter Wright. *Manzanar.* New York: Vintage Books, 1988.
Bishop, Ronald, et al. *Community Newspapers and the Japanese-American Incarceration Camps.* Lanham, MD: Lexington Books, 2015.
Chuman, Frank F. *Manzanar and Beyond: Memoirs of Frank F. Chuman, Nisei Attorney.* San Mateo, CA: Asian American Curriculum Project, 2011.
Garrett, Jessie A., and Ronald C. Larson. *Camp and Community: Manzanar and the Owens Valley.* Fullerton: Japanese American Oral History Project, Oral History Program, California State University, Fullerton, 1977.

Hansen, Arthur A. *Barbed Voices: Oral History, Resistance, and the World War II Japanese American Social Disaster*. Louisville: University Press of Colorado, 2018.
Hansen, Arthur A., and Betty E. Mitson, eds. *Voices Long Silent: An Oral Inquiry into the Japanese American Evacuation*. Fullerton: Oral History Program, California State University, Fullerton, 1974.
Harth, Erica. *Last Witnesses: Reflections on the Wartime Internment of Japanese Americans*. New York: Palgrave, 2001.
Hirahara, Naomi, and Heather C. Lindquist. *Life after Manzanar*. Berkeley, CA: Heyday, 2018.
Irwin, Catherine. *Twice Orphaned: Voices from the Children's Village of Manzanar*. Fullerton: Center for Oral and Public History, California State University, Fullerton, 2008.
Kitayama, Glen. "Manzanar." *Densho Encyclopedia*. https://encyclopedia.densho.org/Manzanar/ (accessed July 31, 2020).
Lindquist, Heather C., ed. *Children of Manzanar*. Berkeley, CA: Heyday, 2012.
Murray, Alice Yang. *Historical Memories of the Japanese American Internment and the Struggle for Redress*. Stanford, CA: Stanford University Press, 2008.
Nakamura, Samuel. *Nurse of Manzanar: A Japanese American's World War II Journey*. Bellingham, WA: Self-published, 2009.
Tateishi, John. *And Justice for All: An Oral History of the Japanese American Detention Camps*. New York: Random House, 1984.
Unrau, Harlan. *Manzanar National Historic Site, California: The Evacuation and Relocation of Persons of Japanese Ancestry during World War II: A Historical Study of the Manzanar War Relocation Center*. 2 vols. Washington, DC: US Department of Interior, National Park Service, 1996. Available online at: https://www.nps.gov/parkhistory/online_books/manz/hrst.htm (accessed July 31, 2020). This is the most comprehensive study of the Manzanar War Relocation Center.
Wehrey, Jane. *Manzanar*. Charleston, SC: Arcadia, 2008.
Wehrey, Jane. *Voices from This Long Brown Land: Oral Recollections of Owens Valley Lives and Manzanar Pasts*. New York: Palgrave Macmillan, 2006.
Williams, Arthur L. *Reflecting on WWII, Manzanar, and the WRA*. Victoria, BC: Friesenpress, 2014.

MANZANAR REVOLT

Hayashi, Brian Masaru. *Democratizing the Enemy: The Japanese American Internment*. Princeton, NJ: Princeton University Press, 2004.
Kurashige, Lon. *Japanese American Celebration and Conflict: A History of Ethnic Identity and Festival in Los Angeles, 1934–1990*. Berkeley: University of California Press, 2002.
Kurashige, Lon. "Resistance, Collaboration, and Manzanar Protest." *Pacific Historical Review* 3 (August 2001): 387–417.

Niiya, Brian. "Manzanar Riot/Uprising." *Densho* Encyclopedia, http://encyclopedia.densho.org/Manzanar_riot/uprising/ (accessed July 31, 2020).

Oda, James. "Manzanar." Chapter 2 of *Heroic Struggles of Japanese Americans: Partisan Fighters from America's Concentration Camps*. North Hollywood, CA: Self-published, 1980.

Tamura, Eileen H. *In Defense of Justice: Joseph Kurihara and the Japanese American Struggle for Equality*. Urbana: University of Illinois Press, 2013.

Unrau, Harlan. "Violence at Manzanar on December 6, 1942: An Examination of the Event, Its Underlying Causes, and Historical Interpretation." Chapter 11 of *Manzanar National Historic Site, California: The Evacuation and Relocation of Persons of Japanese Ancestry during World War II: A Historical Study of the Manzanar War Relocation Center*. Vol 2. Washington, DC: US Department of the Interior, National Park Service, 1996. Available online at: https://www.nps.gov/parkhistory/online_books/manz/hrs11.htm (accessed March 26, 2021).

Yoneda, Karl. "Volunteer for U.S. Military Intelligence Service." Chapter 8 of *Ganbatte: Sixty-Year Struggle of a Kibei Worker*, 145–65. Los Angeles: Asian American Studies Center, UCLA, 1983.

DOHO NEWSPAPER

Oda, James. "Topics, Pre-War and Post-War." Chapter 6 of *Heroic Struggles of Japanese Americans: Partisan Fighters from America's Concentration Camps*, 236–67. North Hollywood, CA: Self-published, 1980.

Mizuno, Takeya. "The Doho: An American Guardian." Chapter 6 of "The Civil Libertarian Press, Japanese American Press, and Japanese American Mass Evacuation," 246–83. PhD diss., University of Missouri, 2000.

Sue Kunitomi Embrey

Bahr, Diana Meyers. *Unquiet Nisei: An Oral History of the Life of Sue Kunitomi Embrey*. New York: Palgrave Macmillan, 2007.

Nakagawa, Martha. "Sue Kunitomi Embrey." *Densho Encyclopedia*, https://encyclopedia.densho.org/Sue_Kunitomi_Embrey/ (accessed July 31, 2020).

Togo Tanaka

Niiya, Brian. "Togo Tanaka." *Densho Encyclopedia*, http://encyclopedia.densho.org/Togo%20Tanaka/ (accessed July 31, 2020).

Karl Yoneda

Omatsu, Glenn. "Karl Yoneda." *Densho Encyclopedia*, https://encyclopedia.densho.org/Karl%20Yoneda/ (accessed July 31, 2020).

Yoneda, Karl G. *Ganbatte: Sixty-Year Struggle of a Kibei Worker*. Los Angeles: Asian American Studies Center, UCLA, 1983.

Elaine Black Yoneda

Raineri, Vivian McGuckin. *The Red Angel: The Life and Times of Elaine Black Yoneda, 1906–1988*. New York: International Publishers, 1991.

Harry Ueno

Embrey, Sue Kunitomi, Arthur A. Hansen, and Betty E. Mitson, eds. *Manzanar Martyr: An Interview with Harry Y. Ueno*. Fullerton: Oral History Program, California State University, Fullerton, 1986.

Hansen, Arthur A. "Harry Ueno." *Densho Encyclopedia*, http://encyclopedia.densho.org/Harry_Ueno/ (accessed July 31, 2020).

Index

Note: page numbers in italics refer to images. Those followed by *n* refer to notes, with note number.

AFL. *See* American Federation of Labor
agricultural workers in California, and Japanese American labor unions, 32–34
aka (Red) as term, 160, 173, 212–13
Akahoshi, Ted, 97–98, 218, 220, 221
Alaska Cannery Union: *Doho* and, 41–42, 44, 51; Yoneda and, 190, 195–96, 199–200
American Federation of Labor (AFL), 38, 42–43
American Historical Explanations (Wise), 74–75
America's Concentration Camps (Bosworth), 157
Ariyoshi, Koji: and arrests after Pearl Harbor, 207; and Block Leaders Council, 102; on "death list" of rioters, 115; Embrey on, 142, 146; as friend of Yonedas, 259; hostility to JACLers, 125*n*71; and Manzanar Citizens Federation, 102, 172–73, 222, 223; marriage, 273; and petition calling for second front, 103, 259; and recruiting for US Army, 273; Tanaka on, 173, 217; volunteer for military service, 274, 276; work as longshoreman, 238; work in Military Intelligence Service, 142, 177; work to save crops in Idaho, 224, 258, 273
arrests after Pearl Harbor attack, 46–47, 91, 163, 206–9, 210, 242
assimilation of Japanese, *Doho*'s support for, 22, 23

Black Dragons: effort to stop Yoneda's election as block leader, 268; freedom to act without administration response, 260, 265, 269; head of Block 4 kitchen crew as, 277; in Japan, 203; Kibei in, 260; threats and violence against pro-US inmates, 131*n*109, 137, 262, 265, 268–69, 274; undermining of self-government effort, 108; as well-organized, 271
Blamey, Joe, 125*n*71, 149, 152, 170–71, 174, 216, 255
block leaders: directive barring Issei from, 97, 106; director's change to adminis-

trative body, 106–7; Manzanar Citizens Federation as counter to, 222; pay for, 252; power of, 97; as predominantly Issei, 96, 97, 147, 220, 221–22; selection process for, 254–55. *See also* Yoneda, Karl, as block leader

Block Leaders Council: Embrey on, 146; JACLers maneuvered out of, 102; Masaoka and, 102; replacement by Community Council, 106; rule requiring English in meetings of, 97–99, 221–22; vocal members of, 221; Yoneda on, 220–22; Yoneda's report of Kibei mass meeting to, 232

Blood Brothers, 108, 225, 279, 281

Browder, Earl, 29, 44, 46

Brown, Bob: Hansen on, 152, 159; inmates' dislike of, 170, 171; oral history of, 293–94; supervision of *Manzanar Free Press*, 148, 149, 150, 170, 179–80, 294; Tanaka on, 170–71, 179–80

Bulletin 22, 103, 153

Campbell, Ned: contemptuous attitude toward inmates, 81; Elaine Yoneda on, 264–65; and Elaine Yoneda's plan to leave Manzanar, 275, 282–83; Embrey on, 152–53; failure to send protection to Yoneda home during Riot, 278; inmates' dislike of, 116, 171; inmates friendly with, 84; oral history of, 293–94; role at Manzanar, 294; and rule requiring English in block leader meetings, 97; Tanaka on, 178–79; Ueno's corruption charge against, 110, 116, 153, 179, 294

Central California Contractor's Association, 32–34

Chaffey, George, 16, 17

Chester, Edward, 276, 279

Chuman, Frank, 175, 294

CIO. *See* Congress of Industrial Organizations

Committee of Five, 76–77, 115, 132n132, 286

communism, historians' tendency to criticize, 57–58

Communist International: control of CPUSA policy, 27–29; Seventh World Congress, 27; Stalin's contempt for, 68n81. *See also* Popular Front policy

Communist Party of America (CPUSA): agents of Japanese government in, 66n63; foreign language sections, 33; growth in Popular Front era, 27–28; and Japanese American labor activism, 33–34; and Popular Front policy, 43, 46, 49–51; Russian control of policy, 26, 27–29, 44; and Soviet nonengagement policy after Nazi-Soviet pact, 46

communists, Japanese American, fear of deportation, 191, 241

Community Council, replacement of Block Leaders Council, 106

Congress, US, awareness of struggle between loyal and disloyal Japanese, 50

Congress of Industrial Organizations (CIO), 38, 41, 44

Coverley, Harvey N., 17, 106

Cow Creek Camp (Death Valley): facilities at, Elaine Yoneda on, 282; Tad Uyeno on, 164, 172; pro-American Manzanar inmates moved to protective custody at, 19, 78, 116, 137, 152, 281–82; schism among inmates at, 281–82

CPUSA. *See* Communist Party of America

Daniels, Roger, 10–11, 80, 90–91

Death Valley. *See* Cow Creek Camp (Death Valley)

Democratizing the Enemy (Hayashi), 24–25

DeWitt, John L., 96, 126n72, 149–50

Doho newspaper: advertisement as "progressive" newspaper, 192; and arrests following Pearl Harbor, 46–47, 52; attacks on reactionaries, 41; attacks on Sei Fujii, 50–51, 52–53, 60, 193–94, 200; attacks on Tayama, 41, 51, 112, 169–70, 196–97; attacks on Tolan Committee, 169–70; attacks on Uno, 197–98; broad leftist coalition served by, 35, 62; circulation, 191; commitment to "American Way," 38–40; contents of early editions, 190–91; cooperation with other papers on issue-by-issue basis, 203; costs and income,

39, 47, 69n97; editorial policy, in sync with Soviet policy, 26, 35, 39–40, 44, 46, 49–50, 57; employees sent to Manzanar, 56, 215; founders of, 29–30; and JACL, 39, 44–46, 48–50, 56, 69n103, 70n112, 204; and Japanese assimilation, support for, 22, 23; Kibei staff members, 70n112; name, selection of, 34, 190; national circulation of, 214; on Nazi-Soviet Non-Aggression Pact, 44, 68n83; and New Deal, support for, 39–40; opposition to peacetime draft, 46; as political, labor, and community newspaper, 198–99; rally sponsored by (June 1939), 199; readers' circles, 65n42, 196, 213–14; readership, 35, 213; rival newspapers in Los Angeles, 36–37; as *Rodo Shimbun* reborn in Los Angeles, 190; roots in Japanese-American socialism, 22, 29–30; sources on, 21–22; Soviet double agent working at, 169; as spokesperson for all Japanese people, 66n63; sponsorship of anti-Fascist rally in Los Angeles, 43; staff of, 34, 36; support for Japanese American Citizens League, 39; support for racial equality, 62, 68–69n88; Tanaka on, 169; telegram to US officials pledging support for US, 52; as voice of working class and progressives, 37; war coverage, 51–52; Yoneda and, 136, 190–97, 209; *Zenshin* as original name of, 34, 190. *See also* Fujii, Shuji

Doho newspaper, and JAI: reporting on, 55–56; staff visit to Manzanar, 56; support for, 23, 53–54, 215

Doho newspaper, and Japan: agents of Japanese government on staff, 66–67n63; anti-fifth-column campaign, 45, 48–51, 52, 53–54, 62; coverage of fifth-column activities, 201–2, 205; criticism of Japanese imperialism, 44, 48, 66n63, 199–200; criticism of pro-Japan newspapers in California, 37, 200; criticism of supporters of Japanese fascism, 40, 43–44, 67–68n77; on Japan's plan to recruit and train Japanese American students, 43–44, 202–3; on Kibei and Japanese fifth column, 48, 69n103, 70n112; on militarists' exploitation of people in Japan, 36, 40; policy on war with Japan, 214; and Popular Front policy, 35–36, 37, 39–40, 43, 195; pro-Japan sentiment, opposition to, 22; support for US war effort, 22–23, 53, 56

Doho newspaper, as community newspaper, 22, 26–27, 58, 62; communities' view of, Yoneda on, 213; and value of alternative to mainstream vernacular press, 58–62

Doho newspaper, communist stance of, 57–58; and communist candidates, support for, 195; as disputed, 22; distancing from CPUSA activities, 22, 64n37; editor's denial of, 39; labeling as *Aka* (Red) paper, 36–37, 51, 212; as underplayed, to avoid backlash, 191

Doho newspaper, English section of, 22; addition of, in second year, 34; first issue of, 35–36, 65n47; as not representative of whole, 22; suspension of, for financial reasons, 47–48

Doho newspaper, labor union activism by, 37–38, 40–43, 44, 45–46, 68n79, 196; criticisms of SCRPWU, 47; government efforts to suppress, 46–47; and labeling as *Aka* (Red) paper, 51; support for AFL over SCRPWU, 49; turn from, with advent of war, 51–52

Doho newspaper, turn to antiwar/noninvolvement policy, 44–45, 46; alienation of liberal supporters by, 47–48, 69n97; modulation of, to avoid subscriber loss, 48; and turn against Roosevelt, 46

Domei Japanese News Agency, 60, 200, 212

drafting of Nisei: *Doho* opposition to peacetime draft, 46; inmates' resistance to, 19; JACL call for, at convention of 1942, 230; Manzanar Citizens Federation petition calling for, 102–3, 222–23, 259, 265; resumption in 1944, 19

Elenbaas, Jack, 4–5, 5

Embrey, Sue Kunitomi, 139, 291; age, while at Manzanar, 136; on *Aka* (Red) as term, 160; background and education, 138–40;

on Brown, 152; on Chiye Mori, 141, 148–50, 174; on family's Los Angeles grocery store, 140–41; interview of, 3–4, 7; interviews conducted by, 8; lectures on JAI, 6; on Masaoka, 152; on Nisei cultural confusion, 88; on protective removal of JACLers to Cow Creek, 152; on removal to Manzanar, 142–43; on Slocum, 152; on Tanaka, 151–52; tours of Manzanar led by, 6; on Ueno, 156–57

Embrey, on JACL: inmates' lack of sympathy for beatings of, 19; leftists allied with, 141–42; members of, 141; reputation as sell-outs, 141

Embrey, on Manzanar: on block leaders and block meetings, 146; on conflict between Bainbridge Island and Terminal Island groups, 143–44, 145; contact with camp administrators, 158–59; departure from, 140, 159; group solidarity among housing blocks, 146; her housing block, and neighboring blocks, 143; her jobs at, 147; her work at *Manzanar Free Press*, 145; inmates' places of origin, 145–46; Issei leadership in, 146–47; lack of privacy at, 153, 158; many rumors at, 153; notable leaders at, as unknown to girl of her age, 151; poor food at, 153; views about camp administrators, 152–53

Embrey, on *Manzanar Free Press*: administration censorship of, 150; beating of staff, 149; editorial writers at, 150; her work for, 136, 147–48, 150–51; post-Riot issue, impounding of, 155–56; removal of staff to protective custody at Cow Creek, 152; staff of, 141, 144, 148–49; suspension of publication after Riot, 155–56; Tanaka and Masaoka's role at, 150–51; threats against staff, 152; views on pro-administration stance, 149–50

Embrey, on Manzanar Riot, 153–55; casualties in, 154–55, 156; causes of, 153, 158; leaders of, 157–58; number of participants, 153

Emperor Meiji, Shakai Kakumeito's threat against, 31–32

ethnic perspective on Manzanar Riot, 85–117; administrators targeted, as typical *keto* (white man, hairy beast), 116; on beating of Tayama, as just punishment, 114; and conflict in cultural loyalties in Japanese Americans, 88–94; and context of larger resistance movement, 86; and cultural meaning in Japanese American Community, 85–86; heightened ethnic consciousness of crowd, 116; and Japanese American conflict over cultural boundaries, 94–95; and Japanese prioritization of group well-being, 87, 89–91; and Manzanar inmates' struggle for control of community, 95–117; and rigid social hierarchy of Japanese society, 87; Riot as culmination of long-brewing resentments, 114–15; Riot as defense of cultural heritage and identity, 116; Riot as unrelated to loyalty issue, 115; rioters' "death list" and, 115–16; and six themes in prewar Japanese American culture, 86–87; sources for, 86; terminology used in, 86

Executive Order 9066, 23, 163

Farewell to Manzanar (1976 film), 8, 284

Farewell to Manzanar (Houston and Houston), 3–4, 284

Fresno Rodo Domei Kai (Fresno Labor League), 32–33

Fujii, Sei: *Doho*'s attacks on, 50–51, 52–53, 60, 193–94, 200; as interpreter and legal advisor to Japanese Americans, 193; as *Kashu Mainichi* editor, 36; as pro-militarist, 36, 194

Fujii, Shuji, 35; anti-fifth-column campaign of, 54; and arrests of Japanese Americans after Pearl Harbor, 52; attacks on Tayama, 196–97; attacks on Tolan Committee, 169–70; as communist, 193; as *Doho* editor, 34–35, 36, 66n63, 190, 191; Elaine Yoneda on, 244–45; family and background of, 35; and JACL anti-Axis Committee, 54–55, 131n118; as Kibei, 36, 70n112, 193; popularity with other editors, 203–4; at Santa Anita

Assembly Center, 57; and Santa Anita Riot, 57; Tanaka and, 68–69n88, 203–4; telegram supporting US war effort, 52; warnings about Japanese American fifth-columnists, 48–49; wartime military career, 57; wartime truce with Tayama, 53; Yoneda on, 191, 193, 201
Fukasawa, George, 128n87, 293–94

Garrett, Jessie A., 7, 8
Gilkey, John W., 275, 276, 288
Grodzins, Morton, 114, 115, 124n68

Hacker, David A., 3, 6, 7, 8, 19, 159–60
Hansen, Art, 8, 285, 291
Hasuike, George, 38, 41, 49
Hawai'i Japanese Americans, volunteers for military service, 146
Hearst family and newspapers, leftists' condemnation of, 39, 168, 181–82, 247, 264
Heroic Struggles of Japanese Americans (Oda), 21, 22
Higashi, Kiyoshi, 110–11, 171–72
historical interpretation: perspectivist model of, 75, 117n2; progressive view of, and Manzanar Riot, 83–84, 85; and search for objective truth through primary sources, 74–75
A History of One Hundred Years (Katō), 212
History of the Three Internationals (Foster), 27
Houston, James D., 3–4, 284
Houston, Jeanne Wakatsuki, 3–4, 284

ILD. *See* International Labor Defense
incarceration camp inmates: registration of, 19; resistance to drafting of Nisei, 19. *See also* Manzanar inmates
incarceration camps: author's study of, 4–12; building of, by first inmates, 55–56; *Doho*'s support for, 23; locations of, 4–11; mix of Issei, Nisei, Sansei and Yonsei in, 16; number of inmates, 16. *See also* Manzanar War Relocation Center
incarceration of Japanese Americans. *See* Japanese American Incarceration (JAI)
Issei. *See* Manzanar inmates, Issei

In Defense of Justice (Tamura), 25
Information Center in Manzanar, as JACL-led, 96–97
International Conference on Relocation and Redress (1983), 10
International Labor Defense (ILD), 47, 237, 241, 242
Itami, David Akira, 56, 71–72n131, 96–97, 205, 206
Ito, James, 156, 277, 278, 288
Iwasa, Sakutaro, 31, 32–33

JACL (Japanese American Citizens League): Anti-Axis Committee, 53, 91, 92, 112–13, 182–83, 540–44; call for end to dual citizenship, 43; disavowal of traditional Japanese customs and values, 82; *Doho* and, 39, 44–46, 48–50, 56, 69n103, 70n112, 204; historians' conflation with Nisei as whole, 80; Kibei division, concerns about, 48, 50, 56, 69–70n103, 70n112, 204–6; left-wing's de facto alliance with, 96, 125n71, 131n118, 141–42; and Manzanar Citizens Federation, 99, 102; reputation as sell-outs, 141; support for JAI, 82–83, 93; Tanaka as national publicity officer of, 162; Tayama as vice president of Los Angeles chapter, 41
JACL members: arrests after Pearl Harbor attack, 91; assistance with camp construction, 95–96; beating of, in Manzanar Riot, 18–19; challenging of Issei leadership, 90–91, 92; and "death list" of rioters, 115–16; distrust of Kibei, 94–95, 123–24n66; Embrey on, 19, 141–42; exposure of disloyal community members, as setting of cultural boundaries, 94–95; favorable Manzanar jobs given to, for demonstrations of loyalty, 96, 124–25n71; inmates' resentment of, 96, 103; move away from Japanese culture, 89–90; number in Los Angeles, 182; as officials' primary source of information, 84; ousting from leadership positions by Issei-Kibei coalition, 105–6, 130n99; positive view of aiding FBI anti-fifth-column

work, 122–23n59; as pro-American collaborators, in inmates' view, 18, 75–76, 82, 91–94, 110–11, 122–23n59, 123n62; removal to protective custody at Cow Creek, 19, 78, 116; as staff of *Manzanar Free Press*, 84, 96; support for rule requiring English in block leader meetings, 99; turn from Japanese to US cultural ties, 89–92. *See also* "WRA-JACL" perspective on Manzanar Riot

JAI. *See* Japanese American Incarceration

Japan, militarism of 1930s, 193

Japanese American Celebration and Conflict (Kurashige), 24

Japanese American Citizens League. *See* JACL

Japanese American Evacuation and Resettlement Study (JERS), 21, 136

Japanese American Incarceration (JAI): first inmates' construction of camps, 55–56, 95–96, 141–42; JACL support for, 82–83, 93; and Japanese American left, as under-studied, 125n71; meetings with Japanese American leaders prior to, 54; perspectives on, 84–85; support for, in Japanese American community, 53–56

"Japanese American Internment during World War II" (1973 lecture series), 6

Japanese-American left (1904–37): CPUSA and, 33–34; founders of *Doho* and, 29–30; labor union activism, 32–34; reaction against violence advocated by, 31–32; Shakai Kakumeito, 30–32; and US as base for Japanese revolution, 30

Japanese American Oral History Project, 3, 6, 7, 8, 293–94

Japanese Americans: From Relocation to Redress (Daniels, Taylor, and Kitano, eds), 10

Japanese Americans in California, expected arrival of Japanese forces, 208, 242

Japanese American society, pre-war: conflict over cultural loyalties, 88–94; forces pushing Nisei back toward Japanese community, 88, 121n44; group solidarity and Japanese culture in, 58, 87; influence of publications from Japan on, 73n150; and Kibei, balance of Japanese and American cultures in, 88–89, 122n47; Nisei challenges to Issei authority, 87–88; Nisei subgroups, 88–90; power of Issei in rigid social hierarchy, 87; power of vernacular press in, 58–60; prioritization of group well-being, 87; setting of social boundaries in, 94–95; six themes in, 86–87

Japanese American World War II Evacuation Oral History Project (Hansen and Jesch), 10

Japanese Association: collection of funds for support of Japan, 210; data on Japanese American incomes, 211–12; and *Doho* labor activism, 44; funding of Tanaka's trip to Washington, DC, 169, 204; Issei leadership in, 87

Japanese Labor Union, 32

Japanese Military Service Men's League (Heimusha-kai), 50; US fundraising to support Japan, 201–2, 203, 205

JERS. *See* Japanese American Evacuation and Resettlement Study

Kaikyu Sen (Class War) journal, 33, 192

Kakumei (Revolution), 31

Kanchi, Shunsei (Toshi Miyajima), 49

Kashu Mainichi (Japan-California Daily News), 36–37, 45, 50–53, 56, 59, 60, 65n47, 200, 203, 212

Katayama, Sen, 29–30, 33, 63n19

Kibei. *See* Manzanar inmates, Kibei

Kido, Saburo, 165, 204–5

Kikuchi, Yoriyuki, 293–94

Kishi, Ben: anger at treatment by US, 103; in Idaho to save crops, 226; as Kibei leader, 103, 105; and Manzanar Citizens Federation, 223–24; pro-Japan statements by, 105; Sonoda on, 129–30n97; strong-arm tactics used by, 129–30n97, 226, 231–32; Tanaka on, 176; Yoneda on, 129n97, 224, 225–26, 228

Kitahara, John: as pseudonym, 66n63, 194; writing for *Doho*, 39, 40, 45–46, 65n47, 66n63, 67n65, 193

Kitchen Workers Union at Manzanar camp: as alternative to Manzanar Work Corps, 285; and Committee of Five, 115; founding of, 107, 137; as index of rising anti-JACL sentiment, 108; limited worker support for, 107, 224–25; as power base for Ueno, 107; role in Manzanar Riot, 18, 76; Tanaka on, 177, 178; Yoneda on, 107, 224–25

Koide, Joe: as agent of Japanese or American government, 66–67n63, 194–95; pseudonyms used by, 70n112, 194, 195; writing for *Doho*, 66–67n63, 194. *See also* Kitahara, John; Tanaka, Fumio

Komai, H. T., 60, 162, 200

Konarita, Tsunero, 30, 32–33

Kuramochi, Zensaburo, 30, 32–33

Kurihara, Joe, 25, 100, 104; allegations of Slocum's "double agent" work, 167–68; and Committee of Five, 115; credibility as Army veteran, 215; Embrey on, 157; and Manzanar Citizens Federation, 223–24; and Manzanar Riot, 76, 276; network of contacts in Manzanar, 167; prewar success in business, 228; resentment of government's lack of trust, 100–102; Tanaka on, 175, 176; targeting of Tayama, 129n95; turn to pro-Japan, 102, 228; Yoneda on, 228

labor union activism: Japanese-American left and, 32–34; Japanese American resistance to, in Los Angeles, 37; Karl Yoneda and, 187–88, 190, 195–96, 199–200; prewar characterization as *aka* (Red), 61. *See also Doho* newspaper, labor union activism by

Larson, Ronald, 6, 7, 8

Lone Pine Railroad depot, as arrival point for Manzanar, 6

Los Angeles: Japanese American newspapers in, 36–38; Japanese group solidarity and culture in, 58; as origin of most Manzanar inmates, 18, 95; police Red Squad, 189; and power of Japanese American vernacular press, 58–60; wartime dismissal of Japanese American employees, 53

Manzanar administration: administrators targeted for removal by Manzanar rioters, 116; ban on use of Japanese in public meetings, 97–99, 105, 221–22; Embrey on contact with, 158–59; Embrey on opinions of, 152–53; frequent changes in, 95; inmates' view of as typical *keto* (white man, hairy beast), 116; on Manzanar as model community, 83–84; preferential treatment for JACLers, 96, 124–25n71; small group of inmates providing information to, 84; Tanaka on, 178–79

Manzanar Citizens Federation, 99–102, 172–73; as counter to Block Leaders Council, 222; Elaine Yoneda and, 261, 266; founding meeting of, 99–102; goals of, 99, 128n86; JACL and, 99, 102, 222, 223; leftist pro-Americans as driving force in, 102–3; meetings, minutes of, 225; opposition to, 223–24; petition calling for opening of second front and drafting of Japanese Americans, 102–3, 222–23, 259, 265; and volunteers to save crops in Idaho and Wyoming, 224; Yoneda on, 222–24

Manzanar Committee: annual pilgrimages to Manzanar site, 8, 20; Sue Embrey and, 3

Manzanar Free Press: administration censorship of, 150; *aka* (Red) inmates' monopolizing of positions at, 174; beatings of staff, 149, 152; Brown as administration supervisor of, 148, 149, 150, 170, 179–80, 294; coverage of awards for productive camouflage factory workers, 265–66; and "death list" of rioters, 115; editorial "thank you" to Army, 96, 126n72, 149–50; editorial writers at, 150; Elaine Yoneda's work at, 255; Embrey on, 141; former *Doho* staff members at, 215–16; JACL members as staff of, 84, 96; Mori as editor of, 141, 148–50, 174; post-Riot issue, impounding of, 155–56; staff of, 136, 144, 148, 148–49, 255; support for administration policies, 96, 149–50; support for self-governing charter, 108; suspension of publication after Riot, 155–56; Takeno as editor of, 170

Manzanar inmates: area of origin, 18, 95; closing of cultural circle against non-Japanese, 98, 105, 106; conflict between different cultural groups, 143–45; general peacefulness of, 18; historians' mishandling of, 85; and letting go of memories, 4; and "missing generation" of Japanese Americans, 261; percentage volunteering for military service, 19; places of origin, 145–46; registration of, 19; release of workers and students, 19; repudiation by some of US ties, 102, 104–5, 131n112; resentment of internment, and refusal to serve in military, 19, 146; resentment of Nisei anti-fifth-column activities, 98; restoration of group solidarity and Japanese culture after Riot, 116–17; rise of pro-Axis sentiment in, 99; some historians' heroic portrayal of, 85; struggle for control of community, 95–117; transfer of "disloyal" to Tule Lake Segregation Center, 19, 175, 290; veterans, views on JAI, 101; work to save crops in Idaho and Wyoming, 224, 258, 273–74. *See also* JACL members

Manzanar inmates, Issei: as block leaders, 96, 97, 147, 220, 221–22; changes designed to undermine authority of, 97–99, 105, 106–7, 221–22; and government directive barring noncitizens from leadership roles, 97, 106; leadership role in camp, 96, 146–47; pro-Japan sentiment in, 221–22, 228–29; resentment of JACL members' cooperation with administration, 96; return to power after JACLers' removal from camp, 116; Riot as response to administration's removal from authority, 116, 153

Manzanar inmates, Kibei: calls to "strike down" Nisei collaborators, 104; causes of anger in, 96, 97–99, 103, 182; demand for complete camp self-rule, 104; directive blocking participation in leave program, 103, 153; followers of Kishi, 226; group meeting to air grievances (August 1942), 103–5, 226–27; increased determination to punish "informers" in mid-1942, 105; increased intolerance of opposing viewpoints mid-1942, 105–6; and Kitchen Workers Union, 107; number of, 103; pro-Japan views among, 250–51, 260, 261; spearheading of opposition to JACLers, 103; turn toward Issei leadership, 98

Manzanar inmates, left-wing: as among first arrivals, 141–42; community's dislike of, 142; de facto alliance with JACL, 96, 125n71, 141–42; hostility toward JACL, 125n71; support for JAI, 96, 125–26n71, 142; volunteers for military service, 142–43

Manzanar inmates, Nisei: administration's favoring of, 124–25n71; resentment of JACL members' cooperation with administration, 96; turn toward Issei leadership, 96, 102, 126n74

Manzanar inmates, pro-Japan: high school-age boys as, 227; Issei and, 221–22, 228–29; Kibei and, 250–51, 260, 261; at Kibei group meeting to air grievances (August 1942), 226–27; leaders of, 129–30n97, 224, 225–26; organization of, 225; power to influence larger group, 269–71; threats and violence against pro-US inmates, 131n109, 137, 229–32, 262, 265, 267–69, 274–77

Manzanar inmates, resistance by, 18–19; and Manzanar Underground, 108, 130–31n109; opposition to drafting of Nisei, 19; refusal to serve in military, 19, 146; refusal to sign loyalty pledge, 19, 119n15; threats against volunteers for military service, 275–76. *See also* Manzanar inmates, pro-Japan; Manzanar Riot

Manzanar Martyr (Embrey, Hansen, and Mitson, eds.), 8, 9, 135

Manzanar National Historical Site, California (Unrau), 23

Manzanar Riot (December 6, 1942): administration negotiations with crowd, 77, 78; administrators targeted for removal by rioters, 116; casualties in, 18–19, 78, 154–55, 156, 286, 288; causes of, 18, 76, 137, 153, 158; class overtones in, 24, 25; Committee of Five negotiating for inmates, 76–77, 115, 132n132, 286; as culmination of long-brewing resentments, 114–15; Embrey on, 153–55; events leading to, 18, 75–78; guards' effort to defend jail, 287–88; JERS report on, 21; leaders of, Embrey on, 157–58; night of violence following, 78; and Nisei's racial embitterment, 24; number of participants, Embrey on, 153; police use of force to disperse crowd, 78, 117n4; portion of crowd seeking collaborators to beat/kill, 78, 91, 154, 286; portion of crowd trying to free Ueno from jail, 78, 286; reason for shots fired, 277–78, 288–89; release of tear gas into crowd, 287–88; removal of pro-American inmates to protective custody at Cow Creek, 19, 78, 115, 152, 281–82; removal of "troublemakers" to other camps, 19, 89, 156–57, 175–76; rioters' attack on jail with truck, 277–78, 289; rioters' "death list" of collaborators, 78, 91, 115–16, 128n87, 136, 171, 176, 177; scholarship on, 23–25; state of mourning in camp, after Riot, 156; summary of, 75–78; Ueno's description of, from jail, 286–89; unresolved facts in, 117n4. *See also* ethnic perspective on Manzanar Riot; "WRA-JACL" perspective on Manzanar Riot

Manzanar Riot, Elaine Yoneda on, 276–81; on casualties, 277–78; flight with son to administration building, 278–79; packing of possessions with armed escort, 278–81; reason for shots fired, 277–78; rioters' effort to run over MPs with truck, 277–78; threats to her family, 277

Manzanar Underground, 108, 130–31n109

Manzanar War Relocation Center: agricultural land, 18; Ansel Adams photos of, 5; author's study of, 4–9, 5, 11–12; block meetings, 146; camouflage net factory in, 137, 147, 255–56, 259, 261–63, 265–66; camouflage factory, threats against workers in, 131n109, 259, 262–63; climate at, 18, 95, 253; directors of, 17; *Doho* newspaper's report on conditions at, 215; dust storms at, 253, 255; first baby born at, 255; as first-build camp, 16; group solidarity among housing blocks, 146; as historical landmark, 1, 20; infections diseases in, 265; labor unrest at, 266–67; local residents' hostility to inmates, 124n69; location and history of property, 16–17, 17, 18, 95; Manzanar Committee, 20; number of inmates, 18; original use as assembly center, 17, 95; pervasiveness of rumors in, 153, 218–19; postwar abandonment of, 19–20; security at, 18; site, in 1970s, 4–5; sources of news in, 254, 264; teachers and social workers at, 159; war-related industries in, 18

Manzanar War Relocation Center, living conditions in, 19; apartments, described, 251; facilities in, 18, 95, 252; lack of privacy, 153, 158, 251, 252, 253; and psychological tension, 252; reckless driving in camp, 253; water supply and toilets, 252–53

Manzanar Work Corps: Issei and Kibei opposition to, 107; Ueno's Kitchen Workers Union as alternative to, 285

Masaoka, Joe Grant: and Block Leaders Council, 102; on "death list" of rioters, 115, 171; dislike of Brown, 170; friendship with Tanaka, 171; and JACL Anti-Axis Committee, 91; and Manzanar Citizens Federation, 99, 102, 103, 222, 223, 225; as Manzanar co-documentary historian, 136, 151, 163–64, 175, 180; and petition calling for second front, 103; refusal of military service, 230; reputation as stool pigeon, 152; support of anti-fifth-column efforts, 91; work delivering papers for *Manzanar Free Press*, 150–51; work with Yoneda, 231

Merritt, Ralph P.: on Manzanar Citizens Federation, 99; as Manzanar director, 5, 17; and Manzanar Riot, 76–77, 78, 137, 286, 288; and Opler's report on Manzanar, 126–27n76; and self-rule charter for Manzanar, 109; and Slocum, 167, 168; Tanaka's postwar friendship with, 167, 168

military service for Japanese Americans: families of volunteers, plans to leave

310   INDEX

Manzanar, 279; Manzanar Citizens Federation petition on, 102–3, 222–23, 259, 265; threats against volunteers by pro-Japan inmates, 275–76; volunteers from Manzanar, 19, 274. *See also* drafting of Nisei
Minidoka War Relocation Center (Idaho), transfer of Bainbridge Island Japanese Americans to, 143
Mission to Moscow (1943 film), 173
Mitson, Betty E., 3, 6, 7, 291
Mizuno, Takeya, 21–23
Moab (Utah), relocation of Manzanar "troublemakers" to, 19, 156–57, 175–76
Mori, Chiye: beating of, 152; as editor of *Manzanar Free Press*, 141, 148–50, 174; Elaine Yoneda on, 245; Embrey on, 141, 148–50; hostility to JACLers, 125n71; and JACL Anti-Axis Committee, 183; removal to protective custody at Cow Creek, 152; Tanaka on, 172, 173, 174; Yoneda on, 216

Nash, Roy, 17, 97, 104
National Council for Japanese American Redress/Reparations, 291
Nazi-Soviet Non-Aggression Pact, 28, 44, 68n81
Neeno, Hiro, 99, 171, 222
newspapers, Japanese vernacular, on West Coast: as anti-labor, 61; competitors of *Doho*, 36; different perspectives in English and Japanese sections of, 60; *Doho*'s alternative perspective as balance to, 60, 61–62; *Doho*'s stance in opposition to, 38; power to shape opinion, 58–60; as pro-Japan, 60–61; support for status quo, 37; taboo on criticism of Japan's imperialist policies, 36–37; tacit acceptance of status quo racial discrimination, 61
Nisei. *See* Manzanar inmates, Nisei
"The Nisei in War Time" (radio show), 53
Nisei Writers and Artists Mobilization for Democracy group, 53, 54

Oda, James: alliance with JACL, 131n118; and Block Leaders Council, 102; on "death list" of rioters, 115; on *Doho*, 22, 39; as friend of Yonedas, 259; hostility to JACLers, 125n71; on Itami, 72n131; as Kibei, 70n112; at Kibei group meeting to air grievances (August 1942), 227; and Kibei JACL, 205; on Koide, 66–67n63; at Manzanar camp, 56; and Manzanar Citizens Federation, 102, 222; and *Manzanar Free Press*, 149, 215; memoir of, 21; Tanaka on, 217; as volunteer for military service, 276; wartime military career, 56; work for Military Intelligence, 149; Yoneda and, 229, 232
Ogawa, Kinji, 31, 32–33
Olson, Culbert, 52, 53, 169
Opler, Morris E., 97, 106, 108, 113, 126–27n76, 294
oral histories: on Manzanar, availability online, 293–94; and perspectivist model of history, 117n2
Oriental Restaurant Employees Union, 41, 51
Owens Valley Reception Center, 17, 95, 163

Pearl Harbor, Japanese attack on: arrests of Japanese Americans following, 206–8, 242; *Doho*'s focus on war following, 51; and increased Issei isolation, 90; and Japanese fifth column, 69n88; and Nisei's forced choice between US and Japanese allegiance, 90; roundup of suspected Japanese subversives following, 52; and US suspicions about Japanese Americans, 51
perspectivist model of historical interpretation, 75, 117n2. *See also* ethnic perspective on Manzanar Riot; "WRA-JACL" perspective on Manzanar Riot
"Point of No Return" (Uyeno), 164, 172
"Political and Socio-Cultural Issues at Poston and Manzanar Relocation Centers" (Yatsushiro), 86–87
Popular Front policy: adoption of, 27; and boycott of Japan and Germany, 43; defeating Fascism as priority in, 27; *Doho*'s support of, 35–36, 37, 39–40, 43, 195; and growth of CPUSA support, 27–28; pause in, with Nazi-Soviet Non-Aggression Pact, 28, 44, 68n81; return to, after German invasion, 28–29

Poston Relocation Center: author's study of, 9–10; as destination for Orange County residents, 9

racism in America, importance of recognizing, 4
Rafu Nichibei, 200, 212
Rafu Nihonjin Rodo Kyokai (Los Angeles Japanese Laborers Association), 33
Rafu Nihonjin Yoshokuten Jugyoin Kumiai (Los Angeles Restaurant Workers Union), 34
Rafu Shimpo (Los Angeles Japanese Daily News), 36–37, 43, 45, 48, 58–61, 59, 68–69n88, 90, 136, 163, 212
"Report on the Manzanar Riot of Sunday, December 6, 1942" (Tanaka), 21
"Resistance, Collaboration, and Manzanar Protest" (Kurashige), 23–24
Rodo Domei Kai (Labor League), 32–33
Rodo (Labor) newspaper, 32–33
Rodo Shimbun (Labor News), 34, 35, 64n37, 189–92, 241
Roosevelt, Eleanor, 162–63
Roosevelt, Franklin D., 23, 28, 31, 46, 163

Sango [Sangyo] Nippo (Southern California Industrial Daily), 36–37, 59, 61, 212
SCRPWU. *See* Southern California Retail Produce Workers Union
second front, opening of: leftist support for, to relieve pressure on Soviet Union, 102–3, 223, 264; Manzanar Citizens Federation petition on, 102–3, 222–23, 259, 265
self-government charter at Manzanar, 106–10; director's appointment of Nisei to drafting commission (Charter Commission), 106; elected block representatives' opposition to plan, 109–10; inmates' resentment of JACL influence on drafting of, 108; inmates' underground campaign against, 108–9, 130–31n109; as perceived effort to oust Issei leadership, 106, 110; replacement of appointed commission with elected group, 108–9; Tanaka's recollections of, 181; Yoneda on, 218, 231

Shakai Kakumeito (Social Revolutionary Party), 30–33
Shibutani, Tamotsu, 90, 94
Shin Sekai Asahi (New World), 215–16
Slocum, Tokie (Tokutaro), 55, 101; adoptive parents of, as Caucasian, 165; as advocate for turning in disloyal Japanese Americans, 164, 165, 166–67; on "death list" of rioters, 78, 115, 128n87, 154; efforts to deflect rioters' wrath, 129n95; and JACL, 54–55, 91, 92, 112–13, 123n59, 141, 164, 165, 214; lack of friends at Manzanar, 164–65; lobbying for citizenship for Japanese American World War I veterans, 165; as loner, 164; marriage to Caucasian, 165; patriotism of, 71n128; post-Riot removal to New Mexico, 164; as *Rafu* employee, 91; relocation to New Mexico following Riot, 281, 282; reputation as stool pigeon, 152; rumors about "double agent" work by, 167–68; rumors about FBI collaboration by, 165–67; support for JAI, 100–101; Tanaka on, 164–68; as target at Manzanar, 164; Tolan Committee testimony, 54–55, 92, 166; work for *Rafu Shimpo*, 164, 165; Yoneda on, 214–15; Yonedas' dislike of, 281
Socialist Party of America (SPA): Japanese American involvement in, 29–30; opposition to Popular Front policy, 28
Soko Rodo Kyokai (San Francisco Labor Association), 34
Sonoda, John, 129–30n97, 279
Southern California Retail Produce Workers Union (SCRPWU), 38, 40–41, 42–43, 47, 49, 67n66
Sugahara, Kay, 42, 183
Suski, Louise, 59, 141, 161–62

Takeno, Roy, 56, 72n132, 96–97, 149, 150, 152, 170
Takeuchi, Tetsugoro, 30, 31, 32
Tanaka, Fumio, 66n63, 195, 197–98
Tanaka, Togo, 7, 59, 162; as advocate for Japanese American military service, 176; age, while at Manzanar camp, 136; on *aka*

(Red) as term, 173; on anti-JACL group at Cow Creek Camp, 172, 173; arrest after Pearl Harbor attack, 91, 163; background and career of, 136, 161–62; on Brown, 170, 171, 179–80; on Campbell, 81, 171, 178–79; *Doho* and, 68–69n88, 169–70; as editor of *Rafu Shimpo*, 48, 136, 150, 161–62, 163; friendship with Masaoka, 171; on Higashi, 171–72; and JACL, 91, 92, 141, 182–83; and Japanese American Citizens League, 162; on Japanese American leaders in Los Angeles *vs.* Manzanar camp, 168; on Kibei survey, prewar plan for, 182; on Koide, 66–67n63; lectures on Japanese American internment, 6; as Manzanar co-documentary historian, 136, 151, 163, 175, 180, 216; on Mori, 172, 174; and Nisei challenging of Issei leadership, 90–91; on Nisei's prewar plight, 121n44; and petition calling for second front, 103; postwar friendship with Merritt, 167, 168; pro-Americanism stance at *Rafu Shimpo*, 162; refusal of military service, 230; removal with family to Manzanar, 163; reputation as stool pigeon, 151–52; Shuji Fujii and, 68–69n88, 203–4; on Slocum, 164–68; study of Japanese American vernacular press, 58–61; on Takeno, 170; on Tayama, 168–70; Tolan Committee testimony, 92, 166, 168–69, 181–82; trip to Washington, DC, seeking permission to publish *Rafu Shimpo* in wartime, 162–63, 204; on "troublemakers" relocated to Moab (Utah), 175–76; on Ueno, 175, 177–78; and United Citizens Federation, 163; on US-Soviet friendship in World War II, 173; Yoneda on, 200–201

Tanaka, Togo, on Manzanar: on administrators, 178–79; anti-JACL group at, 172–75, 216–18; and Block Leaders Council, 102; brother at, 177; complaints about food in, 178; as ephemeral experience, 174; JACL group at, 163–72, 183, 217; Kibei in, 176–77; Kitchen Workers Union at, 177, 178; leaving, as sole goal of inmates, 174; and left wing inmates' hostility to JACLers, 125n71; and Manzanar Citizens Federation, 99, 102, 222, 223; report on, written for Japanese American Evacuation and Resettlement Study, 136; self-government charter at, 108, 109–10, 181, 231; on third group (anti-JACL, anti-administration) at, 175–78; three groups of inmates at, 163, 216; work delivering papers for *Manzanar Free Press*, 150–51, 170, 174, 179

Tanaka, Togo, on Manzanar Riot: on "death list" of rioters, 115, 136, 171, 176, 177; neighbor's warning about, 177; portion of crowd hoping to find and kill him, 78; reasons for popular support of, 178; report on, 21, 119n18, 163, 216; tensions building prior to, 180–81

Tayama, Fred, 42; as advocate for turning in fifth-columnists, 112–13, 214; and allegations of Slocum's "double agent" work, 167; as anti-union, 197; and Block Leaders Council, 102; causes of ordinary Japanese Americans' resentment of, 111–13; chain of cafes in Little Tokyo owned by, 41, 51, 112, 169, 197; and Citizens Federation, 113; claimed exploitation of Issei during evacuation, 112; on "death list" of rioters, 115, 129n95, 286; as delegate to JACL National Convention, 110–11, 113; *Doho*'s attacks on, 41, 51, 112, 169–70, 196–97; *Doho*'s wartime truce with, 53; Elaine Yoneda on, 281; Higashi and, 171; and JACL, 41, 75–76, 111, 168, 169, 197; and JACL Anti-Axis Committee, 54–55, 91, 92, 122–23n59, 214; and Kibei group meeting to air grievances (August 1942), 227; and Kibei meeting (August 1942), 103–5; and Manzanar Citizens Federation, 102, 103, 222; and Manzanar Riot, portion of crowd hoping to find and kill him, 78; and Manzanar Work Corps, 107; prewar work with Naval Intelligence, Japanese American resentment of, 170; public opinion's turn against, 214; as scapegoat for JAI, 169; support for drafting of Nisei inmates, 285; support for JAI, 113; Tanaka on, 168–70; Tolan Committee testimony, 92, 168–69; and Work Corps, 113; work

for *Rafu Shimpo*, 91, 168; Yoneda on, 197, 214, 231
Tayama, Fred, beating at Manzanar, 285; broad inmate support for, 114, 285; due to role as collaborator and informer, 18, 75–76, 78; Elaine Yoneda on, 276; sheltering at administration building following, 278–79; and start of Manzanar Riot, 114, 153, 285–86; Tanaka's views on, 168, 169
Terminal Island (San Pedro) Japanese Americans: at Manzanar, 143–45, 171–72, 226; mass arrests of, 210; pro-Japan sentiment among, 210–11
Three Star Produce Company, and Japanese American labor activism, 37–38, 40
Tolan Committee, 54, 92, 165, *166*, 168–69, 181–82, 243, 244
Topaz Relocation Center, author's study of, 11
Treaty of Commerce and Navigation (1911) with Japan, US abrogation of, 61
Tule Lake Segregation Center, 11, 19, 175, 290

Ueno, Harry Y., *285*, *291*; age, while at Manzanar, 137; on Campbell, 81, 179; challenging of camp administrators, popular support for, 110, 285–86; charge of corruption against camp administrators, 110, 116, 153, 294; as cultural hero, 110; Embrey on, 156–57; interview of, 8, 9; and Kitchen Workers Union, founding of, 107, 137, 285; on Manzanar Riot, description of, from jail, 286–89; and Manzanar Work Corps, 107; opposition to Manzanar self-government charter, 109; renunciation of US citizenship, 290; return to Manzanar jail, 77, 286; Tanaka on, 175, 177–78; transfer from Manzanar, to series of jails and detention camps, 19, 290–91; Yoneda on, 224–25
Ueno, and beating of Tayama, 285; as false charge, in inmates' view, 76, 137, 285–86; inmates' support for, 114, 115, 285; jailing for, as cause of Manzanar Riot, 18, 76, 137, 153, 285–86; later confession of role in, 117*n*4, 291

Ukita, Yo, 258, 259, 276, 277, 279
Uno, Buddy, 197–98
Uno, Kasimuro. *See* Uno, Buddy
Uyeno, Tad, 91, 164, 171, 172, 281–82

War Relocation Authority (WRA), 17, 19, 76, 82, 95, 97, 110, 113; directive barring noncitizens from leadership roles, 97, 106; rule requiring English in inmate meetings, 97–99, 221–22. *See also* Manzanar administration; "WRA-JACL" perspective on Manzanar Riot
Wartime Civil Control Administration (WCCA), 17, 95
Weglyn, Michi, 24–25, 287
Winchester, Joe, 110, 116, 133*n*136
WRA. *See* War Relocation Authority
"WRA-JACL" perspective on Manzanar Riot, 78–85, 118*n*12; chauvinistic oversimplification of issues, 80; downplaying of mass participation, 80; focus on meaning within American society, 85; as historical mainstream, 78–79; ignoring of causation, 79, 86; and JACL disavowal of traditional Japanese customs and values, 82; and JACL members as officials' primary source of information, 84; and JACL support for internment, 82–83; main features of, 79–80; progressive view of American history in, 83–84, 85; separation of Riot from larger resistance movement, 79, 119*n*16; terminology used in, 79, 83–84; trivialization of cultural significance in, 79, 119*n*18; use by historians opposed to internment, 84–85; and WRA goal of Americanizing inmates, 82; and WRA staff's objectification of Japanese, 80–82

Yada, Kinji, 4–5, *5*
Yamaguchi, Genji, 109, 176, 276
Yamamoto, Louis, 46–47
Yamazaki, Ruth, 172, 253, 259
Yamazaki, Tomomasa "Tom": as anti-JACL, 125*n*71; and Block Leaders Council, 128*n*82, 221; as friend of Yonedas, 253,

259; and *Manzanar Free Press*, 215–16; and Manzanar Riot, 279; pro-employer article by, 67n66; as progressive in San Francisco, 240–41; Tanaka on, 172, 173, 175, 217; Uyeno on, 281–82

Yoneda, Elaine, 219, 236, 280; activism, 237; age, while at Manzanar, 136; arrests for activism, 237; on Campbell, 264–65; as communist, 136, 237; daughter by first marriage, 237, 244, 267, 271–73, 274; family and background, 235–37; on FBI visit to home, after Pearl Harbor, 238–39; first marriage, 237; on incarceration camps, quality of life in, 272; interview of, 7; on JACLers' lack of program for inmates, 270; on Japanese American doctors tricked into leaving for Manzanar without managing their affairs, 249; on Japanese Americans alienated by Karl's activism, 240; on Japanese American solidarity after JAI, 243; on Japanese fear of being treated like Native Americans, 239–40; on Karl's election as block leader, 254–55, 256, 265; on Karl's trip to Manzanar, 245; on Manzanar administrators, limited contact with, 260; on *Manzanar Free Press*, 253; marriage, vs. traditional Japanese marriage, 256; marriage of, Japanese American views on, 243; meeting of Karl Yoneda, and marriage, 189, 237; move to San Francisco, 241; on progressive Japanese Americans in San Francisco, 240–41; on pro-Japan sentiment among Japanese Americans, 242; protective custody at Cow Creek camp, 137, 281, 282–83; on racism underlying JAI, 247; on reaction to Pearl Harbor attack, 238; return home to parents in California, 283; on Shuji Fujii, 244–45; on Slocum, 281; on Tayama, 281; on types of groups volunteering for Manzanar, 248–49; on women volunteering for Manzanar, 248–49

Yoneda, Elaine, on "evacuation": arrival at Manzanar with son, 249–50, 253; choice to accompany son, 245–48; inmates driving to Manzanar, 249; plan to stay in Los Angeles with son, 244; pointlessness of resistance to, 243–44

Yoneda, Elaine, at Manzanar: activism, 218, 266–67; call for US flag to be raised over camp, 255, 264; and daughter's disappearances from Los Angeles, 267, 271–73; as defender of democracy but not capitalism, 263–64; encouragement of inmates to maintain voting rights, 260–61; and fight for justice, 255; friends and social group, 256, 258–59, 261; friends from home at, 253; furlough to seek missing daughter, 271–73; inmates' awareness of her political past, 260; on inmates' work to save crops in Idaho and Wyoming, 258; and JACLers, lack of contact with, 261; and Japanese tradition of elder father as household head, 258–59; jobs held by, 251, 255, 259, 273; and Karl's absentee voting in San Francisco, 256; Karl's help with household chores, 256; and Manzanar Citizens Federation meetings, 261, 266; as one of two Caucasian women, 247–48, 251; parents' attempts to visit, 256, 264, 265; and petition calling for second front, 259, 264, 265; return home, after Karl's enlistment, 274–75; as target of pro-Japan elements, 137; on threats and violence by pro-Japan inmates, 267–69, 275–77; vocal support for Allies, 259

Yoneda, Elaine, on Manzanar: beating of policeman who confiscated whiskey, 273–74; and dust storms, 253, 255; hospital facilities in, 265; infections diseases in, 265; Karl as volunteer for, 244; lack of instruction for young people about the war, 269–70; on politically inert inmates as largest group, 270; and pro-Japan Black Dragon group, 260; and pro-Japan group's power to influence larger group, 269–71; rumors at, 254; sources of news in, 254; weather at, 253

Yoneda, Elaine, and Manzanar camouflage net factory, work at, 137, 255–56, 259, 261–63, 273; and allergic reaction to dyes,

259, 265–66; recognition for high productivity, 265–66; and threats from pro-Japan inmates, 259, 262

Yoneda, Elaine, on Manzanar living conditions: complaints to administration about, 253, 254, 259; housing, 251–52; lack of privacy, 251, 252, 253; and psychological tension, 252; reckless driving in camp, 253; water supply and toilets, 252–53

Yoneda, Elaine, on Manzanar Riot, 276–81; on casualties, 277–78; familiarity with events of, 137; flight with son to administration building, 278–79; packing of possessions with armed escort, 278–81; reason for shots fired, 277–78; relocation to Cow Creek Camp (Death Valley) following, 281, 282; rioters' effort to run over MPs with truck, 277–78; threats to her family, 277

Yoneda, Karl, 52, 57, 186, 219, 280; activism against Japanese imperialism, 188–89; age, while at Manzanar, 136; on *aka* (Red) as term, 212–13; arrest after Pearl Harbor attack, 206–9, 242; arrests for activism, 237, 239; on arrests of Japanese Americans *vs.* German and Italian Americans, 210; on Chiye Mori, 216; as communist, 136, 188, 189–90; communist and anarchist ties as youth, 187; disruptive behavior as youth, 187; as editor of *Rodo Shimbun*, 34, 241; Embrey on, 142, 145–46; family and early life, 185–86; in Idaho to save crops, 226, 258, 273–74; interview of, 7; on JACL, 217–18; and JACL Anti-Axis Committee, 183; on JACL Kibei chapters, 204–6; on Japanese American fishermen, 211–12; on Japanese American fundraising to support Japan, 201–2, 203, 205; Japanese Americans alienated by activism of, 240; on Japanese militarism, 65n45; Japanese threats against family in Japan, 239; on Kibei and pro-Japan sentiment, 250–51; on Kibei group meeting to air grievances (August 1942), 226–27; on Kishi, 129–30n97, 224, 225–26, 228; on Koide, 66n63; on Kurihara, 228; labor union activism, 187–88, 190, 195–96, 199–200; and Manzanar Citizens Federation, 99, 102–3, 104, 222–24; on *Manzanar Free Press*, 215–16; meeting of Elaine, and marriage, 189, 237; memoir by, 21; move to San Francisco, 241; move to US, 188; names used by, 237, 239, 256; as political candidate in San Francisco, 189–90, 240; pro-Americanism of, 98, 127–28n82, 229–30; on pro-Japan Japanese Americans on West Coast, 209–10, 211; *Rodo Shimbun* and, 189, 190, 192; schooling in US and Japan, 186–87; on Shuji Fujii, 191, 193, 201, 203–4; on Sino-Japan War, Japanese crimes in, 202; on Slocum, 214–15, 281; on support for JAI, 125–26n71; on Tanaka, 200–201, 203–4; Tanaka on, 172, 173, 177, 217; on Tanaka's account of groups at Manzanar, 216–18; on Tayama, 197, 231; threats from pro-Japan Japanese Americans in San Francisco, 242; and Tolan Committee, 243; trip to Manzanar, 245; on Ueno and Kitchen Workers Union, 107, 224–25; as volunteer for Manzanar, 244; wartime military career, 56, 137, 142, 177; on wife's activism at Manzanar, 218; work as longshoreman in San Francisco, 238

Yoneda, Karl, as block leader, 219–22; and Block Leader Council, policy requiring English in, 98–99, 221–22; duties, 256; election, 219–20, 254–55, 256, 268; pay for, 251; pro-Japan inmates' campaign against, 268

Yoneda, Karl, on *Doho* newspaper, 190–97; and attacks on conservatives, 193–94, 196–98, 200; communities' view on, 213; content and circulation, 190–91; cooperation with other papers on issue-by-issue basis, 203; coverage of fifth-column activities, 201–2, 205; criticism of imperial Japan, 199–200; downplaying of communist bent of, 191; end of, with removals to Manzanar, 215; exposure of Japan's plan to recruit and train Japanese American students, 202–3; Joe Koide as writer for, 194–95; and labor union activism, 196; national circulation of, 214; origin and history of, 190, 192–93; policy on Japanese American removal, 215; policy on war with Japan, 214; as political, labor, and community newspaper, 198–99; and Popular Front policies, 195; readers' circles, 196, 213–14; readership, 213; and Shuji Fujii, 191, 193, 201, 203–4; views on JACL, 204; work as correspondent for, 136, 196, 209

Yoneda, Karl, at Manzanar: absentee voting in San Francisco, 256, 260–61; active political role, 56; and anti-JACL Issei-Kibei coalition, 105–6; on "death list" of rioters, 115; familiarity with events of Riot, 137; help with household chores, 256; inmates' awareness of her political past, 260; JACLers and, 125n71, 131n118; and Manzanar self-government charter, 218; and petition calling for second front, 259; reaction to wife and son's arrival, 250; and recruiting for US Army, 273, 274; as target of pro-Japan group, 137, 271; volunteer for military service, and threats from pro-Japan inmates, 274–76

Yoneda, Karl, on Manzanar: Issei pro-Japan sentiment in, 228–29; rumors at, 218–19; threats and intimidation from pro-Japan group, 229, 230, 231–32, 268–69

Yoneda, Tommy (son), 280; allergies and asthma problems, as issue for Manzanar residence, 245, 248, 250, 251–52, 253; emotional distress at separation from father, 273; Manzanar incarceration, mother's decision to join, 245–48; and Manzanar Riot, 277, 278, 279; threats against, for father's joining of Army, 276

Young Democrats, 174–75

Zaibei Rodo Shimbun (American Labor News), 33–34

Zeibei Nihonjin Rodo Domeikai (Japanese Labor League of America), 33

Zeibei Rodo Shimbun, 192

Zenshin (Progress), 34, 64n37, 190

www.ingramcontent.com/pod-product-compliance
Lightning Source LLC
Chambersburg PA
CBHW071229070526
44583CB00017B/2107